HENRY
MORGENTHAU, JR.

HENRY MORGENTHAU, JR.

THE REMARKABLE LIFE OF FDR'S SECRETARY OF THE TREASURY

HERBERT LEVY

Skyhorse Publishing

Skyhorse Publishing books may be purchased in bulk at special discounts
for sales promotion, corporate gifts, fund-raising, or educational purposes.
Special editions can also be created to specifications.
For details, contact the Special Sales Department,
Skyhorse Publishing, 555 Eighth Avenue, Suite 903, New York, NY 10018
or info@skyhorsepublishing.com.

www.skyhorsepublishing.com

10 9 8 7 6 5 4 3 2 1

Library of Congress Cataloging-in-Publication Data

Levy, Herbert, 1927-
Henry Morgenthau, Jr. : the remarkable life of FDR's Secretary of the
Treasury / Herbert Levy.
p. cm.
Includes bibliographical references and index.
ISBN 978-1-60239-971-6 (hardcover : alk. paper)
1. Morgenthau, Henry, 1891-1967. 2. Cabinet officers--United States--
Biography. 3. United States. Office of the Treasurer--Biography. 4. United
States--Economic policy--1933-1945. 5. United States--Politics and
government--1933-1945. 6. Roosevelt, Franklin D. (Franklin Delano),
1882-1945--Friends and associates. I. Title.
E748.M73L48 2010
973.917092--dc22
[B]
2010013226

Printed in the United States of America

For Barbara
with whom I have spent a lifetime

Contents

AUTHOR'S NOTE

This book is an effort to summarize how Henry Morgenthau, Jr., understood his role as a technocrat during the presidential administration of Franklin Delano Roosevelt and an attempt at defining Social Darwinism as the concept that most affected Morgenthau's life.

Introduction

Henry Morgenthau, Jr., lived a life of quiet heroism. Mocked in his Washington years as a fuddy-duddy for his unyielding rectitude, in fact, he experienced youthful and unfulfilled passion. Put to the test on a moral issue—the creation by presidential executive order of the War Refugee Board—he risked losing his most important friendship, that with Franklin Delano Roosevelt, and his position as secretary of the Treasury. He is responsible for the huge success of Roosevelt's New York State gubernatorial administrations, which led to Roosevelt's national prominence and the presidency of the United States. Aside from his contributions to Roosevelt's New Deal fiscal programs and the financing of the United States' war effort during World War II, neither the International Monetary Fund nor the World Bank would have come into existence except for his interest and encouragement. He also played a crucial role in the survival of the country of Israel and its escape from national bankruptcy in its infant years.

Today, Henry Morgenthau, Jr., is seen as the advocate of an approach to the reconstitution of Germany after World War II that is presently damned and dismissed variously as callous, vengeful, and vindictive, altogether inappropriate, and, luckily, never seriously considered. As will be seen in the last chapter of this book, elements of Morgenthau's plan were put into effect through the efforts of Josef Stalin in ways more savage than Morgenthau ever envisioned, and were acquiesced to by Roosevelt and Churchill at Tehran and Yalta, and Truman, the latter in the Potsdam Agreement of July 1945 governing military government of a conquered Nazi Germany.[1] Morgenthau's plan to contain anticipated, recurrent military aggression and genocide by his generation of Germans was atypical and a measure of the vast, traumatic shock engendered by a realization of the dimensions of the Holocaust wrought by Hitler and the Nazis in Europe. That was almost the only time Morgenthau was seriously engaged—with a personal sense of commitment—in a policy issue.

Well aware of the limitations of his personality, the way of life Morgenthau had consciously chosen for himself was the role of a nonparticipant in the clash of events. He was an onlooker to his father's participation in Democratic Party politics through the latter's connection with Woodrow Wilson—first, with Wilson's efforts to secure the nomination, and then, Wilson's election in 1912 as president of the United States. Morgenthau's father acquired farmland at his son's request in the lower Hudson River Valley. He found great joy in being a farmer.

This work focuses on Morgenthau's response to the social and political myths of the period in which he lived. In some respects, Morgenthau was insulated, by his connection with Roosevelt, from some of the most egregious forms discrimination took in his lifetime. Certainly, as Roosevelt's secretary of the treasury, he had a very special position in the social hierarchy in the nation's capital. That said, there can be no question but that Morgenthau was acquainted with the social and political anti-Semitism of the first half of the twentieth century. If nothing else, as the result of an agreement between Paderewski—the internationally acclaimed pianist who was then co-heading the Polish delegation to the Paris Peace Conference after World War I—and a group of American diplomats under President Wilson, had not his father been appointed in an official position to lead an American delegation authorized to investigate pogroms against Jews in the reemergent Polish Republic?

The recognition in Woodrow Wilson's Fourteen Points of the right of Poles and other ethnic groups in Central and Eastern Europe to form their own independent nations led to the concomitant minority rights treaties, to which each of the newly emergent states was a signatory. The purpose of these minority rights treaties ostensibly was to safeguard and guarantee the rights of other ethnic minorities (or nationalities) found in those newly emergent countries—among which were included Jews in Eastern Europe. Still, the only practical result of the treaties was that work was provided to the staff of a section of the respective foreign ministries required annually to submit reports to the League of Nations at Geneva. The procedure lasted for perhaps fifteen years. In the late 1930s, with the rise of government-sanctioned anti-Semitism in Germany and Hitler's removal of Germany from continuing membership in the League of Nations, the uselessness and absurdity of the process led to its abandonment.[2]

Edna Lonigan had a PhD degree in economics and worked in the United States Department of the Treasury. I met her in Washington, D.C., in October 1951. Notwithstanding her far-right-wing political allegiance, Ms. Lonigan told me with quiet pride that she understood Mr. Morgenthau had mentioned her in his diary. Her voice expressed at once respect for a competent administrator and the pleasure a government employee takes in the recognition by one's supervisor of work well done. Four separate drawers of memoranda in the documents that Morgenthau deposited in the Roosevelt Presidential Library at Hyde Park, New York, are labeled "Edna Lonigan." This suggests that Morgenthau regarded her as a valued member of the department staff and that his respect for her abilities was reciprocated. What is interesting in Ms. Lonigan's regard for Morgenthau is that more times than not, government employees' opinion of prior supervisors is more negative than otherwise.

Franklin Roosevelt was primarily concerned in filling cabinet posts to put into place first-rate administrators to run the federal departments in the most effective manner possible. In modern jargon, Roosevelt was seeking "technocrats"—capable, competent, nonpolitical administrators without political agendas—who were there to implement policies as Roosevelt might choose to set them. Although Roosevelt held regular cabinet sessions at which political and governmental issues were discussed, basically Roosevelt was his own man. Harold Ickes, his longtime secretary of the interior, observed in his *Secret Diary*, "The President is all too prone to decide important questions either alone or with the particular Cabinet officer who is interested." In connection with Roosevelt's commenting at a cabinet session on the question of the international embargo on the sale of munitions to either side during the contemporaneous Spanish Civil War, Ickes wrote, "What I cannot understand is why such an important policy should not have been decided upon without a full and frank discussion in the Cabinet."[3]

If one considers the political milieu from which Roosevelt had to choose cabinet members—except for Frances Perkins and Henry Woodin, a Republican then-president of the American Car and Foundry Company—he was remarkably lucky in the quality of his appointees. By contrast, his successor Harry Truman saw his military aide Harry Vaughan indicted and a congressional investigation of the Bureau of Internal Revenue (now, the Internal Revenue Service) by the King Subcommittee of the House of Representatives. And only Secretary of the Treasury Woodin and his deputy, Dean Acheson, had the temerity to oppose Roosevelt's determination to "go off" the gold standard as the basis for issuing paper money. (No matter that today, in a manner of speaking, American currency is based on nothing so much as the votes of its members at the periodic meetings of the Federal Reserve Board's Open Market Committee. James Grant is somewhat more expansive in his view of the matter. He writes, "[T]he post-1971 dollar is purely faith-based."[4] In the year 1971 President Nixon gave legal recognition to the ban on the interchangeability of American currency for gold for *any* purpose, and abrogated the limits within which international currencies could trade against one another, instituted as a result of the Bretton Woods Agreement in 1944—perhaps Morgenthau's finest hour as secretary of the treasury.)

Roosevelt had decided on a policy, and, like the fabled Hollywood movie producers of the era, after he decided on a policy, he preferred "yes-men" around him. He did not brook opposition once he had made up his mind on a course of action.

Acheson—brought up as a Connecticut gentleman, and finding himself out of sympathy with the monetary policies of the president—ended up resigning. Treasury Secretary Woodin was ill—indeed, slowly dying of cancer—separating Woodin from any day-to-day supervision of the operation of the Treasury Department he nominally headed.[5] Roosevelt had the opportunity to appoint a successor to Acheson. Roosevelt was determined to appoint someone he could trust to loyally implement his ideas without the potential of coming up with any passionately held ideas of his own. And so, Roosevelt came to focus his attention on his Dutchess County neighbor, Henry Morgenthau, Jr., whose qualifications for the job of Treasury secretary were more apparent than real.

Politically, Morgenthau had inherited a connection with the Democratic Party. His father had been a generous-enough contributor of both his time and money to the campaign of presidential candidate Woodrow Wilson that Henry Morgenthau, Sr., had become the American ambassador to the Ottoman Empire, where he was one of two persons to publicize the Armenian massacres in 1915, a most undiplomatic, if morally admirable, posture. Morgenthau, Jr., was extremely helpful to Roosevelt by securing information about farm problems in the Midwest during the 1932 presidential campaign. Morgenthau's inherited wealth allowed him to have a certain social independence, appropriate for a leading government figure in Washington. Most important was Morgenthau's total lack of political ambition, and his utter and complete loyalty to the president.

On the debit side was Morgenthau's lack of experience academically and professionally in the world of finance. That lack strengthened the probability that he would have no ideas of his own in the area of Treasury Department policy. The one other disqualification that Morgenthau exhibited was his Jewish background. It is apparent that this factor meant little to Roosevelt, so Morgenthau was nominated by Roosevelt to be undersecretary of the Treasury. Having finally decided on his successor, Roosevelt accepted Woodin's resignation in November of 1933. Roosevelt then sent Morgenthau's nomination to succeed Woodin to the Senate. After confirmation, Morgenthau was sworn in as the new secretary of the treasury on January 1, 1934.[6]

Morgenthau's life cannot be understood except in terms of the ideas that permeated the period in which he lived.[7]

In this respect, consider a news article in the *New York Times* describing a newsperson's visit to the factory site (turned rocket museum) on Usedom Island in Germany. This is where the Nazi government during World War II developed and constructed the V1 and V2 rockets which were sent nightly to devastate London during the last year of the war. The last paragraph in the article reads: "Near the museum's exit, a plaque is inscribed with a celebrated passage from the philosopher Immanuel Kant. It is his sublime crystallization of the two aspects of his experience that fill him with awe and admiration: 'The starry skies above me and the moral law within me.' Most visitors, it can be hoped at any rate, get the museum's intended message: if the quest to reach the stars takes place in the absence of moral law, it will lead to atrocity."[8]

Rationalist philosophy that had triumphantly animated nine-teenth-century European and American society—the belief that human reason is capable of causing the perfectibility of human society—led to an explosion of technological achievements that separates our world from the world of the eighteenth century—the world that had given birth to that philosophy. But other ideas were taking hold in the years after 1875, derived from Charles Darwin's evolutionary postulates relative to biological develop-ment. Darwin chose to denominate the biological evolutionary development he formulated as *natural selection*. Herbert Spencer was to restate the concept as *survival of the fittest*. (Spencer was less interested in biology than sociology.) Both terms may be said to be in many ways interchangeable[9]—two facets of the same coin—leading to a sense of an inexorable and inescapable process, although that may not be precisely what Darwin intended.[10]

As it turned out, Spencer's choice of phrase proved to be unfortunate. *Natural selection* was intended by Darwin to be understood in an intransitive sense to mean nothing more than that a species whose attributes best fitted the environment in which it found itself, would tend to survive and prosper. In this regard, Hofstadter[11] cites George Nasmyth for the proposition that "the fittest . . . to Darwin . . . meant merely the best adapted to existing conditions."[12]

European civilization had come to exercise dominion over the rest of the globe. Theorists had an itch to explain the phenom-enon, and they had a ready explanation at hand. All that was needed was Spencer's change of Darwin's intransitive phrase into a transitive idea—namely, that the fittest were fated to survive in the sense of prospering to the point of world dominance.

With respect to the prevalence of the sense of an inexorable and inescapable process, Hofstadter quotes,[13] for example, the language used by Captain Alfred Thayer Mahan in his book, *The Interest of America in Sea Power, Present and Future*:[14] "All around us now is strife; 'the struggle of life,' 'the race of life,' are phrases so familiar that we do not feel their significance till we stop to think about them. Everywhere nation is arrayed against nation; our own no less than others." And Hofstadter[15] cites German general Friedrich von Bernhardi's paean to the virtues of warfare,[16] "War is a biological necessity of the first importance, a regulative element in the life of mankind which cannot be dispensed with, since without it an unhealthy development will follow, which excludes every advancement of the race and therefore all real civilization . . . The natural law, to which all the laws of Nature can be reduced, is the law of struggle . . . War will furnish such a nation with favorable vital conditions, enlarge possibilities of expansion and widened influence and thus promote the progress of mankind; for it is clear that those intellectual and moral factors which insure superiority in war are also those which render possible a general progressive development." Hofstadter continues, quoting Bernhardi: "War gives a biologically just decision, since its decisions rest on the very nature of things."[17] And: ". . . it is not only a biological law, but a moral obligation, and as such, an indispensable factor in civilization."[18]

The ambassador to the United States of the Polish government-in-exile during World War II, could write in Social Darwinist terms in his *Memoirs*, ". . . since the fateful mission of Lord Haldane, then British Secretary of War, to Berlin in 1909 to ascertain whether Kaiser Wilhelm II was actually contemplating a war of conquest, the world has not enjoyed one moment of real security.

"This meant that more than thirty years of insecurity had been affecting human psychology and international relations, hampering economic development and cooperation. Mutual suspicion ruled international relations."[19]

William Faulkner, in his celebrated acceptance speech on receiving the Nobel Prize in Literature in 1949, used Social Darwinist language in his memorable peroration, "I believe that man will not merely endure: he will prevail."[20] To be sure, the context in which the words were uttered and understood was no longer Social Darwinist.

There were the splendid examples of the *Risorgimento* in Italy and the seemingly unstoppable military triumphs of Prussia that led to the unification of Germany in a militarist mode. Social Darwinists denominated these as "young" countries with seemingly unlimited futures, not to be compared, say, with the Ottoman Empire that spent the nineteenth century being dismembered, besides being—dread word—*Oriental*; or Spain—humiliated by the United States in 1898 with a concomitant loss of almost all of what remained of its overseas empire—an exhausted remnant of a world power that under Philip the Second had dominated Western Europe in the sixteenth century; or that most wonderful example of a lack of political virility, the island of Sicily, victim of unnumbered invasions over the millennia, never an independent country with an indigenous government, leading to a population (postulated Social Darwinists) of indefinable mixed breeds clearly inferior to the homogeneous "pure" races of northern Europe, like those of Germany and the Nordic lands that had spread terror in the Middle Ages.

Odd Nansen, son of Norwegian arctic explorer and statesman Fridtjof Nansen, whose name was given to the League of Nations identification documents—the so-called "Nansen passports"—had been arrested during the German occupation of Norway in World War II and ended up in the Nazi concentration camp at Sachsenhausen, outside of Berlin. In Odd Nansen's secret diary of that time under detention, he recorded

ironically—considering the plight in which he found himself—
that Norwegians were not only "Aryans," but "moreover belong
to the group of Aryans that is purest and that Germans therefore
envy and admire most."[21] (A striking confirmation of Nansen's
comment is found in an article that appeared in the *New York
Times* some sixty years later, entitled "Results of Secret Nazi
Breeding Program: Ordinary Folks,"[22] describing a conference of persons whom the reporter describes as "the children
of the Lebensborn, an SS program devised to propagate Aryan
traits." The article goes on to observe that Heinrich Himmler,
the leader of the SS and a close associate of Hitler, "valued the
appearance of Scandinavians.") The Norwegian concentration
camp inmates, although they were subject to their share of the
barbarism, sadism, and cruelty that was the lot of all concentration camp inmates, nevertheless alone among the prisoners
were able to receive letters and food and clothing packages from
home, privileges unimaginable for the other inmates.

Social Darwinism inaugurated a species of latter-day provincialism. (Milan Kudera defines the term *provincialism* "as the
inability (or the refusal) to see one's own culture in *the large context*"
[italics in original].[23]) The prevalence of words like "pure" and
"purity," and the popularity of derogatory terms like "half-breed"
and "mongrel races" attested to ever-narrowing circles of exclusion. (So Hitler, coming to Vienna earlier from Upper Austria,
described in *Mein Kampf* [his political testament written in 1923
in prison for the attempted *putsch* in Munich with the nationalist
would-be political adventurer General Ludendorf] how he first
started reading the liberal, more-cosmopolitan Viennese newspapers and then changed to reading the nationalist press.)

Hawkins writes: "Darwin and his supporters were engaged
in the attempt to redefine nature and stress the importance of
struggle, death and extinction."[24] By identifying human beings
in a Darwinist sense as one more biological species comparable

to the biblical "beasts of the field" and extrapolating from animal behavior the "laws of life" to which human beings were inextricably bound, Social Darwinists effectively destroyed any valid basis for moral principles to govern human conduct—to which principles the eighteenth-century rationalists had given their allegiance. Human beings were regarded by Social Darwinists as akin to animals in the jungle. Hofstadter[25] quotes Brooks Adams: "Human societies are forms of animal life . . ."[26] (Sigmund Freud accepted the Social Darwinist concept that human beings were one more animal species and attempted to use the idea that sexual activity, being a natural element in animal behavior, should be considered in a similar fashion by the human species, and it needed to be liberated from Victorian strictures on the subject.)

George Santayana, an American philosopher active in the first half of the twentieth century, could write an essay entitled, "Skepticism and Animal Faith" (1923) in which, speaking of human faculties, he wrote—tongue in cheek but with dead seriousness— "The *animal* [italics added to the word "animal" throughout this paragraph] mind treats its data as facts . . . but the *animal* mind is full of the rashest presumptions. . . ."[27] "Assurance of existence expresses *animal* watchfulness . . ."[28] "*Animals*, being by nature hounded and hungry creatures, spy out and take alarm at any datum of sense or fancy . . ."[29] Professor Edman in his introductory essay speaks of "the human animal" and explains pedagogically, "Essences serve as signs, portents for the precarious *animal* life . . ." He goes on to quote Santayana, "There is . . . a circle of material events called nature, to which all minds belonging to the same society are responsive in common." Also, quoting Santayana: "Assuming such a common world, it is easy to see how *animals* may acquire knowledge of it and may communicate it."[30] Professor Edman then explains somberly and without any sense of Santayana's irony, "Material events arouse intuitions, and the interests and necessities of *animal* psyches will compel them to regard those of the essences given to them as intuitions, as signs for the environment in which they act and undergo, do and suffer."[31]

The "laws of life" derived from an examination of jungle observation were thereby not merely the most atavistic, but also the most biologically true, human instincts. Indeed, Freud came to write a whole book on a theory of the interconnection between animal instincts and human behavior titled *Totem and Taboo*. Animal instinct is, by definition, separate and apart from moral precepts of good and evil. Implicit in those animal instincts was the need to protect one's own flock, pride, troop, or ethnic group against the predatory instincts of others. Eric Hoffer puts the matter in this fashion:[32] "The puzzling thing is that when our hatred does not spring from a visible grievance and does not seem justified, the desire for allies becomes more pressing . . . Whence comes these unreasonable hatreds, and why their unifying effect? They are an expression of a desperate effort to suppress an awareness of our inadequacy, worthlessness, guilt and shortcomings of the self." The "awareness of inadequacy, worthlessness, guilt and shortcomings of the self" during this period included a dimension of sexual inadequacy. John Dollard[33] alludes *en passant* to a sense of physically inadequate sexual dimension in Caucasian male responses to African American male sex organs, usually expressed as the reason why Caucasian women would be attracted to African American men. Some element of this colored Nazi diatribes against Jews.

By the nature of Social Darwinist dogma, there must always be *others* whom one must fear will seek by innate instinct to take from you what is yours. Hawkins writes:[34] "Human brains are programmed to divide people into friends and aliens . . . Hence [quoting Edward O. Wilson[35]], 'We tend to fear deeply the actions of strangers and to solve conflict by aggression.'" *Social Darwinism*, as noted, was ultimately validated in the minds of its adherents by reference to the scientific investigations of Darwin so as to suggest the scientific inevitability of the message Social Darwinists advocated (just as the phrase "scientific socialism" buttressed the economic determinism that Karl Marx proclaimed with the certainty of a latter-day prophet). Written from the point of view of the *others,* does not the sense of an inescapable doom sheathed in a civilized velvet glove permeate the stories of Franz Kafka, the author who gave the world the adjective *Kafkaesque*?[36]

The basic amorality of the ideas of the Social Darwinist period is illustrated by such fin de siècle literary works as Guy de Maupassant's forgotten novel *Bel Ami* and Arthur Schnitzler's play *Das weite Land.* More important, the tone of each work suggests an ambiguous respect for the accomplishments described. The former delineates a young man "on the make," who lies, cheats, and betrays to achieve success, covering his tracks all the while. The book ends as he is about to marry the daughter of a prominent publisher. The latter portrays an outwardly charming Viennese manufacturer who betrays his wife constantly, and also his best friend, an utterly decent doctor, by seducing the young woman with whom the doctor is in love, hoping to persuade her to marry him. At the play's end, the protagonist pushes a young soldier into a fatal duel that leads to the young man's death, just as he was about to leave for several years on a scientific expedition—and all because the protagonist's wife had taken the young man to bed one night.

The timbre of such works is a world removed from, say, Donizetti's comic opera *L'Elisir d'Amore*, or Thackeray's novel, *Vanity Fair.* The character Becky Sharp in the latter work is a young person equally on the make, except that her adventures are viewed with indulgent amusement as simple human foibles. Thackeray's prose does not convey those dreary overtones of a dreaded causality resting on the scientific inevitability of evolutionary biology which colors *Bel Ami* and *Das weite Land*. It is the difference in tone between *L'Elisir d'Amore* and *Tristan*. In theory, both describe young love—although one does not think of the music of the "Liebeslied" and the "Liebestodt" in *Tristan* as the expression of young love. Rather, it is the irresistible, evolutionary instinct of the mature "Life Force" (to use George Bernard Shaw's phrase in *Man and Superman*). While Donizetti's music is all gaiety and fun, Wagner—however resplendent the sound—conveys the cataclysmic portentousness and doom implicit in the ideas symbolized by the words *the laws of life*.[37] It is a message of Social Darwinism expressed in music composed by someone who understood he was one of the Social Darwinist *elect*.[38]

By identifying with the *ferae naturae* as an explanation for the structure of society and postulating an amoral world in which concepts of good and evil are irrelevant—and not merely observed in the breach—Social Darwinists created a psychological frame of reference in which one could identify and trust only one's own ethnic kin. Other persons were, per force, the *enemy*. The corollary to such a concept is that one must come to dislike, fear, and, finally, hate others because of their postulated undesirable, amoral, acquisitive instincts. Eric Hoffer, observing the events of the first half of the twentieth century, commented, "Hatred is the most accessible and comprehensive of all unifying agents. It pulls and whirls the individual away from his own self, makes him oblivious of his weal and future, frees him of jealousies and self-seeking . . . Heine suggests that what Christian love cannot do is effected by a common hatred."[39]

The sense of an implacable inexorability, exuded by the scientism that enveloped the playing out of the concept of Social Darwinism, is reflected by the curious instance of Anne Morrow Lindbergh's reaction to the outbreak of World War II. After it began on September 1, 1939, with the German invasion of Poland, her husband Charles A. Lindbergh, the celebrated aviator who flew the first solo transatlantic flight to Paris in 1927, became an active participant in the activities of the America First Committee, whose members were bitterly opposed to President Roosevelt's sympathies for Great Britain.

Mrs. Lindbergh felt compelled as a loyal wife—a popular ideal in the 1930s—to produce a book reflecting her husband's isolationist America First views. The result was a volume to which—with what must appear to us as unintentional irony—she gave the title *The Wave of the Future—A Confession of Faith*.[40] The title reflects nothing so much as the sense of an overwhelming fate implicit in the concept of Social Darwinism. Curiously, she opened her discussion with the figure of Boethius, a fifth-century Roman scholar who was also a servitor to an Ostrogoth king. Amid the societal anarchy and political upheaval following the barbarian conquest of the city of Rome in 451, Boethius wrote that it was the duty of those who could to salvage and preserve what was best of the fallen Roman civilization in the face of the barbarian onslaught. Mrs. Lindbergh's choice of analogy is telling. It reflected contemporaneous events in Europe. The victorious barbarian conquerors of Rome were obviously of Germanic origin and represented a Social Darwinist inevitability. Britain in this view was analogous to a vanquished Rome.

So she wrote: "In the Greek tragedies the gods never forgave the sin of *pride*" (italics in original). "And there is no sin punished more implacably than the sin of resistance to change. For change [Mrs. Lindbergh's genteel euphemism for the Social Darwinists' *struggle*] is the very essence of living matter. To resist change is to sin against life itself."[41] She continued: "The wave of the future is coming and there is no fighting it."[42] In the best Social Darwinist fashion, she concludes, "Man has never conquered the underlying forces of nature."[43]

Mrs. Lindbergh accepts the unspoken premise that reality is a Social Darwinist world. It followed that the contemporaneous, political systems of Germany and Italy were more in keeping with the fundamental and true animalistic nature of the human species. A democratic way of life was hopelessly inefficient and old-fashioned. (There was Winston Churchill's sardonic comment that democracy was the worst of all political systems, except for all the others.)

And yet, Mrs. Lindbergh was identifying with Boethius, seeking to save what was possible of decency and culture. She described him as living in a time during which ". . . a dream of civilized order and unity was dying," noting that "[he] sat at his desk and contemplated his changing world with a troubled and uneasy mind."[44] And so—even though it violated every value with which she had grown up and to which she had given allegiance—as a writer, she sought to justify her husband's goal of a "Fortress America" awaiting the onslaught of the contemporaneous Social Darwinist barbarians. Uneasily she wrote, "France, England and America were not perfect, perhaps, but they made possible a mode of life I shall look back to the rest of my days with nostalgia."[45] She must regret "[t]he tragedy is, to the honest spectator, that there is so much that is good in the 'Forces of the Past,' and so much that is evil in the 'Forces of the Future.'" Faithful to her purpose of justifying her husband's political goals, she concludes, in a Social Darwinist world, ". . . I do feel that it is futile to get into a hopeless 'crusade' to 'save civilization.'"[46]

In retrospect, the book *The Wave of the Future* is an astonishing defense of a political cause, albeit the only possible escape hatch for Social Darwinists to employ in order to avoid—to mix one's pickles—Marx's "dustbin of history."

Note may be taken of a certain irony in Western attitudes of condescension during that period toward what was regarded as the fatalism inherent in the philosophies and religions of Asia and what were referred to as "primitive peoples"—a fatalism so very akin to the European peasant idea of *Malocchio*, or the evil eye. This condescension went along with the unthinking European acceptance of the inexorability implicit in those Social Darwinian laws of life based on the concepts of *natural selection* and *survival of the fittest*. If anyone in those years was to be so bold as to remark on the essentially similar fatalism of all, such comment would have been met with indignant protest that there was no similarity at all. One was mere superstition, while the other was based on the indisputable "science" inherent in evolutionary biology. Besides, the Social Darwinist laws of life allowed for, involved, and most definitely encouraged individual initiatives to survive and prevail.

It must be noted that Hofstadter, writing after 1945, concludes:[47] "Spencer's impersonal view of history is a brand of oriental fatalism"(!), " 'a metaphysical creed and nothing else . . . ,'" quoting William James, *The Will to Believe*.[48] Hofstadter[49] had already quoted Spencer: "'Not simply do we see that in the competition among individuals of the same kind, survival of the fittest has from the beginning furthered production of a higher type; but we see that to the unceasing warfare between species is mainly due both growth and organization. Without universal conflict there would have been no development of the active powers.'"[50]

Without question, the nadir of the Social Darwinist belief in the need to survive and prevail was reached in Nazi concentration and death camps. The Norwegian Odd Nansen in his surreptitious diary tells the story of how a nineteen-year-old Ukrainian was apprehended in the Sachsenhausen concentration camp stealing a leather bag from which he planned to make himself a pair of shoes. The punishment was death by hanging. Nansen writes, "When the Ukrainian boy and the hangman appeared under the gallows there was a noise and hubbub somewhere on the square. It was a Dutchman, one of the Bible-searchers, screaming a protest against this infamy. One man—of 17,000—dared to react normally! 'It's shameful! It's vile!' he screamed. He was seized and led away."[51]

Nansen had earlier explained in his diary how the prisoners were divided into various groups or categories, each with its own identifying colored triangle. He had written, ". . . there are the Bible-searchers, a strange little flock [who would appear to be similar to American evangelical Christians] who might be released if only they would abjure their 'Bible–searching,' one of whose tenets is that Hitler is a false prophet, a danger and disaster to Germany. But none of them will give up this odd conviction."[52]

Later, Nansen made inquiries through a Norwegian friend who worked in the camp's secretariat as to the fate of that one man who had dared to speak up. The friend "looked up the Dutchman's card. It said, 'Subjected to mental examination.'" Nansen then wrote ironically, "The only man in camp who reacted normally must be out of his mind."[53]

Perhaps Hofstadter's final value judgment on the concept of Social Darwinism[54] is the quotation he takes from George Nasmyth: "Instead of subjecting it to the searching analysis demanded by its practical social importance . . . the intellectual world and public opinion has accepted 'Social Darwinism' uncritically and by almost unanimous consent as an integral part of the theory of evolution."

Concomitant with the development of Social Darwinian ideas was the changeover in the course of the nineteenth century of the societal image in Europe of those who till the soil. Historically, such folk were dismissed as "peasants"—uncouth, coarse, brutal, and violent. Whether because of Rousseau's idea of natural innocence, or because of a concept of animal territoriality implicit in the Social Darwinist laws of life—and thereby applied by extension to the human species—a connection with the soil acquired the aura of authenticity with biological roots in the animal world, to which the human species was linked. Tillers of the soil were no longer considered uncouth peasants; they had become "farmers." Contact with the soil lent a natural nobility and a societal superiority as compared with the moral and physical decadence that was associated with urban life.

The late-nineteenth-century Viennese composer Gustav Mahler, considering a title for the symphonic song cycle he had composed based on German translations of Chinese poems, could think of no more profound an image than the concept of animal territoriality so central to the contemporaneous, Social Darwinist image of an animalistically oriented human society, and so named the symphonic work *Das Lied von der Erde* ("The Song of the Earth").

The idea that tillers of the soil are superior members of the body politic and that connection with the soil must be encouraged (that is, the political concept of "family farms") continues to this day, as evidenced by the large sums of money allocated annually to farm subsidies by the European Union and the Congress of the United States.

Once, so sophisticated an observer as Freud expressed astonishment that such morally objectionable (and criminal) conduct as incest was found as well among rural folk. In one of his early works he introduces a case study by reporting that he went on vacation to get away from medicine, and, more particularly, neuroses. Climbing a mountain known for the views afforded from its summit, he was approached by a young woman, possibly eighteen years old, whose face Freud describes as sullen. Recognizing him as a physician, she complained that her nerves were bad. Freud comments, "So there I was with the neuroses once again . . . I was interested to find that neuroses could flourish in this way at a height of over 6,000 feet . . ."[55]

Perhaps the apotheosis of the supposed greater moral worth of people living on the land as contrasted with city decadence is found in Knut Hamsun's novel, *The Growth of the Soil* (1917). The work so impressed his contemporaries that it won a Nobel Prize in Literature! One may take note that first, the protagonist in the novel is a social isolate and a misogamist; and second, that the author, a Norwegian living in Norway, ended his life as a Nazi sympathizer during the German occupation of his country in World War II. So, too, at the end of *Der Zauberberg* (*The Magic Mountain*), Thomas Mann's allegory illustrating Europe's descent into World War I, Settembrini (in the novel, the apostle of European rationalism), when bidding farewell to Hans Castorp (who was on his way back to his German homeland to volunteer as a soldier), tells Castorp: "You go to fight among your kindred . . . it is your blood that calls . . ."[56]

What may be the last literary expression given to the postulates that underlie the amorality of Social Darwinist laws of life occurs in the climactic scene of the pseudonymous Pauline Réage pornographic novel, *Story of O*.[57] The scene is a vast *demimonde* party at which O (who at the opening of the story was portrayed as an independent, professional photographer) is reduced to the dimensions of a naked sex slave led by a young girl holding a leash attached to O's genital flesh. Using a cliché popular in the middle third of the twentieth century: The naive American juxtaposed against a knowing and experienced Europe—the anonymous, drunken American male is described as instantly sobered by the spectacle of tethered, naked flesh.[58] The symbolism of the drunken American represents the naiveté of a Wilsonian rationalist belief in the perfectibility of the human species reflected against a sophisticated and disillusioned Europe steeped in the miasma of Social Darwinism—with the whole incongruously transposed to a sexual context. It is that substratum of ideas, one suspects, that proved so disturbing to readers, ultimately lifting the work from the realm of mere pornography to eventually be reviewed in that bastion of respectability, the *New York Times Book Review*.

Perhaps the last evidences in the "real" world of Social Darwinism in Europe were the public statements that heralded the dawn of Stalin's last, aborted purge, the so-called "Doctors' Plot." Most of those arrested were Jews. In Eastern Europe, Jewish ethnicity had been regarded as a "nationality," and in the Soviet Union, their internal passports were so marked.[59]

Now, suddenly, as a prelude to the initial revelations of the "Doctors' Plot," Moscow newspapers began to print articles declaring—as proof of their nature as "outsiders," inherently incapable of loyalty to the motherland—that Jews were *rootless cosmopolitans*, not people rooted to the soil.

By the 1890s, the acceptance of the postulates underlying Social Darwinism had led to a most shocking and virulent species of racism in the United States, including the institutionalization of lynching as a form of extralegal societal control.[60] Words like *pure* and *purity* were popularly applied to everything from morals and religion to "womanhood," "race," and soap,[61] while fears were voiced about the consequences of undesirable behavior by half-breeds and mongrel races—the former a derogatory appellation applied to the children and grandchildren of American Indians and Caucasians, while the latter term was applied to groups as diverse as African Americans, Jews, and Sicilians. By the end of the nineteenth century, words like *quadroon* and *octoroon* fell into disuse—even as the effort was made in state constitutions and statutes in the American South to define the exact measure of ancestry necessary to determine racial classification.[62]

The pervasiveness of Social Darwinist modes of thinking extended even into the precincts of the Supreme Court of the United States. So that Court could write, "Legislation [*sic*] is powerless to eradicate racial instincts . . ."[63] These words revealed a negation of the purpose in the late 1860s of congressman

Thaddeus Stevens and the other "Radical Republicans" to secure the adoption of the Fourteenth Amendment to the Federal Constitution after the end of the American Civil War.

The majority members of the Court do not appear to have applied their own rule correctly—for example, the need for "separate but *equal*" accommodations to satisfy the constitutional provision. Plessy had purchased a first-class ticket for his railroad trip, and there were apparently no separate, first-class accommodations for African-American passengers.[64] The state law would have required the railroad company to have put up a partition in the first-class coach—something, it appears, the railroad company failed to do. The court's failure to recognize Plessy's first-class ticket encouraged the institution of a caste system. There was no longer legal recognition of African-American class rights in a Caucasian society. All African Americans were herded into a Jim Crow coach.

Indeed, it was no accident that in the opening years of the twentieth century, American sociologist William Graham Sumner coined a distinction between *folkways* and *mores* to underline the difference between those standards by which people professed to live, and those other standards in accordance with which people *actually* acted in the world in which they lived. Professor Sumner regarded the power of those unspoken societal customs or standards to be so fundamental as to negate and render useless any efforts at contemporaneous social reform.[65] In that respect, Hawkins finds: "The foundation of his work, from his essays during the 1880s to the publication of his study of folkways in 1906, was the assumption that Darwinism was as relevant to an understanding of social life as it was to the organic world."[66]

The effect of Social Darwinist thinking in the United States was so profound that a private college was not permitted by the United States Supreme Court to entertain a biracial student body, holding that the state of Kentucky did not violate the mandate of the Fourteenth Amendment that purported to limit state action by its—the state of Kentucky's—adoption of legislation resulting in the prohibition of such enrollment, and did not thereby deny the equal protection of the laws—a result concurred with by the liberally-revered Justice Oliver Wendell Holmes Jr.[67] What is astonishing about the language of the Court's opinion is that although the ostensible reason for the case being considered by the Supreme Court was whether there was a possible violation of the Constitution of the United States, the opinion of the Court did not see fit to explicitly state that it found no such violation—although that, in its narrowest sense, is what the court actually concluded! (It is perhaps almost superfluous to add that the court has since changed its mind.)

So all-encompassing were Social Darwinist habits of thought that even Franklin Roosevelt was capable on occasion of speaking as a Social Darwinist. Beschloss writes: "Just after Pearl Harbor, Roosevelt lunched with [Treasury Secretary] Morgenthau and Leo Crowley, a Catholic who was Custodian of Alien Property. As Morgenthau later recorded, the President told them, 'You know this is a Protestant country, and the Catholics and Jews are here on sufferance.'"[68] The remark was not entirely isolated. In many ways Roosevelt—however empathetic, democratically oriented, and liberal-minded he was—thought in conventional Social Darwinist terms. One of Roosevelt's biographers, Allan M. Winkler, writes, "He read Alfred Thayer Mahan's important book *The Influence of Sea Power on History* and later corresponded with the admiral himself."[69] While the focus of Roosevelt's interest was undoubtedly on the importance of sea power, the context, as the quotations from Mahan given earlier indicate, was a Social Darwinist understanding of human society.

Once a Social Darwinist configuration of narrowing social groupings was melded into a perception of reality, it was perhaps inevitable that social distinctions should develop in the last years of the nineteenth century in the United States that emphasized and enforced social differences between Gentiles and Jews. The latter were commonly regarded as loud, pushy, vulgar in their clothes and manners, questionable in their business dealings— and altogether foreign to what were deemed to be the cardinal virtues of discretion, consideration, and moderation. Also, for those of a religious bent who were concerned with such matters, there was the Jewish failure to acknowledge the last and truest religious revelation. This was expressed in the thought that the New Testament revealed a higher development of the concept of divine love and forgiveness than was to be found in the pages of the Hebrew Bible. The latter was held to exhibit a vindictive emphasis focused on a stern justice. Professor Vernon Louis Parrington, in his vastly popular survey, *Main Currents in American Literature*,[70] commented on Jonathan Odell, a Loyalist satirist during the American Revolution. Parrington wrote of Odell as "possessing a clear intellect and a heart little touched by Christian charity—a stern Hebraist [*sic*] who would sweep away with the besom of wrath all the enemies of his God and his King"[71] and also: "No Christian charity spread its mantle over the shortcomings of his enemies, no Christian forgiveness found lodgment in his unforgiving heart. He was a son of the Old Testament and he girded his righteousness with prayer."[72]

One may note the currency in the first half of the twentieth century of the theological idea that found a distinction between the higher and more-civilized ideal of "Christian charity" as contrasted with the "unforgiving sternness" that was popularly associated with Jews and the Old Testament. In this scheme of things, the expressions of forgiveness, humility, and mercy that are found in the words of the Hebrew Bible were considered merely as intimations of the truer and greater revelation related in the Gospels. The concept of Old Testament unforgiving sternness was closely merged with the idea of vengeance. (The

popular image of Jewish vengefulness is iconized in the characters of Shylock and Barabas found in the Elizabethan plays by
Shakespeare and Marlowe that we know as *The Merchant of Venice*
and *The Jew of Malta*.) So, Henry Stimson, then secretary of state
in the cabinet of President Herbert Hoover, given the suggestion
that mail to suspected spies ought to be opened, was reported to
have responded with the comment that "gentlemen do not open
other people's mail." He did not hesitate to dismiss Morgenthau's
plan for the reconstitution of Germany after World War II as a
species of Jewish vengeance.[73]

While the dimensions of this work do not permit any extensive comment on the development of the social prejudices against
Jews that were rampant in the United States by the opening
years of the twentieth century, one may take note that as late as
the administration of President John Fitzgerald Kennedy in the
early 1960s, Arthur Krock, the Washington correspondent for
the *New York Times*, allowed himself on one occasion to write,
"[A]lthough the Attorney-General has, on his official stationery,
remonstrated with a private Washington club to which he belongs
for its tradition against Negro guests and members, he did not
deny its legal right to make distinctions which, in some other
Washington clubs as elsewhere, extend to persons calculated to
have more than x per cent of 'non-Aryan' Caucasian ancestry.
Recently, even by meeting the 'x' test, a prominent official of this
and the previous Administration encountered some opposition
to his admission to one of these."[74]

Still, it is valid to say that the 1960s saw the beginnings of the
dissolution of such social prejudices.

If one would seek to understand why such prejudices started
to disappear in the 1960s, it is perhaps useful to start by noting
that the generation coming of age in the years of that decade had
no personal experience with the events and the attitudes contemporaneous with World War II and the decades preceding it. It

was a generation that was acutely sensitive to the consequences of that war, both in terms of the atrocities perpetrated by the Nazi government of Germany and the vast international realignments resulting from that war. What had not been apparent at the end of World War I was very much apparent by 1960—namely, that Europe was no longer the "kingpin" of the globe. The "young nations" that Social Darwinists had earlier celebrated were by 1960 second-tier participants of a politically exhausted Western Europe that was slowly finding its way into an economic and political confederation in the face of a Cold War, on a continent divided by an Iron Curtain. The prior European generation had left to its children a legacy of moral and political failure that had led to death and destruction on an almost unimaginable scale—a source of deep shame.

Not that it mattered to Henry Morgenthau, Jr. By February 6, 1967, he was dead and no longer concerned.[75]

CHAPTER I

The Founding Father

Founders of American dynasties are more fun to read about than their progeny. Their children grow up with wealth and/ or power and in the process learn discretion. They tend to take their worldly advantages for granted, and avoid calling attention to themselves. The maker of the family fortune, starting out with little or nothing, has an innate gift, or, at the school of hard knocks, learns to create assets by seizing whatever opportunities there be to get ahead. Unclouded by doubt, founding fathers tend to enjoy their accomplishments as these accumulate during their lifetime.

Before the age of periodic blood tests, pharmaceutical products, and diets to keep tabs on cholesterol and blood pressure and what-have-you, eating what he would, oblivious to the dietary consequences, Henry Morgenthau, Sr., lived for ninety years and enjoyed his life. He says as much to those who take the trouble to read his various stabs at autobiography. While these are written in the sober-sided style of the early twentieth century, they reveal a personality quietly satisfied with himself and not a little amused by his experiences.[76] His grandson Henry III's own volume expresses regret that his grandfather's sense of merriment—which he found so immediate in his grandfather's ordinary interchange with people—is missing from his grandfather's written pages. Henry III says, "[I]n person my grandfather displayed a sense of humor and zest that got lost in his writing. As an older man, 'he was fun to be with,' recalled his granddaughter, [historian] Barbara Tuchman . . ."[77]

Freud says that a mother's favorite child is destined for success. Henry III records how "[a]t a very early age [his grandfather] gained his mother's special attention," and how "[f]rom the beginning he seemed to have an instinct for attracting people and making them smile."[78] Henry III attributes his grandfather's happy disposition to his "pleasant memories of his Mannheim childhood, [which] provided a sense of security that would stay with him all his life . . . the ebb of the family fortunes in the New World inspired his irrepressible ambitions . . ."[79]

In his autobiography *All in a Lifetime*,[80] Henry Sr. recounts how he was asked in 1919 to chair a three-person American commission to investigate atrocities against Jews within the geographical boundaries of the resurgent Polish Republic. Unsure that their dream of a restored Polish Republic would at long last be made a reality, the Polish Nationalists asked the eminent pianist Ignace Paderewski to co-lead their delegation to the Paris Peace Conference, hoping his worldwide prestige would secure them a felicitous hearing. Locally, in a Social Darwinist world, these idealistic dreamers embraced a virulent, self-identifying form of nationalism that excluded the one-third of the population identifiable as other, non-Polish ethnics. This led to local anti-Semitic excesses. American Jews, also at the Paris Peace Conference, protested the inconsistency between an insistence on justice for one's own ethnic group and physical acts of intolerance toward others.

Paderewski recognized the problem. He suggested the formation of a commission composed of Americans to investigate the alleged atrocities. Wilson was determined to appoint a Jewish chairman and offered the post to Henry Sr., probably because of his role, while the American ambassador to the Ottoman Empire, in publicizing the Armenian massacres by the Ottoman government in 1915. That action had established his bona fides as a humanitarian.[81] Somewhat reluctantly,[82] Henry Sr. accepted the appointment. His reluctance must be understood in the context of Social Darwinist societal attitudes that mitigated against too public a specifically Jewish identification. These had not prevented him from making his fortune by age fifty. He explained, "I had a special gift for making money. By the time I had attained the [financial] competency which had been my ambition, I had become fascinated with moneymaking as a game."[83] But he had become bored and set about focusing on community affairs. He became the president of Rabbi Stephen Wise's Free Synagogue.[84]

Governor Woodrow Wilson of New Jersey agreed to speak at the fourth anniversary dinner of the Free Synagogue. Henry Sr. was impressed.[85] He wrote to Wilson, expressing his interest in the governor's ideas. Wilson invited Henry Sr. to join his campaign committee to secure the Democratic Party's nomination for the presidency. Henry Sr. was liberal with his time and financial contributions, and was the Democratic Party's Finance Committee chairman during Wilson's presidential campaign.[86] With Theodore Roosevelt running on the "Bull Moose" ticket and splitting the Republican vote, Woodrow Wilson found himself elected president in 1912. Other members of Wilson's campaign committee came to be appointed presidential cabinet members.[87] Henry Sr. in all fairness might have hoped for a similar post.

Harold Ickes in his *Secret Diary*[88] describes how the foregoing became political folklore. In 1937, Senator Robert Wagner of New York had been lobbying both President Roosevelt and Ickes in support of the appointment of Nathan Straus as the first administrator of the federal public housing program created as a result of the enactment of the United States Housing Act of 1937. Ickes was unenthusiastic about Straus, regarding him as a dilettante. Roosevelt ultimately appointed Straus. Ickes wrote,

> During my talk with Senator Wagner about ten days ago, he gave me an interesting sidelight on Henry Morgenthau, Sr. . . . After Wilson's election Morgenthau told Wilson he would like to be named Secretary of the Treasury. Wilson said: "Mr. Morgenthau, I have heard that you are a very rich man, that you are worth more than ten million dollars." (Wagner said it may have been only five, but he thinks that it was ten.) Morgenthau admitted the soft impeachment, whereupon Wilson said: "I am afraid that you are not qualified to be Secretary of the Treasury. I don't think that any man could earn such a sum of money honestly."[89]

That Wagner told a discreditable story about Henry Sr. is curious, since he helped Wagner's political career in no small measure.

In the Triangle Shirtwaist Factory fire in New York City in 1911, 160 young women died in particularly horrifying circumstances because the factory owners had locked the doors leading to the fire escape in order to prevent the young seamstresses from taking unauthorized smoking breaks. The factory owners were indicted for criminal homicide.

As Henry Sr. writes,[90]

> That resulted in a public protest against inadequate factory inspection and the creation of a "Committee of Safety" in which I served. . . . When Henry L. Stimson relinquished his duties as chairman to become Secretary of War, I succeeded him. We were instrumental in having

the [New York State] legislature appoint a factory investigating committee of which Alfred E. Smith was chairman and Robert Wagner vice-chairman.

These men came to see me soon after their appointment in some embarrassment. They seemed sincerely desirous of performing their duties, but said they were badly handicapped.

"Are you folks going to finance this investigation?" they asked. "Because, if you aren't, we don't see how it is to be carried on. The legislature appropriated only $10,000, and it will take all that to pay a good attorney to do the necessary legal work."

"I can get you a first-class lawyer who will not demand any fee," I said, "and he will be satisfactory to everybody concerned, including Tammany Hall."

The man I had in mind was Abram I. Elkus. He agreed with me as to the good he could do in this capacity, and the public honour to be won if he would volunteer his services. Within two hours after my interview with Smith and Wagner, Mr. Elkus assumed the post. The result was thirty-one successful bills constituting what is to my mind the best labour legislation ever passed by a State Legislature.

This led Smith to the governor's office and nomination in 1928 as the Democratic candidate for president of the United States, while Wagner went from the anonymity of the state legislature to the stature of a distinguished member of the United States Senate.

Henry Sr. recounted what happened next: "In April, 1913, Senator O'Gorman telephoned me from Washington that he had been requested by the President to offer me the Ambassadorship to Turkey. I apparently astonished him when I told him please to thank the President for me, but that I would not accept.

O'Gorman, whom I had known for many years, urged me to discuss the matter with him. He told me that I had no right to refuse such a tender over the telephone."[91]

The senator had not anticipated a refusal. He was a longtime national public official and understood the deference due the office of President of the United States. He understood that recommendations made by him to fill federal offices in New York State had to be accepted by the president. Failing a presidential assignment was a bad start. So he urged Henry Sr. to come to Washington to talk, and that ended with a conversation with Wilson.

In the context of the prejudices generated by a Social Darwinist world, Henry Sr. explained to the President,

> "The Jews of this country have become very sensitive (and I think properly so) over the impression which has been created by successive Jewish appointments to Turkey, that that is the only diplomatic post to which a Jew can aspire . . ."
>
> Mr. Wilson's reply was aggressive in manner and almost angry in tone.
>
> "I should have hoped," he said, "that you had a higher opinion of my open-mindedness and freedom from prejudice than this. I certainly draw no such distinctions, and I am sorry that you should have thought so."[92]

Accepting that Henry Sr. was neither naive nor paranoid and that Wilson was sincere, the latter revealed his lack of anti-Semitic prejudice by nominating Louis Dembitz Brandeis in 1916 for a seat on the United States Supreme Court as its first Jewish member.

An explanation for Wilson's failure to propose one of the more-glittering European capitals for Henry Sr. is found in Allan Nevins's biography of Grover Cleveland. What happened took place in 1885 at the beginning of Cleveland's first term. Nevins writes:[93]

> The one bad error in the diplomatic field lay in the selection of Anthony M. Keily as minister first to Italy and then to Austria. Keily was a Virginia Catholic with an unfortunate record. Attending a public meeting in Richmond in 1871 to protest against the destruction of the Pope's temporal authority, he made a speech denouncing the Italian government as a usurper.[94] Now [Keily's] harsh utterances regarding Victor Emmanuel and Italian unity were dug up and given wide publicity. It is strange that Keily himself had not realized that they would debar him. The Quirinal naturally refused to receive him and the appointment, to the chagrin of Archbishop Gibbons, who had urged it upon Cleveland, had to be revoked.
>
> This would have been a trifle had not Cleveland immediately made the mistake of appointing Keily as minister to Austria. Had he given the matter careful consideration, or received proper advice from [Secretary of State] Bayard, he would not have done this. Austria had to reject Keily not because she was in close relations with Italy, but because her relations were exceedingly strained. On both sides of the Italo-Austrian border Irredentism persisted and despite all repressive measures was continually breaking out. There was constant danger that some "incident" would bring the two nations close to war. Under these circumstances Austria could not afford to accept as minister a man whose insulting references to Italy had just been given the widest publicity in Europe. To do so would have been regarded by even sober Italians as a needless affront. When [the Austrian Foreign Minister] Count Kalnóky came to reject Mr. Keily, he felt the dignity of

the Dual Empire would not permit him to disclose this real reason, and hence took refuge in allegations touching on the social ineligibility of Mrs. Keily; she was a Jewess, and he declared that she would not be acceptable in the diplomatic circle of Vienna. The State Department rejoined with asperity that the American Government could tolerate no religious test in such a matter, but Keily never reached Vienna. The whole episode was unfortunate. No experienced European government would have made the error of choosing for the foreign service a man with Keily's record.

If Wilson was unaware of the incident, bureaucrats in the State Department would surely call it to the new president's attention. It goes without saying that Wilson was anxious to avoid an experience similar to Cleveland's. Although Henry Sr.'s first language was German, which would have made him a natural choice for Berlin or Vienna, caution would seem to have prevailed. Constantinople, on the other hand, offered an ambassadorial appointment with the knowledge that there would be no possible objection to someone who was Jewish. At least one member of the Turkish government was Jewish, while another was a member of the Döenmeh, a heretical Jewish sect that originated in Salonika in 1683.[95] So that a post Henry Sr. regarded as a diplomatic ghetto for Jews, Wilson could regard as a safe diplomatic setting for him. At the same time, Wilson would not want to embarrass Morgenthau or himself by having to explain that there was a fear on Wilson's part of a refusal by a foreign government to accept Morgenthau as an ambassador because of his ethnic identity. That would explain why Wilson could ignore what was impertinence on the part of Henry Sr. and leave the post open notwithstanding Henry Sr.'s refusal to accept it.

But Henry Sr. remained firm in his resolve. In a Social Darwinist world, social prejudice hurt. On a personal level, he had been enormously helpful to the president and thought he deserved better. Henry Sr. reports (this after the death of Wilson), "As I left the President, he gave me a look which is hardly describable. He was sadly disappointed that he had not been able to dominate my decision." (Perhaps there was also an element of astonishment that Henry Sr. would have the temerity to refuse a request from the president of the United States to accept a not-ungenerous appointment.) Nevertheless, Henry Sr. reported that Wilson apparently also showed "a deep affection for me, and it was evident how much he regretted that his arguments had failed to persuade me. On the other hand, I felt sorry, and it probably showed in my face, that I appeared so ungrateful at not promptly complying with his request, and abiding by his judgment that Turkey was the best place in which I could serve the country."[96]

He gave up on his ambition for public service and followed through with his personal plans to take his wife and daughter Ruth to Europe for the summer. There, at Aix-les-Bains, he met Myron T. Herrick, President Taft's former ambassador to France, who would be reappointed to that post by Warren Harding. Henry Sr. writes, "I mentioned to him that I had refused the Ambassadorship to Turkey. He told me that I had made a grievous mistake, and probably from ignorance; that I did not comprehend what a splendid position that of Ambassador was . . . He ended by urging me that if I still could obtain the post, I should take steps to secure it."

Henry Sr. was greatly impressed by Herrick's words but he was still not entirely convinced. He knew that Rabbi Wise, the spiritual leader of his congregation, was in Paris at that moment. Henry Sr. wrote to Rabbi Wise, summoning him for a consultation. Rabbi Wise was somewhat pressed for time, so they agreed to meet midway at the Dijon railroad station. Wise had just come from a visit to Palestine and was concerned about the circumstances in which the Jews lived there. As Henry Sr. describes it, "Dr. Wise urged me with all the force of his eloquence to rescind my declination."[97] But Henry Sr. was not to be stampeded. He writes, "[I] told Dr. Wise that I would be back in America in September, and if the position had not yet been filled . . . I would reconsider it. On the strength of this statement, Dr. Wise telegraphed the President that I would accept. Within three days I received a cable from the President, again tendering me the position, and I accepted it."[98] Within a few months of his arrival in Constantinople, he was writing to his family at home on December 23, 1913: "I am *very glad* I came."[99]

And so Henry Sr. now found himself the chairman of an American commission assigned to investigate anti-Semitic excesses in the re-emerging Polish Republic. The nature of the virulent, self-identifying Polish nationalism that then colored public life in Poland may be gleaned from the comments Oscar Halecki included in his *A History of Poland.*[100] Halecki, an apologist for the Polish government of the years 1919–1939, protests in an aggrieved tone that ". . . Poland had to sign a special treaty which imposed upon her far-reaching obligations in the matter of the protection of minorities. . . . [T]he procedure was humiliating in this respect, that it placed Poland, as well as a few other states unjustly termed 'new,' under international control, which was not provided for as regards Germany."[101] Halecki could discreetly admit, "The problem of national minorities" [as noted, then aggregating as much as one-third of the population of the country] "was . . . less successfully handled during that score of years."[102] He added somewhat ruefully, "The question of the Ukrainian minority was . . . generally speaking, not properly appreciated . . . and in contradistinction to the Germans and the Jews, it was composed, not of immigrants, but of immemorial inhabitants of these lands. . . . [I]t is to be regretted that neither successive governments [i.e., Cabinets] nor the Polish nation [i.e., Polish nationalists] achieved in regard to the Ukrainians a consistent programme which might have reconciled them to the Republic."[103]

Halecki dismissed the members of the German and Jewish ethnic communities in Poland as alien nationalities, going so far as to use the term *immigrants*—implying (at least to an American) "foreigners of recent arrival," as if successive generations of these ethnic communities had not been living within the country's geographical boundaries for a millennium. Halecki granted a greater legitimacy to the Ukrainians retrospectively, possibly because they were principally rural (and descended from the first human inhabitants in the area; in a Social Darwinist sense, they had a true and authentic connection with the land they occupied). He may also have identified the Ukrainians with the ancient Grand Duchy of Lithuania, separate but still part of the historic Polish Realm, if independent after 1920.[104]

Halecki accepted without question the nascent Polish government's actions in 1919–1922 to seize and retain the city of Vilnius (Vilna/Vilno), the historic and present-day capital of Lithuania. Polish leader Marshal Jozef Pilsudski was born there, and at the time, Polish-speaking persons accounted for a significant proportion of its polyglot inhabitants. The Poles would be expelled after World War II when the Soviet Union, retaining the Baltic States first seized in 1940, once again made Vilnius the capital of Lithuania.

Halecki also commented on what proved to be a temporary occupation by Poland—until the outbreak of hostilities on September 1, 1939—of the remainder of the Teschen (Tesin/Cieszyn) coal-mining district that had been apportioned between Czechoslovakia and Poland after World War I. He accepted that the temporary occupation of the remainder of the Teschen district "was notably avenged," but in Social Darwinist fashion, approving of its basic amorality and cynicism (if not recognizing its plain stupidity), he describes the seizure as a "small and illusive success" if a "most regrettable step," because it seemingly gave Hitler, as if he needed it, an opportunity to complain of Polish ill treatment of its German minority.[105]

Reflecting on the plight in which Polish Jews after 1919 then found themselves, in a virulently nationalist Polish State, Halecki wrote: "The Jewish question became particularly acute . . . it was indeed, a very considerable one, having regard to the fact that over three million Jews—almost ten percent of the entire population—were living scattered all over the country, constituting a far higher percentage still among the populations of the towns, in trade and industry, and in certain professions, and that only an insignificant number of them were really assimilated. Under these conditions the rise of an anti-Semitic movement on economic, rather than racial, grounds, was unfortunately almost inevitable."[106]

Today Poland has an ethnically cohesive population; its Jews were almost all murdered by the Nazis. The Germans were expelled after World War II, not only from prewar Poland, but also from those prewar German territories—a portion of East Prussia, the remainder of Silesia and Pomerania to the Oder River—that were awarded to Poland after the war by Stalin. The Ukrainians and their lands were recovered by the Soviet Union in September of 1939, to become part of a consolidated Ukraine, consequent upon the Russo-German Non-Aggression Pact signed in August, 1939. The arrangements were ratified first by Roosevelt and Churchill at Yalta in February of 1945, and accepted later that year by Truman at the Potsdam Conference.

But all of the foregoing lay in the future. In 1919, President Wilson, acceding to Paderewski's suggestion of an American investigatory commission, decided it should be chaired by an American Jew and chose Henry Morgenthau, Sr., Morgenthau accepted the assignment, securing two American non-Jews for the two other seats on the commission. Reaching Warsaw on July 13, 1919, and recognizing the rather nasty dimensions of the situation in which he now found himself, Morgenthau commented, "Far from depressing me, this juxtaposition had a stimulating effect."[107]

His first act was to establish his American identity in the matter of his breakfast. He announced that he expected to have an American breakfast consisting of juice, cereal, bacon and eggs, and coffee. Thereafter the commission members set about interviewing various government members and representatives of the Jewish community. The representative of the Vilnius Jewish community urged the commission members to visit Vilnius, explaining they had prepared a full legal case, including documents and the testimony of actual witnesses. Henry Sr., impressed with the representative's earnestness, agreed to conduct hearings there.

The Polish chief of state was Jozef Pilsudski, who had been born in Vilnius. When the American commission members arrived there, they learned that he had preceded them. Henry Sr. wrote, "Etiquette required that [General] Jadwin and I should call upon him."[108] So they went. As Henry Sr. described the encounter,[109]

> The president was quartered in the Bishop's Palace. We were received with great formality and ushered through several vast rooms before we reached the audience chamber. A storm was brewing, the light was dim. We found ourselves in a great big uninviting room . . .
>
> He had evidently been reading the anti-Semitic newspapers to advantage and was determined to give me a piece

of his mind. The storm from heaven broke just as the verbal torrent began . . . He spoke in German . . . [Pilsudski had been released from a German prison to assume the leadership of the Polish Nationalists.]

He declared he was the chosen head of 20,000,000 people and would defend their dignity. He represented the Polish Government, the ruling power of a people that had been a nation when America was unknown, and here was a committee of Americans stepping between the elected Government of Poland and the Polish electors—positively belittling the former to the latter. He dismissed as unfounded the stories of bad treatment of prisoners. He asserted that, considering Vilna's population of 150,000, civilian casualties had been comparatively few. Excesses? . . . the occurrences had been mere trifles inevitably incident to any conquest.

"These little mishaps," he said, "were all over, and now you come here to stir the whole thing up again . . . The Polish people resent even the charge of ever having deserved distrust: how then can your activities have any other effect than to increase the racial antipathy that you say you want to end?"

"Why not trust to Poland's honour?" he shouted. "Don't plead that the [treaty] article's concessions are few in number or negative in character! Let them be as small or as negative as you please, that article creates an authority—a power to which to appeal—outside the laws of this country! Every [true ethnic Polish] faction within Poland was agreed on doing justice to the Jew, and yet the Peace Conference, at the insistence of America, insults us by telling us that we *must* do justice. That was a public insult to my country just as she was assuming her rightful place among the sovereign states of the world!"

Pilsudski spoke as a true Social Darwinist—determined to be protective of his particular ethnic group's right to act as it chose, decorated though his thoughts were by the language of national sovereignty. It was the Poles' country to do with as their representatives saw fit, and not a confederation of foreign, "other" ethnics, who might claim to share together in the legacy of a Renaissance Great Power. For Pilsudski, non-Polish ethnic groups—although physically present within the country's borders as its present government took form—were aliens, living there on sufferance, dependent on the goodwill and generosity of those who considered themselves its true citizens.

As Morgenthau described the encounter, "For fully ten minutes [Pilsudski] continued his tirade. Nothing could have stopped him and I didn't try. When he was out of breath, I said quietly [responding quite obviously also in German], 'Well, General, you've made good use of your opportunity; you've gotten rid of all your gall. Now, let's talk from heart to heart . . .'"[110]

Henry Sr. writes that he suited the expression of his face to his words. One imagines that he sat patiently as Pilsudski spoke, softening the expression on his face to the benign smile of the avuncular "Uncle Henry," as he was known to his political friends at home in the United States. One does not know what Pilsudski intended by his passionate outburst. On a narrative level, it would seem that Paderewski had convinced the Polish nationalists (probably against their passionately held feelings for their absolute right to an unlimited exercise of sovereignty) of the necessity of conciliating President Wilson, who had championed the independence of Poland. Pilsudski was therefore attempting to argue the justice of his position as he saw it to the American proconsul.

The identification of Pilsudski and the other Polish national-ists with Polish ethnicity and their commitment to Polish national independence did not go so far as to include a restoration of the eighteenth-century political structure of the Polish Republic. The final solution to the problem of royal election had been the designation of Saxon—non-Polish, *German*—royalty as hereditary kings. That was unacceptable to Social Darwinist nationalists. Nor were they prepared to surrender the national legislature to the surviving Polish gentry who had been its members earlier. These might be given their due in a social sphere, but what was politically accepted in the eighteenth century was obviously unacceptable in a contemporaneous Social Darwinist world.

One does not know if General Jadwin, sitting with Morgenthau, spoke German. If not, he could only guess at what was transpiring. As Morgenthau describes the conversation, the effect of his dismissing Pilsudski's diatribe and his suggestion they talk "heart to heart" "was surprising." Pilsudski "stared at me for a moment with unbelieving eyes and then threw back his head and burst into a giant laugh."[111] What exactly Pilsudski was responding to, what he found to laugh about, is an interesting question.

Morgenthau then proceeded as if against a Social Darwinist "true believer," to carry the flag of an older, eighteenth-century, rationalist ideal. He said, ". . . in my official capacity, I was no Jew, was not even an American, but a representative of all civilized nations and their religions. I stood for tolerance in its broadest sense." The commission "was not there to injure Poland but to help her."[112]

Pilsudski had to be aware of the idealism that animated Woodrow Wilson, which had led to American support for the reemergence of Polish independence after 125 years of ineffectual efforts by successive Polish patriots. It would not have done at all for Morgenthau and the other members of the commission to report back to Wilson that the Polish nationalists were ungrateful wretches. So Henry Sr. was able to conclude his description of his interview with Pilsudski in Vilnius by writing, "Pilsudski's entire attitude changed; before I left him, he consented to release the Jewish prisoners still in custody since April, 1919," adding the caveat, to save face, "as rapidly as each case can be investigated."[113]

Henry Sr. spoke of rumors he had heard of Paderewski's purported anti-Semitism that arose out of Paderewski's connection with the anti-Semitic Polish nationalists. "How ridiculous!" was Paderewski's honest response. Henry Sr. then proposed that he and Paderewski should attend Friday-night Sabbath services at the great synagogue in Warsaw, symbolically to dissipate any thought of Paderewski's being anti-Semitic.[114]

Morgenthau wrote, "Paderewski at once saw the point. He was anxious to refute the charge against him, yet his caution prompted him to consult his political associates, who advised against his adoption of my suggestion."[115] The Polish nationalists regarded implementation of Morgenthau's suggestion as a species of ethnic treason.[116] Paderewski may have been able to convince them to go along with an American commission; they were as yet unsure of themselves in the international sphere. But locally, in Warsaw, they were not prepared to allow Paderewski to treat with persons the Polish nationalists regarded as undesirable aliens, whatever his personal needs or desires.

Morgenthau's somewhat-visionary suggestion that a Polish public figure attend Jewish Sabbath prayers would eventually come to pass. But, again, it would be in a vastly different world, some three generations later. The place was not to be Warsaw, but rather Rome in the year 1986, and the public figure would be the Polish-born Pope John Paul II, who attended Sabbath services at the main synagogue there, near the Tiber River.

In any case, the visit could not have taken place in what had been the great synagogue on Tlomackie Street in Warsaw. It was no longer extant. It was destroyed on May 16, 1943, at the end of the Warsaw Ghetto Uprising. Although the abandoned synagogue stood outside the physical confines of the ghetto walls, in a fit of pique, Wehrmacht soldiers had dynamited the building and reduced it to rubble. After the war, although the Polish government had restored the medieval synagogue at Krakow as a tourist attraction—there no longer being a congregation to use the building for its intended purpose—the same policy was not operative in Warsaw. This is possibly because the Warsaw synagogue, a wonderful nineteenth-century Second Empire structure in photographs, was subject to the general twentieth-century prejudice against Victorian architecture, which regarded such buildings as the nadir of taste. The Communist government finally used the empty site for a nondescript office building.

Paderewski recognized that he had been discourteous to Henry Sr.'s efforts to be helpful to his needs. "Never mind," he reassured him. "I'll find another way." The occasion was Herbert Hoover's visit to Warsaw in connection with Hoover's relief activities. Paderewski gave a state dinner in Hoover's honor at the prime minister's official residence. Paderewski invited Henry Sr. and the other members of the American commission.[117]

Morgenthau wrote, "That dinner was a gorgeous affair. Everybody of political, financial, and social importance was there; the representatives of the old aristocracy, the makers of the new republic . . . Paderewski had personally arranged the seating: on his right sat [commission member] Gibson, at his left [commission member] Jadwin; Mme. Paderewska was at the table's head; Hoover sat at her left; General Pilsudski, as Chief-of-State, sat at her right; and at his right was the place that the Premier had given me."[118] Henry Sr. reports that he and Pilsudski conversed intimately and almost incessantly.

The terrible Chief-of-State was telling me, quite simply the story of his adventurous life: how he had fought always for Polish liberty, how he suffered imprisonment at Magdeburg.

"But, even when there seemed no hope for either my country or me," he declared, "I never lost my faith. A marvelous gypsy palmist had assured me that I was destined to be dictator of Poland."

[Henry Sr.] looked at him in amazement.

"The palmist," he continued, with the simplicity of a child, "found that the lines at the base of my right forefinger formed a star. That is a sure sign that the lucky bearer is to rise to mastery."

He held his hand out to me. I could almost hear the rustle of excitement among the watching guests to whom, of course, his words were inaudible.

The star was there. Then, inquisitively, I looked at my own right hand, and to my great surprise I also found a star!

"I have the mark as well as you," I laughingly proclaimed, "but the nearest approach I ever made to a dictatorship was when the British were expected in Constantinople in 1915, and I was to be in control of the city between the departure of the Turks and the British occupation."[119]

Paderewski had killed two birds with one stone. He had mollified Henry Sr., and he was able to give public recognition to Pilsudski's acceptance of the American commission's presence in Poland, notwithstanding the opposition of other Polish nationalists to it. For Paderewski himself, it represented a validation of his judgment in urging Polish nationalist acceptance of the commission's presence.

Finally, it may be asked, what did the American commission do that was of any lasting value? Henry Sr. produced a report accepting that there were anti-Semitic excesses, although the two other commission members disagreed in writing. Henry Sr. provided some consolation to Polish Jews, and he may have tempered some of Pilsudski's attitudes. In a sense, Pilsudski had made a commitment to fair treatment of Poland's Jews, and, until his death in 1935, he tried, within rigid limits, to live up to that.

CHAPTER 2

Of Birth and Growing Up

Henry Morgenthau, Jr., was born on May 11, 1891. Family and friends sent his parents congratulatory telegrams. His son, Henry III, wrote that Morgenthau was his father's favorite child—the first and only boy after three girls.[120] The record of Morgenthau's growing up is found in a series of postcards and letters he wrote to his parents over the years that are deposited in the Roosevelt Library at Hyde Park, New York.

On a paper dated September 19, 1902, eleven-year-old Henry Jr. promises he will not smoke or gamble [until he] is twenty-two, and solemnly signs his name.

May 11, 1904, finds young Henry at the Baths and Grand Hôtel des Salines at Bex-les-Bains in the Rhone River Valley of Switzerland with his mother and sisters. He reports to his father he had a miserable birthday and decides it was because he is thirteen years old.

In an undated letter (marked "1904?" possibly by an archivist), a young Morgenthau writes to his parents in pencil that he has just taken an exam and feels pretty sure he passed it. He adds: "Now, if by some chance I did not pass, please do not feel disappointed, but I am almost positive that I did pass it." He feels fine and reports he is getting his room into shape. Tomorrow classes would begin. The letter suggests it was written from a school, heralding Morgenthau's entrance into the very posh Phillips Exeter Academy in New Hampshire. Henry Sr. had the mad idea that his son should enter that most fashionable of WASP boarding schools. What Papa could not do was change the perceptions of young Henry's fellow students. They *knew* Jews were déclassé. One did not associate with them socially. Faced with the unconscious cruelty of his fellow adolescents, young Henry was to often find himself treated as a non-person by his peers.

In a letter dated September 20 (and again marked "1904?" probably by an archivist), young Henry reports that on the preceding afternoon, he'd had a great and pleasant surprise: a visit from Charlie Weil Jr., his first cousin, come to Exeter on business. Young Henry goes on to say that the dormitory had organized a self-government. It then gave a boy named Rosenberg "his last warning." Henry writes: "The committee decided that fresh boys get three [underlining in original] dunks in the river".

Another letter details young Henry's encounter with the school's genteel, religious anti-Semitism. The school chaplain, he reports, told the students all about Christ and his good points, "and then [he] goes to work and tells all the bad points of the Jews." The sermon apparently was to be repeated the following Sunday. Young Henry adds: "I will not go again. Now do you not think I am right. You said you would like to have me taught about the bible and not Christ."

He continues with this extraordinary passage: "This afternoon I had nothing to do, so I took the trolley to the ocean beach with Mr. Aimen's permission [underlining in original]. I remembered that you did not want me to go out of town, but I thought you would not object to a trolley ride". He adds: "I have not made any particular friends yet."

The foregoing is an artless adolescent confession of feeling out of place in the little society of "H. M. Dunbar Hall, Exeter,

N.H.," from which he sought to escape if only for an afternoon. He seeks to hide the full dimensions of his feelings by making it seem like a spur-of-the-moment whim, as he adds that he has not made any friends yet.

In a letter dated September 22, 1904, Henry writes that he has just returned from a school meeting. (He has trouble writing the word "school.") He reports that he played a little football that afternoon, and goes on to say that he received a nice letter from his sister Helen, adding: "Please write oftener." He mentions he saw his cousin Sumner Weil in his auto, who said he would come around to see him that evening but never turned up.

Henry reports that he passed his entrance exam in "Arith" but flunked history and English—contrary to his expectations. He adds hopefully: "I guess I have been good in my other studies, for they have not said anything to me besides telling me I flunked." In large letters he writes: "Please send me something to eat [underlining in original]." He recounts that that morning, "they" (otherwise unidentified) had a football meeting where he gave ten dollars for a season ticket to attend all of the school football games, except the one with Andover. He writes that he went to the New Hampshire–Exeter game. Exeter won. "It was a fine game," he goes on, vicariously participating in the school society. He returns to a major preoccupation: "I wish you people at home would please write more [underlining in original]," and adds: "I want some more." After starting in a peremptory tone, in his misery he is reduced to quiet pleading.

There is a stark postscript: "The committee called down Rosenberg again. I do not speak to him anymore." We are never told what young Rosenberg's particular offenses were, other than earlier when it was implied that he was "fresh." Morgenthau never identifies any other classmate by name in his letters.

Henry's October 4, 1904, letter reports that he went canoeing the preceding Sunday and enjoyed it, and expresses the wish that his father could see the river. He confesses: "I can see it will take a pretty long time before I get in with the old fellows." He adds: "I am not worrying at all because it is the same with all the younger boys." He comes back to his crying need: "I have been away almost three weeks and Mamma has only written me twice." He pens a detail especially for his father: "Listen, Papa: I take a <u>cold</u> <u>shower</u> <u>every</u> [underlining in original] morning and brush my teeth." Again he adds: "Please write often." There is a postscript: "What do you think about my going to Boston on Saturday [to visit relatives]?"

On October 30, 1904, Henry writes that he has just returned from Boston where he "had just a fine time." He arrived at four o'clock and took a cab to his Aunt Carrie's home. On the way he stopped to buy flowers for her. He took tea with his aunt, and at five o'clock, he reports, his cousin Charlie Weil walked in, "sad and dejected." His cousin was disappointed with the results of the college football game. Young Henry then took supper with his aunt and cousin. Afterward, they walked to the theater and had front-row seats. He enjoyed the show and thought it was "great." Then he went with cousin Charlie to the Adams House for oysters and Welsh rabbit to appease the voracious appetites of the young. A reader may imagine how much thirteen-year-old Henry enjoyed his evening with his nineteen- or twenty-year-old cousin. It more than made up for the snubs of his classmates.

That Sunday morning Henry visited other relatives and then walked to the Sunday school where cousin Charlie taught. Afterward, they visited still other relatives, the Eisemans, but did not have time to call upon the Dreyfuses. He had caught up with his aunt Carrie earlier, and later had Sunday dinner at her home. Cousin Sumner and some of his friends from Harvard and (cousins) Catherine and Helen Filene were also there. He stayed till 5:30 PM, after which he went to the station with cousin Sumner and took the 6:00 PM train back to Exeter, arriving safely.

Henry III explains the family relationships: His paternal grandmother's "oldest sister [was] Carrie, and the Filene, Eiseman, and Dreyfus cousins [were] families of Carrie's three daughters by Charles Weil, whom Carrie married in 1874."[121]

On November 13, 1904, Henry writes to his parents: "Well, well, 35 [underlining in original] to 10, Exeter's favor. How's that. I was never so surprised in my life. I suppose you read all about it in the paper . . . Through the whole game Exeter had it easy. After the game we marched all around the Andover campus and then walked four abreast to the station. We had a special train and got back to Exeter about 7:10 PM. We then had supper."

On January 12, 1905, Henry writes to his parents: "I hope you received my telegram O.K. Last night I was so homesick, I have not got over it yet. It was hard for me to get back to serious work after having so much fun. I tell you what: there is no place like home [underlining in original]." He reports: "It snowed last night and this morning the snow changed to rain, so you can imagine how dreary and what it is here. How is everybody at home? Tell Grandmamma I was sorry that I was not able to see her again." He reverts to his fundamental concern: "I have never been so [underlining in original] homesick . . . my whole life."

But lest there be any implied criticism of his father's decision to send him to Phillips Exeter, he adds: "It is not that," and here he repeats himself as if he were hesitating to add what he really wanted to say: "that the boys are not nice to me. It is that being with you so long, it is hard to leave you. But I guess I will get over it in a day or two. At least I hope so."

On January 15, 1905, Henry writes to his parents: "Last Friday afternoon I went to the Doctor because I had a rash on my body. He said he could not tell what it is and that I should go to bed and stay there until he came next morning. Saturday 14, in the morning the doctor came and said it was nothing. I still am very [underlining in original] homesick. I wish you would take me home. But I guess you think it is best for me here. I do not think I will go another year. Home is the best place for me". He adds a postscript: "If Papa can come to Boston on the 21 Jan. I would be <u>ever</u> and <u>ever</u> so <u>happy</u> [underlining in original] to see him."

His mother must have decided that it was imperative to pay her son a quick visit, since Henry Jr. writes to his parents on 18 January 1905: "I hope, Mamma, that you arrived safely in New York. I was so glad to see you . . . It is snowing hard up here and looks like a blizzard." A faint suggestion of acceptance by some of his classmates at the school is reported in a letter dated January 20, 1905, and he responded accordingly: "A few boys up here are going to have a feast. I would like you to send me a Harmony basket which will hold enough for 6. The other boys are going to furnish the dessert and drinks. Please send it as soon as possible . . ."

Morgenthau never again refers to a group of his classmates getting together with him.

On March 13, 1905, Henry writes a letter to his father: "Thank you ever and ever so much for the fine time you gave me in Boston." He allows himself a small criticism: "I think the next time you come to Boston we will not do so much family calling" so that "we can be more together."[122] He continues happily, "Three more weeks and I will be coming home." He asks his father to "remember your promise and answer every letter I write to you," and pleads, "Please write soon."

Young Henry went home for spring break in April of 1905. On Thursday, May 13, 1905, he writes to his parents: "It feels funny to be again at old Exeter. This is the last term and is the shortest of all three terms." He goes on to write: "Mamma was worrying about gymnasium. Well, instead of working inside the gym for three quarters of an hour, we go outside and run for twenty minutes and that makes me very tired." He then adds: "See if you can get a certificate from the doctor, and send it to me, and I will try and get excused from gymnasium."

He includes in a new paragraph: "I saw Charlie and Ludwig. Charlie and Sumner [Weil] will come this summer and want to thank you."

On May 18, 1905, Henry writes to "Dear Papa" to say he received candy, adding, "[T]hank you ever and ever so much." He refers to his learning problems and confides: "I find I am able to concentrate my mind, and it is only a matter of want[ing] to. I do not put three hours work on my Latin, but one hour's good hard [underlining in original] work. I think that your plan of coming up in the automobile is O.K. And that you should come up to Exeter on the 21st because if you come up on the 20th, the girls would have to stay a[t] the Hotel, which, as you know, is nothing extra." He mentions his health: "Yesterday, I stayed in bed all day with a bad cold, but I am up again today." He is concerned about his parents' reaction as he writes: "Do not get worried like you did the last time I was sick, because it is nothing serious."

On May 30, 1905, he writes to his father and his sister "Ruth" [underlining in original] and asks that his mother write a definite invitation to Charlie and Sumner Weil for the summer, although he wonders whether Charlie Weil can take the time away from his business. Henry adds: "[I am] very sorry that I was not able to speak to you over the phone last Saturday night . . . we had a party and dance here at Dunbar Hall and we certainly had fun. Today, from ten o'clock on, we have a holiday." He returns to summer invitations. "Also, I believe Aunt Belle Buchman has invited all the Trounsteins except Paul, [underlining in orginial] and if you should send me his address and the time Mamma wanted him, I would write him an invitation. Do you not think it would be best for him to come on with Mr. Trounstein?"

A happier letter in some respects is dated October 1, 1905. Henry writes to his parents: "I was very glad indeed to receive your letter, Mamma, seeing it was the first letter I had received from you. You can not imagine how happy I was when you called me up. I was just about going to bed and had given up the idea of hearing from you, when I received word that I was wanted at the telephone. I was glad to be able to say goodbye to Alma." He continues: "Please let me know her address in Europe so that I can write to her on her birthday, also what steamers sail this week." He continues to his parents: "In my last letter, [I] wrote to you asking you to come up to the Andover football game on Jan. 11. It is really on <u>November</u> [underlining in original] 11, 1905.And seeing you might come up here in November, you might as well come then and see a good game." He goes on to focus on his real social life at school: "I think I will go to Boston next Saturday if you have no objections."

There is a rare letter to his sister Helen, dated October 9, 1905, in which Henry writes: "You are a peach. Thanks ever and ever so much for the candy. It was just great and it tasted the better because it came from you. I have sent you a few flowers from Exeter in return for the candy and I hope you will like them." He reports: "I had a fine time in Boston." One may imagine the thrill of a fourteen-year-old, spending the night in the room of his nineteen-year-old cousin Sumner Weil at Cambridge. He passes on gossip: "All the relations in Boston seemed to think Papa and Mamma were coming on to Boston . . . but that was the first I had heard if it: was there any truth in it?"

On October 25, 1905, he writes to his father: "I was delighted to receive your letter, and am very glad that all of you are coming up to Boston. I most likely will be able to go down to Boston to meet you." He reports proudly: "I am still off study hours and intend to stay off. I got C+ in a Latin exam the other day but am doing nothing extra in the rest of the classes."

On October 29, 1905, Henry writes: "I am sorry to hear that Mamma will not be able to come up. I could not make out in your letter at what hotel you are going to stop at. Please let me know." He goes on to make one request: "When you come up, please bring my large yellow automobile gloves with you." It is important to him and he tries to be precise: "You know, the ones I got at Sacks [*sic*] last year." There is momentous news on the education front: "Listen, I received <u>B+</u> [underlining in original] in my Latin exam." He adds: "I was not doing so well in Mathematics about a week ago, so I took a few tutor lessons and am doing O.K. now."

On January 23, 1906, he writes to his parents: "I am glad you and Alma are coming up here to see me. I am sorry, Ma, that you have so much trouble with your servants." He continues: "I have enclosed the house key in this letter and am sorry I did not send it to you before." Apologies done, he goes on: "If it is not too much trouble, would you mind forwarding my fur gloves as it is rather cold up here now." He reports on the state of his health: "I am feeling more like myself today than I have since I am out of the hospital. I went to the doctor yesterday and my throat is O.K. I have not been taking gymnasium up here the last two days on account of being just out of the hospital."

On January 29, 1906, Henry writes a postcard to report: "I have been in my room almost the whole day on account of being ill. The doctor says I have no fever and that my pulse is alright [*sic*] but most likely I have just a slight cold." He gets to what is important to him although it is at least five months into the future: "I would like to know what time during the summer you and I will go to Blue Mountain. Because Bernice Marks would like to know, so that she could have Louise L. there at the same time I am."

There is a cryptic postcard (possibly postmarked February 6, 1906) that begins rather formally: "My dear Papa, Please excuse any-thing I said in my letter but my eyes trouble me. Then being sick and this last thing put me out of sorts as you can imagine, but I will stick it out to the last day of school."

An undated letter believed by the archivist to belong to this period is addressed to "Dear Papa & Mamma." It reads: "You do not know how happy I was to hear your voices once more, even if it was over the telephone." He goes on to family gossip: "I am very glad to hear that Aunt Sophy is engaged to be married, and I suppose you all are pleased also." He goes on to report on his schoolwork: "I had a geometry exam in which I received a D+ which is poor, but I will do better next time. I also had a Latin exam and I am pretty sure I passed that, but I have not received my mark as yet." He goes on to something more interesting: "I am glad to hear the Mercedes is running so well . . ." He addresses his mother: "Mamma, I do not think I will find time to take up piano, so please do not feel disappointed." He turns to a burning theme with his father: "I hope, Papa, that you will come up to see me in about two weeks from today, as I will have been away from home almost five weeks, and it will be pretty near a month from that time when you are coming up here for the Andover game, so please consider the matter."

On March 23, 1906, he writes: "You can imagine how glad I was to hear from Alma and you over the telephone the other night. I have been studying very hard for the last two days for examinations. I have taken one in Latin and one in Algebra. Both were pretty hard, and in Algebra I got a 'C-' and I do not know yet what I will receive in Latin, but it ought to be a pretty good one. Tonight I will take a German exam and intend to pass it."

On March 30, 1906, he writes to his father: "I received your letter and am willing not to go to Ehrick's wedding, [although] I would have liked to." He goes on to education matters: "This afternoon I took an examination to decide whether I should get a 'D' or a 'C' for a term mark in German. In the whole examination I had only one little slip so I will get a 'C.'" Having finished with education matters, he goes on: "I will take the one [under-lining in original] o'clock train from Boston and will arrive on

New York at about <u>6:10</u> [underlining in original] p.m. I wish that you could have the Mercedes there at the station for me, and if it will be too much trouble for anybody to meet me there, why alright, although I would be very glad if someone was there." He goes on with adolescent logic: "If you will send me $10.00 for my carfare home, as I do not see why I should pay my own fare out of my pocket money." He adds: "But I will have enough . . . to pay my fare and you could give it back to me when I got home, if that way would be more suitable to you than the other." He adds: "I can not wait till I get home for I am pretty sick of this place and I would like to be back home for a little while."

On April 16, 1906, he writes to his mother and sisters, Alma and Ruth, saying that he regrets he is unable to wish them good-bye in person before they sail to Europe. He promises to write to them and asks them to write regularly. With adolescent bravado, he continues: "P.S. Do not worry about Papa, Mamma. I will take good care of him."

On April 21, 1906, he writes to his father: "I ordered my summer suit, and it will be finished by next Wednesday; it will cost $38.00 which I think is rather reasonable and if that suit for every day fits me, I will get another suit for the same price for my good suit." He hastens to add: "if you do not object." He returns to an urgent need: "Please write often to me and I will surely write often to you." He reports on his health: "Today I have a cold but I am going to school anyway. I saw the doctor, so do not worry as I am taking good care of myself." Ever looking for ways and means to escape from the boarding school, he adds: "Now, don't forget, any time you get lonely, why just telegraph me <u>and I will come at once</u> [underlining in original]." He ends: "P.P.S.: Please become lonely."

On April 25, 1906, he writes to his "Dear Papa": "Heartiest congratulations for your fiftieth birthday, and I hope you will have <u>many, many</u> [underlining in original] more birthdays." He adds: "I do wish that I could spend tomorrow with you, but I am sorry to say that I can not." He reports: "I will try to get permission to come to New York. I do not think it will be necessary that you write to Mr. Armen." He goes on to a financial matter: "I am glad to hear that my property is turning out so well and I have to thank you very much for giving it to me." He adds: "I will apply for a room in one of the dormitories as soon as possible."

On April 27, 1906, Henry writes to his father: "I forgot to say in my last letter that I received my wash and the food, and I thank you ever so much. The squab was just great as well as the tongue. I was very sorry to have missed you yesterday over the phone as I would [have] liked very much to have congratulated you. Robert [whom Henry III identifies as Robert Simon, the nephew of Henry Sr., with whom the latter entered into a partnership named the Henry Morgenthau Company to conduct a real estate business[123]] wanted me to come down to your surprise party (which I hope was a great success), but that was out of the question, notwithstanding that I would [have] liked to have come very much." He goes on: "I think that there will be [no?] doubt about my coming to New York on my [fifteenth] birthday, as I have received permission from Mr. Rogers, and as I will miss two classes, I will have to see my instructors, one of whom I have already seen and have received his permission; now I have only to see Dr. Klark." He ends: "I envy Mr. Marks for being able to go up to Blue Mountain so early, don't you?"

On May 3, 1906, comes a rather different letter to his father: "I went to Boston yesterday and had my eyes attended to. The doctor did [not?] know how my eyes would adapt themselves to glasses, and [said] that if I was his son, he would have me leave school." There is some question about young Henry's reaction to the new glasses. He asked the oculist "to write to you. I do not know if he did." While Henry thinks he should remain at school to the end of the term, he first has to see how well he adjusts to the glasses. He continues on a more dismal note: "I had to return last night on account of being on probation, and I guess it was a good thing as I did not have a chance to get to the theatre. Today my eyes are recovering from belladonna and I have to wear dark glasses in the strong light. My regular glass[es] will not be ready till tomorrow." He goes on to an awkward subject: "That letter I sent, I see now is perfectly foolish [underlining in original] and please do tear it up. I wrote it when I had the blues, as you can well imagine, after what I went through last week. If my eyes last out, I will stay here till the school closes, as I think it would be cowardly to stop now." He closes on a happier note: "I hope you had a great time at West End and enjoyed it thoroughly."

The reference in the preceding letter to the oculist's comment (that if Henry were his son, he would have him leave school) suggests that young Henry, sensing a sympathetic soul, had poured out his misery and the oculist had responded to his young patient's psychological need. Henry Sr. wanted the satisfaction of having his son at a fashionable boarding school. He had great affection for his son, and was quite generous, but he refused to recognize the price his son was paying to satisfy his own ambition.

On May 8, 1906, young Henry writes: "Frank Koch sails for Europe this coming Thursday on 'S.S. Lorraine,' and I would like you to send him a couple of books or whatever you think is most suitable, and send it on board ship. You will find my card enclosed." The language is such as one might use to a "personal shopper" or to a busy executive's administrative assistant. His father might insist he stay at Exeter, but in exchange, his son knows he may depend on his father to do things for him.

Evidently, in response to his father's inquiry, he writes: "I am not sure what I will want for my birthday, and it will be much more fun for you and I to select it together. I shall telegraph you as you desired, and I am going to make all preparations possible to catch that 2:00 train, and as I was told, another boy has done the same thing, I hope I will be able to do the same. I hope the Mercedes will be in first-class condition so that we can have a fine ride together. I am glad that 'we' are going to the theatre together Friday night, and 'we' can go again on Saturday night."

On May 19, 1906, Henry writes again to his father: "I . . . was very sorry to leave you and New York, and its inhabitance [*sic*]. . ." He adds loyally: "but I felt better when I once got back to Exeter." That said, he asks: "Are we going to Europe?" He affects nonchalance: "I really do not care whether we go or not." He records an odd comment: "One of the boy[s] suggested that I should call for Mamma alone but I suppose I am to[o] young, not withstanding that I would like to do that." He comes finally to important matters: ". . . if you wish to meet me in Boston next Saturday or do you wish to come later, but the 26th would be just in the middle between the last time I saw you and the time you will be coming up in June."

On May 25, 1906, Henry Jr. writes: "I intend to leave Exeter tomorrow afternoon at 2:45 PM and arrive in Boston at 4:05 <u>sharp</u> [underlining in original] as that train is usually on time". He adds: "I think it would be a good idea if I should telephone you at the hotel at 9:00 AM tomorrow morning, so you may expect to hear my musical voice." (Although written with adolescent humor, Henry III has written that his father did have a fine baritone voice.)

Henry continues: "I have no particular reason for telephoning but I can speak to you so much the sooner and it might not make your wait in Boston for me quite so long." He adds with anticipation and regret: "I wish I could get there earlier but I have two classes, one at eleven and one at twelve, so I guess I will have to wait till the afternoon before I can see you." It is apparent that it is his own long wait, and not so much his father's, that is his real concern; he has a great affection for his father. Then to a most immediate interest: "Look up what shows you want to see and we can decide over the telephone the one we'll go to see." He is confident that his father will want to go to the theater.

He goes on to suggest to his father: "You could see the Weils in the morning and so be free for the rest of your stay in Boston" [presumably, to devote the rest of his time to his son Henry]. He goes on earnestly to affect modesty: "I certainly appreciate your taking all the trouble to come up to see your loafer of a son, and I will try to make your trip worthwhile." He wants to nail down the arrangements: "Now do not forget about my telephoning to you at 9:00 AM." The young man is anxious his father will go out for his family visits with no telling when his son could catch up with his father. Henry adds, out of concern for his father's convenience: "I took that hour as being most suitable and I hope it will be."

In a letter dated "Exeter 28, 1906" [the archivist adds: "May?"], young Henry writes: "I . . . hope that Mr. Smith decided to take the Altman place, as I know it will be a great relief to you." He goes on with his health: "I took my water to the doctor to see how I am after my trip to Boston and I will let you know what he says." Returning to his father, he writes: "It must have been comfortable traveling for you when it started to rain. It has rained here all day." He returns to his health: "My eyes trouble me quite a little but I will try my best to study hard." He changes key to humility: "Please excuse this awful scrawl but I am in an awful hurry." He goes to gossip: "I received a very nice letter from Louise and she sails for Europe on the [sic] June 11, and I will ask you later to send her something."

In a letter dated June 1, 1906, young Henry copes with a crisis: "After lunch I went down to see Mr. Rogers. Well, he asked me all the different circumstances, and I told him what you thought (not mentioning that I wished to leave school). Well, he told me finally that I deserved 'probation' and I took it. He is going to write to you and tell you briefly the different things." (The nature of the pranks is not described.)

Henry continues: "I wish I know [sic] just how you felt towards me after doing such a thing. It certainly is not anything actually wrong but just a foolish thing to do." In despair he writes: "please write to me just how you feel about it, and if you [feel] any different[ly] towards me, after doing such a thing." With that off his chest, he can write: "I now have a rather good piece of news. I asked my advisor to find out what my marks are going to be and they are as follows: Latin D-E, German D (I am pretty sure I will get a C), English composition D, English Literature C-, Mathematics D." He notes humbly: "They are not extra good marks . . . I am very sorry that you were under the impression that I had failed all together here. Of course," he continues, trying to throw out some hope to his father, "some of those marks I will perhaps be able to raze [sic], [but] at least I am not a failure all together."

His fears come out: "Over the telephone you sought [sic] of impressed me to think that you did not expect much more from me and that you seemed to take it for granted that I had failed in this school and could not come back. I know you did not seem entirely that way at Boston but today you seemed different." In supplication, he begs: "Please write to me, and I feel sure that you do not feel that way towards me." He adds a postscript: "I do <u>not</u> <u>mean</u> [underlining in original] what I said above. [You] seemed so awful[ly] indifferent".

Young Henry's grades were a disappointment to his father. Henry III thought his father was dyslexic. At that time, the disability was not fully recognized.

In a note dated February 16, 1906, Henry writes a sad confession that must have been difficult to make: "Now, Papa, if I write to you about my studies, please do not worry about them for it makes it only harder for me to write to you." He explains: "I have had a certain spell which comes over me at certain times," and goes on, seeking to reassure his parent: "and I am going to break away from it, let's hope, for good."

It is clear that young Henry was miserable at Exeter, with his constant mentions of homesickness, loneliness, and feeling "blue"; his psychosomatic illnesses—constant colds, eye problems, feelings of physical exhaustion—and his failure in all the years he was at Exeter to personalize even one of his classmates by name. His academic work suffered as a result. Henry often tried to suggest to his father, without success, that he would do better at school if he were permitted to live at home.

In this respect, there is an op-ed article in the *New York Times*[124] that casts light on Morgenthau's adolescent difficulties. The authors report that educational studies have revealed that children who "feel safe, valued, confident and challenged, will exhibit better school behavior and learn more to boot." The authors conclude: ". . . promoting students' social and emotional skills plays a critical role in improving their academic performance."

It is apparent that while young Morgenthau was living at home—attending the Sachs Collegiate Institute, and learning in an environment among young people who were part of his own social group, who related to him, and with whom he felt comfortable—his academic performance, if not breathtaking, was, at the very least, adequate. It is also clear that Henry Sr. had no conception of the emotional trauma to which he was exposing his son, imposing a stark apprenticeship in stoicism at a tender age.

Apparently, Henry Sr. responded to his son's May 1, 1906, letter in a forgiving fashion. Young Henry's next letter reveals a less-tragic tone. In a letter dated June 7, 1906, young Henry tries to soften the blow to his father's pride in family intellectual skills: "[B]ut do you not worry about your old loafer of a son, he will get through alright." He explains: "You know, if you are on probation you are not supposed to leave town, so I can not go down to Andover when we play them next Saturday in baseball." He adds: "Is that not a shame." There follows a not-so-subtle hint with respect to his anticipated summer activities: "If my health is not all right when I return to New York, do you think it would be best for me to go rushing around in the auto (seeing that Louise is at Blue Mountain), and do you not think it would be better for us to go right to Blue Mountain."

Evidently Henry Sr. acceded to his son's request to go to Blue Mountain quickly, and at last young Henry is able to show his father some tangible accomplishment. On July 22, 1906, fifteen-year-old Henry writes to his "dear Papa" on the stationery of the Eagle's Nest Country Club in the Adirondack Mountains in northern New York State, where the family has a cottage: "I won [underlining in original] the tournament, just think, is that not fine." He goes on: "Enclosed you will find it explained. Please save it. Also, please save the score cards." He reports: "Grandma is much better." He returns to his triumph: "Mr. Hochschild was asked by me to telephone you tomorrow, that I had won as I thought you would be pleased to hear it." He goes on to country club gossip: "Ethel Ehrmann's friend is here, and she seems to be a real nice girl. But I hardly know her as yet." He reports: "Uncle Julius M—[125] and I will meet [underlining in original] you and the family at the carry [?], so please let us know as soon as possible what day they are coming".

Morgenthau's next letter is dated September 11, 1906. He tells of his roommate who "as far as I know him, seems to be very nice, and I think I will get along with him O.K. His mother is here with him and she also seems very nice." The relationship would seem to be impersonal, for he continues: "I am just a little homesick but will get over that allright [sic]."

On September 19, 1906, Henry writes, "I am enjoying life much more this year than I ever have before, the change of being out of Dunbar, and I seem to get along a little better with the fellows. My roommate's mother is back again and is at present fixing our couch."

On October 2, 1906, he writes, "I am very glad to hear that you and Mamma decided to come up and see me. I really have no preference whether you come this Saturday . . . but if you should come the Saturday following, I would have some good clothes to wear, which I certainly have not got now. And I would hate to go to Boston looking like a bum."

He goes on to a serious concern: "I am sorry [to] say that I find that I have not got myself under perfect control yet, as last night, I went out walking with another boy, and there were a couple of girls ahead of us, and we spoke a few words to them, and I had a desire to speak more to them (but nothing more), but luckily we did not get the chance. Which proves to me that not [*sic*] matter how careful you are, your passions will spring up, but that was a good lesson to me and showed me that I did not have myself under control and I feel assured that I will abstain from such temptation the next time."

He writes to both parents on December 5, 1906: "I certainly want to thank you both for the lovely time you gave me [at] Thanksgiving. I received a letter of thanks from Elsie E—, so I suppose you must have given her a present for me. I thank you again." He goes on to apologize for disappointing his parents: "I am sorry that I am so poor in my studies and sometimes I despair about myself, whether I will ever amount to anything or not." There is a revealing postscript: "I am going to talk with you about my not going back to Exeter next year. I have been thinking that perhaps I would be able to study better if I was near the family, and then I would not feel so home-sick."

One may imagine his parents' consternation upon reading the foregoing letter, for on December 7, 1906, he writes: ". . . I should not really have written that last letter to you but I had a bad case of the blues. I am, as I told you, or ought to have told you, pretty near failing in Latin and will fail in geometry unless I take care. I am glad to say that in the last few days, I have done some good work. I took an exam in geometry this morning and I think I passed it. I hope by working hard these last few days before Xmas to be able to pass everything." There is a revealing apology at the end: "I am sorry to have caused Mamma or you any pain and I hope that in the future you will have no cause to complain, for as you said, I must knuckle down to work."

There is a six-month break in Morgenthau's letters to his parents, with the next letter in the archive dated June 27, 1907. Morgenthau is now sixteen years old, and he's writing from the Eagle's Nest Country Club in the Adirondack Mountains, where his family has a summer cottage. "I am sorry to hear that you are so angry at me. I was so busy during the week that I kept putting it off . . . You wrote to Ruth that you did not know how I came out in my examination, and I thought I told you that I will not find out until July or August." Ever the optimist, he continues: "I think I passed my Latin grammar, English & German, and perhaps Caesar and Algebra . . ."

Henry III reports: "At the end of the school year, Henry Sr., Henry Jr., and Exeter agreed that young Henry would not return in the fall." What is not clear is how Henry Sr. was persuaded to let his son drop out of Exeter. Apparently, the school was the determining factor. The faculty, one may gather, became tired of young Morgenthau's lack of scholarly accomplishment. Henry III explains: "[H]e was readmitted to the Sachs Collegiate Institute [and] after two years . . . Henry was ready to graduate, but was still not qualified to enroll as a student of architecture at Cornell, the route he and his father had chosen. To ease the transition, he attended Cascadilla, a cram school in Ithaca . . . Edward Bernays, the public relations genius, was Henry Jr.'s age and was among his classmates at Cascadilla (and then at Cornell)." Professor Blum describes Morgenthau as having reached a height of over six feet by the age of fourteen years.[126] "The diminutive Bernays remembers looking up admiringly to Henry: 'He was tall, handsome, very personable; no table-pounder or 'go-to-hell' kind of person, affable and gentle.'"[127]

The next letter is dated September 13, 1907, from the summer cottage in the Adirondacks: "At last we have got[ten] fine weather, and it looks as if it would last; Aunt Bella and Mamma had a picnic today, just for the family, and it was lots of fun. I was at Mark's for dinner yesterday and [cousin] Sumner went to the Naumburgs'. Tomorrow we are all going to a picnic given by [the] Sterns on their island . . . Miss Wallach, Alma, Sumner and I intend to sleep out tonight, and I am sure that we will have a great time. I have decided to use part of the money I won from you to get for myself a new camera."

On September 15, 1907, Henry writes to his father: "I am very glad to hear that you are going to bring Nelson up with you, and Mr. Ford and his son. Yesterday we all went to [the] Sterns' picnic and it was lots of fun . . . Tomorrow morning at five o'clock I am going to start out for the woods. I am going with Dr. Keery and Mr. Stern and Edward [?]. The idea is that the men will drive the deer towards us and then we will have an opportunity to shoot them. I intend to stay in the woods at least two or three days. Hoping that Greenhut's opening will be a success . . ."

On Sunday night, December 22, 1907, he writes from the Lakewood Hotel in Lakewood, New Jersey: "Mamma is fine, and looks better than she has in a long time. She was very much surprised and pleased to see me . . ."

The next time Morgenthau had occasion to write to his parents was on August 10, 1908. He was now seventeen years old, and the letter was written from the summer cottage: "We were all ever so glad to hear from you and to hear what a fine trip you had, across the water. Rob let us know that you went to Aix-les-Bains, and I wonder if you gave up your automobile trip. I want to say that Ruth and I sent the watermelon and the eggs and fruit from Acker & Merrill, and I am glad to hear you all enjoyed them." He promises: "From now on I write twice a week regularly and I am ashamed of myself for having written so few times."

On August 26, 1908, still at the family summer cottage, he writes: "I just received Papa's letter and I feel that I have been very neglectful in my correspondence this summer; however, from now on I will make up for it by writing regularly and often." He and his sister Helen are having a pleasant summer. He reports: "I must say [we] have very few fights seeing that we have no [word unintelligible] father and mother. Helen has been lovely and has tried very hard to keep us all on the right path."

He envies his parents and sister Alma, taking all those fine auto trips. He wonders why his father would think he would use the automobile. He announces that he intends to go directly from Eagle's Nest to Ithaca on or about September 13, where he expects to put in one week of hard studying. His college exams come September 20 through 25, and college does not start until the 29th. If he passes his exams, he is sure his father would not be "so cruel" as to refuse him the use of his automobile for a few days. He reports that they have had beautiful weather: "fine, clear, cold days, the kind that make you feel good." He goes on to social gossip: "Alice & Arthur Saks are here and they are lots of fun. Alice has great fun at table by first ruf-housing [sic] Arthur and then me. She waits until my mouth is full and then tickles me and you can imagine the rest." He ends with the hope that this long "epistle and those which are to follow shortly will quiet" his dear parents' concerns.

On September 7, 1908, on the stationery of the Eagle's Nest Country Club, young Morgenthau reports to his "dear Mamma & Papa": "Roby Simon [his cousin and his father's business partner] came up Saturday morning and is staying [at the Morgenthau cottage] until Monday night; [his sister Helen's husband] Morty goes down Monday also." He reports: "Today being Sunday, I worked in the morning and not in the afternoon." He crosses out: "I work about an hour and half this evening. So about three and half" and continues: "Two hours for a Sunday is fair."

He is hoping to enter Cornell University that fall, for he writes: "I am getting a double bed," and he explains: "one over the other as you saw when you were up at Ithaca, so that when you come to visit me, which I hope you will, you can stay right with me. I am going to send home for some linen and bed covers as I will need them. I suppose Mamma will not mind. I will not take the best if I can help it."

He discusses his travel plans, noting that he expects to be in Ithaca for eight days, and then intends to go on to New York for a little vacation and to buy a few necessities. He writes: "If I pass my exams, I have to register on the 29th, and if I do not, I will enter high school on about October 1." He tells how his tutor Mr. Kraemer "has made my work very pleasant and nice for me," and he thinks it will be very nice living with him next school year. He confesses: "I think [I] have become more sensible and have learned how little I know and how much can be done in this world." He expresses optimism: "I think if I get in [to the college], I will make good all right and stay in the College, if I only could get in." He tries to encourage his parents: "Just do not worry for I think I have got a good chance."

He turns to his relations with his sisters: "I have not written much about Ruth, for if I know Helen, she has done her share. On the [w]hole, Ruth and I have got[ten] along O.K. In fact, I very seldom tease her, and we seldom scrap. I have had numerous talks with her, but lately I have left her alone for I thought it was for the best. When I see you personally, I will tell you more." There is a postscript: "Mamma, you have not written me a letter this summer."

Henry III writes: "Eventually Henry Jr. was accepted by Cornell, where a private tutor engaged by the Morgenthaus remained on duty. When Henry's grades were poor and he failed to get into a fraternity, his father blamed the tutor . . . Henry soon realized that he was once again fighting a losing battle . . . By the Spring of 1911, Henry Jr., discouraged by his books and drawing board, left Cornell."[128]

Earlier, on November 15, 1908, he wrote to his "Dear Papa":

I enjoyed Mamma's visit ever so much. I think she [is] very much less nervous than she used to be, and I suppose it is due to Christian Science. I noticed at once that there was a change. She has mostly likely told you everything by the time you receive this letter, so I have not much else to tell you. I wish you would decide where you are going Thanksgiving as I would love to go somewhere very much. Mamma told me that the last plan was off. And decide soon. I hope your latest deal will go through, as it would be a big thing I should think, to have such a large factory in the Bronx. If you get time, I would like it very much if you would keep me posted more or less on your business.

On November 22, 1908, he writes to his parents:

I got back from Syracuse this evening at eight o'clock. Phil and I had a very nice time together. He is coming to see us Thanksgiving, and will write to you himself. He will get in about 10:00 PM Wednesday night and will come right up to the house. He does not want anyone to call for him. Now, please do <u>not</u> [underlining in original] get up any parties, as I spoke to Phil and he agreed that we would enjoy ourselves more alone. Of course, I [k]now Mamma would do it only to please me, but ——! I have decided not to come down until Thursday morning, unless you have some definite object which would be worth my while to come down for.

I have changed my mind, for I found out that we have no school on Dec. 3 or 4, as the teachers of the school have to attend a meeting in town, so the school will close down. And if you have no objections I will come down again for the four days, as I think I might see as much of you all as circumstances will allow. And I think under these conditions you would be displeased if I missed any school unnecessarily. So that accounts for my change in plans.

I hope you will take an automobile trip as I would enjoy it ever so much. And if you left early and went to the Berkshires, I could go there directly and meet you. I decided that I was old enough to decide for myself in the case I mentioned to you, so I have dropped my glee-club work as that took three to four hours a week and I needed that time. Mr. Kraemer had advised me to do it quite often, and as it was only a question of making up my mind, I thought it was up to me and not to Papa to make it for me.

There is a postscript: "I am looking forward to seeing you all again. I read in the paper about the big deal. Mamma and [I] will have to take a taxi."

On January 14, 1909, ensconced at Cornell University, Morgenthau writes a short note to his "Dear Papa": "I am awfully glad that you are going to come up and see me. I will be at the station. Drop me a line letting me know on what line you are coming, as they [sic] are two roads coming into Ithaca . . . I have two exams tomorrow, French and American Civics, so I have to hustle tonight."

On January 24, 1909, he writes:

. . . Alma is engaged. Mamma, your misgivings have at last been quieted, and now you only have Ruth and myself to worry about. I am sure you must all be delighted and are going around with the smile that will not come off. I myself cannot quite place him in my mind, so I am sorry to say I do not know whether I like him or not. But I am sure I will, for Alma has such good artistic taste, and I am sure she did not let —— [blank in original] mislead her in this most important step . . . I obeyed Papa's instructions in his last letter. I slept eleven hours last night, walked four miles this morning and slept two more hours this afternoon. I feel fairly confidant [*sic*] about my exams, hope to pass them all. Well, I wish you all kinds [of] joy. Please send me all the facts and particulars that you know of as I am naturally interested.

Henry writes to his father on February 2, 1909: "I received your telegram, and am much obliged to you for getting a Jap[anese houseman] for us. Mr. Kraemer will meet him at the station." (So much for the racist language of the period.) There is a sad bit of school news he feels obligated to pass along: "I received 70% in [F]rench, but 75% is [the] passing mark." He hastens to add: "I, however, still have hopes as they may make a new rule, and then my [F]rench might be passed. But I have continued it again in school." He adds: "I am working hard. The exam which I expected to take last Monday was not given and I did not work much on Sunday, but I at least got rested up. I gave 'Little Joey' yesterday and have to give it again Thursday before a public speaking class. I will be able to tell you more about it when I come down."

There is a short, rather desperate note dated February 14, 1909:

I have been working all Saturday & Sunday. And tonight I am tired. I had to make four maps and I have pretty nearly completed them. I have not got[ten] to my other work and that is just an example of the trouble I have. I try to do one thing well [and] it takes up all my time and I do not get to the rest of my work. I do not want you to think I am not getting along, but just want you to understand the conditions under which I am laboring. I received 80% in a Civics exam—and did not do well in a [F]rench exam. I have not yet heard my mark. I will let you know whether I will be able to use those opera tickets. I am much obliged to you for offering them to me.

On February 16, 1909, there is a pathetic note to his father: "I am sorry that I will not be able to use the opera tickets on next Saturday. Bernice has another date and her mother does not approve." There follows a sad confession that must have been difficult to make:

Now, Papa, if I write to you about my studies, please do not worry about them, for it makes it only harder for me to write it to you. I have not done well in two historie [*sic*] exams which I took a week ago. I have had a certain spell which comes over me at certain times and I am going to break away from it, let's hope, for good. I want you to understand clearly my case. I work hard in school. I have been doing my work pretty regularly with Mr. Kraemer. That much of my work with school takes up my time till supper. Then after supper perhaps I have two hours to do my homework in, which is not always enough. My conscience has been bothering me that I have not always got[ten] my work done, and that I have not spent as much time <u>after</u> <u>supper</u> [underlining in original] as I should have. I hope I will be able to drop my French and that will clear matters up. You see, I really have no more studies this term than last, but two of my subjects, Advanced Algebra and Solid Geometry, are brand new, and that's where the trouble lies.

On March 2, 1909, he writes: "I spoke [to Mr.] Boynton about my work, and [b]y [?] the beginning of next w[ee]k [?] I will know whether they will [ac]cept my [F]rench at Cornell or not. Until then I can really do nothing. I also mentioned to [Mr.] Boynton that [I] might stop school in April. I will know everything by next week. I told you I did badly last month, but I did not do as badly as I expected. I passed for the month in French, Algebra, & perhaps history. However, that is doubtful, but I know I flunked Solid Geometry. Of course, that can all be made up as I get time, and I am going to do my best until next week now."

There is a postscript: "By next Friday, I have [to] decide on a subject which I wish to write on for my graduation Thesis. I have to have two subjects and then the teacher makes a choice of one. Perhaps you can suggest one or two to me."

On March 4, 1909, he writes to his father: "I have two more opportunities to come to New York before I come home for good: namely either May 8 or 15 and May 30. Now, if I come down May 15, I may not come again till June 20. But maybe it is best for me to come May 15, and if it is possible, why I will come May 30, also. It is understood then that I will be in New York at 7:30 PM May 14. I will let Bianca [k]now that I will come. I have spoken to Kraemer, and as I want to talk to you about my work and get your advice, I will call you up at 30 West 72nd St., May 5 at 6:35 PM."

He gives a report on his schoolwork: "My work has been coming along much better the last few days. And it is the first time really since Xmas that I have been getting all of my lessons prepared."

On March 15, 1909, he writes to his "Dear Mamma & Papa": "I want to thank you both again, ever so much for the lovely time

I have just had. I really enjoy myself so much in New York that when I get back here I feel like working. At least I know for the rest of [the] time, until Easter, I am going to apply myself. It is quite cold up here and it snowed a while today." School affairs intrude: "I will send you my report to sign shortly." He admits the bitter truth: "I know it is very poor." He tries to leave his parents with something in the way of hope for them to grasp: "I also know the next one is going to be better."

He writes to his "Dear Papa" on April 8, 1909: "I am working well this week and I am glad of it. One feels good when one knows that one is doing one's duty. That is the feeling which I have had a slight taste of in the last few days. My teacher told me I stand third in my class in Solid Geometry and he expects to call on me when a hard knot comes up." Having come to this not-insignificant achievement, he goes on to general matters: "We are having beautiful warm weather. I took a nap this afternoon for I was very tired. My singing teacher is away this week, so I take no lessons. Mr. Kraemer & I have been working pretty near two hours every afternoon this week on mechanical drawing." There is a postscript: "Please write!"

On April 29, 1909, almost eighteen years old, he writes to his father: "Well, sir, have you forgotten that I am alive. I thought that my request for money might stir you up. I enclosed a letter from Alma and Maurice, it is certainly very funny. Please keep it, and in fact all their letters that I send you, as I want them." He reports on schoolwork: "I dropped my [F]rench and have now got most of my afternoons off. In fact, on Thursday and Friday I do not have to go back in the afternoon at all. At last my composition got finished. I had a typewritten copy made of it and will send it to you [two words illegible] when it is returned to me." He reports that he has been aching the last few mornings, but feels it is much better. He had two exams that day and did fairly well in one and not so well in the other. He reports that Mr.

George spoke at the high school the other day, the founder of the George Junior Republic. He writes: "I am going there some day and while anyone can be shown through, I would like it very much if you could get for me a letter of introduction. [B]ut if it is any trouble, why do not bother."

On April 30, 1909, he writes a fairly long letter to his father that begins:

> You have partly misunderstood me. I told Mr. Kraemer that I thought there would be no trouble in getting the money. That is not entirely final and I could back out if I wanted to. The money would not be alone for his patent but to give him enough to live on while he is learning the business of some company at naturally small wages. I think this is a worthy cause and so will you if you look at it in the right light. I am not by any means taken away by the man, but I want to help him where the money is mine and not being used. I should have spoken to you first and will do so in the future, if another case should happen to come up.

That said, he continues with less-controversial matters: "Thanks for the check. I heard a concert given by the Boston Festival Orchestra. It was a pretty good concert. The orchestra and a large chorus is here as they have a spring music festival here every year at this time. I will be able to leave here next Friday on the 12:15 PM Lackawanna train. It arrives in New York at 7:30 PM I will come right out to Ardsley or do whatever you suggest."

There is a postscript: "This evening I am going up and spend this evening with Auerbach. [H]e is giving a little party. I sent some flowers to Alma today. Please do me a favor and send one of Alma's pictures to Sumner Weil at once. [Y]ou will oblige me by doing so."

It is apparent that the teenage Morgenthau has come to understand that his father would permit certain actions by his son and not others, such as giving money to a tutor who was already being paid what Henry Sr. must have considered a fairly liberal salary, with not very satisfactory results.

To anticipate for a moment, there is one other letter in which young Morgenthau exhibits his fledgling efforts to engage his father's connections to assist a business enterprise for charitable purposes. On February 2, 1910, he writes in a long letter to his father:

> I was very glad to hear from you, and I am sorry that you miss me so. I wrote in an awful hurry, which accounts for my mistakes in spelling. I will try and do better this time.
>
> I want to ask you for your aid in a little business I am trying to put through. R. Neuburger, a graduate of Sachs [Collegiate Institute, the private high school that Morgenthau himself had attended both prior and subsequent to his matriculation at Phillips Exeter], is the manager of the English Dramatic Club play. He came to me and wanted to know whether I knew of any charity which would want an organization of such a character to give a benefit performance. I told him all I could do for him would be a Jewish Charity, which might be offensive to some member of the cast. He agreed with me.

What is extraordinary today is how casually both young men accept the fact that Gentile cast members could object to being the beneficiaries of charity from a *Jewish* organization, and that such Social Darwinist prejudice was the norm.

Morgenthau continues:

But coming up on the train (Neuburger talked to me on the train), I could not sleep at once and so I thought the matter over and hit upon this idea. It seems to be that either Chas. Frohman or Klaw & Erlanger [Broadway producers of the period] if properly approached would consider the following proposition. Namely, to [give] the Cornell Dramatic Club a play house for a Friday afternoon (so as not to interfere with [the] regular performance that might be going on) for the production of *An Enemy of the People* by Henrik Ibsen. For the Society to come to <u>Brooklyn</u> [underlining in original] their expenses for the day would be $100.00. They would want a guarantee of $100.00, the manager to first take from the gate receipts his expenses for opening the theatre, and then 2/5 of what would remain should come to Cornell Society. It can not cost at the most $200.00 to open a theatre, plus $100.00 for [the] Societies [*sic*] expenses [that] would make $300.00. From the Cornell Alumni and the Brooklyn School children, the latter having shoun [*sic*] their interest in the Society; [there] could easily be drawn upon an audience of three to seven hundred people.

Clearly, Henry is so caught up in his ideas, he has difficulty fitting them into coherent sentences, and thus omits words. He continues: "The play, *An Enemy of the People*, was given here [at the Cornell campus] with success. The same cast will practically take part again this year, especially the leading man of last year's performance. Now, I want you to try for me, whether you can [get] some manager to undertake this proposition. I was given to understand that the *Brooklyn Eagle* would back the Society, which means much, and I thought I could get Ox [?] to take an interest also. They want the theatre for Friday afternoon, April 7, if possible, or else a day sooner or later would not matter. If any manager will listen to my proposition, let me know and I [underlining in original] will write [to] him".

Morgenthau goes on to defend his enthusiasm:

The players are good and can be depended upon. Any manager ought to want to give high-class drama a boost, without any risk or expense to himself. He would get a lot of good advertisement out of it, for the Society would come each year, if they made good. I would like to know, if it is possible by this Monday, but if it [is] necessary to wait, I could do so for a month or more. I hope it will not be of too much trouble to you, but it will mean a lot to me, as I may be made manager of [the] show next year. I would prefer you not to say anything to anyone, for it is all so uncertain. I want to make out of the Dramatic Society, what you are doing with the Underwood and at the same time bring myself into prominence. All I want is for you to start the ball rolling (this most [underlining in original] important part), and I will take care of the details. If I was in New York, I could go and see the men, with letters of introduction, but I can not do that from here. It will mean quite a lot to me if you can put it through. Please give it your immediate attention, if you will bother with it at all, and let me know the results.

Young Morgenthau explains to his father by way of justification:

If I do get this, I will start into a competition for manager with some other boys, who have been at it for a month or more. It will give [me] a big advantage over them. And is it fair? The competition is naturally made to bring out the business ability of the boys. The boy who can give them [the] best advantages is the boy they want. But am I not showing my business knowledge by thinking out such a scheme alone? The head man of the Society jumped at it when I told him about [it]. And he told me to get the theatre for them if possible. Of course, for a play like this which goes to the big cities, they want a man of influence from the cities. The present manager having his position because he is capable of getting a theatre and [a] good audience in New York. While another boy would not be able to make an entrance into New York for the play. So I am not really using those powers which I have within my grasp to further their interest and really make them a successful organiz[ation]. Please let me know soon, as I am naturally anxious to get word.

From your troublesome but appreciative son,
Henry.

There is a postscript: "Theatre to be in Brooklyn, L.I." Crossed out is: "New York City." Young Morgenthau has forgotten for the moment that the five boroughs of the city were consolidated in 1898 into a single municipality.

Morgenthau apparently received a noncommittal response, for he adverts to the Cornell Drama Society once more in an undated letter to his father. He writes:

I was certainly glad to be able to talk to you as you could easily hear. I was only sorry I could not talk with Ma and Ruthy. Enclosed you will find clippings from the *Ithaca Journal* and the *Cornell Daily Sun*, a student paper. The clippings speak for themselves. I spoke to them about a vaudeville house, but he said he did not think it [would be appropriate]. The thing is to get a theatre in a good part of the town, it is an advertisement in itself. They want it for a matinee or evening on the last Thursday in March, I believe it is March 31. Please do not put yourself out, and I can wait until it is convenient for you. One of the boys wrote Erlanger and he said he would know by the end of this month whether he would have a theatre or not. But this boy is a total stranger and it might come to naught. There is little doubt but what they can draw at least 500 people. The girl parts are taken by girls from the college, something unusual in college theatricals. There is no doubt but what they will give an <u>excellent</u> [underlining in original] performance. For I was at the first rehearsal and any doubts I had myself were brushed aside.

I am feeling O.K.

Love from Henry.

Morgenthau was now about to reach his eighteenth birthday, and on May 2, 1909, he writes to his father: "I saw 'The Thief' last night. It was the second company but I enjoyed it. Mr. Kraemer invited one of the actors here for supper and he was a very nice gentleman. He gave us passes for the performance." He reports on the weather: "We have had quite a bit of snow up here lately and it certainly seems out of place." A most important matter must be taken up. He writes: "I have used most of the money you sent me in paying bills. I have kept account of it. I find that, counting $120.00 for board for this next month plus other expenses, I will have to have about $150.00, not now but just before I leave here."

An awkward subject must be addressed: "I have not studied much over Saturday and Sunday, but I will get quite some work done before I go to bed tonight." He waxes philosophical to suggest his recreation was not an entire waste of time: "That play I saw teaches a great lesson, and as I suppose you have seen the play, you will understand what I mean. Not only the relationship between father and son, but the way a young matron can lead a young man astray." He goes on to his studies: "In school we have started on a review of algebra and will, I expect [word unintelligible] to begin to review Solid Geometry before the week is up." Finally, there are practical details: "Please ask Mamma not to put anything of mine away and to leave everything where it is, as I want to do it myself. I intend storing a lot of my things here in Ithaca so that I will have everything where I want next fall. My housekeeper said I could put anything I wanted in my future rooms and her attic over the summer." There is the usual *envoi*.

There is a short note dated June 13, 1909, addressed to his "Dear Papa": "I told the Jap [!] that I would take him and I will bring him with me when I come. I have been doing quite some work and I am ready to do my best at my exams. I will write you tomorrow night how I did. Yesterday I played tennis. The weather is fairly cool here. I hope it will be so tomorrow. Well, Papa, love to all from your son Henry."

The next day, June 14, 1909, he is as good as his word and writes to his father, but in a disheartened tone of voice: "I took an examination in Advanced Algebra, Solid Geometry and American History and Civics. The only one I feel reasonably positive about is American History and Civics. I find out early tomorrow morning whether I passed Geometry or not. If I passed it I need not take the examination in Geometry with the Board Examiners. I did my best & I hope for the best. I feel somewhat tired as I took exams from 9:15 to 5:30 with only a half hour for lunch. I will write to you as soon [as] I hear definitely."

There is a break in the letters that suggests Morgenthau spent the summer with his family at their summer cottage in the compound at Blue Mountain.

The next letter is dated Sunday, October 17, 1909. It is unusual in that Morgenthau has now discovered real paragraphing. It is also addressed to both his parents:

I received only one letter from you, Papa, last week. You must have been very busy. Please write to me occasionally, a long letter from at home, and keep me in touch with the general situations, financial and political, etc., because you know it interests me. Today, I got up late and read most of the day. You know we have an exam every Friday in Analytic Geometry. They mark us as follows: A = 100%; B = 80%–60%; C = 60%–40% and D is below 40%. Well, in the first exam I got an A. But in last Friday['s] exam I know I failed.

The reason is simple. I have not studied. You know I told you it is hard for me to work at nights [*sic*]. Well, I think the trouble is that I have not started soon enough after supper. I am going to try my best to get settled down to my homework this week in all my subjects.

P.S. You know, Papa, that the twenty-four [hours?] we spent together were one of the most pleasant times I ever had. When I awoke, in the following morning, I had to rub my eyes & think just where I was. It seemed like a dream.

On October 21, 1909, he writes to his father:

I am sorry I neglected to write to you last night. Last night the Sophomores came into the Freshman drawing rooms and wrecked up the whole room. Things were on the roof, outside the windows and in fact every place but where they should be. But I finally got together most everything that belonged to me. I have not mastered myself yet, but it is going to come, for it has to—enough said. You can not tell me what to do, or anyone else, for I know only too well what I ought to do, and I am going to fight to the finish. I look at it as another part of myself which must be killed once & for all, and then I will be free to apply myself.

Love, Henry

There is an ominous postscript: "I am having a lot of work fired at me, but I think it will not be too much."

What happened next is described by Henry III: "[He] soon realized that he was once again fighting a losing battle. . . .[129] By the spring of 1911, Henry Jr., discouraged by his books and drawing board, left Cornell."[130] At loose ends, for a time Henry became a timekeeper on a construction project. Then, at his father's suggestion, he tried volunteering his services for social work that summer at the Henry Street Settlement House.[131]

Without any real sense of direction, Henry took advantage of his father's business connections to get a job with the Underwood Typewriter Company in Hartford, Connecticut, where he came down with typhus. When he was sufficiently recovered, Henry Sr. insisted his son go to a Texas ranch for several weeks of recuperation.[132]

The letter that follows, dated January 8, 1910,[133] provides evidence that young Morgenthau—just four months shy of his twentieth birthday—has experienced a kind of revelation. The tone is vastly different from his previous letters; even the salutation has changed. It is looser, simpler:

Dear Ma & Pa,

Although I have only been here two days, I begin to feel at home. This country and the life is wonderful to me, who has always lived in the city. It is just six, and we have finish[ed] our supper and the sun has set. I stood at the gate and watched the sun go down slowly. It is wonderful.

I will not attempt to describe this place to you all at once, for I have not been here long enough to have set views about the place.

My trip here in the train was uneventful so I will not say anything about it. The ranch is twenty-five miles from town and we came out here in the auto. We are connected by telephone to Midland, so a telegram will <u>always</u> [underlining in original] reach me. I live in a small one-story house with Leonard Pence [w]ho is twenty-two and practically runs the place, as his father W. Pence is away most of the time taking care of [name illegible] ranches in Mexico and other places. They have a house w[h]ere we eat right with the men. Then they have a house where all the men sleep, and a couple of hundred feet away is the corral and barns and blacksmith shop. For breakfast we get eggs, bacon, potatoes, coffee and <u>no</u> [underlining in original] milk or butter. For lunch we have bacon, kidney beans, potatoes, coffee, molasses. Supper: pork, potatoes, beans, molasses, cabbage. If I am not a different boy when I get back with this fresh air, frugal food and exercise, there will be something wrong. I will describe [to] you the rest in the next few days. I have heard from no one as yet. Please write, and you, Ma, please write more than once a month.

My very best love to you all,
from your loving son,
Henry

CHAPTER 3

Love, Marriage, and Property

Morgenthau's stay at the Pence ranch in Texas proved to be decisive in his life. Writing to his parents on Sunday, April 4, 1915 [year identified by the archivist], Morgenthau takes note that his sister Ruth was planning to visit him in ten days at his farm in the Hudson River Valley of New York State. Concerned with social proprieties, Morgenthau had arranged for the wife of his head foreman to sleep at the house whenever Ruth had both "boys and girls staying there." On the other hand, if Ruth brought along only a girlfriend, a chaperone was unnecessary in his opinion. It is entirely possible that Morgenthau envisioned his sister and her friend sharing one bedroom together, providing a lack of privacy for untoward events. In any case, the reason he gives as explanation for his thought on the matter of social propriety is, interestingly, "[b]ecause, supposing I had a ranch in Texas, Ruth might come out to visit me with some girl and no one would say a word." That said, he hopes his parents will agree.

Professor Blum, in writing his biography of Morgenthau, asked the deceptively simple question: How did Morgenthau come to take up farming as a vocation? It was a fundamental decision, and, as with most people who are unable to express the nature of deep-seated perceptions in their lives—why else the need for Freudian psychoanalysis—Morgenthau, in *his* conversations with Blum, could make a joke to cover his inarticulateness. "In a desperate move to get out from under [my father's intention to have me in business with him], I moved to the country . . ." As Blum put it, Morgenthau "was determined to be in a business about which his father knew nothing . . ."[134]

In truth, Morgenthau himself knew nothing about farming, any more than he knew anything about property management or the buying and selling of real property, matters that were at the core of what had become his father's business operation. The motivation for Morgenthau's determination to become a farmer lay elsewhere, in a Social Darwinist mode.

Professor Blum writes, "In 1912, he told his father he had decided to become a farmer."[135] Henry III adds, "With this purpose clearly in his mind, he returned to Cornell [University] to enroll in the School of Agriculture."[136] Morgenthau was twenty-one years old. What is remarkable is that Morgenthau was able to convince his father, and that Henry Sr. went along with the idea. Whether Henry Sr. realized immediately that his son envisioned a major business enterprise involving no small investment of money is an interesting question. The point is that Morgenthau had become mature and forceful enough so that his father accepted his son's decision.

That Henry Sr. had doubts is evidenced by a letter of Morgenthau's addressed to his parents, dated July 20 (1915). Morgenthau (among other matters) writes directly for his father's eyes: "I have yours of May 8th, 18th & 30th & June 6th before me and will try and answer any direct questions you may have put.

"First, in regard to the farm, I am not or trying not to spend a red cent unless there is an absolute need for it. Second, I am absolutely of one accord with you, that is, if the farm does not pay soon, to shut down on it. I can not afford to spend the best of my years at something that will not give tangible results [in dollars and cents]."

Yet that is exactly how Morgenthau was to spend his life.

He had earlier written to his father, explaining his interest in his father's political adventures in connection with Woodrow Wilson's efforts to secure the Democratic nomination for president in 1912, and asked to be kept informed. Political activities fascinated Morgenthau without in the least inciting any desire within him to become an active participant as a candidate or a political party official. His experiences at boarding school were too strongly imprinted in his mind. *He had learned to get along by going along.*

As it happened, Henry Sr. had become one of a small group of men whom Woodrow Wilson had recruited to support him in his somewhat quixotic quest for the Democratic presidential nomination in 1912. Henry Sr. describes how, after Wilson had wrested the nomination, as was then the custom, his defeated competitors at the national convention came to the Wilson summer home at Sea Girt, New Jersey, to tender "their hearty congratulations." Wilson's most formidable opponent, Senator Champ Clark of Missouri, "could not master his disappointment, nor conceal it. His depression lay upon the gathering like a cloud."

Joe Tumulty, later Wilson's White House personal secretary (who today would probably be called his "chief of staff") came to Henry Sr. to suggest Clark be invited for an automobile ride. Clark accepted, saying he wanted to see his daughter who was visiting in the neighborhood. Apparently, Clark was as anxious to get away as Tumulty was to see him leave. Clark and his friends filled the car and off they drove with young Morgenthau at the wheel.[137] Henry Sr. recounts how: "[w]hen my son came back, he had a broad smile on his countenance. 'Where do you suppose,' he exclaimed, 'Clark asked me to take him? His daughter is staying with George Harvey's daughter!'"[138] Henry Sr. goes on to explain that Harvey was one of Wilson's early supporters who "broke" with him and later ended up as the future President Harding's ambassador to London.[139]

Henry III writes: "In the fall of 1913, a few months after finishing up at Cornell (without a degree), Henry Morgenthau, Jr., then twenty-two, acquired some one thousand acres of farmland in the township of East Fishkill, about fifteen miles south of Poughkeepsie, New York."[140] In those years, southern Dutchess County had the advantage of being entirely rural in character while still within (if barely) commuting distance of New York City. Henry III explains: "The Fishkill Farms, paid for by the senior Morgenthau, was at first a joint father and son enterprise."[141] This did not suggest any lessening of the close relationship that existed between the two of them. For good measure, Henry Sr. also "arranged for a junior staff member [of the United States Department of Agriculture] Carl Schurz Scofield to take a leave of absence so that Morgenthau could retain him as an advisor. So the two young men, accompanied by Scofield's male secretary, J. A. Taylor, took off on a transcontinental grand tour."[142]

On April 24, 1913, Morgenthau wrote to his parents from the city of St. Joseph, Missouri:

> I spent four days in and around Fargo, North Dakota. Monday noon we got into a hired auto . . . and went about 100 miles across the State. On account of bad roads, we did not reach our destination until 12 that night. About 10 PM we got stuck in a mudhole and it took four horses, supplied by the farmers, to pull us out. The moon came out and from 10:30 to 12 we ran under the guidance of 3/4 full moon. It was a wonderful experience.

Morgenthau also recorded his impressions of farming practices in North Dakota. He noted: "[T]he general run of farmers are not making any money out of their farming operations . . . mainly because they grow only one crop, wheat, and in a [*sic*] unfavorable wheat season they go broke. For the last two or three years they have not had a really good wheat crop . . ." He writes that land values are increasing rapidly so that the farmers are becoming wealthier yearly, on paper. He notes local banks pay "big dividends . . . 6% and up for deposits, so you can see what they must demand on loans." He observes that "[a]s you go west in North Dakota money gradually goes up to 10% [for interest rates], as the country is newer and less developed, the risks being proportionately greater."

Actually seeing the land to which those judgments applied allowed Morgenthau to retain the abstract information he was receiving in a way that had not been possible in a classroom setting.

Taking into account his father's large investment in the Underwood Typewriter Company, Morgenthau reports that he had several talks with the Underwood manager at Fargo, who expressed his disappointment that no officer or company official ever visited the Midwest. Sympathetic, Morgenthau wonders whether that was a good thing. He also includes the information that the manager had become familiar with the new Royal typewriter, then on the market for six months, and it seemed so much like the Underwood model that the manager feared it could develop into a serious competitor.

Morgenthau also asks his father to tell him about financial conditions in the country. He recounts how they wanted to see a large corn farm that day, but "the roads were so bad, we did not attempt it." He tells of their present plans to go on to St. Louis, adding: "[I]f the Mississippi Valley is flooded, we will go right through to New Orleans." He wanted to visit two of the large ranches in Texas and have the party work its way up to San Antonio. He is "mighty glad" to get his father's letter.

Morgenthau adds that he thinks he is learning a great deal. His health has improved greatly from his adolescent years. He is once again what he calls "his normal self." He goes to bed and rises early. He is reading quite a bit on agricultural subjects. He is having Mr. Scofield's secretary Taylor prepare a great number of statistics that should be interesting. He acknowledges that it is hard for him to accustom himself to having someone do the little things for him, as he is used to doing for himself. He reports Mr. Scofield as saying it is harder to get yourself out of the habit of doing things than into it.

Since his father is paying for the trip, Morgenthau is careful to include: "So far I feel that the expedition is being run on fairly efficient lines. I am keeping strict account of the parties' [*sic*] expenses and we know exactly what we are spending, which is a new experience for me, and has a good influence not only on me, but the whole party."

He ends by telling his father: "I believe this is the longest letter I have ever written to you but I am bubbling over with enthusiasm, new ideas and energy."

The answer to the question that Professor Blum put to him—How did you decide to become a farmer?—has complex Social Darwinist roots, reflecting Morgenthau's adolescent life experience within the currents of contemporaneous society, as he found how social attitudes ebbed and flowed in the little adolescent world at boarding school. His letters portray not an effort to escape his father's interest, but rather a desire to share with his father, as his closest friend, the discoveries he was making about the larger world in which he found himself, and how he could find an accommodation to it and the means of discretely participating in that world.

The trip west with Scofield took three and a half months. Morgenthau "investigated farms producing wheat, potatoes, alfalfa, milk and cream, cattle, sugar, rice and citrus fruits. He gave special attention to the mechanization of agriculture, to scientific farming, to canning for home consumption and to rural schools."[143]

In the early fall of 1913, Henry Sr. arrived at Constantinople as the new American ambassador to the Ottoman Empire.

On November 24, 1913, Morgenthau writes to his father and sister Helen, her husband, and their sons, who are visiting the new ambassador: "We have just received your first batch of letters and we are all mighty glad to hear from you, as it is almost three weeks since you left. It must be simply great to meet all the people and to be so extremely busy." Henry's letter continues:

As I wrote to you before, if I am wanted I would be very glad and anxious to come out about January first, to visit you for about a month at Constantinople. I have spoken to Mama about it several times and she is determined that she will not go out before January twenty-eighth. Of course, she has a good many reasons for this, but Alma and I think we know the one reason why she wants to stay as long as possible. As I have to be back in the United States on or before March first, to look after our farm, it seems to me only fair that I should take this opportunity and come out as soon as I can, because if I wait for Mama and Ruth, to bring them out, they will want to spend a week in Paris, and so on, and it would, therefore, not be worth my while to come at all. I think, under the circumstances, you will be apt to agree with me, that it will be all right for me to come as soon as I can leave.

I spent Wednesday at [the segregated] Hampton Institute in Virginia, and had a most interesting and uplifting day. On that day they had a farmers conference, at which a great many of the negroes and farming demonstrating agents throughout the state were present. Some of the guests were Governor Mann of Virginia, Mr. Butterick and Mr. Green, the Executive Secretary and Treasurer, respectively, of the General Board of Education, and several educational men of Virginia. Doctor Flexner was there and sent you his warm regards. We all sat down to lunch together, and after lunch they had a big meeting at which Governor Mann spoke very well. I brought back with me an invitation for Doctor Wise to speak down there on the Founders Day Celebration and I think he will do so. They were very anxious to have me stay several days longer but it was necessary for me to come back on account of previous engagements. After seeing their work and how responsive the negroes were, I am very much inclined to accept the trusteeship which Dr. Peabody offered me.

Morgenthau now announces what will prove to be a disastrous business venture: "I have bought thirty-two steers at the Buffalo market and have them now on our place and intend to try the experiment of fattening them this winter. I do not know yet just what they cost me, as I have not seen Mr. Brill, the cattle buyer who bought them for me . . . It has aroused a great deal of interest in the neighborhood . . ." Morgenthau continues:

I have made no progress so far with Mrs. Van Wyck. We have not made any offer and she has been so high in her price that Mr. Perkins felt that rather than offer a sum for her place and then have her refuse it, thereby breaking off negotiations, it would be better just to keep in friendly communication with her.

My neighbor, Mr. Minton, wrote me a letter, with a note of introduction from Mr. Freddie Allen. I had a long talk with Minton. It seems that Mrs. Van Wyck was playing him against me in her effort to sell her property and he has practically agreed to keep his hands off and leave the field open to me, so I hope that after she sees that we really do not have to have her property she will be sensible about her price.

I am going to take the family up this Saturday to see the place for the first time and am anxious to see what they think of it.

Morgenthau then reports to his father that he has prudently asked Mr. Scofield to look at the farm: "Mr. Scofield spent Sunday and Monday up there and he said that the farm, as a whole, looked very good to him, and especially liked the looks of the soil. In fact, he said, that with the land and labor so reasonable and the farmers in that locality getting top price for their produce, it was almost too good to be true. He told me that he will be glad to come up next spring and look the place over again and help me with advice . . ."

Writing to his parents on April 23, 1914, Morgenthau begs off meeting them in London because he was busy with the farm.

On May 6, 1914, Morgenthau writes to his father:

. . . I can get away from the farm about Dec. 15, but not much sooner than that. However, I am not able to look that far ahead, because we may have a late or early fall and that makes a large difference.

The work on the farm is coming along fairly well. Of course, certain things have transpired, which if I had had previous experience could have foreseen. I made a mistake in the type of plow I bought. It did the work fairly well on our dandy land, but when it came to the stony ground it was not good for very much. I had bought 9, and succeeded in swapping and trading in 7 for 7 good plows. Also I was a little slow in having my fertilizer mixed and potato seed cut. But up to date I am proud to say I have not kept my men waiting for seed or anything else. But they have been able to go ahead with their work, weather permitting. One other feature has been a problem. I have undertaken to set out some 1,400 fruit trees (apple trees) which cover some 47–48 acres. And it was a big job, bigger than I had any idea of. But I secured for this job the services of a fruit man, who has a 30-acre fruit farm of his own right near me. And he took charge of the work. We had planted: 700 Baldwin (Permanents), 300 McIntosh, 200 Rome Beauties, 200 Opalescents [the latter] Fillers. The Baldwins are what we call "Permanents" in that we plan to leave them in [the] ground permanently. The Baldwin comes into bearing from its eighth to 12th year, depending a great deal on what kind of treatment it receives. The other three varieties are supposed to come into bearing 2 or 3 years earlier, and we call them "fillers."

Morgenthau now explains the details of the operation on the ground:

I have been able to put the spring work through so far by employing every man in the neighborhood who would work and by going to N.Y. City and Poughkeepsie, and getting temporary help. Instead of working 10 men, our regular number, the last few days I have averaged 20 or more, but that will last only a few days.

The mixing of fertilizer should be done in the winter time and we will do so next winter.

Last week I came to New York for Aline Dreyfus' wedding to Mergan Gunst. And Saturday I got to Helen's [around] 7:30 PM . . . I am cutting off more and more of my N.Y. connections, as it is very difficult for me to leave the place just now and I always have a guilty conscience when I am away . . . I do intend to come to N.Y. once in a while but just at present my place is on the farm.

My cook Eva, her husband and little boy have been on my place about a week and you may feel rest assured that I am in good trustworthy hands . . . Stephan, Eva's husband, has started to paint and fix up the house. It will take a month or so before we are finally settled in our new home.

With respect to servants, Henry III comments wryly: "Most households had more full-time servants than family members . . . servants were considered a necessity—the status of a family freed from all manual labor had to be upheld at all costs. Wages paid to the help were meager, although their physical needs were supplied: lodgings, food, uniforms, hand-me-down clothes for 'days off,' medical services . . . Servants had no rights, only privileges and a homemade safety net of sorts. Most were single women. A few had been deserted by men. None were expected to have any close relationships with the opposite sex."[144]

In a letter dated May 24, 1914, Morgenthau writes: ". . . I am writing this letter under the trees on our farm. The country is beautiful early in the morning (6:30–7:30). We had ten days without any rain and that enabled us to get a lot of work done. I have practically all my potatoes in and about half my corn. The season has been an unusually late one. But on account of the very wet spring we had, although it held us back for quite a while, I think we are going to have a very good season."

Writing in a letter dated June 12, 1914, Morgenthau reports he spent the weekend at the country house of the Nathan Strausses. He goes on to say: "Everything on the farm is coming along fine. We had very beneficial rains last Thurs[day], which has helped us a lot." He adds: "I am going to write regular [*sic*] from now on."

Professor Blum comments:

Morgenthau's progress in his new life caught the attention of the Poughkeepsie *Sunday Courier* in June, 1914. "His first venture," a long article explained, "was in the raising of steers and last fall he went to the western market . . . and purchased a carload of . . . fine animals . . . already butchers are hastening . . . to secure them. The success of the venture is assured and Mr. Morgenthau has the credit of again starting what may become one of the chief factors in giving our people better meat at cheaper prices . . . He is an enthusiast over farming for profit . . . He has no new-fangled ideas—he keeps no livery, no high-priced chauffeur or landscape gardeners or unnecessary help but is directing his time to plain, simple, practical farming . . . He is using the most modern machinery . . . has become a member of the local Wiccoppee Grange . . . and is fast acquiring a large host of friends . . . He has recently been made a Deputy Sheriff." This was a lot to show for less than a year in the country.[145]

Along those lines, there is an undated flyer in the Morgenthau Archives at the Roosevelt Library at Hyde Park, New York, that most probably dates from this period. It announces Fishkill Farms' acquisition of a Holstein bull named "Dutchland Colantha Sir Inka," identifying it as a proven sire and inviting requests for impregnation.

Morgenthau's ongoing, committed, interpersonal relationship with his father is illustrated in a letter dated Wednesday, August 12, 1914. He writes:

> I received your nice letter of July 24th. You may not know it but in all your letters you hardly ever mention anything about your personal thoughts. In fact, your silence to me is a bad omen. Because if you were really happy and enjoying yourself to the full[est] extent you would say so. But from your reference in your last letter to the faults of society, I have found the first symptoms of a long extended disease. My only hope is that you will be really satisfied with life here in America after your sojourn abroad, your contact with nobility & your taste of political success. One thing is certain. As soon as you come home, you must become connected with some large enterprise, either financial or philanthropic. [W]ork and hard brain work alone will keep you happy here and contented. A man of less balance than you possess might spend the rest of his life in constant, unsatiated ambition. Of course I would be glad to see you go on & upward in political life but is the game worth the candle? Are the hurts, the cuts, filled up and healed by final success. I don't know? You may be surprised to see me write to you in this strain, but I can foresee your coming home and then what?

Curiously, Morgenthau is unknowingly prophesying the course of his own life thirty years into the future, after the death of Franklin Roosevelt, whom Morgenthau has then barely met.
Morgenthau goes on:

> My one hope and desire is that our paths of work & play & endeavor may soon come together & that we may run a

double-track railroad side by side through life. I certainly, as the younger, will be only too glad to do more than my share to shape the future so that it will converge with yours. The only way we may differ is that whatever enterprise we go into, I would like to feel that there is some chance of financial return while you may want to have it purely philanthropic. But is not true constructive welfare work necessarily one which is self-supporting. You certainly must know by this time that the mere giving of money is not always a benefit to them on whom it is bestowed. However, whether it is a large farm or a model city, the future will work itself out for us.

So Morgenthau ends the thought with the optimism of youth and concludes with what is important to him: "In any case, I am with you [underlining in original]."

To digress for a moment: It is fortunate that Harold Ickes, future Roosevelt Secretary of the Interior, like the good heresy hunter that he was, never saw the preceding paragraph with its vaguely patronizing, rich-man's-son flavor in the comments about "constructive welfare work" and how "the mere giving of money is not always a benefit to them on whom it is bestowed". As it was, in his diary for Wednesday, March 27, 1935, Ickes quoted with relish the comment of Vice President John Nance Garner, that "[h]e does not believe Morgenthau has any sympathy with progressive ideas. [Garner] believes that in his heart [Morgenthau] is against the bill to abolish the holding companies, and that in general his sympathies are with the big interests of Wall Street."[146]

To return to Morgenthau's letter of August 12, 1914: There is one other curious detail. Morgenthau wrote: "The only way we may differ is that whatever enterprise we may go into, I would like to feel that there is some chance of financial return while you may want to have it purely philanthropic." If anything, this represents a curious reversal of roles between Morgenthau and his father, as between them, it was Henry Sr. who focused on financial return and his son who allowed other considerations to govern his judgment.

After the expression of filial sentiment ("I am <u>with you</u>"), Morgenthau turns to practical matters. He gratefully recognizes his father's appreciation of his activities. He continues: "The very fact that I am so tied down with the business of the farm will keep me from taking any active interest in politics for the time being."

Young Morgenthau now arrives at the subject of the fair sex. He writes: "The fact that I have no real good girl friends available is one that I deplore . . . You & I both realize the importance of the influence of a fine girl or girls . . ." Young Morgenthau continues: "I have recently met a Mrs. Thomas (widow) and her sister Miss Brinkerhoff, young people, of old stock around here. Miss Brinkerhoff is a gorgeous creature, beautiful in every way to the eye, but the fine spirit is lacking." Morgenthau explains at this point to his father: "(By sitting down and writing this way to you, it is the next best thing to having a talk with you and it will give me moral courage)" [parentheses in original].

Morgenthau explains further:

I met Mrs. Thomas at a dinner given by Mrs. Courtney, her aunt, in Fishkill Village. Then last Sunday I called Mrs. Thomas and went down to see her. She invited me to go for supper with them to a relative of theirs. It was lots of fun. We had supper out on the lawn. I met Miss Beatrice Brinkerhoff at their house. Tomorrow, Thursday, I am taking Mrs. Thomas & Miss Brinkerhoff over to Monroe (near Goshen) to see the trotting races. The skeleton in the Brinkerhoff closet is this: Mrs. Thomas comes first, third a Mrs. Fitzgerald (husband Irishman, gentle man), fourth Miss Beatrice. The second sister is supposed to be friendly with a Mr. Jones of Fishkill, who, dame gossip says, has been very attentive to her, and has instantly given up living with his own wife and baby.

Young Morgenthau comes to the point of his story: "I was thinking only last night that you, Ma & Ruth, especially Ruth, will be coming up here to live for a while, & so I must be very careful what sort of friends I make. Because when you come up here the friends I have made I naturally expect to be your friends." It is with relief that he concludes: "Well, Pa, I have got it down [in] black & white now and can not desert the ship. You can see my object."

In these perilous waters young Morgenthau regards his father as a beacon in the night, a moral compass in his life. Filled with emotion, he finishes: "Good night, dear Pa, I will finish this tomorrow." But it was not finished the next day. What he adds is: "I have re-read this letter a week later and am sending it now. I will write a conclusion to it in a day or two." He ends: "I would not mind your reading parts of this letter to the family, but most of it is for you and you alone. For reasons you well know."

The letter reeks of Victorian reticence.

In a Social Darwinist world, marrying "out" promised untoward consequences. Morgenthau was at the portal of entering into what promised to become a relationship with an unsuitable young woman. Temptation was rearing its ugly head. Now, at the age of twenty-three, it could have serious consequences for him. Like Tannhäuser in Wagner's opera, Morgenthau was being exposed to the temptations of the Venusberg. He turned to his father for moral certitude.

And what of Miss Brinkerhoff?

Young Morgenthau was certainly an eligible bachelor, and a young woman in that era needed a husband who could support her. Moreover, in young Morgenthau's case, such support promised to be handsome. Personality was also a consideration for a young woman possibly contemplating marriage. According to Edward Bernays—who would become a brilliant public relations consultant in the middle years of the twentieth century—Henry's personality was engaging (if we can take his description at face value). Bernays was young Morgenthau's classmate at Cascadilla, a cram school in Ithaca both attended prior to their entrances to Cornell University. The diminutive Bernays remembers looking up admiringly to the six-foot-one-and-a-half-inch[147] Morgenthau: "He was tall, handsome, very personable, no table-pounder or 'go-to-hell' kind of person, affable and gentle."[148]

As to the matter of young Morgenthau's Jewish identity, if Miss Brinkerhoff had any attitudes of social anti-Semitism, these remained muted. And in Miss Brinkerhoff's case, prevailing social attitudes may have meant little or nothing, especially when it came to the serious matter of finding a husband.

In the same way that Giuseppe Tomasi di Lampedusa in his novel *Il Gattopardo* ("The Leopard") has the young Tancredi say to his Uncle Fabrizio, the august, Sicilian *Principe di Salina* and a vast land owner, as Tancredi was going off in 1860 to join the Garabaldini invaders who were preparing to further the political dimensions of the Italian *Risorgimento* by overthrowing Franceschiello II (the Bourbon ruler of the Kingdom of the Two Sicilies on behalf of Vittori Emanueli, sovereign of the Piedmontese Kingdom of Sardinia), so Miss Brinkerhoff could say with Tancredi, "*Se vogliamo che tutto rimange come è, bisogna che tutto cambi.*"[149] ("If we'd have all remain as is, then all needs change.")

As a matter of practicality, the family had accepted the marriage of Miss Brinkerhoff's sister to the Irish (presumably Catholic) Mr. Fitzgerald, which probably did not affect either her sister's religious or social identification, even if it represented a step down in the era of the WASP Ascendancy in society—as

John O'Hara makes acidly clear in his novels and stories. One may conclude in the circumstances that young Morgenthau himself could be regarded as a "good catch."

So Mrs. Courtney arranged for her niece to meet young Mr. Morgenthau, and her niece Mrs. Thomas could arrange with all propriety for the young Mr. Morgenthau to become acquainted with her younger sister by means of encouraging him to go with her to a family supper taken on the lawn, and he could then take the young ladies to the trotting races across the Hudson River at Monroe near Goshen.

One could imagine oneself in an updated version of Jane Austen's *Pride and Prejudice* except they were contemporaries of the very cynical novelist Edith Wharton in a Social Darwinist world. Young Morgenthau's adolescent life experience had given him an understanding that the WASP Ascendancy dominated a society in which he was an outsider. As was his father, young Morgenthau might be attracted by the glitter and glamour emanating from the WASP world, yet he remained wary of it, and, in an ultimate sense, untrusting. So he could take a guilty pleasure in the company of Miss Brinkerhoff, whom he described in the discreet language of the period as "a gorgeous creature, beautiful in every way to the eye." But—to use more of the language of the period—*racial instinct* held him back. Self-preservation required he find some fault. And he concluded: "the fine spirit is lacking."

Real intimacy could realize the unspoken fear that in a moment of anger or annoyance she could think to call him a *dirty Jew*. With Social Darwinist logic in a world of social anti-Semitism, and his adolescent experience at boarding school from which he was but a few years removed, it would seem very probable that he sensed something of the sort. Some fear of the consequences must have arrested any move toward continued social intimacy with the Brinkerhoff ladies, and led him to seek out his father as a sort of confessor. Henry knew he could safely confide his fears to his father, who would instinctively understand his concerns; he could safely reveal his anxieties in the matter, knowing his father could save him from the deep emotional waters in which he was finding himself.

Late in his life, Morgenthau could still express, in an ironic sort of way, concern about marrying "out." Henry III recounts the following: "Once after [Professor Blum, his biographer who was of Jewish antecedents] and my father had become comfortable with each other, Morgenthau broached the subject rather obliquely. 'One of my children tells me that your wife's Christian. Is that true?' Blum said, yes, it was true. Morgenthau said cheerfully, 'My God, you're as bad as my son Bob.'"[150]

What in 1914 in a Social Darwinist world might be a source of deep-seated anxiety, could be described, almost a century later in a vastly different world, as the "claustrophobic and mild insanity of our anxious parents and grandparents"[151] and become a source of ribald humor. Commenting on the publication of the first two volumes of the novelist Philip Roth's collected works in the "Library of America" series, a reviewer could write: "Forget *Catcher in the Rye*, with that handsome, melancholy preppie and his so-called problems and desires. We wanted shiksas, and as Alexander Portnoy finds out to his and our delight, they wanted us. Three decades before gentile women started cruising jdate.com en masse hoping to find a sober, funny, successful little someone, Portnoy got the picture: 'Who knew that the secret to a shiksa's heart,' he said, 'was not to pretend to be some hook-nosed variety of goy, as boring and vacuous as her own brother, but . . . to be whatever one was oneself? That is to say, a Jew."

The reviewer goes on: "Roth is documenting (and in the end, putting to rest) a hysterical fear of the outside, of anything unknown, forbidden or *tref* [in a Judaic religious sense, ritually impure and therefore to be avoided], a vestigial instinct designed to protect, yet inflicting untold psychic violence of its own."[152] (Without seeking to belittle Roth's comedy—so difficult to write well and at which Roth has succeeded so brilliantly—one cannot leave the matter without commenting that the reviewer lacks the life experience of inhabiting a Social Darwinist world.)

So young Morgenthau gave up any romantic notions of developing a tender friendship with Miss Brinkerhoff—just as young Winnie in Joseph Conrad's *The Secret Agent* gave up the very attractive young butcher because he let it be understood there would be no place in their life together for Winnie's developmentally challenged younger brother, for whom she cherished a fierce maternal concern. Winnie settled for the sober-sided, older gentleman who showed no annoyance and was willing to accept her brother as a member of their household.

Morgenthau understood intuitively that he must seek out someone from his own social group. He could only feel comfortable, relaxed, and secure with a young woman who was from the same milieu, who would instinctively understand and share the sense of being regarded as an outsider—a separate race—by members of the WASP Ascendancy.

Morgenthau had a birthright entry into the active social world in New York City of economically successful American Jews. Writer Stephen Birmingham would later characterize this group in his book—quoting the visiting Prince Poniatowski, descended from the last Polish king, Stanislaus II—as a kind of provincial aristocracy, although he gave them the modest appellation *Our Crowd*. (They might more accurately have called themselves *Unser Leute*—since the members hailed from Germany, retained the language, and tended to vacation at German spas.) Henry III writes that Birmingham took the term *Our Crowd* for the title of his book from Henry III's great-aunt Hattie Goodhart, born a Lehman of Lehman Brothers, the fabled private merchant bankers.[153] On May 6, 1915, Morgenthau writes to his parents of his first social engagement after his return from his first trip to Constantinople: "Elly Fatman gave a theatre party. We met at the theatre, saw Arnold Daly in the Bernard Shaw play, *Arms & the Man* [that most wry of romantic comedies]. . . . After theatre we went to the Plaza [Hotel] Grill & the bunch danced. I will try & narrate the names of those present. Margaret Fatman, Elinore Kaskel, Peggy Wolf, Lucy Loeb, Ethel Ehrman, Mr. & Mrs. Howard Goodhart, & one more. Men as usual. I resolved as usual after this party that it was a fearful waste of time & energy and swore as usual never again. I would rather call on a girl if I really want to see her."

In a letter to his parents dated July 15, 1915, Morgenthau wrote: "Over the fourth of July, I visited Helen Hammerschlags at Deal [New Jersey]. Ely Fatman and Will Scholle were the other guests . . . Saturday night we were all invited over to Harry Saks . . . Those present were Annette Goldenburg, Carola Warburg, Margariute Seligman, Edith Saks . . . The men were Robert Stern, Maurice Neustadt, Arthur Goodhart. After supper, we all had been invited to the coming-out party of Elenore Guggenheim, daughter I believe of Simon G." The letter goes on to say he left a family gathering that Sunday "about three and arrived at Ely Fatman about five. They have the same house they used to have at Oriente Point, Mamaroneck. We went in swimming & I was invited to stay for supper, which I did. Had an awfully good time. Returned to the farm Monday morning."

He ends the letter by saying he is trying to give his parents a little idea of what he does with himself. He goes on to say he has taken quite an interest in the Surprise Lake Camp (an *Our Crowd* charity for poor, underprivileged children), and that while he was at the Guggenheims' at Elberon (in New Jersey), Felix

Warburg spoke approvingly of that activity. In his postscript he writes that he is feeling much better in every way.

Professor Blum writes: "From the farm Morgenthau had written to his parents two years earlier about a weekend spent at the [country] home of the Herbert Lehmans [at Pleasantville, New York], relatives of his wife-to-be: 'I was asked to come over the telephone, the bait being Ely Fatman . . . I bit.'"[154] This is a simplified statement of, and a bit of a joke about, the help Miss Fatman secured from her uncle Herbert Lehman in her various efforts to bring herself to young Morgenthau's attention. (Herbert Lehman was later to go into public life, eventually becoming governor of New York State, and afterwards, a United States senator.) Among the Morgenthau archives in the Roosevelt Library at Hyde Park, for example, are two very stiff, hand-engraved, formal invitations from Mr. and Mrs. Herbert Henry Lehman to fancy-dress dinners at (the then very fashionable) Sherry's Restaurant that Morgenthau preserved.

Henry III tells the charming story of his parents' engagement. In 1915, young Morgenthau had gone a second time to Constantinople to serve as his father's aide. There he revealed his intentions to his father, who had serious misgivings, as Henry III writes—not because Henry Sr. objected to the young lady, but on general principles. " 'I have often thought lately what a mistake it would have been for you to have married too young,' he had written his son in 1914."[155] As Henry III then tells it, Henry Jr. proceeded to disregard his father's comments. Henry III continues:

[O]n February 22, 1916, while the dockside ceremonies for the returning ambassador were in progress, Henry Jr. slipped away . . . to the Fatman brownstone at 23 West Eighty-first Street to call on Ellie. [The building is no longer extant—pulled down perhaps a decade later as part of an assemblage for a high-rise apartment house.] She was pleased but not surprised to see him. Henry, however, was speechless. She suggested a walk around the Central Park Reservoir [that lies just north of the Eighty-sixth Street transverse passage across the Park]. After they had silently circled the entire half-mile perimeter . . . [as she recalled] 'I broke the ice by proposing marriage. Henry was greatly relieved.'"[156]

And so Henry Jr. and Elinor Fatman were married on April 17, 1916.[157] Morgenthau had asked his father, really his closest friend, to be his best man. The officiant was Rabbi Wise,[158] with whom Henry Sr. had not yet broken any connection over the matter of Wise's commitment to Zionist ideology.[159]

The year 1914 saw war break out at the beginning of August with the Western Allies, England and France, and Tsarist Russia opposing Germany and the Austro-Hungarian Empire on the other side. In November of that year, Russia declared war on the Ottoman Empire, which then declared its solidarity with the Germans.

Morgenthau writes to his father from Bar Harbor, Maine, on September 5, 1914: "Quite a spell has passed since I have last written [to] you. But then we have not heard from you in ages and the chances of your receiving this letter at all seems [sic] slight." Expressing his doubts about his father's receipt of the letter does not inhibit Morgenthau from proceeding to write an exceedingly lengthy missal:

Many things have happened since I last wrote to you.

First, the Democratic Conference took place at Saratoga. I believe it was on August 19 [1914]. Mr. Perkins [a local Democratic political figure] & I motored up there from Poughkeepsie. We arrived about nine in the evening, having had supper at Albany. We mixed in with the crowd in the lobby & Perkins introduced me to lots of the people. They all seemed to know you [underlining in original]. You must have made a host of acquaintances & friends while you were at national headquarters. I spoke to McCoombs & he asked after you. Also met W. C. Osborn. Then Charlie White, sergeant at arms of Dem[ocratic] conventions, etc. asked Perkins whether he did not want to see the "Chief." I do not know who asked—White or Perkins—but anyway, first thing I know I was on my way up with Perkins. We were admitted into a bedroom where five or six men were sitting & lounging about. One, C. Truman, of Ithaca, & another, Fitzgerald of Buffalo, both of whom I met.

After about ten minutes, we were shown "Chief" Murphy's room. [Murphy was then the very powerful leader of Tammany Hall in New York City, and thereby Democratic Party leader of the state.] He said, "I know your father very well." Perkins asked him how about the Senatorship. [This was the first year there would be a direct election of United States senators. Theretofore, they had been elected by the state legislature.] Murphy said, "I have no candidate. Who do you think is best?" The whole conference was a cooked up & dried performance . . .

The foregoing political gossip suggests that Henry Sr. and probably his son had been liberal in their political contributions on the local and state levels.

Morgenthau continues with details of his social life.

I am here with Frances Sullivan at Bar Harbor. I got here Thursday morning and am staying until Monday after-noon. They have George Vanderbilt's cottage, the one

Otto Kahn had for two years. Bar Harbor is one of the most picturesque places I have ever been at. It is really lovely and the weather has been wonderful.

I knew Miss [Lillian] Wald [of neighborhood settlement house fame, where Morgenthau had earlier been a volunteer] was staying here with Miss Jane Ad[d]ams [the originator of the neighborhood settlement house concept in poor neighborhoods in Chicago]. I called up Miss Wald and she invited me for lunch. I went and had an unusual and [up]lifting meeting. The[y] are really charming people. We talked about politics & you & Turkey. Miss Wald told me she is going to Grand View with a secretary, & cook, & work, on Sept. 17 for some time, and asked if I would not come down and call for her and take her up to my place, which I said I would be delighted to do.

Last night they had a Democratic Rally here. As the election for Gov[ernor] is on Sept. 14, [Josephus] Daniels [Secretary of the Navy] & [Senator] Gore spoke. Gore left right after his speech.

But as Daniels spoke last Miss Sullivan and I went up & spoke to him. I asked him whether he was going to send you a battleship and he said he could not, as the Turks had objected—saying if they let one in they would have to let all. But he said things were getting better out there. He said: "Send your father my love." Was that not nice and genuine?

In a letter to his father in November or December of 1914, Morgenthau details the continuation of his relationship with Franklin Roosevelt:

I forget [*sic*] to write I was in Washington about two weeks before this on Agricultural business. Thought I would drop in and see F. Roosevelt [then Assistant Secretary of the Navy]. This was after he was defeated. [Roosevelt had chosen to run almost impulsively at the last minute in the Democratic primary election that year for the nomination as a reform candidate for the United States Senate against Tammany Hall's candidate, John Watson Gerard, then ambassador to Germany; he lost.] I asked him how they felt about your work in Washington. He said Billy Phillips (3d Ass. Sec.) says that your father's dispatches are always cool and business-like, and that is a great deal more than you can say about some of the rest. He (F. Roosevelt) said it in such a nice, full hearted manner, that it carried a great deal more conviction than I can put into mere words. I told the family about it and they were very much pleased.

It is entirely possible that Roosevelt was grateful and showed his appreciation that Morgenthau had not forgotten him (as so often happens in political life) after he lost the election.

A postscript reads: "Wrote this letter without a dictionary so excuse misspelt [*sic*] words. On receipt of your letter this week asking for information about election, I cabled you at once but do not know, of course, if it went through." The 1914 election was a so-called "midterm" election for the House of Representatives, as well as for state government officers. It was evidence of how the electorate evaluated the first two years of the Wilson administration.

To follow the development of Morgenthau's connection with Roosevelt, in a letter dated July 20, 1915, Morgenthau tells how he "was at Franklin Roosevelt's for luncheon. [Roosevelt] had the following interesting story to tell. He said: 'I asked one of the most important men in our army and one in our navy if they had to bet a thousand dollars on one of the three following propositions, which one would they choose: 1st, will the Allies win? 2d, will the War be a draw? 3d, will Germany win? He said each man was dependent on his salary and balked at the sum, but when pinned right down . . . would bet that Germany will win this war.'"

Morgenthau comments to his father that he thinks it very significant because, he believes, both the Army and Navy Departments must be getting confidential reports about the progress of the war from both sides.

This July 20th letter is also interesting because it reveals that Morgenthau has mastered the art of classifying information and statistics into charts and tables. He writes: "You may remember that in speaking of the possibilities of Pres. Wilson being reelected, you & others stated that one of the most important requirements would be a good crop. The following figures copied from the Crop Report published by the Department of Agriculture at Washington, July 15, 1915, would lead one to believe that we will have the largest crop in the history of the country. I might add that in such a problematical function as forecasting crops they are fair."

There follows a chart covering wheat, corn, oats, potatoes, and rice, listing the projected percentage increase in 1915 over the 1914 figures, the acreage given over to each crop, the numbers of anticipated bushels in 1915, a comparison of the final estimates of production of each crop for 1914, the average production for each crop for the years 1909–1913, the July forecast for 1915, etc. He comments that Europe has absorbed the American agricultural surpluses produced in 1914 and paid for the produce in gold, not using American securities as many people had assumed, including Morgenthau himself.

In a letter dated late November/December 1914, Morgenthau reports on personal finances: "I asked Rob [Simon, his cousin and his father's nephew and business manager] to let me have $500.00, which he did, for household expenses for April &

May." He notes the farmhouse is being refurbished under his sister Ruth's guidance, and that his parents will reap the benefit when they come. The house now had four master bedrooms and one bathroom, with two servant's rooms and bath, "so you see we can accommodate you quite nicely when you come."

So Morgenthau took the first of his two trips to assist his father at the American Embassy in Constantinople and consumed the winter and early spring months of 1914–15 with the trip. In what would appear to be a letter from the Athénée Palace Hotel in Bucharest, Romania, to his parents—still in Constantinople—on his way home from his first visit to see them, Morgenthau writes:

The trip as far as Adrianople was uneventful. With the exception that the apple tart that Ma gave me made a great hit with the Courier, so did the rest of goodies later on, for which many thanks. (I have since heard that on the train that left on the following day, 20 people were taken off the train because they had suspicious letters, so advise everybody who is leaving to leave their letters at home.)

Thursday night we had to change sleeping cars; the one to Sofia [Bulgaria] is a miserable old antediluvian affair without individual was[h] stands.

Friday morning we arrived at Sofia, with which city I was charmed. It is situated on a gentle slope overlooking a beautiful valley, with high snowcapped mountains right close by. The air is very invigorating and stimulating . . . Although the new city is only twenty years old, it is well paved and up to date. It has a public Turkish Bath with swimming pool etc. for men and women, a Public Market, a National Museum, a museum of costumes & peasant industries which was beautifully arranged. All these I visited as well as Parliament (they only have a lower house, no higher house at all, which makes it very democratic). The house was very orderly & never have I seen the people in the galleries watch & listen with such rapt attention, although they were composed of entirely the "peasant class." If one sees a country like Bulgaria, which has been freed from the Turks only 30 years or so, there well tilled fields alongside the barren hill of European Turkey, one must stop & think: is it really wise for the sake of civilization & progress that Turkey should continue as an Empire. There must be something about their religion that is radically wrong or at least does not fit the twentieth century. The Turks were not born to rule today.

After his return from Constantinople, in a letter dated June 2, 1915, Morgenthau finally faces the need to give his father a full accounting of the moneys spent for the farm. He writes: "I will try and give you just a rough estimate of how H[enry] M[orgenthau] & Son stands financially. We have, of course, used up all of our original balance in [thc] Bank and besides we have put in the [proceeds] of Underwood Dividends [in addition to other moneys]."

Morgenthau now "bites the bullet" and painfully admits the consequences of "playing hooky" from the farm over the winter, during his first visit to his parents in Turkey. He writes:

Some of the reasons why we ran behind so last year were, first, the disease trouble which we had with our potatoes cut our estimated yield down one-third. Second, the prices of potatoes were lower last year than they have been in years. Next, strange as it may seem, beef prices were exceptionally low. And last, I had counted on the cordwood which I expected my men to cut during the winter to amount to

$3,000.00–$4,000.00. In my absence, they spent all winter sorting potatoes & did not cut any cordwood at all.

This year I have made every effort to correct my mistakes of the season past.

I have bought my seed potatoes from a new source & have every reason to believe that I will not have the same trouble as last year. I have also treated all the potato seed with a solution of corrosive sulfate which helps to control disease troubles. Last year we did not treat our seed. The market is still hard to judge, but on account of the low prices as of the year past, the reports show that the planting is smaller than it was last year in sections that compete with us. Although the cotton states have planted more than last year, due to the agitation against the single crop system in the south. Generally we look for higher prices this fall. Things look very much better than they did some time ago.

By making a rough budget for the next six months I feel that the Underwood dividends will carry us along, without the aid of outside capital.

Although I personally have depended on my H[enry] M[orgenthau] Co. dividends for my living expenses, I expect to get along on less this year, if possible. Also, if necessary, sell some more Underwood Common [stock shares]. I do not feel that I will have to continue to sell Underwood indefinitely, as the farm will not & must [not] continue after this year to use up $16,000.00 a year.

So you see, if anyone has an object to make the farm go, I have.

(To get an idea of what $16,000 means in contemporary terms, Beschloss speaks of Henry Sr. contributing $20,000 to Wilson's campaign for the Democratic Party's presidential nomination, and describes it as "almost $200,000 in 2002 dollars."[160])

Morgenthau continues: "I have bought a small piece [of land near the] Railroad station. It includes a corner house on the state highway & runs back to the R.R. I bought it for us because it will permit us to have a siding at the R.R. and for the future it will come in very handy. I am negotiating now with a blacksmith to rent the corner house for $300.00 a year on condition we put up a shed to cost about $1,000.00. The property cost $2,500.00. I take title on or before April 1st, 1916. The seller puts a mortgage of $1,000.00 on the property for three years at 5½%. I think the deal is O.K. & you can judge it when you see it."

Morgenthau's determination to make the farm succeed as a paying business proposition would appear to have been an abiding concern throughout his life—even after his father was no longer alive. Henry III writes: "In fact, the farm sustained huge losses most of the time, but its fabled success was accepted by almost everyone . . . although [my father] was always very thin-skinned when anyone dared to question him closely on this score."[161]

Henry III goes on: "My father selected two principal endeavors: dairy farming and apple growing. During the first years he concentrated on his dairy, beginning by building up a herd of registered Holstein cattle . . . and soon reached the desired level of fifty head. For a short time he sold his milk very profitably, a few miles down [and across] the Hudson River to the West Point Military Academy."[162]

The real meaning of the farm for Morgenthau lay elsewhere than in bookkeeping entries. Henry III wrote: "He loved nothing better than to ride horseback through the rows of apple trees at all seasons. Twice a year the problems dissolved in a moment of sheer ecstasy. For a few spring days—usually bracketing his birthday on May 11—the trees would burst forth in a pink-white haze of delicately scented blossoms. Then at the end of the season, the boughs would be bent down, heavy with red, golden yellow, and green apples ready to be plucked for market. Those few days made all the drudgery, disappointment and expense worth enduring."[163]

CHAPTER 4

Life in Dutchess County

The relatively few letters of Elinor Morgenthau found in her husband's archives in the Roosevelt Library reveal her to be enamored of her husband and desperately lonely in his absence, even to the point where she feels ill. She writes how meaningless her life becomes in his absence and how she must struggle to get through her social activities. Henry III quotes from one of the letters his mother wrote from Augusta, Georgia, to her husband during the winter of 1923–24, when she took Henry III there to recuperate in warmer weather than could be found in New York at that time of year. He had suffered a skull fracture in a riding accident on their farm. Henry III writes, "[S]he had 'become awfully morose and depressed . . . without you nothing is really worthwhile,'" and in a later letter she writes, "Don't let's ever be separated so long again—ever—ever—ever!"[164]

A large part of the romance Elinor Morgenthau shared with her husband, who towered over her physically, emanated from their farm in Dutchess County. Later, when they were in New York City, or later in Washington, D.C., after Roosevelt had chosen him to be secretary of the treasury, Morgenthau rented housing accommodations. He regarded these homes as temporary residences; they lived there only because circumstances required his presence. He considered the farm in Dutchess County his true home, the place where he had put down deep roots of identity.

Henry III and Beschloss both have it that he never bought a home during the years he spent in Washington because he was terrified he could be dismissed at any time—except this logic does not apply to the apartments Morgenthau rented over the years in New York City, beginning with his marriage, and continuing even after he resigned his post at the Treasury and left Washington forever.

Also, a residential lease runs for one or more years, periods of time that do not necessarily coincide with a date of dismissal from a job. If one were to be dismissed, most likely, one would still have to cope with the remaining months in the lease period. Also, officeholders in Washington periodically leave town, so there is a regular turnover in housing ownership. (At least in the case of foreign diplomats, the practice existed in mid-twentieth century Washington, D.C., where diplomats were immune from local legal proceedings; diplomats renting housing accommodations had to deposit rent security amounting to four months' rent to cover a landlord's losses, should a diplomat be transferred before the lease ended.)

More important than any fear of dismissal had to be Morgenthau's fierce attachment to, and identification with, Fishkill Farms in Dutchess County, New York—for him, his true home. In New York City, that identification was not menaced because the convention was to rent apartments. In Washington, if one could afford it, one owned one's own home. Still, it would appear that Morgenthau regarded multi-residence ownership as a form of social pretension, and by the same token, wanted no psychological threat in his own mind—in the form of property ownership in other places—to his committed identity as a farmer.

Other public personages in Washington, D.C., in those years might have occupied residential quarters in the Mayflower and other hotels, but the more-conventional residence in the nation's capital was a private dwelling. So Morgenthau as secretary of the treasury took annual rentals in fashionable private homes in northwest Washington. Indeed, such was Morgenthau's commitment to Fishkill Farms that he did not own a *dacha* at the shore or in the mountains. His immediate family's vacations were at suitable hotels that did not threaten his rural identification.

After his wife's death, Morgenthau told his biographer, Professor Blum: "I was fortunate in marrying Elinor Fatman in 1916. We lived happily together for thirty-three years until she died after a long illness. My inclination as a young man was to hop from one venture to another. It was Elinor more than anybody else who kept my nose to the grindstone. She had a brilliant mind and insisted that I, having selected farming as a way of life, stick to it. I am deeply indebted for her help and advice during our married life."[165]

It is a heartfelt and obviously sincere tribute to a deceased spouse. Henry III called theirs, "a true love match."[166] And yet, one's curiosity is aroused—as much as by what is left unsaid as to the way he chose to phrase his appreciation. Earlier in this study, it was suggested that one remark made by Morgenthau to Professor Blum was not entirely accurate—namely, that his primary motivation for convincing his father to purchase the farm for him was to escape Henry Sr.'s plan for arranging his life. Henry Sr. wanted Henry Jr. to join his real estate ventures by becoming an architect, so as to allow them to become builders and developers without the need for outside consultants to develop construction projects—a mode of real estate business operation Henry Sr. had never previously entertained.

Rather, it would appear that Morgenthau's primary motivation for wanting to become a farmer germinated from an effort

to escape the social humiliations incident to a Jewish ethnic identification in the Social Darwinist world of the late nineteenth and
early twentieth centuries in the United States. Both Morgenthau
and his wife Elinor could take great satisfaction in Morgenthau's
participation in the dairymen's cooperative and the local Grange,
and when they were asked, they served on the boards of rural
schools and state fairs, establishing a visiting nurse service and a
mobile library in Dutchess County.[167] Their community service
represented a visible acceptance of them by elements of Gentile
society in Dutchess County.

The operation of Social Darwinist prejudices in the
consciousness of both his parents is illustrated by Henry III
when he describes their response to their ethnic background.
He wrote (and Beschloss quotes): "Early in life, I sensed my
parents' malaise in their Jewishness, which they mocked
good-humoredly, while remaining fiercely alert to attack from
outsiders. To them, he said, being Jewish was 'a kind of birth
defect that could not be eradicated, but with proper treatment,
could be overcome. If not in this generation, then probably in
the next.'"[168] Beschloss continues with Henry III's comments:
" 'Almost all of my parents' friends were Jewish,' [he] recalled,
'but they never talked about anything Jewish' [at least in a religious sense], and 'there were no Jewish [religious] artifacts or
anything around.'" He recalled that when his mother took him
for the winter to Augusta, Georgia, to recuperate from a riding
accident [that had resulted in a fractured skull], she "really
resented [it when] the Jewish community there [reached] out to
her," and "kept her distance."[169]

Beschloss describes Elinor Morgenthau as "more 'firmly
assimilationist' than her husband . . . As the son recalled, his
parents did not attend a synagogue as he was growing up, and
'tended to avoid' the city and country clubs, the American-
ized Temple Emanu-El, and the country places in Westchester

County that gave wellborn New York German Jews a comforting sense of community."[170]

Morgenthau, yet unmarried, wrote to his father, then ambassador in Constantinople, in a letter dating from late November or early December, 1914: "The weekend that Turkey went to war, that same weekend Mr. Wertheim received word that [his son] Maurice [the husband of Morgenthau's sister Alma] & family had left Turkey. I made up my mind that if you knew that I could get away, you might want me to come over."

He continues:

I jumped on the train and went down to Washington. As I did not know anyone well in the State Department, I went over to see Mr. Tumulty [in the White House], after first telephoning to see if he was in . . . I told him I wanted to cable you . . . He was extremely nice. Called up Mr. Phillips, 3d Ass[istant] Sec[retary] of State, told him I was coming over. He then wrote on a card marked "President of the United States" my name, and with that introduction, I marched over to the State Depart[ment]. [At this time, this building was located next to the White House in what is now known as the Executive Office Building—a marvelous Victorian Second Empire pile barely saved from the wrecker's ball in the 1960s, during that period's wildly exuberant infatuation with urban renewal]. Mr. Phillips saw me at once. I sat down in his office and wrote the cable which he said he would send.

Morgenthau tries to explain his purpose:

I wanted to make it clear in the cable that I did not wish to come over [to Constantinople] for pleasure or personal reasons. But if I could be of service to you and help you in any way I felt it was my duty in these times of danger and stress to be by your side. And I was ready to let all my personal business slide.

Of course, before the war had come on I had pretty well made up my mind that I ought to stay in this country and see my products of the farm sold. And especially as I had to go into debt. And I still feel the same way about it. Namely, if you feel I can't be of any <u>real</u> [underlining in orginial] service—why I had better stay here and see the farm business through.

Morgenthau then allows himself to express the depth of his feeling toward his father: "God knows that there is nothing I would rather do than be with you and Ma if only for a few days. My flesh hungers for your affection, which I have so long been used [to] and never have been without so long. But I have my battle[171] to fight here," Henry adds.

These words are typical Social Darwinist language of the day. So Hofstadter, for example, speaks of William Graham Sumner's view of Social Darwinism—that it "could serve only to cause men to face up to the inherent hardship of the *battle of life*"[172] (emphasis added). Morgenthau himself goes on to finish his sentence: ". . . and I am going to win out. That is the only way." The martial language is obliquely adverting to his challenge to make the farm operation a paying proposition.

The second and last trip to Constantinople ended with Morgenthau accompanying his father as the latter returned home in early 1916 antecedent to submitting his resignation as ambassador to the Ottoman Empire. For Morgenthau himself, the return led to his engagement and marriage.

The entrance of the United States into World War I in 1917 was to divert Morgenthau's attention—first, to his joint efforts with his wife in Dutchess County to organize large-scale local family food-canning activities by encouraging local women to undertake the cultivation of their own kitchen gardens, growing vegetables and engaging in serious canning efforts with the vegetables they had grown, as a civilian contribution to the war effort. The second instance occurred in 1918, when he developed his idea to provide the French Republic with mechanized farm tractors/cultivators to help alleviate the rural manpower shortage there that resulted from the absence of young French farmers drafted to serve in the French armies.

With respect to the former, Henry III comments: "My mother, who had never stepped inside the kitchen either in her own mother's home or in her own [it being the workplace of the family's cook and the social domain of the other household servants], applied herself diligently to learning the technique of canning as though it were another foreign language, and she was soon teaching it."[173] Henry III lists the household help at one stage in their home in Dutchess County: "There was a basic cadre of five live-in maids, plus a full-time chauffeur and a caretaker" living with his family in the farmhouse they occupied on the property.[174]

Henry III writes that his grandfather prodded his son in 1917 to make a larger contribution to the war effort.[175] Possibly, Henry Sr. felt the exigencies of a wartime economy created opportunities for advancement in the public sphere, and possibly Henry Sr. was feeling a surge of old-fashioned patriotism and wanted to encourage his son to share his feelings. Certainly, notwithstanding his foreign birth, Henry Sr. identified himself as "100% American" (as Henry III describes him[176]). Henry Sr. had good reason to feel patriotic, and was enormously grateful for the financial success the United States had afforded him, as compared with the insolvency in Germany that had caused his own father to bring his family to the New World in 1866[177]—providently as it turned out, when one considers what happened to Jews in Germany with the advent of the Nazi regime on January 30, 1933.

Morgenthau himself was appointed chairman of the Dutchess County Committee on Conservation and Food.[178] Morgenthau focused on the state of the agrarian economy in the United States, since this directly affected the prices he would receive for the crops he grew on his farm. He began to realize that after the United States entered World War I in April 1917, large quantities of agricultural produce were being shipped to France over German submarine–infested waters. This was because the government in France had mobilized all able-bodied men between the ages of eighteen and fifty into the French armies, creating a shortage of rural manpower. Fully one-quarter of French farmland lay uncultivated. It seemed obvious to Morgenthau that with the importation and use of American tractors, the existing manpower in the rural areas of France would be able to cultivate much of the abandoned French farmland, thereby reducing the need for imported food.[179]

The idea appeared so simple to Morgenthau that he wondered why it had not already been proposed. Fearful he had overlooked some major difficulty, he turned to his closest friend, his father, for the latter's reaction. Henry III writes: "The old man was duly impressed, seeing the scheme as a great opportunity for his son. He went straight to President Wilson, [who] referred him to Secretary of Agriculture Houston, who was not impressed. But the senior Morgenthau persisted, going to see the newly appointed food administrator, Herbert Hoover . . . who was enthusiastic . . ." Henry III continues: "In mid-December 1917 . . . Morgenthau arrived in Washington to effect his plan." Henry III then allows himself to express an accolade for his father's efforts: "It was a bold and complex undertaking for an inexperienced twenty-six-year-old."[180]

Henry III continues: "The French High Commissioner in Washington (and later premier of France), André Tardieu, expressed the French government's willingness to purchase tractors with funds...loaned by the U.S. government...Morgenthau went to Detroit to call on Henry Ford, the leading tractor manufacturer, and secured his promise of cooperation."[181]

Tardieu wrote to Hoover to say the plan had been implemented, and he gave generous credit to Morgenthau, "who had kept in touch with the transaction through all stages of allotting contracts, manufacture and shipping by rail and water." The French high commissioner then continued: "With a view to carrying out this enterprise to a successful issue, may I suggest it would be advisable to have Mr. Morgenthau go to France."[182] And so, early in March 1918, Morgenthau sailed off. Henry III observes that his father felt constrained to write to his mother: "I am the only married man on board [ship] I have seen so far who wears a wedding ring and I am proud of it."[183]

In this latter respect, Henry III writes that his mother "had encouraged her husband's adventure abroad, yet she couldn't help reminding him that while he was enjoying Paris [going to the Opera and the like], her life on the farm was pretty austere—albeit with a nurse, a cook, and a maid. She was spending a good deal of time managing the farm, especially minding the accounts." She took a daily course in automobile repair, anticipating ambulance driving and repair. Henry III reports that his mother learned to remove and repair an automobile tire, and comments it was "no mean trick in those days." He adds: "[I]n later years 'she would sometimes remind her husband that never in his life had he changed a tire.'"[184]

It is not certain why High Commissioner Tardieu came to endorse the tractor plan and recommend that Morgenthau be dispatched to France. It is entirely possible that Tardieu recognized the seriousness of the rural manpower shortage and was willing to endorse any promise of a successful resolution, especially one that would have no immediate financial cost. In recommending Morgenthau's presence in France, it would appear that Tardieu hoped Morgenthau's enthusiasm would serve to surmount local French difficulties. Some of the local problems Tardieu may have anticipated are suggested by Henry III: "The second day Morgenthau was in Paris he met with a Captain Goudard, the chief of Culture de Terre, to discuss the tractor project . . . [T]here were serious problems with spare parts and qualified mechanics, even with the three-wheeled tractors themselves, which were difficult to turn on wet ground." Morgenthau concluded that "our tractor plan must have appeared to Goudard as a criticism of his agency."[185]

Morgenthau had no way of knowing that an older generation of French farmers, disqualified by age for military duty, would be more set in their habits, with less occasion to have learned to use motorized equipment. Their work experience was focused on the use of a horse to pull a plow. They could not imagine using a motor vehicle to cultivate farmland. Unfortunately, that bottleneck was less easy to remove than bringing the tractors to France. The absence of younger French farmers, who might have been tempted to seize the opportunity to experiment with learning to use freely offered American farm tractors, both created the problem and prevented its resolution. Morgenthau could recognize he had neither the knowledge nor experience to deal with that local French difficulty. He returned home in May, 1918. Henry III comments, "He wisely chose not to become further involved . . ."[186]

Back home, Morgenthau once more sought his father's help to secure a commission in the army. Henry Sr. went to Secretary of War Baker. Before Baker acted, Josephus Daniels, secretary of the navy, "came through." Louis Howe, then assistant to Assistant Secretary Franklin Roosevelt, let Morgenthau know "the Bureau of Navigation had waived his deferment."[187]

Why Louis Howe, then assistant to Franklin Roosevelt, would have been the messenger raises an interesting point. Henry III quotes from a letter dated December 11, 1914, from Roosevelt, on the letterhead stationery of the assistant secretary of the navy. It is addressed formally to "My dear Mr. Morgenthau." Roosevelt inquires about one "John Dugan, the Blacksmith," then put forward by the local Democratic Party for appointment as postmaster in Fishkill. Henry III writes that Roosevelt "understood that there was some opposition: 'I should very much like to have your personal and confidential judgment on the matter . . . of course, if possible, I should like to have everybody united in the Township of East Fishkill.'"[188]

Although Henry III does not quite suggest the idea, it is probable that Assistant Secretary Roosevelt recognized Morgenthau as a political resource early on. Professor Blum writes:[189] "Morgenthau did not meet his Dutchess County neighbor until 1915, when Roosevelt at luncheon at Hyde Park tried without success to persuade him to run for sheriff."[190] [It is not easy to get people to agree to run as candidates for minor public office with the sure knowledge they are going to lose the election because voters in the area consistently vote for the other party. This is especially the case when the person who is sought after has "other fish to fry," as Morgenthau did.]

Blum continues quoting Roosevelt: " 'He is an awfully nice fellow,' Roosevelt judged after this first meeting, 'and one who will be a tremendous asset to us in the county. . . . Certainly we ought to do everything possible to keep him interested.'" If that consideration hovered in the picture, arranging for Morgenthau to receive an officer's commission was a small gesture that promised future benefits. There would be no occasion to put such an understanding in writing. Quite the reverse. The only other evidence that could shed some light on the subject is the comment Louis Howe made several years later, when Roosevelt appointed Morgenthau as Secretary of the Treasury. Beschloss reports, "The President's longtime political adviser and éminence grise . . . told Morgenthau he had 'earned' his new job with his 'loyalty' while others had let Roosevelt down."[191] Those words are nothing if not political jargon and suggest a longtime political connection.

So the commandant of the Third Naval District enrolled Morgenthau as a lieutenant junior grade in September 1918, and for two months, wearing his blue serge uniform, he "busied himself inspecting cargo on the city docks, returning each evening to his wife and son at their apartment on Broadway"[192]—until the Armistice was signed on November 11, 1918, after which his services were no longer needed.

Henry III writes that in those years, the teens and the 1920s, his family spent the winter months in an apartment in New York City and the summer on the farm. Weekends and holidays found them in the country.[193] Henry III goes on to say that his nuclear family was "leading a double life. In the city my mother maintained warm relations with a network of her relatives and family friends," whereas in Dutchess County they "were on undiscovered territory," since most of their relatives and friends entertained each other in their country houses, located in Westchester County, just above the city's northern boundary. In summer, many (including Henry Sr., as noted in an earlier chapter) participated in rustic "camps" in the Adirondack Mountains in northern New York, just below the Canadian border, although a minority still went to the Jersey shore.[194]

In 1922, Morgenthau acquired the money-losing weekly farm newspaper, *American Agriculturist*.[195]

Many persons of wealth have been fascinated by the idea of publishing a newspaper. Being connected to the "press" exudes a romantic ideal in our society that is hard to resist—if one has the money to indulge one's fancy. There was the case of department-store heir Marshall Field in Chicago with the *Sun*, merged into the Chicago *Times;* there was Eugene Meyer with the *Washington Post* (the most successful of the lot), and venture capitalist John Hay Whitney, who, in 1938–39, was a major financier of the movie *Gone With the Wind*, to his great profit. Whitney acquired the New York City newspaper, the *Herald-Tribune*, from the heirs of its fabled editor, Ogden Reid. To his later regret, after six years, he followed the advice of his financial advisors and terminated publication of the newspaper. His obituary in the *New York Times* concluded: "He had one great disappointment—his inability to save the *New York Herald-Tribune*, which he took over as editor in chief and publisher in 1961. E. J. Kahn Jr., his biographer, said the paper 'meant the most to him of any of his enterprises,' and Whitney Communications poured $40 million into the effort."[196]

Morgenthau's efforts were on a more modest scale.[197] Beschloss writes that the acquisition of the rural newspaper was a means to advance Morgenthau's ambition to be Roosevelt's farm expert.[198] An interesting idea. By 1922, one may say that Roosevelt found himself in a difficult position. In some ways, he had had a meteoric political career. At a relatively young age, in 1910, as a Democrat in Republican-majority Dutchess County, Roosevelt had won election to the state Senate. Perhaps his victory was partly due to the strength of his name, which conjured up the magic of Theodore Roosevelt. Nonetheless, he earned the undying enmity of Tammany Hall by succeeding in putting together a coalition of legislators that defeated Tammany Hall's candidate, William F. ("Blue-eyed Billy") Sheehan, in the last New York state legislative election of a United States senator. Afterwards, United States senators would be popularly elected.

In 1914, Roosevelt's political ambitions had led him, somewhat impulsively, to run in the first direct primary election for the Democratic nomination for United States senator against Tammany Hall's candidate.[199] The latter won the primary but lost the general election. Robert Caro records what was probably the politest comment made by a Tammany Hall adherent when he quotes one "Big Tim" Sullivan as saying: "Awful arrogant fellow, that Roosevelt."[200] It was not merely Roosevelt's political heresy of being identified as a reformer. There was also the Irish, Roman Catholic response in a Social Darwinist era to the condescension of the WASP Ascendancy toward them.

The election of Woodrow Wilson to the presidency in 1912 led to Roosevelt's opportunity to become the assistant secretary of the navy. As such, and perhaps because he was a quintessential member of the WASP Ascendancy—and could be identified as an upstate Democrat (the only one of any note)—he had been tapped by the Irish, Roman Catholic leaders of the New York Democratic Party organization at the Democratic national convention in 1920 to second the token nomination of Al Smith for the presidential nomination. Caro called it "an effective speech."[201] It may have been the sudden and unexpected death in 1919 of the charismatic Theodore Roosevelt—who had captured the imagination of the American public by his exploits as president and, afterwards, as an explorer of the unknown sources of the Amazon River in South America—that led to his namesake, Franklin Roosevelt, being selected as the Democratic vice presidential candidate that year.

The American electorate chose Calvin Coolidge in the general election as the next vice president of the United States, and in 1921, Roosevelt found himself out of a job. He retired to New York State to rest on his laurels and face the reality that the state Democratic organization rested in the Irish, Roman Catholic hands of Tammany Hall, whose public image was the down-to-earth, Lower East Side, New York City slum-born-and-bred Al Smith. That summer, while swimming in the Bay of Fundy at the family's summer home at Campobello in Canada, Roosevelt contracted a crippling case of infantile paralysis that immobilized him physically and left him to spend hours in bed trying to wriggle one toe.

In a sense, that catastrophic illness—however crushing it may have been on a personal level—could be said to have created some element of pity and compassion for him in his Tammany adversaries. In July, 1922, with Smith then out of office, Roosevelt was given the task of getting Smith's gubernatorial campaign started with an open letter calling upon Smith to run again. And in 1924, Roosevelt was delegated to act as floor manager for Smith at the Democratic national convention. Caro writes: "swinging to the platform on crutches and delivering a speech . . . [Roosevelt] dubbed the Governor 'the Happy Warrior of the Political Battlefield.'" Caro also records that "[a]mong Smith's happier moments during the convention's interminable 103 ballots were Roosevelt's appearances at the microphone to rally his supporters.[202] But," Caro continues, "Roosevelt was never really part of the Smith inner circle."[203]

In 1923, Roosevelt was able to make his way with enormous difficulty on crutches, heavy iron braces on his legs. Like the medieval Holy Roman Emperor Henry IV—who stood barefoot in the snow at Canossa for three days in January of 1077 as penance, to beg Pope Gregory VII to withdraw a ban of excommunication—Roosevelt must have recognized that he had to make his own "pilgrimage to Canossa." He had to visit Smith's suite at the Biltmore Hotel on East 42nd Street in Manhattan, where Smith entertained his Irish, Roman Catholic, political cronies. As Caro describes it, "feeling awkward about going there alone, Roosevelt would . . . often telephone [Robert] Moses in the late afternoon from his office at 120 Broadway and ask if he might stop by, pick him up and go up to the hotel with him." Caro adds that Moses generously took Roosevelt along. Moses was born Jewish, (although he apparently converted to the Episcopalian communion at some point in his life[204]) so did not have what was the impediment in that context of birth and identification as part of the WASP Ascendancy.

In that respect, there have been others who were Protestant by religion; for example, Erastus Corning, who for some thirty years in the third quarter of the twentieth century, was mayor of the city of Albany, New York. Although Corning had been born into the local WASP aristocracy in Albany, he had been sponsored by the local Democratic Party organization that was headed by the very Irish, Roman Catholic Daniel Patrick O'Connell. Grondahl, in his biography of the mayor, says: "Corning, in keeping with O'Connell's political philosophy, ruled a backwards-looking administration that ran and won on the old verities of the Democratic machine: low taxes, marginal services, patronage rewards for loyalty to the party, punishments for anyone who challenged the machines's manifesto."[205]

Then there was Harry Truman, whose career led him to the White House. He had been initiated into public office by the local Democratic machine in Kansas City, Missouri, headed by the Irish, Roman Catholic Thomas J. Pendergast. Pendergast, later criminally prosecuted by the Roosevelt administration, went to prison after being found guilty by a jury.[206] Men like Corning and Truman, whatever their personal sense of probity, recognized and needed the power of the local political machine that in turn recognized their talents. So Truman, although vice president of the United States by that time, flew back to Kansas City to attend the funeral for Pendergast, a convicted felon, knowing full well that it would subject him to criticism in some quarters.

With respect to Roosevelt, Caro writes: "In Albany, his haughty manner, accentuated by 'his habit of throwing up his head so as to give the appearance of looking down his nose, his pince-nez—all this, combined with his leadership in the anti-Sheehan fight, stamped him as a snob . . .'" Caro adds: "Once, with regret in his voice, Smith told a friend: 'Franklin just isn't the kind of man you can take into the pissroom and talk intimately with.'"[207]

To return to Morgenthau: In a letter dated August 21, 1922, on stationery of the *American Agriculturist*, Henry writes to his parents, who were on vacation:

> Elinor & I enjoyed your letters very much. I am sending this to Paris, hope that is right. Thanks very much for the check for [son] Robert, in which he joins me. This will be only a short note as I will have to rush for the train.
>
> This last week we had four very hot days and Elinor felt the heat very much. [This was in the days before air-conditioning was available as a matter of course.] But fortunately Sunday the weather changed and now it is really cold.
>
> The subscriptions [to the weekly newspaper] continue to come in nicely. I told a real estate man who has been looking [at] a corner for me to wait until you came back. There is no hurry and I do not want to buy any real estate without you.
>
> I hope Ma and you are feeling real well. What steamer are you coming home on?
>
> I thought the enclosed from *N.Y. Times* is so interesting as it simply says O.K. to what you have been saying right along about Palestine. [Henry Sr. was vehemently opposed to the concept of a Jewish homeland in the British League of Nations Mandate territory of Palestine.]

On February 7, 1924, Morgenthau writes to his father in care of the American Legation in Athens:

We were all thrilled today to learn from the newspapers that you had been able to get the Bank of England to intervene in behalf of the Greeks, provided that they declare themselves a Republic. I congratulate you on being made an honorary citizen of the City of Athens. I have no doubt but what you will be able to put the Greeks on a sound basis, and if you do, you will certainly accomplish one of the most difficult propositions that you ever went against, but after all, each proposition that you conquer ought to make the next one that much easier.

I sent you a cable from Chicago telling you about our big increase in advertising revenue for January—80% to be exact. I wonder if you ever received it . . . [It] looks as though February will be even a better month than January.

Murphy has most likely notified you that I took $10,000 in January from you. This makes a total of $201,000 that you have put into the *American Agriculturist* . . . The Hunts Point Palace account loaned the *American Agriculturist* $4,000 yesterday until Monday, when we will receive $20,000 from our January revenue. I would have loaned it to them personally, but I only had $3,500 in the bank. I feel fairly confidant [*sic*] that we will make money January, February and March. Our present plans are to go to a semi-monthly during June, July and August. By doing so, we figure we will save $14,000 or $15,000. It is too early yet to make any prophecies, but it does look as though we had [*sic*] the *American Agriculturist* under control and that our losses, if any, will be limited this year. Every year that we are in business we will be able to make headway, and convince the advertiser that the old *American Agriculturist* is a thing of the past and that this is really a new paper with new blood and new readers . . .

He goes on to other business matters:

I do not know whether I wrote you that Underwood Type-writer has not appropriated any money as yet for advertising.

I guess Robert [Dowling] keeps you posted on 61 Broadway. I understand that they have rented up to date $1,700,000 and I think they most likely will rent another $100,000. I understand that this will give us a profit of half-a-million dollars or more. [As the scion of wealth and not its creator, he goes on to write:] I cannot see why we do not increase the dividend from 24% to 30% beginning with the first of April.

Morgenthau then goes on to defer to his senior partner: "Inasmuch as it seems to be your policy to want to accumulate cash, I will leave the money that we have in the Hunts Point Palace account in the bank for the present."

Morgenthau next turns to national political gossip, speculating about the identity of the Democratic presidential candidate that year: "Now that McAdoo seems to be definitely out of the running, I imagine that you will come home for the Democratic [national] convention." [He interrupts his train of thought with:] "All of your children are anxiously awaiting the message from our respective parents as to their future plans."

Returning to the political scene, he continues: "On account of the [Teapot Dome] oil scandal and the feeling that it will sooner or later be traced to Wall Street, the people that [sic] I have talked to feel Davis' chances are very poor on account of his J. Pierpont Morgan affiliations . . . I still feel if Coolidge handles the oil situation well . . . his chances for re-election are excellent." (Morgenthau was proved wrong about John W. Davis, who received the Democratic nomination for president in 1924, and right about Coolidge's reelection.)

He goes on about family matters: "Elly has just completed her ten days' visit with me and I have enjoyed having her tremendously." [Theirs was an active, sexual relationship.[208]]

He finishes the letter with the most important matter of money: "I do not figure that I will need any more money from you at least for three or four months, and I want to take this opportunity to tell you how much I appreciate the wonderful way in which you have stayed back of me in the past year and a half [in connection with the purchase and operation of the farm newspaper, *American Agriculturist*]. It has been a tremendously trying period and I hope that the time, effort, money and sweat put into this paper will come back to us in the form of satisfaction of a difficult job well done.

March 23, 1924, finds Morgenthau visiting his immediate family, who were spending the winter months in Augusta, Georgia, and he has the time to write another letter to his father:

> I am afraid I have been a very bad son, because I have not written to you in some time. Frankly, I was awfully disappointed because we lost [$]1,300.00 in January, but now that I know we made $4,300.00 in Feb[ruary] and most likely do as well in March, I feel much more encouraged over the *A[merican] A[griculturist]*. With any kind of luck, we ought to go along without any help until July 1st. I have not been able to return the $4,000.00 I borrowed from Hunts Point Palace, but I will be able to take care of it later. My main job is to find a place where the paper can be printed for less money. I believe I can cut the printing cost by 50%. I have two people figuring on it now and they are quite encouraging. Our advertising continues

to run 50% ahead of last year which speaks for itself. I really think some of the issues this spring have been quite good.

We have been urging our readers to sign a petition for general [rural] tax reduction. It was signed and sent to Gov[ernor] Smith. He was sufficiently interested to send for Eastman [the editor] and myself and kept us there from 12:00 PM to 2:40 PM. During this time he talked on his pets: 1. the executive budget; 2. consolidation of 160 Departments into 20; 3. 4 year term. We agreed to support him editorially on his first two plans.[209]

I then suggested to him why did he not call a meeting of upstate newspaper owners and farm leaders and give them the same talk he gave us. He said fine, please prepare a list for me, which we did. He has called the meeting for next Wednesday and it ought to be a very interesting one. He asked after you.

Morgenthau is careful to add: "So you see I am making a position for myself thru the paper." Never mind the cost.

Morgenthau then continues: "Saw [Senators] Copeland and Carter Glass in Washington on my way South. They also asked after you." He continues: "By the way, at the last 61 B'way [board of directors'] meeting, they reported that on June 1, 1924, after making all payments and dividends, we would have a surplus of $234,000.00. That they have all but 7,000 feet rented. R[obert] D[owling—the co-owner of the building] has to rent his office out of the 7,000 feet left. It looks as though we would make over $600,000.00 this coming year. It is certainly a wonderful proposition & it seems as though your wildest forecasts will be more than fulfilled."

Morgenthau then turns to family matters:

For the week you went to London no one knew where you were. I cabled to you to our embassy at London but no answer. You really ought to let us know here when and where you go.

I certainly would be awfully glad to see Ma and you come home. Hunts Point Palace is doing fine and is no trouble. Once & a while I have to attend to something.

Well, my dear parents, I hope you will let us know soon what your plans are.

I am here [in Augusta, Georgia] for four days only. Elinor has been quite sick for ten days with the grippe. But she is much better now. The children are darlings. Joan walks and is too cute for words.

We leave here April 15th for N.Y. We stay there two weeks and move to the farm on May 1st.

Morgenthau's letters in the 1920s turn more and more to business matters. Henry Sr. has made his son his business partner and divided his assets, with a substantial part going to Henry Jr., who has taken over direct management of their joint affairs. His father is now in semi-retirement, enjoying public honors and private travel.

In a letter dated April 3, 1925, Morgenthau writes to his father:

I thought you would be interested in knowing how we stand on Hunts Point, as of April 1st. I figure that from April 1st to December 1st inclusive, our rents will be $37,000—our expenses will be $11,000—leaving a balance to distribute of $26,000. As we have already distributed $4,000, there remains a balance of $22,000 to distribute between you and myself.

I am sending you herewith 7 shares of Title Guarantee & Trust Co. and 5 shares of Southwestern Bell Telephone. I suggest that you sell these stocks and that we deposit the money in the Hunts Point account and then divide it up. [In the margin next to this paragraph is the handwritten notation: 'Sold.']

If you have the 100 shares of City Investing stock which belongs to the Hunts Point, I would appreciate it if you would have 50 shares of it transferred to me personally, as that would clear up that account.

In a handwritten letter dated Friday, July 3, 1925, Morgenthau writes to his parents:

I was delighted to get your letter and learn that you had such a fine trip to Bar Harbor.

I spent Saturday evening with Elinor upstate. She and Marion Dickerman spent a whole week upstate. They had a very good trip. Elinor has 32 junior [women's Democratic political] clubs organized now.

I then went to Ithaca Sunday night. Monday & Tuesday we really had a wonderful conference composed of our circulation men. 50 in all were there. On June 27, we had 93,800 [subscriptions] in N[ew] Y[ork] State. We will easily have over 100,000 [subscriptions] by Jan[uary] 1, 1926 and a total of 140,000+.

I read with great interest what you wrote about 61 B'way. I hope that just as soon as you hear any news you will relay it along to me.

The children are fine. They finished our pool yesterday and we ought to be able to swim in it tomorrow.

Elinor & I expect to hear Gov. Smith & ex-Gov. Miller debate next week. It ought to be very interesting.

I saw [brother-in-law] Morty yesterday and said goodbye to [sister] Helen today. New York will be quite lonely with all my family and family-in-law away.

Roosevelt's reward for his efforts in initiating the reelection campaign of Governor Smith (by writing a public letter calling upon him to run) was appointment by Smith as the chairman of the Taconic State Parkway Commission. The Commission was "mandated to build a highway set in continuous parkland from Westchester County to Albany."[210]

While the state legislature allocated funding to the better politically connected Robert Moses and his Long Island State Park Commission, Roosevelt found himself bereft of state funding to hire a staff to proceed with the planning of the highway he had been authorized to construct—a state of affairs for which Roosevelt somewhat irrationally never forgave Moses. Nevertheless, undaunted, Roosevelt, driving the hand-operated touring car he had secured to cope with his infirmity, set out to preliminarily survey a possible route for the Taconic Parkway.[211] Morgenthau sometimes joined Roosevelt's expeditions,[212] probably at Roosevelt's invitation.

More important, during Roosevelt's mapping trips through southern Dutchess County, Roosevelt and his wife Eleanor "would often come to our farm for dinner."[213] Mrs. Morgenthau thoroughly understood the importance of the friendship such visits offered and rose to the occasion. Henry III comments, "My mother always made sure [the dinner] was a good one."

Henry III quotes a letter dated July 16, 1925, that Roosevelt (and not his wife—as is more usual with couples in American social life) wrote to Mrs. Morgenthau: "We are looking forward to the pool and supper with you on Saturday . . . I will telephone you from Hyde Park on Friday (to confirm how many of us are coming) so you can kill the fatted calf for us!"[214] Henry III concludes: "[T]here was never a better example of finding a way to a man's heart than through his stomach than the food and drink served up in our crowded little dining room,"[215] in the original house Morgenthau acquired in 1913.

Morgenthau's letter to his father, dated July 10, 1925, acknowledges that he has taken over Henry Sr.'s business affairs from Robert Simon, Henry Sr.'s nephew, who had held the job for many years. The letter is addressed to a hotel at Bar Harbor, Maine. Morgenthau writes:

I had lunch this week with Rob Simon, who wished to consult me about some parent's magazine he was thinking of going into. Rob told me how glad he was that he was through with Dowling and that for the first time in 20 odd years, he was no longer in business with you. He said he was very glad of this, as now he could see you and Mamma as a nephew, and not for any business reasons. He also said that he could see something of me, as cousin, even though I had bought him out of two pieces of property.

Robert [Simon] was down to dinner with Otto Kahn[216] to see him and a group of Kahn's friends about renting them Carnegie Hall for 10 years on a guarantee rental plus a profit sharing basis.

I told Elinor about your proposed trip to Athens, and she is very keen on having us go along with you, if we receive an invitation. She is crazy to go to Athens and see it all, and she is quite thrilled at your getting a degree in the University of Athens.

Our swimming pool is a great success and we are enjoying it tremendously. The children are all well.

We have received some very large orders for advertising to run for a full year in the *American Agriculturist*. These orders are mostly new business.

If you have any ideas or suggestions on 61 Broadway, I would be glad to receive them.

On July 23, 1925, Morgenthau writes a business letter to his father, still at Bar Harbor, Maine:

I went down to call on Mr. Dowling today and he had just time to tell me that he had not heard a word from J. P. Day or Mr. Emanuel . . . At 2:30 sharp, in walked Mr. Weber of the Allied Chemical Company, and Mr. Dowling asked me to excuse him for a few minutes. A few minutes lasted an hour. Mr. Weber's office called him up several times to remind him that he had an appointment at 3 o'clock, but he stayed until 3:30 with Dowling.

After Weber left, Dowling had me come in to see him. (While waiting for him, I went through the engine [boiler?] room, and it was in very good shape.) Mr. Weber had come in to see Dowling about buying 61 Broadway . . . Dowling was tremendously elated. He told me that he read an extract from your letter to Mr. Weber in which you said you were not anxious to sell unless you got a big price. Dowling told Weber furthermore that we had refused $14,000,000 and that we had been offered $14,250,000, but that the tax question had kept us from selling . . .

Dowling thinks that Weber may have heard something about Emanuel dickering for 61 Broadway. The Allied Chemical Company, as you may know, own their building on West Street, free and clear, and Dowling thinks that they could borrow $3,000,000 on this building in the present market.

I have not gotten very excited about any of the other many prospective purchasers of 61 Broadway, but I really believe that Mr. Weber's coming in on his own accord at this time is very significant. Possibly I am simply falling under the influence of Mr. Dowling in that I see things through rosy glasses.

Morgenthau now comes to what is obviously an important, emotional matter:

In your last letter to me you said that I should not sign any contract for the sale of 61 Broadway, without first speaking to you over the telephone. My dear father, any such thought was furthermost from my mind. Before signing any contract, I will not only have you on the telephone, but I will give you plenty of opportunity to get on board of [*sic*] a train and come to New York yourself, if you so desire [this last phrase added to the typewritten text in handwritten ink].

That sentiment expressed, a calmer tone reappears: "In answer to your other question, 'should you buy any Dairy Products,' I really cannot advice [*sic*] you one way or the other."

Morgenthau then returns to the matter of 61 Broadway: "Now, don't get excited about the information contained in this letter, because the chances are that if Weber is really interested, there will be plenty of time for you to get your finger in the pie before the deal is closed."

Morgenthau interjects a family note: "The children are fine and so is Ellie. We are leaving for Weekapaug Inn, Westerly, R.I. on August 6th and I expect to stay with my family at Weekapaug until August 17th."

The somewhat stiff reference to the Weekapaug Inn is amplified by a comment Henry III makes about the choice of summer resort his parents patronized. He writes they chose "to penetrate some of the less-fashionable New England resorts, gaining entry through my mother's Vassar College chums, a number of whom were daughters of Protestant clerics. Thus we spent several seasons at the Quaker-owned Weekapaug Inn, a few miles down the Rhode Island coast from tightly restricted, posh Watch Hill and light years away from Newport."[217] In a sense, it was a social game Elinor Morgenthau played in a Social Darwinist world, relishing the satisfaction of escaping unspoken, restrictive, social codes of behavior.

On July 28, 1925, Morgenthau writes to Henry Sr., still at Bar Harbor:

> You will be interested to know, for your information, that I had lunch with Uncle Mengo yesterday [Henry Sr.'s brother Max]. He told me that my prophesy in regard to the Dusting Aeroplanes had unfortunately proven to be correct. Due to the dry weather the boll weevil has failed to appear this year so far, so that they have no call for their Aeroplane Dusters.
>
> Uncle Mengo told me that he has $100,000 tied up in this Dusting enterprise, and I think he feels pretty sick about it. Of course they will try to sell the planes and get back what money they can.
>
> I think it is wonderful that Dr. Fosdick has accepted your invitation, and Elinor and I expect to go with you, unless something unforeseen comes up. Once you learn on what date you are going to receive your degree from Athens, I would like to discuss with you the best time to leave for Europe.
>
> For your information, [eight-year-old grandson] Henry composed his letter entirely alone.
>
> I am just writing this as a short note to you, as I am leaving on the train in a couple of minutes.

The point of the letter comes at the end: "I expect to see Dowling on Thursday and will tell him that you are willing to sell your half-interest at the rate of $14,250,000 to the Allied Chemical Co., but you do not care to stay in for ¼ interest."

On August 3, 1925, Morgenthau writes:

The building in which [the *American Agriculturist*] is in [at 461 Fourth Avenue] was sold last Friday to J. C. & M. G. Mayer. As you will see from the enclosed letter, Edgar A. Manning, Broker, has offered me this property, which was assessed for 1925 at $380,000. With the present rentals, it will show about 15% return on the money . . . As an investment, it looks pretty good to me.

There is nothing new to report on 61 Broadway. Robert Dowling simply said that Mr. Clark had asked for a new set of figures, but did not say for whom they were for.

I do not know whether I wrote you that I called up [Elinor Morgenthau's uncle] Herbert Lehman from Robert Dowling's office and asked him whether his firm was interested. He told me that Mr. Ball informed Lehman Bros. that 61 Broadway could be bought by them without any cash. Herbert Lehman said that of course he was interested on such a basis . . . that they had been mislead [*sic*] into believing that the building could be bought without any cash—and under the circumstances—they were not interested.

There is a handwritten postscript: "Just got thru talking [with] Aaron Rabinovitz. He said they paid $540,000.00 for the property. Which he thinks is more than it is worth."

Morgenthau later writes to his father on August 7, 1925, from the Weekapaug Inn: "They forwarded me your letter here. You are right. I was not very keen about 461 Fourth Ave[nue]." Not so cryptically he adds: "Off with the old and on with the new."

He continues: "We arrived here in fine shape. All stood the trip well. Two days before we left the farm both cars broke down. But we were able to get them fixed to leave on time."

He goes on to the business matter that appears to be the focus of their attention:

During one of the many talks I had with R[obert] E. D[owling] he told me what a good chance the City Inv[esting] Co[mpany] had to sell 46 Str[eet] & B'way and 56 Str[eet] & 5th Ave[nue]. He said, "Of course if we did, what a lot of cash we would have on hand. Then maybe we could afford to buy your half of 61 B'way." Or words to that effect. I believe that in [h]is heart he would like to buy us out. But maybe I am wrong. What do you think? In the meantime the <u>whole</u> [underlining in original] family is enjoying the best of health and a <u>darn</u> <u>good</u> <u>income</u> [underlining in original]. So why worry?

Would you and Ma be in favor of taking one of the Italian liners right to Naples. Or would [you] prefer to take a fast steamer to France [on the way to Athens]? We will be ready some time in October.

Now for a brief account about the *A[merican] A[griculturist]*. On August 1st for the first time we were able to stop everyone's subscription when it expired. You know we have been carrying them about three months over. Advertising for Sept[ember], Oct[ober] & Nov[ember] looks good. I think we will have considerably more than last year. We need it. For the first time since I have owned the paper our readers have got a little money to spend. I see this reflected in the sale of my surplus cattle on the farm which has been very good. The farm has had the best year so far since 1920. I am feeling very optimistic about my own affairs and have a good lot of cash in the bank.

By August 20, 1925, Morgenthau is back at his office at the *American Agriculturist*. He has now put the name of his editor, E. R. Eastman, in the upper-right corner of the company letterhead besides keeping his own name as publisher in the upper-left corner. He is clearly upset with his father. His secretary typewrites a letter to his father on that date. It begins:

I was quite disturbed by the letter which Jesse Ehrich wrote to you and your answer to him.

If you do not mind my saying so, I think you made a mistake in answering him at all. I have been trying to handle the Hunts Point Palace to the best of my ability and I believe to your entire satisfaction. I think you should have written Jesse Ehrich that the matter was in my hands and that he should deal with me exclusively. You could have then written to me any suggestion which you might [the last word is handwritten in] have had in mind, and in this way kept Jesse from trying to play you against me.

I will do nothing in the matter until I hear from you, instructing me whether you wish me to continue the negotiations for renting the stores, or whether you prefer to handle the whole matter yourself. If you wish me to continue to handle Hunts Point Palace, I would like you to write Jesse Ehrich at once that all negotiations are in my hands and that both he and Mr. Lerner will have to see me . . .

In a more-relaxed mode, Morgenthau writes to his father on September 3, 1925: "You will be interested to know that I met Lerner and his lawyer at Lachman & Goldsmith's [law] office this morning. They asked for a few changes, which I agreed to. I received your telegram, and with this in mind, I asked them to pay us three months' rent in advance instead of depositing three months' rent [as security], and they agreed to this. The leases are being changed, and I expect to have them signed within a day or two."

After discussing new prospects for the sale of 61 Broadway, Morgenthau then goes on with what is more congenial to him: "The [a]dvertising for Sept[ember] in our paper looks good. I believe we will make a little money in September. It is too early to say yet about October. On account of the small amount of advertising we carried in July and August, I will have to put some money into the *A[merican]* *A[griculturist]* during September. Once the revenue for the advertising for September comes in [i]n October, we will again be in good shape, and the paper ought to be able to carry itself for the rest of the year. I believe you will agree that this is a wonderful improvement over last year. You will remember when I started out to save $25,000 of manufacturing expenses, you told me that that was a nice mark to aim for, but you doubted if I would be able to accomplish this. You will be pleased to learn that I will save at least $25,000 in the manufacturing department, and maybe more."

It is evident that Morgenthau was very conscious of his father's jeremiads about the farm weekly's recurrent deficits. Henry III quotes a letter dated January 24, 1924, which his grandfather wrote while in Athens on his Greek refugee resettlement mission: "It is not much of a business that produces $185,000 and costs over $200,000 to do so."[218] Still, Henry III writes, his "grandfather continued to put up with the drain on the family's funds"[219] just as he continued to put up with the deficits his son's farm venture incurred every year.

Having patted himself on the back for reducing the deficit in the costs of continuing to publish the "paper," as he called it, Morgenthau now ends the letter with a discussion of the details of accompanying his parents on their trip to Athens, where Henry Sr. is to receive an honorary degree: "I understand that the *Leviathan* is an excellent steamer, and I believe that at that time of year we would get the best accommodations for a very reasonable sum. Elinor and I will be absolutely ready to sail on [the] day [designated by Henry Sr.], but I want an opportunity to discuss it with her, with you and Mamma before we finally decide what steamer we do sail on."

Henry III gives the background for the honorary degree Henry Sr. received in Athens: "In 1923 [Henry I] accepted the appointment from the League of Nations to be chairman of the Greek Refugee Settlement Commission, which was charged with the task of resettling Greeks who had been expelled from Smyrna [Izmir] by the Turks. [Henry Sr.] proceeded to coordinate the job of housing and rehabilitating what amounted to about a 25 percent increase in the population of Greece. The task required a practiced outside hand. Altogether, the time [Henry Sr.] spent in Greece on behalf of the League of Nations proved to be one of his happier and most effective ventures."[220]

By letter dated January 26, 1926, Morgenthau writes to his parents:

I have been postponing writing to you for some time, as I felt it was very unsatisfactory to write a letter that you would not receive for two months.

I have been extremely busy getting your affairs, mine and the A[merican] A[griculturist]'s into shape. I will take up in my letter business matters first and then will talk about personal affairs afterwards.

I do not believe that you begin to realize the amount of detail there is connected in looking after your and Ma's affairs. There is hardly a day that passes but what something comes up that takes my personal attention, and Miss Stein has been kept quite busy. I think that you must give [nephew] Robert Simon credit for a good deal more work than you ever had any idea was connected in looking after your affairs. During the last two weeks I have taken a young boy out of the Advertising Dept. and let him look after your things every morning. This will cost you the large sum of $12 per week. Just at present he is down at the Customs House trying to get some of Ma's things which she sent from Rome.

I just got some lace through the mail from Belgium for 135 francs. If they send you another bill, I will pay it. The only thing I have done which you may question is the paying of $2,000 to Marcus M. Marks for Eagle's Nest. This correspondence was sent you in another envelope to Hongkong. It seemed most urgent, and inasmuch as the other three had all come across, I felt that you would want to do the same. After I paid this $2,000, Elinor reminded me that you had some row several years ago about paying your share of the deficit each year, and I hope that by paying this $2,000, I have not established a precedent which you do not concur with.

He continues:

In regard to the selling of your Kennecott Copper, I received your cable on a Monday and I called up Lachman and Goldsmith, who referred me to George Naumburg, who referred me to Miss Adelstein, who referred me to the Manufacturers Trust Co. where I finally on Tuesday located Mamma's stocks. I now have a list from Mr. Jewett of the securities which he holds for her. On Tuesday, Kennecott had dropped a couple of points and I hoped that by waiting I could sell for the same price that it was selling on Monday. By the end of the week, the stock was still selling around 54, so I told George Haas to sell it out, which he did, at 54 1/8. I am sorry that I could have gotten the highest price for the week, but this was impossible, as you did not say in your cable how many shares of Kennecott Mamma owned, where her stock was, or who had the power of attorney.

I was delighted to get your cable today from Calcutta: "Feeling scrumptious pay Mount Sinai Great Eastern Hotel until thirty-first love," and I am going to send Mt. Sinai a check for $2,500.

I think it would be to your advantage if you would arrange to have the same person look after your affairs year in and year out, as there are so many things that come up which even I do not know about. I will be very glad to continue to look after them if you want me to, provided that I can hire sufficient help to do the work properly.

Evidently thinking that Morgenthau knew the man better than he did, Morgenthau reports that his brother-in-law Morton Fox "asked me to go down and see Robert Dowling and try and get him to give us a letter to the effect that the City Investing Company stock was worth [$]200 [a share] at the time you gave it to us. I am going to try and see him today. The stock market seems extremely nervous and I believe will go lower."

He says of himself, "You will be glad to learn that I am going two or three times a week to Mcgovern's [sic] gymnasium, that my waist line has gone down 1 1/2 [inches] and I lost 5 lbs., and I feel simply great. Elinor starts tomorrow morning with Mrs. Mcgovern [sic] at 7:30 AM, which means that I have to get out of bed."

Reporting on his farm activities, Morgenthau writes, "After talking the matter over with several people, we have decided to sell all but 12 of our best cows from our dairy, and this will enable me to curtail the terrible work and the loss of money considerably on the farm. At least, I am going to try it out for another year on that basis, and give particular attention to my fruit trees."

Outlining their social calendar, Morgenthau tells how:

Elinor and I spent a most enjoyable evening with [Elinor's uncle, then a judge of New York State's highest court] Irving Lehman [and his wife], at their home in Albany. The Governor and Mrs. Smith were there, also Chief Judge Hiscock, Judge Anderson, Colonel and Mrs. Rice and Colonel Fred Stewart [Stuart?] Greene. [The latter was then the State Superintendent of Public Works.]

The Governor arrived 45 minutes ahead of time and we had to take turns getting dressed for supper, while one of us entertained Governor and Mrs. Smith. He was in great shape and told one [former Governor] Sulzer story after another. He told the one how you came to see him at the time that there was a rumor that Gaffney [who was a partner of Boss Charlie Murphy in a construction company] was going to be appointed for Highway Commissioner. I told one of your favorite stories about the time that Governor Sulzer threw the wet sponge at his wife. On the whole, it was one of the most enjoyable evenings that I have spent in a long time.

Governor William Sulzer has the distinction of being the only government official to have been impeached in the State of New York. Telling stories about him had a risqué quality suggestive of Communist party officials in the Kremlin telling stories about Trotsky during the years Stalin was conducting his Purge Trials of Lenin's Old Bolshevik associates. The *New York Times* has described the circumstances giving rise to the impeachment:[221]

In Governor Sulzer's case, what the charges come down to—in addition, apparently, to arrogance and greed—was a legal coup by Charles F. Murphy, the Tammany Hall leader whom Mr. Sulzer, a fellow Democrat, had defied. Mr. Sulzer not only campaigned for political reform and against corruption—that might have been excusable—but also unforgivably pursued his agenda once he got elected in 1912.

Mr. Sulzer refused to name Mr. Murphy's partner in a contracting business as state highways superintendent.

"When Governor William Sulzer refused to consult the 'ahrganization' on appointments," former Senator Daniel Patrick Moynihan wrote in a 1961 essay, "When the Irish Ran New York," "Murphy did not argue; he impeached and removed him." . . .

Tammany's allies, including Alfred E. Smith Jr., the Assembly speaker, and Senator Robert F. Wagner, the [state] Senate president pro tem, helped engineer the coup. [If the lieutenant governor replaced Governor Sulzer, Senator Wagner would automatically succeed him.]

Morgenthau then goes on to tell of another auspicious social occasion to which they were invited: "Saturday night we attended another nice dinner at the Roosevelts'—at which they announced the engagement of their daughter Anna to a Mr. Dall, who works at Lehman Bros."

Morgenthau goes on to discuss a personal, obviously highly confidential concern of Henry Sr.'s: "You will be interested to know that about two weeks after I got back, I went to see Gov[ernor] Smith about your matter. At first he seemed a little annoyed and said it was too early to say anything. However, I pressed him on the subject. Whereupon he pulled out of his inside pocket an envelope with several notes on it and he pointed to the line which said 'for Congress Henry Morgenthau.' He went on then in a better mood to explain how they really could not tell until they found a vacancy.

"I spoke to him about raising money for his campaign fund, but he said he had decided not to make a pre-nomination fight. I think you can take that with a grain of salt."

Morgenthau then addresses his mother: "Mama Dear: This may be the only letter to reach you in time for your birthday. I want to wish you the happiest of happy days. We all miss you very much. I hope you will come home sooner than you planned. We talk often about our experiences in Greece and how brave you were."

The acquisition of a second thousand acres of farmland took place, along with a residence that was now being purchased.[222] The acquisition of farmland probably did not require a noticeable increase in Morgenthau's costs for farm laborers. The major expenditure was his foreman's salary. If an additional laborer or two was needed for planting and harvesting periods, the wages paid the temporary employees were negligible.

The building that was acquired was larger and more elegant than the one that had come with the initial acquisition of farmland. Robert Morgenthau suggests that with the move to the new house late in 1929, after the alterations to it had been completed, their old home, no longer needed, was sold shortly thereafter.[223] Elinor Morgenthau would appear to have had a large hand in the decision to purchase their new home and the additional acreage.

The idea of being the chatelaine of a large landed estate would have appealed to Elinor Morgenthau as much as to her husband, and money was no problem. Henry III writes: "In 1926 . . . my mother inherited some money from her father, who had succumbed to heart failure . . ."[224]

On the other hand, Morgenthau himself included the information in a letter to his parents, dated July 10, 1930: "I am leaving in a few minutes to fly down to Atlantic City to call on my parents-in-law. Elinor has been with them since Monday. She thinks that Mr. Fatman has improved slightly." If Mr. Fatman was still alive in 1930, Henry III is mistaken as to the source of his mother's inheritance in 1926.

The later date for Mr. Fatman's demise would explain the appropriateness of the use of the adverbs "fortuitously" and "prudently" in Henry III's comment: "Morris Fatman, my mother's father, had fortuitously sold his woolen manufacturing business a few years before he died [well before the stock market collapse in 1929] and prudently invested his profits and his wife's Lehman inheritance in securities that produced relatively stable yields."[225]

A possible explanation for the confusion may be that Henry III was roughly nine years of age in 1926, and he may have overheard a casual reference in a conversation between his parents to an inheritance from a "grandfather." In Henry III's life experience at that age, he would have only known of his own grandfathers and associated the term with them, not understanding that his mother could have had a long-gone grandparent of her own. It is entirely possible that the inheritance Elinor Morgenthau received in 1926, was, in fact, from the termination of a trust fund created by her Lehman grandfather—probably in his will. The money would have been derived from the operations of the fabled private merchant banking firm of Lehman Brothers.

Events recollected in tranquility may suffer a sea change in the telling. So, when Henry III came to put pen to paper as an adult (or fingers to typewriter or computer), he recollected his impressions as a child at nine years of age without considering the matter further.

Since the money to purchase the new house was supplied by Elinor Morgenthau, it saved Morgenthau himself from the burden of appealing to Henry Sr. once more for money, a circumstance for which, one may be sure, he was grateful to his wife.

The building that the Morgenthaus purchased had been owned by the family of a New York City brewer by the name of Adolph Jupfel, who had a substantial house built on the farm in 1884–85 in the Queen Anne style.[226] In turn, the property would be disposed of to a new owner by Morgenthau's family after his death. A field architectural historian would later note that by 1984, "the estate which this house once commanded had been divided and is under development pressure with its orchards and open fields overspreading gentle hills . . . [I]n 2001, much of the area surrounding the estate has been developed."[227]

Henry III explains that the newly acquired house was "located in the middle of the [Morgenthau] farm acres . . ." He goes on to describe the new acquisition: "The property was shaded by mature maple trees and a huge, ancient oak on the south lawn. The north side commanded a view of an artificial pond that had supplied neighborhood icehouses before the advent of the refrigerator. Other buildings on the property included a boat-house, a saw mill, and a large barn with box and straight stalls for horses. For the next couple of years, supervising the remodeling and furnishing of the house and the landscaping of the grounds occupied a great deal of my mother's time."[228]

With Elinor's inheritance in hand, the Morgenthaus had no need for mortgage loans or the like to pay for the services of the architect and the substantial costs of the reconstruction of the building.

Her son notes that Elinor's taste ran to "rustic colonial cottages" rather than to "the pretensions of marble fireplaces and mahogany furniture"[229] (more common twenty-five years earlier), even though the size of the new building required the more-formal style chosen for the remodeling rather than the look of a simple Cape Cod farmhouse. So interior paneling, modeled after the Georgian style of the 1760s, would be "pickled pine" and not walnut, in keeping with the simplified and "dressed-down" aesthetic of the 1920s and 1930s. The knotty pine paneling would then be stained to a warm golden color suggestive of a centuries-old mellowing of raw wood—an instant and effective aging technique.

During the Depression years in the 1930s, the farm and the *American Agriculturist*, both of which Henry III describes as having been "debtor operations all along, didn't seem to be losing any more money than usual." He writes that he does not remember any retrenchment in his family's lifestyle, although his mother in her capacity as watchdog of the family's spending, "continued as always to be extremely careful."[230]

If nothing else, the farm, in large measure, was the means whereby social access was provided to Elinor Morgenthau to meet members of the WASP Ascendancy—namely, Franklin Roosevelt and his family. Her husband had secured social access for several reasons. For one, perhaps minor, there was the prestige that had accrued to Henry Sr. through his ambassadorship to Constantinople and his courageous and morally admirable publicizing of the Christian, Armenian massacres by the Turks in 1915; and then, more important, there were Roosevelt's political ambitions. Political fund-raising is never easy, and Henry Sr. promised to be a source of funding for Democratic reformers' political campaigns, for himself and from soliciting others— a political identity for which Franklin Roosevelt qualified. Access to Henry Sr. promised to be easier through an acquaintance with his son, who also would appear to have been generous with his political contributions. Besides which, the younger Morgenthau showed a discreet, neighborly interest in Roosevelt's political future that was coupled with Morgenthau's own entire disinterest in any political ambition for himself.[231] In that respect, on the Roosevelt front porch, Morgenthau was the committee chairman who led the formal notification ceremonies of Roosevelt's designation as the Democratic Party's vice presidential candidate in 1920 in front of some 8,000 persons.[232]

Both Morgenthau and Roosevelt were "gentleman farmers," not dependent on the sale of their farms' produce for living expenses. For them, their farm operations ended up costing money by the end of the year. Still, they shared a concern that their farms produce income and not become a bottomless pit into which money was continuously being thrown. (Although Roosevelt had gotten the idea that Morgenthau "was the only man he knew who had made a profit farming."[233]) Like all farmers, they learned to look to the weather and the prices farm produce brought.

Most important, Franklin Roosevelt accepted as a matter of course that he lived in a Social Darwinist world that postulated life called for struggle and uncertainty.[234] In that sense, however peaceable the landscape, metaphorically, the barbarians were always at the gates. As Ed Flynn recounts, Roosevelt "liked a fight, especially a political fight. He would fight with all the vigor he could command for what he wished and for what he believed."[235] Regardless of how much Roosevelt may have relished doing battle to achieve his ambitions, in quieter moments he must have taken enormous satisfaction in knowing that the land endured, and that he could point to trees growing on his lawn that had stood there going back to the days when Indians, untouched by a corrupting European civilization, had roamed the forests that then covered the area. That awareness must have been an unspoken source of spiritual kinship he shared with Morgenthau. So in the stress of political battles to come, Roosevelt may have cast aside Morgenthau, but it was afterwards, when calm returned, that he could share with Morgenthau the realization of a promise of peaceable days on the ever-enduring land.

Perhaps once, Roosevelt put into words—however obscurely—that unspoken connection with the land he shared with Morgenthau. In 1934, he gave a picture of himself at the wheel of his automobile with Morgenthau as passenger, inscribed, "For Elinor from one of two of a kind."[236] Beschloss suggests that Roosevelt gave the inscribed photograph to Elinor Morgenthau because he knew "it would delight Morgenthau,"[237] but if so, it would seem the inscription should have been addressed directly to its intended recipient. Roosevelt apparently understood it was Elinor Morgenthau herself who would take unalloyed pleasure upon receiving the picture—a precious acknowledgment of friendship.

So Elinor Morgenthau could find herself invited to tea with her husband at Springwood, the Roosevelt estate overlooking the Hudson River, and seated in the vast library—some thirty-five or forty feet in length and almost as wide, built onto the south side of the building in 1916, when the Regency facade replaced the original Queen Anne–style front. (The Roosevelts thriftily saved money by changing nothing at the rear of the building that faced the river.) The new library effectively substituted the family's social space from the relatively small rooms coming off the large central hall of the original construction plan on the first floor of the house. There Elinor Morgenthau could be a participant in a social gathering that included Mrs. F. W. Vanderbilt and five of the latter's own guests who, one day, paid a call on the matriarchal Sara Delano Roosevelt.[238] (The Vanderbilts had built a vast palazzo a few miles up the road from the Roosevelt estate—like many of the other *palazzi* of that period not otherwise demolished—now become a museum.) Sara Roosevelt would comment in a letter to her daughter-in-law Eleanor, Franklin's wife, "Young Morgenthau was easy and yet modest and serious and intelligent. The wife [*sic*] is very Jewish, but appeared very well."[239]

What may the Roosevelt matriarch have meant by the words she used? We know from his letters that Morgenthau had learned early in adolescence that he would get along with members of the WASP Ascendancy by going along and avoiding its stereotype of Jews—namely, that they were loud, pushy, and vulgar in their manners and dress (i.e., undesirable "alpha" personality types). So in boarding school Morgenthau had learned to be unassuming, mild-mannered, polite, asking questions quietly when appropriate, laughing at Franklin's jokes, showing interest in what was being said by the matriarch of the family, and otherwise being a discreet guest. For Elinor Morgenthau, notwithstanding her middle-class, Protestant, college friends, it had to have been mostly a new experience. She had to have been unsure of herself, ill at ease, trying a little too hard to appear a pleasant and appreciative guest, and the effort must have showed. Sara Roosevelt could dismiss her as a parvenu—except her words were "very Jewish." Still, Elinor passed muster. She was not impossible, and as a social appendage of her husband's, she "appeared very well."

If one seeks to understand what turned out to be Eleanor Roosevelt's rather contrary response from that of her mother-in-law, one should remember the conflicting considerations that influenced the young Eleanor Roosevelt as she was growing up. While there could be no question that she belonged to the WASP Ascendancy, she had to cope early in life with the realization that her father Elliott Roosevelt was a lost soul, a drunkard whose dissipated life ended at an early age. A biographer of Eleanor Roosevelt would write of her father, "[I]n August [1894], he fell into a coma and died—a victim of illness, alcohol and despair."[240] So she had grown up shy, conscious of her physical plainness.

On the other hand, her uncle, the ebullient Theodore, had taken her under his wing. She had come to understand that she was a lesser member of what passes in the United States for royalty. Her cousin, Alice Roosevelt Longworth, Theodore's daughter, married to a Speaker of the United States House of Representatives, knew to the end of her days where she was counted in the social hierarchy in the nation's capital—just as Indira Gandhi's former husband, even after their divorce, understood he had certain privileges that allowed a former son-in-law of Jawaharlal Nehru to make remarks lesser folk would not have dared utter.

People today cannot have any awareness of the charisma Theodore Roosevelt projected in his lifetime. There is good reason that his face was carved by the sculptor Gutzon Borglum on Mount Rushmore in the Black Hills of South Dakota, along with those of national icons Washington, Jefferson, and Lincoln. Her uncle Theodore was the very embodiment of a Social Darwinist ideal. He had successfully struggled to overcome his childhood weaknesses and medical afflictions to become a hero on the Western frontier, when that romantic ideal, involving struggle and conquest, animated the collective American psyche. He was at once energetic and intelligent, a sure protector of his ethnic kin (who were overwhelmingly the majority of the population of the United States). Only he, with his immense charisma, could have succeeded in splitting the Republican Party in 1912, causing men to break with party loyalties to join his "Bull Moose" campaign to regain the presidency of the United States—although the campaign ended with the victory of Woodrow Wilson in the presidential election that year.

Some element of that sense of a special political magic that enfolded Theodore Roosevelt must have entered into his niece's attraction for Franklin Roosevelt, so that he asked for her hand in marriage with a five-carat diamond engagement ring and a wedding that took place in the White House itself.

So, Eleanor Roosevelt could regard herself as American royalty, and at the same time be subjected to the social tyranny of her mother-in-law, in whose house she lived at Hyde Park. Sara had also provided her son with a house in New York City, with a connecting doorway to her own home next door. Sara Roosevelt might dote on her only child, Franklin, but she would expect her daughter-in-law to have a suitable regard for the wishes of the older woman, who was providing much of the money to fund her son and his family's lifestyle at Hyde Park. (Outside observers and her daughter-in-law might think of Sara Delano Roosevelt's expectations as requiring an unconscionable level of deference. To be sure, this social interchange between mother and daughter-in-law would be carried out under a cover of genteel good manners and general affability.)

With royalty, class distinctions tend to lose their importance, since everyone else is socially inferior. Louis XIV at his morning *levée*, looking over the crowd of noblemen at his bedside who were straining to be given the honor of presenting the king with his shirt, did not need to consider the difference in social precedence between one title and another. Beschloss describes the matter, saying that Eleanor Roosevelt had shed the genteel anti-Semitism of her class,[241] perhaps forgetting that she was not only a part of the WASP Ascendancy, but, by connection with her uncle, above it.

So Eleanor Roosevelt could recognize the young Mrs. Morgenthau as being the chatelaine of an estate comparable to that of her husband and his mother. She also had to be aware of, and join in, her husband's political ambitions, and be certain that Morgenthau had not dropped her husband, as political "fellow travelers" were wont to do after Franklin's embarrassing political defeat in the Democratic Party's first direct-election United States Senate primary race in 1914. And in the desperate months after the onset of her husband's infantile paralysis in

1921, Morgenthau unselfishly had spent countless hours playing Parcheesi with him. That was on a disinterested, personal level. Morgenthau could probably be counted on for contributions to future political campaigns—this assuming Eleanor's husband recovered sufficiently to be able to consider returning to active political endeavors.

Eleanor was probably also aware of her mother-in-law's disdain for the unsure and socially awkward young woman who was their guest for tea. Some memory of her own social insecurity while growing up may also have created sympathy for the other woman. And so, probably, for both psychological and mundane political reasons, Eleanor Roosevelt wanted to reach out to the young Mrs. Morgenthau as a friend.

Henry III adds that his mother was "an obvious exception" to Eleanor Roosevelt's early perception as she was growing up of Jewish "devotion to 'money, jewels and sables.'" He notes that both women had a disdain for fashion, and writes that his "mother seldom wore any jewelry other than her diamond engagement ring, a wedding band, and occasionally an amber or crystal necklace or a small brooch. And the house at Fishkill Farms was in every way unostentatious."[242] (At the time of which Henry III writes, the house would have been the earlier Greek Revival farmhouse—dating probably from the second quarter of the nineteenth century—that came with the initial purchase of farmland in 1913, rather than the building later acquired in the 1920s.)

With regard to Elinor Morgenthau's social insecurities, to anticipate, Henry III describes how during the 1928 election campaign, when Al Smith was running as the Democratic candidate for the presidency of the United States, and Franklin Roosevelt, as an upstate WASP, had been chosen by Smith to run as the Democratic candidate for governor of the state of New York to buttress Smith's position in the state, Morgenthau served as Roosevelt's "advance man." This meant that he traveled across the state, sizing up the political situation in the locations where Roosevelt expected to campaign, alerting local party leaders when to expect a visit from the candidate, arranging for political rallies, hiring brass bands where appropriate, and briefing the candidate on the local situation in the town upon his arrival.

Elinor played a role in the women's division of the state party organization along with another of Mrs. Roosevelt's friends, Nancy Cook. Ms. Cook appeared to be taking over control of the women's division, easing out Ms. Morgenthau, who became disenchanted by her fellow volunteer's activities. Leaving the scene at the women's division to Ms. Cook, Elinor Morgenthau started traveling around the state with her husband.

Henry III suggests that his mother encouraged his father on October 17, 1928, to telegraph Eleanor Roosevelt (who was in overall charge of the women's division) to complain that his arrangements for women campaign speakers were being upstaged by Ms. Cook. Ms. Roosevelt's response was to telegraph her husband that she was ready to resign. Roosevelt then sided with his wife with the face-saving addendum that Morgenthau be told in advance of any change in speaker arrangements.

Faced with the realization that things would remain as they were in the women's division, Elinor Morgenthau began to understand she had uselessly irritated her friend and was aghast as she foresaw the rupture of their friendship. Seeking to repair the damage, Ms. Morgenthau then wrote what was apparently a contrite letter, although Henry III conjectures that it still radiated animosity toward Ms. Cook.

Ms. Roosevelt replied with a lengthy letter to let Ms. Morgenthau understand that none of Ms. Roosevelt's separate female friendships precluded other friendships, and she did not intend to have to choose between them. Then, focusing in on Ms. Cook, Ms. Roosevelt very pointedly wrote, "I am devoted to her and it will be wiser for you not to talk to me about it as you cannot expect me to agree with you or to be influenced by your feelings." Ms. Roosevelt then proceeded to give Ms. Morgenthau some advice, suggesting the latter was "hurt often by imaginary things . . . But if one is to have a healthy, normal relationship . . . you simply cannot be so easily hurt. Life is too short to cope with it. Cheer up and forget about it . . ." So royalty deals with social impertinence before a regal expression of forgiveness: "I'll be home for lunch tomorrow and Thursday at 1:30 but must work from three on."[243]

Beschloss tells how Eleanor Roosevelt once wrote to another of her friends, who was a Gentile, "You are worse than Elinor Morgenthau and haven't her reason!"[244]

Beschloss quotes Professor Blum as suggesting that the "bond of affection" that developed over time between Ms. Roosevelt and Ms. Morgenthau was "much greater" than that between their husbands.[245] Certainly, the connections were rather different. Roosevelt did not suffer fools gladly. None of Eleanor Roosevelt's friends—with the possible exception of Elinor Morgenthau—interested her husband. Perhaps Roosevelt's own closest friend was his maiden cousin Margaret Suckley, to whom he wrote letters throughout his life and who was one of the guests at Roosevelt's cottage at Warm Springs, Georgia, when he suffered his fatal stroke in 1945. In a sense, she filled the role of the sister he never had. (Apparently, she had kept his letters in a valise under her bed and these were only recently discovered.)

Henry III writes how, during the 1920s, his parents "dined frequently [with the Roosevelts] and were guests on the Roosevelt houseboat, *Larooco*, anchored off the Florida Keys, as well as at Hyde Park." He adds: "Yet neither of them ever felt secure." Henry III describes the problem in the following words: "In their work relationships each of the two Roosevelts had individual ways of keeping supporters off balance."[246] Perhaps a more-telling analogy lies in the relationship between royalty and their courtiers. Whether Roosevelt himself would ever think of himself in terms comparable to royalty is an interesting question. In the same way, he and Eleanor, without thinking about it, had to feel that, with their "old money" and their connection to Theodore Roosevelt, they were quintessentially at the peak of the WASP Ascendancy. Perhaps the best way to characterize how Roosevelt may have regarded his status is to compare him to the Yussupov princes in Tsarist Russia, who were, without question, the richest and most socially prominent persons, next to the tsar himself. For the Roosevelts, this meant that socially, they could do much as they liked, in the sense of choosing their friendships as they would. By the same token, Franklin and Eleanor would expect people to treat them with a kind of unspoken deference, no more perceptibly expressed than in the use of a certain tone of voice when speaking to them. If people forgot themselves and took, to too great an extent, social liberties of familiarity, why, as Henry III writes, "each of the two Roosevelts had individual ways of keeping supporters off balance."

Henry III describes how Fishkill Farms, life in Dutchess County, and the demands of motherhood dimmed his mother's early interest in the theater. He writes, "[H]er energies were harnessed to activities supportive of my father's career," and how "she later became a popular speaker for the State Democratic Committee, Women's Division." He concludes, "[S]he was serene in her bucolic Dutchess County environs."[247]

Morgenthau writes to his parents in a letter dated March 12, 1926:

I am sending this on the SS *MATSONIA* [*sic*], hoping that it will arrive in Honolulu by April 1st. I hope you got all of our letters in the Philippines which we sent care of Gov[ernor] General Leonard E. Wood, also Thomas

Cook & Son. Some letters may have been sent [to] you care of Thomas Cook & Son, Honolulu, and I suggest that you inquire at the post office . . .

I sent you yesterday by parcel post, Colonel House's two volumes, which I hope you will receive in time, as I thought you would enjoy reading them on the steamer on your way back to the United States [*sic*]. [Morgenthau has forgotten that he is sending the two volumes to the Hawaiian Islands, an American territory. He probably was thinking of the continental forty-eight states.] You will notice that he refers to you several times, but does not give you much credit or anybody else any credit.

Morgenthau now turns to business:

I had a good deal of work, and at the same time satisfaction, in arranging for a loan on Hunts Point Palace. The Bond and Mortgage Co., who [*sic*] now hold the mortgage, offer us $240,000 at 5½% for five years provided that we will pay off $5,000 a year. Several others offered us varied amounts, but all at 5½%. Finally, I called up Mr. Schield of the Mutual Life Insurance Co., as you suggested, and they are making us a loan of $200,000 for five years at 5%, with very reasonable charges. There is very little 5% money around, and if I must say so myself, I think that I made the best loan that could be made in the present market— keeping in mind all the time that you did not care so much about getting a large loan, as you did about getting a loan with a reasonable interest charge. [The foregoing language is that of a subordinate employee reporting how meticulously he has carried out his supervisor's instructions.]

I received a letter from Murphy informing me that the Siden Realty Co. would not go on the bond and mortgage, so naturally it was up to me to find some other way. You, Lachman and Goldsmith [Henry Sr.'s former law partners for some twenty-five years, while he was still engaged in the practice of law] and I had discussed forming a corporation for over a year, so I have gone ahead and taken out corporation papers for "Henry Morgenthau and Son, Inc."

Morgenthau goes on to tell his father: "I personally take a good deal of satisfaction in having a company by the name of Henry Morgenthau & Son, Inc. and I would like to develop it with you into a real estate holding company of modest size." Morgenthau then reports on his parents' household situation:

Helen is looking after your servants, but please let me know if you want me to hire a chauffeur for you and put your Packard into commission.

We have just gone through quite a smash in Wall Street, and I am glad to say that the things I own suffered very little. Underwood Typewriter Co. held up as well as anything. Your idea of keeping together the cash we received from 61 Broadway was certainly the right one, and I believe that when you come back, there will be lots of opportunities to invest it to advantage. Personally, I am of the opinion that business will continue [to be] good for this year anyway.

Morgenthau now turns to his personal favorite enterprise and writes: "The *American Agriculturist* is continuing to do well, and I am sending you under separate cover, the last four issues."

That said, Morgenthau focuses on complimenting his father: "We enjoyed all of your letters very much and I have them copied here in the office and distributed to the family, and keep the originals here, as you requested.

"I understand that the City Investing Company has done nothing this year so far. They also have their money on hand and feel very happy. When you get back, one of the jobs I will give you, will be to see if you can't sell all of our stock through Robert Dowling, because there is absolutely no market at all. I believe that he takes every opportunity he can, to give out b[e]arish statements on his own stock."

Morgenthau now shares his personal news:

The following are some of the things which came in for Mamma: 2 bundles of wool; 1 box containing copper plates; 1 burlap tapestry; some merchandise which Mamma shipped from Rome [that] has now been released [from Customs] and we will send it to the apartment in the next few days [from which we learn that Henry Sr. has sold his town house and moved to live in an apartment house in the fashion of the times]; several pictures of the Temple [?] at Delhi. [Morgenthau may have misspoken: The Red Fort is the noted tourist site at Delhi.]

We are all delighted that you are going to be home in time for your birthday, and we are making preparations to celebrate it with you properly.

By letter dated June 24, 1926, Morgenthau writes: "I understand from Eastman that he is going to run your 4th of July oration next week, even though it will appear in the issue [of the *American Agriculturist*] following the 4th of July. I hope that you will have a few more travel talks for us, as wherever I go upstate, people are talking about them."

He turns to family gossip: "Elinor sprained her ankle last week, but is getting along nicely. Mr. and Mrs. Fatman sail on

the *Majestic* tonight for Europe. We had both the boys vacci-
nated for smallpox, as there is quite a lot of it in Peekskill and
Cold Spring. [Elder son] Henry returns today from his first visit,
at Grant Straus' from Mamaroneck, and I am anxious to see him
and hear about his experiences. The sale of [cattle] purebreds
is picking up considerably and I feel quite encouraged and may
decide to keep my Holsteins after all."

He ends the letter with subtle flattery, although it would appear
quite sincere: "Why don't you write us a family letter from Bar
Harbor similar to the one that you wrote us from Europe, giving
us some idea of what you are doing and what your life is, and I
would be glad to have it typed and sent to my three sisters."

Three weeks later, by letter dated July 13, 1926, Morgenthau
writes to his father:

> George [Naumburg] called me up and told me that he had
> a long letter from you asking him to buy enough more
> shares of Texas Oil to give us 1,000 shares and also 1,000
> shares of American Tele. & Tele., and to sell all the rail-
> road stocks . . .
>
> I defy anybody to invest this money during the next
> six months and guarantee that the stocks will not go
> down, unless one of us knows of some special situation,
> and not just guess. Mr. Heer is going to work out a state-
> ment showing exactly what our income will be for the
> next year if we leave the money as it is. It is my opinion
> that we should keep this money "liquid"—an expression
> which I have heard you use many times—with the hope
> that some fine piece of property or business will come
> along in which we can invest advantageously. If we should
> continue buying 1,000 shares of this and 1,000 shares of
> that, our money will be tied up at just the time that we
> need it.

If I, who has the smallest income of all of you, am willing to be satisfied with 6% on my money for the next year, I should think that the rest of you could well afford to be satisfied with the same amount—with the hope and expectation of investing this large fund permanently.

The above expresses my opinion and I give it to you for what it is worth. I realize that I am only one out of five, and if the rest of you are still of the opinion that we should buy Texas Oil and American Tele. and Tele., why you have my permission and blessing.

By letter dated July 15, 1926, Morgenthau writes to his father:

I was just interrupted by George Naumburg's phone call. He told me that you had written him to sell the rest of the 61 Broadway notes. George was of the opinion that we should hold on to them and I concurred with him.

By now you have my letter which I wrote you a couple of days ago and evidently from your letter of July 12th you have had a complete change of heart in regard to the stock market.

I have just had lunch with Frank Altschul, and he and I both agree that crops are going to be good this Fall, and if this assumption is correct, business ought to continue good for the balance of the year . . .

Eastman is planning to run Miss Muscate's article in our next issue and using extracts from your letter as an introduction . . . Eastman was very enthusiastic about this article and was glad to get it for the *A[merican] A[griculturist]*.

Morgenthau writes a scolding letter to his father on July 19, 1926:

I wish you would start writing a book, or have a flirtation, or do something to take your mind from the stock market. George tells me that he has letters and telegrams contradicting each other as to what to do with Standard Oil of New York.

We had the best advice, and on the strength of it we bought Socony. You have got a hunch that Texas Oil is good, and there is no doubt, with information that I have, that they are selling a lot of gasoline, but I am through playing "hunches." When I buy a stock, I want to know something about it . . .

The only thing I can agree on with you is that I think it is a wise move to let E. Naumburg & Son have our money instead of keeping it in the bank at 3%.

I also can see no reason for our selling $100,000 worth of notes on 61 Broadway.

I went up to Hunts Point Palace Sunday, as Miss Stein was up the week before and told me about the trouble they were having with the Marquise. It will be necessary for us to either have the old Marquise repaired, or get a new one. I am having several people bid on the job. [It would appear that Morgenthau is referring to a *marquee*, a rooflike projection built out from an entrance to a building that protects the space underneath from inclement weather.]

Apparently deciding he had done enough scolding for one letter, Morgenthau changes course and continues in a more conciliatory vein: "We were very glad to get your most recent article, and I am looking forward to reading it with pleasure.

Personally, I have changed my position on the future of business for the next six months. We are facing excellent prospects for crops and I believe that business will continue good for the next six months, and on the strength of this, I have bought some stocks."

On July 20, 1926, Morgenthau writes to his father:

I just got through speaking to Mr. Montgomery. He tells me that he has seen the Heckscher people twice—the last time last night, and he is to see them again this afternoon. He wanted to ask me whether I had heard from you and I told him "yes," and that you had told me that at $6,500,000 you thought the building was a fair buy, and if you had to pay $7,000,000 you wanted to go into the figures very thoroughly. I also told him that you would not pay one penny over $7,000,000.

Mr. Montgomery is going to either call or telephone me on Thursday and let me know the results of his further talk with the Heckscher people . . .

Please let me have a letter Thursday morning informing me whether or not I am following the proper course with Montgomery.

I have not said anything about this to my brothers-in-law, as I do not think they could be of any assistance until we got a definite price and then we could call a family counsel [*sic*].

Morgenthau next writes to his father, still at Bar Harbor, Maine, on July 22, 1926:

I have your letters of July 18th and 19th before me and note what you say.

At noon today, I mailed you a letter from Mr. Montgomery about the Heckscher matter . . . He said he had a long session yesterday with young Heckscher.

If you decide that you are willing to make a firm offer of $7,000,000, I suggest that you ask for a 30-day option in order to enable us to investigate their figures thoroughly . . . Let me know what you answer Mr. Montgomery.

I hate to disagree with as well-known a man as Mr. McFadden on his forecast on the corn and wheat [futures]. Ten days ago I bought 10,000 bushels of corn at 79 [cents per bushel] and at present have a nice profit in it. I believe that in both wheat and corn we can expect a good price this Fall.

George [Naumburg] gave me a copy of the letter he wrote you about swopping Socony with Texas Oil. I would like to make you a little bet that we will make more money out of Socony than we do out of Texas Oil between now and the first of October.

On July 29, 1926, Morgenthau writes to his father about a matter dear to his heart:

I just called up George [Naumburg] and told him that we have a very good chance of receiving the advertising from the Hudson Motor Car Co. and I asked him whether he would be willing to write Mr. Jackson. George was very nice about it and let me dictate the letter over the phone to his secretary.

I sent Mr. Jackson to Detroit a copy of the papers containing all your articles [*sic*]. . . .

I wonder if you would be willing to have Mr. Jackson over to your house, the way you did Mr. Erskine, and fill

Jackson full of the *A[merican] A[griculturist]*. [Morgenthau adds by hand: "and food."]

You will be pleased to know that we have just received a unit order from Buick—nine insertions of approximately three-quarters of a page each, beginning this September . . .

The very next day, July 30, 1926, Morgenthau writes a business letter to his father:

I went up to the Ritz Tower yesterday to see what they had and what they were asking. The thought I had in mind was that we might compare their prices with possible prices that could be asked for the tower of the Heckscher building.

It is perfectly astounding what they are asking for the Ritz Tower. You will note from the enclosed booklet that they are getting approximately $39,000 a floor in the Tower for what looks like 2,000 square feet gross. Of course they have to give service, but even with that, the prices seem unbelievable. The representative on the grounds told me that they have rented 30% of the building.

I believe that we could convert the tower of the Heckscher building into apartments and if we only got one-half of what they are getting at the Ritz Tower, we would be getting a handsome price. [The conversion of commercial and industrial space to residential uses does not appear to be a uniquely contemporary idea.]

Morgenthau, having provided his father with potentially useful business information, adds by hand: "What do you know about Loew's [stock]? I am told it is very good. We leave Monday for Weekapaug, R.I."

On August 31, 1926, he writes to his father: "Frank [Altschul] is still 'bullish' on railroads as I told you over the phone, and he thinks they are going to go still higher between now and election [day]. Please let me know about when we can expect you and Mamma at the farm, as we are looking forward very much to seeing you. Dr. Craig is going to take my tonsils out on September 8th."

By letter dated September 2, 1926, Morgenthau sends his father a dividend check of $2,500 from Hunts Point Palace, and adds as a postscript: "Mr. Montgomery telephoned me and wants to come down and see me tomorrow. I told him that I had a letter from you in which you were not at all enthusiastic about the Heckscher Building and that you did not wish to purchase a 'misfit' at a penny over $6,500,000."

By letter dated November 11, 1926, Morgenthau outlines the stock market profits of Henry Morgenthau and Son, Inc. to that point. Five stocks show a profit of $4,937.28 with a loss of $404 for a net profit of $4,533.28.

What is interesting in the foregoing sequence of letters for the year 1926, is that—except for Morgenthau's indirect query, asking when he might expect his parents to visit the farm—with all the gossip Morgenthau supplies to his father about his own immediate family's activities, nowhere does he find space to mention that he and his wife are planning to acquire a larger and grander home. Perhaps the answer lies in the fact that the money for the purchase is coming from an inheritance to Elinor Morgenthau, left to her by her grandfather, and Morgenthau has no need to plead once more with his father for the money. Morgenthau is, at least in this one instance, finally free from dependency on his parent to pay for something he, or at least his wife, wants. (Perhaps, too, Morgenthau wanted to surprise his parents, once they came to visit, with an automobile ride to see the new house.) And as the money is Elinor's to use as she saw fit, that explains why Henry III reports that his mother took an enormous interest in the details the alteration of the house entailed: It was she who was paying the costs. While Henry III could say that his mother ordinarily kept track of the family expenditures and carefully limited spending within what she considered appropriate bounds, it is evident that she was sparing no expense with the alteration and reconstruction of their new home. It would assuredly measure up to the library wing the Roosevelts attached to their house in 1916.

In the years 1927 and 1928, the flow of letters from Morgenthau to his father thins out. Having had his fling with roaming around the globe, Henry Sr. was now content to remain more of the time close by in New York, facilitating visits and lessening the need to communicate by mail.

On August 8, 1927, Morgenthau writes a handwritten letter to his father on the stationery of the Weekapaug Inn: "We arrived here safely today. Everybody well and happy."

There follows a strange paragraph relating to his cousin Robert Simon:

"I forgot to write you that about a week ago Rob Simon telephoned me to ask the name of the Hotel at Bar Harbor. I told him I did not know it. It seems that Rob & Elsa are leaving on Aug[ust] 10th for a motor trip through Maine. I told Rob I would write you and that I was sure you would want them to spend the night with you. I have delivered the message; the rest is up to you."

It is apparent that Morgenthau does not wish to keep up any social contact with his cousin. One can only guess at the reasons. In the process, he would appear to have been glaringly inconsistent. On the one hand, he said he did not know the name of the hotel at which his parents are staying, and on the other hand, he says he will write to his father to convey his cousin's request, revealing his rather clumsy fabrication. To compound his rudeness, Morgenthau took it upon himself to suggest his father would want to ask his nephew to spend the night at the hotel where his father is staying.

Morgenthau continues with a business matter:

I spoke to Jackson & Davis today. Everything is going along well. They did a splendid business over the weekend.

I am leaving here Wednesday evening to be in N[ew] Y[ork] Thursday to sign our contract with Lehman [Bros.] I had planned a week here with my family, but I must finish this job.

Alfred Jaretzki handled himself very well at our conference. Arthur Lehman is the only member of his firm who is at all interested in Photomaton [an English company in which the Morgenthaus made an investment] and I don't believe he ever would have taken this on if it had not been for the fact that I am married to his niece. Arthur says he has not given any business of this size so much time and attention in years.

Morgenthau then turns to the signing of the contract for consultative services with Lehman Bros.: "I will telephone you Thursday or Friday when we have signed."

Some seven months pass before Morgenthau has occasion to write to his father again. He writes by hand on stationery headed WARM SPRINGS, GEORGIA. Morgenthau is visiting the health resort Roosevelt has put together with a large infusion of his own money. Roosevelt found that the naturally heated spring waters proved extremely beneficial in his physical rehabilitation efforts. Morgenthau's letter is dated March 3, 1928: "I was delighted to have a few minutes talk with you . . . I am <u>simply delighted</u> [underlining in original] the way the whole [Photomaton] matter is turning out. Especially that the whole thing will be settled this month. I did not like the idea at all of having the suspense for one year whether or not we would be paid. This way I gather we will know in two weeks just where we stand . . ."

Morgenthau changes the subject to the resort where he is staying: "This is a wonderful, restful place. I think you would enjoy it. The pool is grand."

Morgenthau writes to his parents by letter dated July 6, 1928: "Hofheimer [their accountant] closed up the deal on Eagle's Nest last Friday. [Apparently that terminated the Morgenthau family's connection with the summer compound. They had outgrown it.] Elinor and I had a very amusing time in Houston [as delegates attending the Democratic national convention that year, at which Al Smith was finally given the nomination for president of the United States]."

In this regard, Henry III quotes from a letter dated April 26, 1928, that Eleanor Roosevelt wrote to her husband: "Elinor and Henry Morgenthau are like children in their joy that she should be made a delegate at large."[248] Mrs. Morgenthau took it surely as a visible acknowledgment of her acceptance into Dutchess County life.

In connection with the Dallas convention, Freidel gives an interesting sidelight on Morgenthau's closeness to Roosevelt. He writes: "Herbert Lehman had Henry Morgenthau, Jr. call Franklin D. Roosevelt's attention to the fact that clergymen of every faith but Jewish had delivered invocations. FDR presided the next morning over the closing session of the convention." He arranged for a local rabbi to correct the omission.[249]

Morgenthau's letter of July 6, 1928, continues:

A great many people inquired after you and wanted to know how you were feeling and where you were. I told everybody that you had gone to Greece to finish your book and that you would be back in September to take an active part in the campaign.

It was not nearly so hot as I thought it would be, as the whole of the United States has been fairly cool during June.

There was very little for us to do at Houston as there was no doubt from the beginning that Smith was to be the candidate . . .

Elinor presented planks for the Women's Democratic Union before the Resolutions Committee and Senator Wagner was the member from New York and was extremely kind to her. Elinor made quite a hit with everybody and they were particularly impressed with her ability and knowledge of political affairs . . .

Morgenthau adverts once more to the Photomaton Corporation: "Mr. Daniels and an associate have arrived from England and will be here for about a month. Davis, Jackson and I had lunch with them today. Mr. Daniels impresses me [as] an extremely shrewd, hard-boiled business man. We discussed the question of the pool today and got nowhere. If anything happens I will cable you. He asked me a good many questions about what we would do and I told him that we would be glad to cooperate with him but that when we finally got a proposition boiled down, I would in the final analysis have to get your O.K. This leaves me in a good trading position."

By letter dated July 13, 1928, Morgenthau writes to his father:

I had a fairly active week, as Mr. Daniels has kept us on the jump. We have agreed to give them an option on your $207,200.00 Debentures, and Klein & Jackson are doing the same . . .

Mr. Daniels accepted my suggestion to have Alfred Jaretzki draw up the agreement, and I am meeting them there at 11:30 this morning . . .

I saw the Governor [Smith] yesterday for about half an hour. I had a most amusing time. As you can well imagine, with the National Committee meeting here in New York, that there was a great number of people who wanted to see him. I asked his secretary to let me know when the Governor was free. A few minutes past 12, the Governor called me up himself. At first I thought somebody was trying to play a joke on me. He told me he was very busy, and he was going over to Bell's to try on a suit. I asked him if I could go along. I had the fun of seeing him try on a couple of suits, and also gave Bell hell because his trousers were too short. I read him part of your telegram, and the Governor said, "Of course I want his help." He also said there will not be much doing for the next six weeks and it is impossible to keep a campaign going for three months. The Governor said, "Tell your father not to rush back but enjoy his vacation, and if he is back by Labor Day it will be plenty of time."

Lastly, Morgenthau adverts to the ending of Uncle Mengo's affairs: "On Tuesday, Rob Simon, Charles Riegelman, James Frank and I met with Uncle Max at his office. I cannot go into the details as they are too complicated and too long, but I have asked James Frank to draw up a summary describing what we have done so I can mail the same to you. They asked for a check today from you of $50,000.00, which I let them have. Uncle Max is sailing for Europe . . . and says he expects to see you in Prague."

By letter dated July 24, 1928, Morgenthau writes to his parents: "I just received your cable announcing that you will sail on the 17th. Of course, we all will be glad to see you back in this country once more, but I am sorry that you are cutting your trip short, as you will arrive in New York while it is still pretty hot.

"Nothing new has happened in Photomaton since Daniels sailed for England. I do not think, if I were you, I would go to England to see the Photomaton crowd, as I believe it would show too much anxiety on our part and there is really nothing that anybody can do at this time . . ."

Morgenthau now turns to the political scene and writes:

Franklin [Roosevelt] will definitely not run for Governor . . . There is quite a little talk about running Senator Wagner for Governor. He would not have to resign as United States Senator in order to run for Governor. In this way it makes it a bigger inducement for Wagner to run because in case he should be defeated for Governor, he still would be U.S. Senator. There is also some talk of putting me on the state ticket with Wagner. Elinor and I are not getting excited over the prospects as there is only one chance in fifty of this coming about. We are not discussing the matter with anybody as I do not want my friends to think that I am seeking this position and then be turned down—so I am giving you this information for what it is worth, but wish to caution you, my dear parents, not to mention it to anyone . . .

I have had two sessions with John Dillon [a rival rural weekly publisher] with the thought of consolidating our two papers. For the first time he admitted that he is interested in this idea. Mr. Dillon told me that the death of Collingwood, his editor, has made a great difference in his outlook. I find Dillon an extremely difficult man to deal with. We are to meet again next Tuesday. I am hopeful that something will come out of these negotiations and will be mighty glad to have you back in order that I can discuss my problems with you and get your advice. What with Photomaton . . . *Rural New Yorker* and the State Ticket all in suspense, I have plenty to keep my mind occupied and out of mischief.

It does not appear that Uncle Max's affairs are fully settled because Morgenthau continues: "Today I sent checks of $1,250 over to James Frank from [sisters] Helen, Alma, Ruth, and myself and also drew on you, as per arrangement, for $5,000 which I gave in my name. When I get the stock certificate for the $5,000 I will endorse it and hand it over to you. Outside of the one meeting which we had, I think I wrote you about that, there has been very little trouble for me in connection with Uncle Max's affairs."

Morgenthau returns to political matters and writes: "With Herbert [Lehman] and Franklin as members of the [state Democratic Party's] Executive Committee, and Eleanor Roosevelt, Chairman of the Women's Advisory Committee, Elinor and I are able to keep in close touch with what is going on in national campaign headquarters."

What actually went on in national campaign headquarters (meeting at Rochester, New York) is given in Robert A. Slayton's biography of Al Smith.[250] He writes:

In the Private Files of the Jim Farley Papers at the Library of Congress, there is a memo recounting an earlier series of conferences "when we met to take up the name of the man to be nominated to succeed Smith."

In his notes on these sessions, Farley told how "all agreed that inasmuch as Smith was a Catholic that a non-Catholic be named." His choice was Franklin Roosevelt, and he presented it to the group.

Smith's reaction to this suggestion was focused and intense: he "threw it out on the theory that it was a mistake to attempt to nominate a man in his physical condition. He stressed the great amount of work attached to the Governorship and said Roosevelt could not be expected to do it." According to Farley, "It was apparent that Smith wanted Lehman."

Following this parlay there were two other meetings to discuss candidates.

By the third one Smith was still supporting Lehman, while others pushed Wagner. Al seemed to be looking for a candidate, any candidate but the inevitable: when George Olvany, reigning head of Tammany Hall, "insisted that Wagner would not run . . . Smith replied that he would not take no for an answer until he had talked to him." "Considerable discussion of candidates" followed, with Smith holding out for Lehman. Finally, after "all recommendations were thrown out," Farley "made a motion that we communicate with Roosevelt and ascertain whether or not he would accept the nomination and the motion was unanimously carried."[241]

In truth, Morgenthau had it right: 1928 was almost the only time that Franklin Roosevelt had no ambition to run for public office. As Slayton quotes him: "[O]n July 4, 1928, he wrote, 'I, myself, am very certain that I cannot be a candidate for the governorship this year'; on July 26, 'I fear it is absolutely impossible for me to undertake the run this year.'"[252]

He had a more consuming passion. Slayton notes he "had retired to Warm Springs [and physical therapy]. On one occasion he had actually taken a few steps without the use of canes (albeit with braces); that was exhilarating, and he believed that another year or two down there might restore the use of his legs."[253] Slayton goes on to say: "Party leaders . . . led by Smith [then meeting at the state Democratic Party convention in Rochester, New York], needed" Roosevelt, who "refused to take their calls." Desperate, they turned to Eleanor Roosevelt, who was present. She did not want to be involved. She understood her husband's reasons and could not gainsay his judgment. Growing more desperate, the party leaders asked her just to bring her husband to speak on the telephone. Reluctantly, she agreed. Slayton writes: "When [after midnight] she at last got him on the line, she recalled, Franklin 'told me with evident glee that he had been keeping out of reach all day and would not have answered the phone if I had not been calling.' There was just enough time to tell him that I had called because Mr. Raskob and Governor Smith begged me to, and I was leaving him to Governor Smith to catch the train [to New York City]. Then I ran."[254]

The ensuing election that year is important in Morgenthau's life because as a consequence, he found his most rewarding vocation: He discovered he had an innate skill to run a bureaucracy.

CHAPTER 5

In State Government

The principal effect of the stock market crash in October 1929 would appear to have made Morgenthau more cautious than ever about the investments of his father, himself and his sisters. So on November 13, 1929, he writes to his father: "I think that you are making a mistake in loaning out money on call for the Josephine Morgenthau trust fund. I would feel happier if at this time we would recall this loan and leave it in the Bankers Trust." He writes by hand under his name: "your ultra conservative son for other people's money."

Once Governor Smith and his advisors were done with nominating Franklin Roosevelt as their candidate to succeed Smith in the governor's office, they turned their attention to Smith's national campaign. Roosevelt was left to his own devices. Smith's biographer Robert A. Slayton writes: "Smith's people ignored Franklin, treating him, according to [Roosevelt's] memory a decade later, as 'one of those pieces of window-dressing that had to be borne with because of a certain political value in non–New York City areas.'"[255] His remark suggests a sense of resentment at once unworthy of the iconic figure that Roosevelt would become.

Once more, Roosevelt would feel left out of Smith's inner circle. But beyond the feeling he was being snubbed, one suspects he was slowly starting to realize the prospect that was opened to him. Given no instructions, Roosevelt was entirely free to fill in the boxes on his campaign schedule as he chose. Accepting that, it is too much to expect of human nature that the ambivalence Roosevelt felt about accepting the nomination, disappeared with the shadows of the night.

There were two significant concerns with which Roosevelt grappled. One was political. So he could write to Josephus Daniels, his boss in the navy department during the Wilson presidency, by letter dated June 23, 1927: "Strictly between ourselves, I am very doubtful whether any Democrat can win in 1928. It will depend somewhat on whether the present undoubted general prosperity of the country continues. You and I may recognize the serious hardships which farmers in the [S]outh and [W]est are laboring under, but the farmers in the [S]outh will vote the Democratic ticket anyway and I do not believe that the farmers of the [W]est will vote the Democratic ticket in sufficient numbers even if they are starving."[256]

Commenting on the thought Roosevelt expressed, Freidel writes: "Undoubtedly the most important factor was that both Roosevelt and Howe manifestly regarded 1928 as a bad political year. For Roosevelt to have gone down to defeat with Smith would have been a disastrous setback. For him to serve as Governor during continuing years of Republican prosperity might bring him to a presidential nomination in a year when he could not possibly win. Roosevelt, as his negotiations for the presidency of a trust company indicate, thought a financial crash was still no immediate likelihood. Howe once told Warren Moscow [a newspaper reporter] that the plan was for Roosevelt to run for governor in 1932, and for President in 1936.[257]

Secondly, on a personal level and in a Social Darwinist world that abhorred physical deformity, his health had to remain a fundamental consideration for Roosevelt. The personal indignities that Roosevelt suffered daily—the lack of the most personal privacy—and the chance that Warm Springs, Georgia, offered a real opportunity to leave these behind and to restore his ability to walk by himself, forged his determination to forego political activity that year. That motivation could not have disappeared from his thoughts. He had agreed to accept the nomination to run for governor with great hesitation. It had to have been done primarily to demonstrate his party loyalty. That said, the necessity to retire afterwards to Warm Springs for an extended period of time to pursue his physical rehabilitation program must have loomed large in his mind.

In that respect, Kenneth S. Davis writes: "In Warm Springs, Missy LeHand told her employer with considerable feeling that she hoped he would lose the election, a hope that Roosevelt himself may have shared at that moment. He may even have told Missy 'just between ourselves' that he did so. Almost certainly he indicated as much to Louis Howe over the telephone, for Howe, when he wrote on the following day to his wife, Grace, said flatly, 'We are much upset and are praying that we get licked.'"[258]

In truth, the days of his youthful insurgency were over. Smith's biographer, Christopher Finan, commented, "At the time of [Tammany Boss Charles] Murphy's death, the *New York Times* had refused to adopt the conciliatory tone used by Franklin Roosevelt and others who had once opposed the boss."[259] Roosevelt had reached the age when he was more than ready to pursue the path of a party loyalist. He could faithfully campaign for Governor Smith and, if he lost the election, he could honorably retire to Warm Springs and recover the movement of his legs. That certainly was the schedule Louis Howe, Roosevelt's own political advisor, had mapped out. Contrary to Freidel's estimation of the consequences of a loss in a gubernatorial election, it is more probable that in Roosevelt's mind, his campaigning for Smith would give him unimpeachable party credentials with which to go forward and, at a later date, seek the gubernatorial nomination from the party chieftains. Then, physically rehabilitated, he could look forward to campaigning vigorously to win. That thinking could explain how Roosevelt came to conceive the campaign trail on which he embarked.

A nominee consumed with a passion to win will focus his attention on energizing his political base, those centers where he and his party are strongest, where the most votes are to be found, where the electorate is potentially most sympathetic to, and most liable to vote for, the candidate. The objective is to encourage one's adherents to "get out the vote"—inducing voters to go to the polls and cast their vote for the candidate. That assuredly is what Smith did. Somewhat condescendingly Slayton, Smith's biographer, comments, "Al stuck to his strategy of few cities and big speeches."[260]

David McCullough, Truman's biographer, commenting on Roosevelt's 1944 presidential election campaign—in which Truman had been substituted as the vice presidential candidate in place of then–vice president Henry Wallace—writes that Roosevelt "made few public appearances."[261] Earlier, as Slayton rather admiringly describes it: In 1928, Roosevelt "pulled into small towns and villages of New York [State] in his special [all hand controls] car, snapped his braces into position, stood up in the back seat and talked about Al [Smith], farming, whatever FDR's research and instincts told him was important to the people of the area."[262] Roosevelt had started his upstate campaign with a total focus on the presidential candidate. Freidel writes, "After four days of what Democratic headquarters feared was a quixotic campaign for Smith, Roosevelt abruptly shifted to state issues."[263] At the end of his speech, "there was usually that joyously triumphant, rhetorical question, 'Not Bad, For a Sick Man?'"[264] The way Freidel describes the onlookers' response, is: ". . . the crowd would laugh appreciatively."[265] (Whether Republican farmers laughed *appreciatively* or otherwise is an interesting question of some importance.)

Freidel writes: "The plan of campaign was simple. While Tammany took care of New York City, Roosevelt would concentrate upon upstate New York where he must pick up large quantities of Republican and independent voters if he were to win. Among the registered voters in the state, the Republicans outnumbered the Democrats by more than 200,000. Roosevelt drew up an itinerary parallel to . . . the campaign of 1920 [when he had been campaigning as the vice presidential candidate]."[266] (The success of that strategy may be gauged by the circumstance that the Republican presidential candidate Warren G. Harding "carried" the state in the earlier election.[267])

What Roosevelt was up against in 1928 as he traveled through the small towns and villages in the Mohawk Valley, the so-called "Southern Tier of New York," is described by Freidel as "a stronghold of both Republicanism and Ku Klux Klan sentiment." Still, Roosevelt "concentrated upon lambasting bigots. Moreover, he was unperturbed by the pictures of Hoover in almost every window and the correspondingly lukewarm attitudes of the small crowds that greeted him, as he stopped at Bath, Corning, Hornell, Wellsville, Olean, Salamanca, and other towns. [After his remarks,] he would sit down again, greet local Democrats with a warm smile and handshake, and nodding enthusiastic appreciation, listen to their reports of progress. Thence to the next town."[268]

Freidel comments: "The next day when he returned to Hyde Park, he pointed out that in many places on his tour the audiences were twice as large as the total number of registered Democrats in the town—proof that he was at least being heard by quantities of Republicans and independents."[269] (The inference is equally plausible that his listeners were curious onlookers captured by the spectacle of public street theater of a political genre, and that

Roosevelt was contributing to establishing his credentials as a loyal party campaigner.)

Roosevelt's biographer, Conrad Black, wrote:

> There is no discernible truth at all in the arguments later presented by some that he really didn't want to win this election. Missy LeHand allegedly said, out of concern for his physical condition, that she hoped he would lose, and Louis Howe expressed a similar hope to his wife in a letter [dated] October 12, but this is almost certainly because of his attachment to his own timetable of waiting another four years for his patron's bid for governor. There is no doubt that Roosevelt, persuaded with the utmost difficulty to make the race, thought that the circumstances just might be right. He thought he had a good underdog's chance, that Smith would lose badly to Hoover, and that this would enable him to judge the best moment to try to make the jump to the White House. The circumstances of Smith's importuning of Roosevelt and the apparent invincibility of the Republicans quickened Roosevelt's ever-active intuition that destiny might, at last be knocking.[270]

If one looks at his words, Black states a thesis, presents two statements seemingly to the contrary, then proceeds to restate his basic proposition affirmatively and engages in hyperbole to purport to explore the subjective workings of Roosevelt's mind. He ends with an *a priori* reference to "Roosevelt's ever-active intuition," as if Roosevelt had *magical* powers (in the medieval and pre-rationalist sense of knowing the ways to arouse the malign forces of the incorporeal sphere of reality to direct the course of the natural world).

Matthew and Hannah Josephson give a more prosaic reason for Roosevelt's win: "In Erie County, at the western corner of the state, a Republican boss had knifed Albert Ottinger, with whom he had a personal vendetta, and swung some 20,000 Republican votes over to the Democratic candidate."[271] Kenneth S. Davis writes: "Hamilton Ward, the Republican candidate for attorney-general . . . in his home area of Buffalo, encouraged a swap of Republican votes to Roosevelt for Democratic votes for himself and managed to squeak through to victory . . ."[272]

The Josephsons modify their comment by also stating: "Many perplexing crosscurrents were revealed in this election contest . . . In New York State, for example, about 100,000 independents who voted for Roosevelt split their tickets to vote for Hoover for President. There was a flurry of anti-Catholic voting upstate, and also some manifestation of anti-Semitism against Ottinger, while Herbert Lehman won Jewish votes for the Democratic ticket in New York City."[273]

If one looks at Roosevelt's campaign performance objectively, he was devoting himself mostly to a relatively few voters in a scattering of small towns and villages in upper New York State. He was looking to farmers who were almost all registered Republicans, basically disinterested if not entirely antagonistic to Democratic candidates.

In a Social Darwinist age, when physical deformity was looked upon with a species of disgust, if not horror,[274] Roosevelt arrived in his open touring car (or in Morgenthau's old Buick) in front of a crowd of curious, local onlookers. He then had to display the full extent of his infirmity by opening the front door, maneuvering his torso to bring his paralyzed legs out of the front seat of the car in full view of his audience, and as they watched, snap his leg braces into place to keep his legs rigid. Then he would raise himself to a vertical position and somehow manage to get to the backseat of the car and climb in—all with a helping hand, and in full view of the local onlookers. He was revealing himself to be a cripple. And at the end of his remarks, again, there was the verbal reference to his physical infirmity.

What is interesting is that, in future years, in all his public appearances, there would never be the slightest reference by him to his paralysis. The press would neither write of his infirmity nor photograph him in an awkward moment that could have suggested his physical impairment. (The only exception would be Roosevelt's speech to the Congress on March 1, 1945, reporting on his trip to Yalta to meet with Stalin and Churchill, when he apologized for sitting down to deliver the speech with the explanation that he had not yet recovered from the rigors of the long trip.)

In a Social Darwinist era that abhorred physical weakness and infirmity, it was a bravura performance. He compounded his confrontation with his audience's prejudices by extolling the virtues of the Tammany Hall, New York City slum-born-and-bred, Irish Catholic, presidential candidate. Some of those present may have voted for Smith for governor, but making him the president of the United States was a different matter. As if determined to bait his audience even more, Roosevelt would go on to discuss the religious issue—the idea that as a practicing Roman Catholic, Smith was duty-bound to follow political direction from the pope in Rome!

If one were to try to list every verbal and nonverbal gesture for a candidate in hostile territory to avoid—especially in a situation when the candidate for state office had no need to refer to his party's national standard-bearer, and it would have been the better part of wisdom to steer clear of the national campaign—Roosevelt plunged ahead, at once heedless of the risks involved in identifying too closely with the locally despised national candidate and heedless in exposing his physical infirmity for all to see. It was a thankless task that Roosevelt had taken upon himself, which promised few rewards—if it was not an outright prescription for disaster. One must ask what it was that made Roosevelt pursue the course he had chosen.

One possibility is that Roosevelt was "a superb campaigner,"[275] fishing for votes among antagonistic voters (much as literary critic Edmund Wilson described his father as a brilliant trial attorney who would succeed in convincing an initially skeptical and even hostile jury to bring back a verdict for his client)— except it is easier to energize voters who are predisposed in favor of a candidate to go to the polls and actually vote than to troll for votes in the countryside, where voters are relatively few, and of those, most are disinclined to vote for a Democratic candidate in any case.

To ignore almost completely the great urban centers in the state—New York City, Buffalo, Rochester, and the Albany-Troy-Schenectady triangle—was foolhardy. If there was a method in Roosevelt's contrariness, where does the logic lie?

Roosevelt had squelched efforts in 1926 to nominate him to run for the post of United States senator,[276] and he was profoundly ambivalent about running for public office in 1928, even to the point of rudely snubbing efforts by the party's national leader, Smith, and his close associates to reach him by telephone. In the end, herself conflicted and against her better judgment as to what was best for her husband's health, Eleanor Roosevelt agreed to get him to take the call and speak to Governor Smith and John J. Raskob, Smith's financial angel and campaign manager. Even then, finally faced with the question of whether he would accept the nomination for governor, Roosevelt equivocated.[277]

Ernest K. Lindley, publishing in 1931, writes:

"I just want to ask you one more question," Smith said finally. "If those fellows nominate you tomorrow and adjourn, will you refuse to run?"

Roosevelt hesitated. They all knew why he did not want to re-enter public life yet, he said, and he could not sanction the presentation of his name. What he would do if he were actually nominated, he didn't know.

"All right," said Smith. "I won't ask you any more questions."[278]

Black suggests that Roosevelt was under some psychological pressure in that there was the unspoken implication that his failure to cooperate with the party leader's wishes could result in Roosevelt's being "blackballed" in any future effort to seek the party's nomination.[279] Smith in desperation took Roosevelt's failure to flatly refuse a proffered nomination as an affirmation that Roosevelt would accept it if offered. Accept it he did,[280] but his reluctance to run that year could not have entirely disappeared.

Luckily for Roosevelt, Smith and his campaign managers became immersed in Smith's national campaign and gave no further thought to Roosevelt. Obviously, they felt they had accomplished their purpose by putting his name on the ballot and bringing the magic of its association with the memory of the revered Theodore Roosevelt to grace the Smith campaign.

With his name to appear on the ballot, Roosevelt would secure political credits that could be applied to "clinching" the nomination in later years, just as his nomination for vice president in 1920 gave him a certain political standing that was not affected by loss in the election itself. Roosevelt could run a pro forma election campaign as the upstate candidate campaigning upstate, where the population was relatively sparse and antagonistic to a Democratic candidate.

That could also explain why he chose a rank amateur, Morgenthau, to be what was effectively his field manager, recognizing that Roosevelt was, ultimately, his own campaign manager. (The contretemps surrounding Morgenthau's telegram to Eleanor Roosevelt on October 17, 1928, objecting to Nancy Cook's inter-ference with his arrangements for women campaign speakers, suggests his responsibilities went beyond merely firming up the details for Roosevelt's campaign appearances.) Formally, Morgenthau operated as Roosevelt's "advance man," performing a relatively minor function. He was given a list of campaign stops prepared by others (Beschloss has Morgenthau actually planning the campaign stops[281]), told to contact local party leaders to give them the date and time of the candidate's expected arrival, and remind them to spread the word about the impending event to get local voters to appear. Morgenthau apparently went further and got the names of local party members who needed to be mentioned and thanked, and identified matters of local interest that could be acknowledged to serve to identify the candidate with the community and particular local concerns that needed to be discussed. As Henry III describes it, "He traveled across the state sizing up the political situation in the places where FDR planned to appear. When Roosevelt arrived, Morgenthau would often be there to brief him."[282]

In the 1920s, as earlier, without television and with radio not yet in operation a decade, public entertainment was at once make-shift and functional. The traveling circus, the touring theatrical company (as, for example, the one that provides the background for the dramatic action in Leoncavallo's opera, *Pagliacci*), and political street rallies were the norm. National political campaigns included special campaign trains—such as the one from which President Truman campaigned in 1948—and candidates were expected to speak from the rear platforms at the end of the last coach of the train to waiting crowds in the railroad yards.

Roosevelt's choice of Morgenthau as his advance man rather than a seasoned political operative is interesting. Morgenthau's practical experience was nil. He could be counted on to provide money, but he had never been involved in the nitty-gritty of political campaigning. He had never been involved in getting nominating petitions signed by eligible voters; he had never herded voters to come out to the polls; he had never watched votes being counted after the polls closed. He had no experience from which to raise objections to whatever Roosevelt was choosing to do. Still, Morgenthau was not stupid, and he was available. Like Louis Howe, Roosevelt's longtime political advisor, he promised unquestioning loyalty, and that was perhaps the most important consideration. If Roosevelt was feeling ambivalent about his election, knowing that Morgenthau was unswervingly loyal suited him fine. It allowed him to feel less burdened by the pressures that a political campaign engenders. He would be developing a record of political fealty more than seeking to be elected.

What may be the final word as to Roosevelt's choice of Morgenthau as his advance man would be written by Arthur Schlesinger Jr.: "At work or at play, [Roosevelt's] defenses remained intact. He appeared almost deliberately to surround himself by incurious people—the Earlys, McIntyres, Watsons—as if to preserve his inner sanctuaries. 'It sometimes seems,' [Rexford] Tugwell has perceptively noted, 'that those who were closest to him for the longest time were kept there because they did not probe or try to understand but rather because they gave an unquestioning service.'"[283] Schlesinger goes on to quote Morgenthau as saying, "but thank God I understand him."[284] Morgenthau's comment was in connection with Roosevelt's statement—almost an unintelligible aphorism—"Never let your left hand know what your right hand is doing." To which Morgenthau responded with an equally ambiguous question, "Which hand am I, Mr. President?" Roosevelt said, "My right hand, but I keep my left hand under the table."[285]

Roosevelt's words can only be understood in that Roosevelt was at once a skilled dissimulator who took a private pleasure in that ability. People could go away from conversations with him thinking he had implied positions, intentions, beliefs, whatever—none of which Roosevelt had come anywhere near saying. He was able to lull visitors into believing a sense of empathy was shared with his listener, who, upon reflection at a later date, could only conclude he had been led unthinkingly to an unwarranted inference solely of the listener's own making.

On occasion, Roosevelt expected Morgenthau to exhibit the same skills. Harold Ickes gives an example of such an occurrence several years in the future. The date was November 29, 1940. Ickes writes:

> Cabinet met Friday afternoon. The first matter under discussion was a credit of $100 million to China, which has long since been announced in the newspapers. The president was keen about this credit and he wanted it right away. . . . The President wanted $50 million from Jesse Jones [i.e., the Reconstruction Finance Corporation that Jones headed] and $50 million from the [Exchange] stabilization fund of the Treasury. Jones had already been brought into camp. He was ready to advance $50 million against oil, tungsten, and one or two other articles that we import from China, even though none of these goods may ever be delivered. However, he had to satisfy the requirement of the law under which he operates, that security must be taken for the loans.
>
> Henry Morgenthau found himself in a very difficult position . . . [H]e had made a commitment to Congress when he was urging a bill up there recently which bound him not to advance any more money out of the [Exchange] stabilization fund without consultation with the appropriate committees of Congress. He had been required to put this in writing in a letter to Speaker Bankhead and also

in one, I believe, to Senator Vandenberg. The President was inclined to insist that Henry advance the $50 million regardless of the word that he had given. Henry argued that this would destroy him and make it impossible for him to approach Congress on any other matter. I made the point that even if Henry did consult the appropriate committees on the Hill, it probably would not be helpful because if he then disregarded the advice of the committees, he would be in a worse spot than ever . . . As matters were left, the President was to talk personally to Senator Wagner, who is the chairman of the Committee on Banking, after Cabinet meeting, and Henry Morgenthau and [Secretary of State] Hull would get in touch with Vandenberg and others . . .

Henry Morgenthau, who is so dependent upon the President and wants to please him—and it must be said in this instance that he was fully sympathetic with the objective—appeared to be in a sad mental state. Later, during the meeting, he sent across to me this note:

Dear Harold,
I will never forget that when I had my back to the wall in order to keep my word with Congress, you were the only Cabinet member who had the guts to come to my support. Thanks,
Henry

I had done nothing to deserve such a note. It only goes to show how hard pressed Henry felt.

I learned later that when Henry went back to his office he sat for a time at his desk with his head between his hands. Shortly he went home and to bed.[286]

Morgenthau, although he was an intimate friend who might think otherwise, never really understood the full contours of

Roosevelt's inner being. If he had, he would not have remained forever insecure in his relationship to Roosevelt. Roosevelt's "sometimes unfeeling ribbing of his associates expressed a thin streak of sadism of which he was intermittently aware and for which he was intermittently remorseful." [Francis Biddle said,] " 'if we came too close I might suffer from his capacity to wound those who loved him.'"[287] Schlesinger adds, "No one came closer than Henry Morgenthau, and no one suffered more. . . . As almost a member of the family, Morgenthau bore more than his share of Roosevelt's excess irritability."[288] Schlesinger cites Tugwell for the thought that it "was up to the President to judge what endangered his essential objectives, and he made the judgment 'in the recesses of his own considering apparatus which no one ever penetrated.'"[289] Morgenthau, looking back, observed with insight, 'He never let anybody around him have complete assurance that he would have the job tomorrow.' Morgenthau added, 'The thing that Roosevelt prided himself the most about was, "I have to have a happy ship." But he never had a happy ship.'"[290]

To continue with the attempt to divine Roosevelt's ultimate purpose as a candidate in the gubernatorial election of 1928: There was the matter of Roosevelt's investment of some $200,000—which Slayton describes as a "good chunk of his fortune"—in the Warm Springs health resort. That historian also would have it that Roosevelt "needed to stay, supervise, and ensure its success."[291] It meant no less than the recovery of his health. That overriding consideration was recognized by Smith and Raskob. A political campaign could not begin to measure up to Roosevelt's fierce determination to regain the use of his legs, and so he stayed away from the telephone, only responding to what he thought was a personal call from his wife. Schlesinger writes, "Years later Roosevelt told [the author] Emil Ludwig, 'I didn't want it,' smiting himself on the knee; 'I wanted, much more, to get my right leg to move! . . . But the moral pressure was too strong.'"[292]

Another piece of the puzzle is supplied by Eleanor Roosevelt's attitudes. Black writes: "Eleanor Roosevelt's performance was undistinguished." [Black does not want to use the word "disloyal" about one who is commonly regarded in her own right as an iconic figure, although that is the import of his full paragraph.] He continues, "She had not campaigned with her husband but entirely for Smith, despite her support of Prohibition. . . . She told a *New York Post* reporter when the results were in: 'I don't care.'" Black then goes on to contrast the conduct of Roosevelt's mother: ". . . Sara had not been enthusiastic at first, but once her son was nominated, she was a fierce partisan and promised that if he were elected she would make good the diminution of his [business] income."[293]

One may speculate, in the whole affair, that Eleanor Roosevelt had felt she had been disloyal to her husband's most important concern: his health. On that crucial night when she acceded to Governor Smith and brought her husband to answer the telephone call, her actions suggested that she had acted contrary to her husband's wishes; she apologized and sought to excuse her behavior in her brief remarks to him before she fled to catch a train. Knowing her husband's passionate focus on his health could only make her feel she was being used as a decoy. Afterwards, she "telegraphed her husband, 'Regret that you had to accept but know that you felt it obligatory . . .'"[294]

With respect to Eleanor Roosevelt's focusing on Smith's national campaign rather than devoting herself to her husband's efforts, Freidel writes: "She was already carrying the main office burden under Mrs. Moscowitz for the women's division of the party. Her husband felt she was obligated to remain there, although it absorbed almost all of her time and attention."[295] If her husband were hell-bent on winning his election, it seems an extraordinarily generous gesture on his part to forego his wife's assistance. For a wife to forego assisting her husband's efforts to win an election seems uncaring and the opposite of what one would expect from a devoted spouse. They both were acting oddly in the circumstances.

Another curious detail is that, when the newspapers at about midnight had it that the election for governor had been lost, after thanking "his supporters and without explicitly conceding the election, Roosevelt [left his campaign headquarters and] went home with Eleanor and [his daughter] Anna."[296]

The failure to publicly concede defeat is hardly a casual or insignificant detail. It is a time-honored custom that is an inescapable moment in election campaigns. It is no mere expression of defeat. It symbolizes a candidate's acceptance of democratic governance, his or her acknowledgment of the "will of the people." It certifies the validity of the electoral process that election day.

If we would accept that Roosevelt had neither the desire for, nor the expectation of, victory, it follows that he had no real interest on a personal level in publicly expressing nonexistent feelings of loss. He could only think he had accomplished his immediate purpose and that the time he gave to campaigning was well spent. He had served the organization as he had been implored and he now had a call on a future gubernatorial nomination.

Unlike Smith, who was devastated by the way the election went, Roosevelt was apparently unfazed by the results; he simply went to sleep. Not so for Roosevelt's political operatives Jim Farley and Ed Flynn, nor his mother Sara Roosevelt nor Frances Perkins. *They* stayed and continued to follow the election returns.

Black continues: "At about one o'clock in the morning, Ed Flynn telephoned Roosevelt's home and had the butler awaken him so Flynn could tell him he was now pulling well ahead of

Smith in New York [State] and had a chance to win. Roosevelt was incredulous and went back to sleep."[297]

If a candidate has a passion to win, the news that he was pulling ahead of a candidate on the same ticket who had unquestionably lost *his* election, should produce *elation*—a sense that he was still in the fight and could look forward to victory. Instead, Roosevelt's reaction is reported as *incredulous*, that is, disbelieving—looking at the prospect the information foretold as being at variance with some preconceived notion the hearer entertained. Roosevelt was unexcited by the news with which Flynn had awakened him, since he was disinterested enough to go back to sleep. It was as if Roosevelt had given himself a task—to conduct an election campaign—and he had done so impeccably, so he was able to go back to sleep with the satisfaction of a job accomplished without flaw.

One might say Roosevelt dismissed Flynn's information as insignificant—much as radio commentators would later dismiss the early election returns on election night in 1948, which reported Truman leading in the count as being unreliable and subject to later correction because the early returns were inconsistent with pre-election day, presidential polling results that had favored Thomas E. Dewey.

Black continues: "Between 2 and 4 AM, the balance [between Roosevelt and Ottinger] slowly shifted as the results from remote areas came in more quickly.

"Shortly after 4, it was clear Roosevelt had won. Sara [Roosevelt] and Frances Perkins toasted him in milk and shared a taxi, dropping Sara first at [her home on] 65th Street . . . It seems to have been Ed Flynn who informed the candidate! He stopped at 65th Street on his way home a little later and awakened Roosevelt to give him the good news, the candidate's mother not having wished to interrupt his sleep . . . Roosevelt won by a razor's edge of 25,564 votes out of 4,234,822 cast."[298]

Deep ambivalence would explain Roosevelt's seemingly "off-the-wall" campaign antics and why Roosevelt did not seem fazed or exhausted by the campaigning he had devised for himself. (The "low-key" automobile travel that called for Roosevelt to speak from the backseat of his car—aside from formal speeches in the major cities of Buffalo and Rochester—also had the virtue of costing little more than the price of gasoline, which was negligible. To the extent that Morgenthau as advance man may be said to figure in the cost equation, there can be no question that he paid his own way.) So Roosevelt could decide to leave campaign headquarters on election night, while the election returns were still coming in. It would appear he was not upset or disappointed in the result to the extent that it interfered with his desire to go home to bed and sleep peacefully.

In a fundamental sense, if one accepts that Roosevelt's primary objective in the campaign had been to establish his bona fides with the party leadership, he had succeeded brilliantly. No one could question his loyalty to Smith's candidacy. Slayton comments, "Franklin seemed to be far more concerned about speaking up for Al Smith than promoting his own candidacy for governor, and even tackled the religious question."[299] Still, in the end, since nothing succeeds like success, Slayton would describe Roosevelt's campaign strategy as "great theatre—[if] not quite Al's style"[300] (nor, for that matter, that of any sensible or even moderately ambitious candidate).

A skeptical reader may rejoin that the foregoing is pure speculation—that Roosevelt was indeed a brilliant political figure, and, having made the decision to run for public office, he swallowed his disappointment at not being able to pursue his health agenda and set his mind on winning the prize,[301] recognizing that he must look for votes among negative-minded voters, as he did in 1910 and 1912, when he ran in his home district for a seat in the state Senate for Dutchess County in what was majority, registered Republican-voter territory. (Indeed, he would never again "carry" Dutchess County in future presidential elections.)

Then, again, on election night, as Black recounts the story, "Ottinger led all evening. Roosevelt telephoned several upstate sheriffs and said he was relying on them to ensure that the fact that returns from their districts were coming in late did not imply skullduggery. He claimed that he could easily prevail on Governor Smith to take over the counting process with the state police."[302] This suggests that Roosevelt was concerned with winning the election if he could.

Still, one must remember the context in which the calls were made. We do not know whether Roosevelt came up with the idea himself. And he had two political operatives with him at his election headquarters, Jim Farley and Ed Flynn, who were working the telephones all night. By the very nature of their work, they wanted to win. They would have been looking for any way to add to, and retain, every last vote they could find for the candidate. It was incumbent upon the candidate to match their enthusiasm and ingenuity. So whether he or one of them came up with the idea of calling upstate sheriffs, Farley and Flynn fairly obviously would urge it upon the candidate. And Roosevelt was in no position to give offense to them by dismissing the idea. In any case, the reference to the governor calling out the state police was hyperbole because even if Smith were amenable to the idea, and it was questionable legally, it would take hours to put it into effective action. So the significance of the gesture, as a practical matter, is obscure. At a moment of great tension, without a doubt, it made committed political professionals happy. That, in itself, had to be an important consideration to the candidate.

If we accept that Roosevelt was powerfully motivated to look to spending most of his time for the next few years at Warm Springs, Georgia, working on the physical rehabilitation of his paralyzed legs, one may only say that life has a way of confounding expectations, and, in Roosevelt's case in 1928, he ended up with an incredible prize about which he had been ambivalent throughout the campaign.[303]

How had Roosevelt pulled the proverbial rabbit out of an election hat?

First is that, in truth, political verities were observed in the campaign. The great urban centers of Democratic Party strength in New York State were energized for Roosevelt after all. This was accomplished by the national campaign in the state that included Roosevelt (and Herbert Lehman for lieutenant governor) in campaign literature and speeches. Party leaders had wanted the benefits of the association with Theodore Roosevelt and the other attributes that FDR contributed (and the Jewish connection that Lehman added to the ticket), and they had to have exploited both in the printed material that was handed out and in the speeches that were made by party orators on street corners and at political meetings in the great urban centers of the state.

There is also the consideration that in 1928, 50,000 fewer voters cast their votes for a gubernatorial candidate than they did for a national candidate. Most of those would probably have been Republican voters influenced by anti-Semitic as well as anti-Catholic prejudice that season, so that they passed over Ottinger's name on the ballot (although a majority of those voters had voted previously for Ottinger when he was elected the state's attorney general). Four years later, many of those same voters would cast their ballots for governor for the Jewish Herbert Lehman—and continue to vote for him for governor for the next eight years. The only explanation is that beginning with the 1930 election, Roosevelt's coattails were very long, and later—with his national New Deal—only grew longer, carrying the entire Democratic slate with him.

All of the foregoing is not to deny the one element that Roosevelt would probably have discounted, which also had to have been felt by Smith and other Irish, Roman Catholic, Tammany Hall Democrats. That had to have been *pity* that infantile paralysis had been inflicted upon him, and a concomitant sense of compassion. The spectacle of his physical helplessness led the Tammany Hall partisans to forgive his prior seeming arrogance. And, also, even if it was not overtly spoken, the voters had watched him painfully getting out of his car and moving with great difficulty to the backseat to use it as an improvised platform from which to speak to the small gatherings he encountered on his trips through the rural counties of the state. Those onlookers had to have been painfully aware of Roosevelt's physical infirmities, the paralysis that had made a cripple of him. In a Social Darwinist world, the Scots-Irish- and English-descended, Protestant farmers and their wives could identify Roosevelt as one of themselves.

Because of the horror in a Social Darwinist world that physical deformity engendered, it was incumbent upon members of a group to want to help one of their own. It was surely a subliminal sentiment to which none of those upstate voters would probably have admitted, if questioned. And when the overwhelming majority of those voters entered the voting booth, their prevailing sentiment would have been to vote against a Roman Catholic candidate for president. But it would appear that a small number of those upstate voters—after they had voted against Smith—rationalized their thinking that it probably did not matter if they gave a consolation vote to Roosevelt.

Operating in his favor, too, had to have been the magic emanating from the aura that Theodore Roosevelt, then deceased not a decade, still projected, and, perhaps, not least, FDR's own hearty, good-humored, if still aristocratic personality. Finally, there was the circumstance that he could speak of himself—not unreasonably—as a farmer (although not in the sense that his listeners, who depended on what their farms produced for their living expenses, understood by the use of the word). It is beyond question that only a very small number of voters who may have been affected by this kind of thinking, acted upon it, but it was enough (taking into account the other factors operating in that campaign), so that when the votes came to be counted, it was Roosevelt and not Ottinger who emerged as the next governor.

Clearly, Morgenthau and his wife Elinor "were overjoyed with this new beginning."[304] Their personal friend was now the governor, and they could take pleasure in that. Beyond personal satisfaction, there was the fact that Morgenthau had contributed not merely his money but also a great deal of his time and effort to help secure the result.[305] A very interesting question is how Roosevelt would recognize that contribution.

In a real sense, Roosevelt tended to regard Morgenthau as Smith felt about Roosevelt. Slayton writes, "Franklin was clearly the object of deep and real tenderness, but at the same time Al felt that the young man 'had milk on his chin.'"[306] In like fashion, Henry III records, "FDR scrawled on the program for the luncheon celebration of his fiftieth birthday at Hyde Park on January 30, [1932]," to which Henry and Elinor Morgenthau had been invited, "Elinor, I want to know what makes Henry argue so. Don't [sic] he get a chance at home to make his opinions known?"[307] Roosevelt was taking an aristocrat's prerogative to make an affectionate, doggerel jest at a friend's expense. Still, as the saying goes, "Much truth is spoken in jest."

On finding himself elected governor, Roosevelt had to decide what programs he wanted to emphasize—something he had not focused on during the campaign. Initially, he fell back on the formula that he would continue Governor Smith's programs.[308] It is apparent that Roosevelt, when he started to consider the programs he wanted to highlight, had to consider programs that would distinguish his administration from that of his predecessor.

The most obvious lacuna in Al Smith's years in office had been his lack of rapport with upstate rural voters. It remained for Morgenthau, as he had written to his father, to suggest that Smith invite farm organization leaders and rural newspaper editors and publishers to a meeting at which Smith might explain the key elements in his legislative programs. And then the governor had to ask Morgenthau to supply him with the names of such persons he might invite to attend the meeting.[309]

In a Social Darwinist world that found a fundamental virtue in a connection with the land, Roosevelt was a person who took his farming seriously—even if he did not depend on it for his income. (Quite the reverse; as in Morgenthau's case, the farm at Hyde Park required an annual financial input.) Roosevelt probably read farm journals and was aware of the difficulties farming entailed in the 1920s, during what was an agrarian business cycle period of economic recession.

With respect to farm journals, Professor Blum writes, "Using the A[merican] A[griculturist] as his platform, [Morgenthau] drew attention to the questions that seemed to him most important for the welfare of the farmers of the state . . . he advocated inexpensive rural credit, lighter rural taxes, rural electrification, reforestation, reclamation, and more efficient utilization of land, construction with state aid of more rural schools. More farm markets, more farm-to-market roads . . ."[310] Evidence of Morgenthau's personal commitment to reforestation is found among his papers in the Roosevelt Library in the form of an order dated March 28, 1933, addressed to the New York State Department of Conservation, for 6,000 four-year trees—mostly red pine and Norway spruce, but also including some black locust seedlings. (The cost was $24. Having his farm workers plant the trees would add something to the cost.)

Within days after the election, Roosevelt decided his focus would be on farm problems. In a legislature that had a large proportion of Republican members who came primarily from rural counties, it was good politics to present them with a legislative agenda that focused on the problems their constituents faced. Roosevelt then had to consider how he was to put such an agrarian agenda together in such a way that the Republican state legislators would be hard-pressed to reject it.

Complicating the difficulty was the matter of money. Roosevelt had to find the money to hire agrarian specialists to put together farm programs to alleviate farmers' difficulties. Approaching the state legislature that included a large proportion of antagonistic Republican members promised charges of threatened wasteful spending of the people's money on ponderous reports that nobody would read.

Many such reports were already available. One example, found among Morgenthau's papers in the Roosevelt Library, was the "Report on the Agricultural Situation by the Special Committee of the Association of Land Grant Colleges-Universities—41st Annual Convention, Chicago, Illinois, November 15–17, 1927." It included among its findings (page 5): "Incomes from farming since 1920 have not been sufficient to pay a fair return on the current value of capital used and a fair wage for the farmers' labor, or to permit farm people to maintain a standard of living comparable with other groups of like ability. Agriculture has received a much smaller share of the national income during this period than during the period prior to the [First] World War."

Even if, after prolonged and acrimonious squabbling, moneys were appropriated by the state legislature in a mean-spirited manner, the money appropriated would be miserly, too little and too late. Roosevelt's term at that time lasted only two years. He had to be up and running with his inauguration on January 1, 1929.

Roosevelt's solution was brilliant: He must create an Agricultural Advisory Commission made up of eminent persons involved with farming whose nonpartisan prestige could provide a gravitas to support a message to the state legislature from the governor calling for legislation.

Professor Blum gives an explanation for the idea: "It was natural . . . that Roosevelt after the election should invite Morgenthau to Warm Springs [Georgia, to which Roosevelt had returned] to discuss New York's agricultural problems . . . It was equally natural for Morgenthau to hurry south. At his urging, Roosevelt agreed to appoint an Agricultural Advisory Commission."[311]

With no moneys appropriated by the state legislature for the Commission, there was one person to whom Roosevelt could turn, who had the background in farming,[312] the time, and who would be happy to be of assistance to Roosevelt by providing space for the Commission to meet[313] and the secretarial help for written reports, as required. Henry III writes that Roosevelt "made Henry chairman of the new Agricultural Advisory Commission. There was no salary and no office space. [After Roosevelt's inauguration,] Henry set up headquarters at a clerk's desk just outside the governor's office [with secretarial services then provided by members of the Governor's staff]. He and Elinor maintained a suite at the DeWitt Clinton Hotel, Albany's finest [since demolished]. The Agricultural [Advisory] Commission sponsored studies of farm problems and initiated a broad program of legislation, much of which was enacted within the two-year gubernatorial term." Henry III adds, "Up until then, the Democrats . . . had ignored the farmers. Roosevelt made them his friends.[314]

"Within his first week as governor, Roosevelt appointed the same people to a second unofficial Agricultural Advisory Commission, again asked Morgenthau to serve as chairman, and requested recommendations for a farm program. It was not much more than a formality, since the previous month the members of the commission had already made proposals which were acceptable to all major farm organizations in the state."[315]

At that point the Republican leaders of the state legislature—then in session—woke up to the circumstance that Governor Roosevelt was in the process of stealing their thunder, and threatening their constituents' allegiance. "The Republican leaders of the legislature promptly announced that they would hold a conference of farm leaders on the opening day of the annual meeting of the state Agricultural Society[316]—the same day that Roosevelt's commission was scheduled to meet." The Republican legislators allowed as how this rendered the governor's unofficial commission superfluous.[317] "To appear above partisan considerations, they invited Governor Roosevelt to address them." Feeling they had extended themselves far enough (from a public relations vantage point), they dispensed with a further invitation to Morgenthau's commission members. "Morgenthau directed attention to this and added: 'I would be glad to go if I had an invitation.'"[318] Apparently, the local newspaper reporters caught up with these interchanges and questioned the omission, whereupon the Republican legislators had to agree and try to excuse the matter by saying "there must have been an oversight."

Freidel comments that the worst mistake of the Republican legislative leaders was "in allowing Roosevelt to appear, for he could so skillfully outplay them at their own game." With everyone's attention focused on him at the rostrum in the legislative chamber, he appeared as an apostle of sweetness and peaceable cooperation. He agreed "that they do what they were already planning to do, appoint a committee of agricultural experts to cooperate with the legislature. For his own part he pledged, 'After I go downstairs to my desk, you will find an Executive who wishes to go along with you the whole way.'" Freidel comments, "Even Republican legislators were forced

to applaud." His final comment was "they would have a difficult time stealing the spotlight back from Roosevelt."[319] The
governor was far more newsworthy to newspaper reporters
than the near-anonymous leaders of the state legislature (and
the legislators probably knew it). It goes without saying that
Roosevelt had no intention of disbanding his unofficial Agricultural Advisory Commission.

There is among Morgenthau's papers in the Roosevelt
Library a transcript of the minutes of a meeting of the members
of the Commission that is addressed to Roosevelt, submitted and
signed by Morgenthau as chairman.[320] The lack of public funding
would appear to explain why Morgenthau acted both as chair-
person and unofficial commission secretary. (Its polished quality
suggests that members of Roosevelt's personal staff helped out in
the writing and typing of the document itself.)

Apparently, Roosevelt, with Morgenthau's probable help, had
put together a list of names of nonpolitical technocrats—in this
instance, college professors—who could make a real contribution in proposing programs for the state legislature to enact and
finance. Since the Agricultural Advisory Commission had no
statutory mandate, and no state financing, there was no need to
secure state Senate confirmation of its membership—removing
them from any legislative oversight. The members would be
performing a pro bono public service, and Roosevelt would
appear to have convinced them to serve as a contribution to the
welfare of the farming community.[321]

While Roosevelt had outwitted his Republican opponents
in the state legislature, they were not prepared to throw in the
towel. Morgenthau sampled farm opinion after the legislature adjourned and discovered the Republicans were trying to
take credit for the legislation adopted in the preceding session.
Once again, the Democratic governor had to counter a Republican gambit so that rural voters understood Republican legisla-

tors merely acquiesced in the recommendations of Roosevelt's Agricultural Advisory Commission but had no part in *initiating* the legislation.

On August 23, 1929, some eight months after his inauguration, "he sent open letters to the taxpayers of each of the fifty-seven counties beyond the Bronx [New York City's northernmost borough], addressed to editors of local papers, calling attention to the savings in their individual counties due to farm-relief legislation."[322]

Roosevelt explained that he thought it was important that people understand the assistance given them. It goes without saying that Republican politicians were outraged and "shouted, 'Politics.'" Editorials printed in rural newspapers claimed Republican credit for the legislation. "Roosevelt countered not only with statements of his own, but by directing his press bureau to 'get local people to write letters to the Republican papers which are getting out the deliberately false statements.'"[323] Needless to add, Morgenthau's *American Agriculturist* gave no such credit to Republican legislators.

To go on with Morgenthau's correspondence with his father, by letter dated April 8, 1930, he writes:

Please pardon my sending you a dictated letter, but I have been so terribly rushed that if I didn't dictate it and waited until I had time to write you a long-hand letter, I am afraid I would not get it off in time for your birthday.

I want to wish you a very very Happy Birthday. You will certainly have to spend your 75th Birthday in the United States with your family or else charter a yacht and take all of us with you.

I was very glad to get your cable that Mamma and you had arrived safely in Athens. We are all wondering how long you expect to stay there. I hope that you get the man out of jail whose brother sent you such nice fruit, even though he was a "bum shot" and missed the man. We are anxiously awaiting your first letters to learn what kind of a trip you had . . .

Elinor went to Mrs. LeRoy's Sanitarium on March 29th on the advice of Dr. Chase. She is receiving treatment for her gall-bladder. She is doing nicely there but I imagine that it will be a matter of at least three weeks before she can leave there.

The children have written you each a letter about their experiences on their trip south. How you would have enjoyed being with us. We were busy every minute and you never saw three children who are more full of life and pep and have sweeter dispositions.

Our family has become quite "horsy." It is the main topic of conversation. So far we have bought two horses for the [two older] children and they are very happy with them.

Leo Klein told me that he cabled you about receiving the money from Photomaton, so I imagine on Thursday, April 10th, the rest of us will make our bow and exit from the stage of Photomaton. Amen!

Freidel gives an interesting sidelight on the matter: "Franklin D. Roosevelt and the younger Morgenthau were directors of Photomaton, Inc. which was placing quarter-in-a-slot automatic cameras in stores and railroad stations. Photomaton . . . was to go into a receivership early in the Depression; but in December, 1928, its stock was rapidly increasing in value: Morgenthau purchased and resold five hundred shares of it for Roosevelt at a profit to him of three thousand dollars. Roosevelt wrote to Morgenthau: " 'It is thrilling about the Photomaton Stock. I had, as usual, entirely forgotten to give you, as I intended . . . a check to cover the transaction and I really feel that as I did not do so, I am scarcely entitled to the profit. Why don't you and I split the profit in this transaction and each give one half of the total to the Patients Aid Fund at Warm Springs? This will cost us nothing and will enable us to deduct a fifteen hundred ($1,500) gift to charity from our income tax reports!'"[324]

Morgenthau continues in his letter to his father: "I had supper last night with [sister] Helen and [nephew] Tim as it was Helen's wedding day. She seemed very happy and looks extremely well. Helen says that [her husband] Morty is like a new man since his trip to Hawaii."

Family and some business matters put to rest, Morgenthau takes up public affairs:

This is the last week that the Legislature sits in Albany and I am not exaggerating when I say that Albany called me at least five times yesterday and I called them as often. Franklin is desperately looking for an Independent Republican to appoint as Public Service Commissioner. I made several suggestions and I have not heard yet whom he has appointed. I am leaving this afternoon for Albany to be on hand in case they need me. The Republicans have not yet made up their minds whether they are going to investigate New York City and if they don't, they certainly will be the laughing stock of everybody after all the fuss that they have made about the so-called graft, etc. in the city.

The stock market continues to rise and if I were to follow my own judgment I certainly would get out, but people on whom I rely seem to think that this is not the time to sell, so I am going to stay in the market until they tell me to get out.

Morgenthau addresses both of his parents in a letter dated May 2, 1930. He writes:

> I certainly envy you your trip, Pa, with Venizelos [a prominent Greek political figure of the period]. I hope you do not run into any storms. Everybody is asking me when you are going to return and I think that once you make up your mind, you might let us in on the secret.
>
> Elinor is feeling much better although she still tires very easily. All three children are very well. Henry has gained over seven pounds during the last six weeks under a special diet from Dr. Kerley. We have secured a very nice tutor for the summer. He is a senior at Hotchkiss and was president of his class and is one of the most popular boys there. I think Henry and Bob will enjoy his companionship.
>
> I do not know whether I wrote and thanked your for your check of $100 for our wedding day. If I have not thanked you before, I thank you now.

His personal family gossip finished, Morgenthau turns to the political scene in Albany: "Franklin approved all of our agricultural bills and he signed them surrounded by his Agricultural Advisory Board [Commission?]. I am enclosing herewith a copy of the statement which he read and gave out to the press at the time of the signing of the bills."

Morgenthau turns to Roosevelt's gesture addressed to Henry Sr.:

> I think that the Commission to which he appointed you is a very nice one and I hope you will accept the appointment. I imagine that there is very little work connected with it and you will find it interesting.

I lunched with [cousin] Rob Simon yesterday and found him in excellent spirits. He is coming up to Vassar next week and we invited him to come down and have a meal at our house.

You may have read in the paper that New York City is trying to tap the Delaware Water Gap for water. Inasmuch as it affects three states they are having hearings before a Federal man. New Jersey retained a couple of Poughkeepsie real estate men to appraise real estate in our district where a large dam could readily be built. Out of curiosity I inquired as to what they had appraised my farm at and was surprised to learn that they had placed a valuation of $500,000 on it. Of course it will be years before they decide what they are going to do, but it gave me a pleasing sensation to think that the appraisers valued our property so highly.

I know that you will be pleased to learn that notwithstanding the depressed period that we have just gone through, the paper did better the first three months of this year than it did last year and I am quite encouraged. Dillon [publisher of the *Rural New Yorker*] continues to lose a large amount of lineage and we are getting closer together each year. I am sure you will be interested in the enclosed chart which shows that for the first time the *A[merican] A[griculturist]* has passed the *Rural New Yorker* in circulation in the State of New York.

I think that this letter ought to reach you on your Wedding Day and in closing I wish to extend to both of you my heartiest congratulations and best wishes. After all, your Wedding Day was a very important occasion for me.

The statement that Morgenthau refers to in this letter was read by Governor Roosevelt, with copies given to the press. This took place when Roosevelt signed all the bills recommended by the Agricultural Advisory Commission in a public ceremony, at which the members of the Commission were present. The statement is found among Morgenthau's papers in the form of an undated draft (with Roosevelt's final corrections). A public relations document and something more than a "press release," it sums up the work of the Agricultural Advisory Commission under Morgenthau's direction, and reflects many of the programs Professor Blum reported that Morgenthau advocated in his farm journal. The public release of the document probably functioned as an opening salvo in Roosevelt's reelection campaign in 1930.

The document confirms that Roosevelt, not expecting to win, had no need in the months prior to Election Day to formulate a gubernatorial legislative program. He "organized . . . the Agricultural Advisory Commission" *only after he won the election.*

The manifesto reads in Roosevelt's recognizable speech rhythms, cadences, and sentence structure (with the format following Roosevelt's original typewritten draft):

Before I assumed the office of Governor, I organized in November 1928 the Agricultural Advisory Commission for the specific purpose of a cooperative study of the outstanding needs of the rural population of New York State. This commission, non-partisan in its every aspect, has now completed its work so far as the two Legislative sessions of the present administration are concerned, and I consider it advisable to draw the attention of the people of the State, particularly those toward whose requirements the work of the commission was directed, to the accomplishments which have followed the commission's work.

The first recommendations of the Commission were made available to the public on November 24, 1928, by

Henry Morgenthau, Jr., the commission's chairman. I feel the most graphic means of presenting the results of its efforts in cooperation with the Legislature, is to state, chronologically and in sequence, the recommendations made before I assumed office, together with the final result that has followed each individual recommendation. The record stands as follows:

1. THAT the counties be relieved of their 35% contribution to the state for the construction of new highways.
RESULT: This was accomplished in 1929.
2. THAT the state assume the cost of removing snow from the state highways.
RESULT: In 1930 the legislature passed a bill authorizing the state to aid the counties for snow removal from state and county highways and requiring that such snow removal be accomplished at the joint expense of the state and the county. This bill is now a law by my signature.
3. THAT the state assume the cost of elimination of grade crossings.
RESULT: In 1929 the counties' share of the cost of eliminating gradecrossings was reduced from 10% to 1%.
4. THAT a readjustment be made for the distribution of moneys for so-called dirt roads under section 101.
RESULT: In 1930 the legislature passed the Pratt Dirt Road Bill which will give the rural counties approximately double the amount of state money which they received heretofore. This bill is now a law by my signature.
5. THAT a gasoline tax be passed.
RESULT: In 1929 a gasoline tax of 2¢[325] was put on the statutes of the state. Owners of farm tractors and stationary

engines are refunded the tax paid for gasoline used. Twenty per cent of the moneys received from the gasoline tax is given to the counties for construction of county highways.

6. THAT a study be made of the cost of local units of government.

RESULT: [Roosevelt's brief, handwritten insert is illegible.]

7. THAT the state assume the minimum salary for rural school teachers.

RESULT: In 1929 a rural school bill was passed equalizing the method of raising rural school taxes. This piece of legislation has meant more in the way of tax relief to the districts that needed it most than almost any other single piece of legislation.

I feel that if the foregoing represented the whole work of the commission, its members might well be proud of their achievements. It does not, however, represent the entire work of the commission. In the Legislature just ended, an additional group of the commission's recommendations were passed and, by my signature, these measures also have been made law. These include the following:

At the January 30, 1930 meeting of the commission, the following recommendation was adopted:

1. THAT Governor Roosevelt be requested by the commission to call as soon as possible a conference of Mayors and health officers of the cities of the State to give consideration to the establishment of such regulations governing the production and sale of milk and cream as will insure consumers the maximum health protection and will enable such cities to take of nearby sources of supply.

RESULT: The conference was held and as a result I have just signed an act entitled: "AN ACT to amend the public health law in relation to the sanitary control and inspection of milk and cream, and making an appropriation for such purposes." (This appropriation is for $90,000.)

At the January 30, 1930 meeting of my commission, they recommended and adopted the following resolution:

a. THAT in view of the serious emergency confronting the peach industry by the widespread injury of oriental peach moth and of the apple industry, particularly in exports from apple maggots and spray residue, we recommend that the budget item of "Investigation of moths and insects, services and expenses, $13,000" be increased to $25,000.

RESULT: I have just signed and it has become a law, an act entitled "AN ACT making appropriation for investigation of certain moths and insects by the New York State Agricultural Experimental Station at Geneva." (The appropriation is for $37,000.)

b. THAT in view of the depressed condition of the potato industry in New York and of new insects and diseases which have appeared, we recommend that additional work in research be carried out by the college at Ithaca and the Geneva Experimental Station, and that a special work on the control of insects or diseases affecting potatoes on Long Island be made by the College of Agriculture at Ithaca.

RESULT: I have just signed an act making an appropriation for research, extension work and investigation by the New York State College of Agriculture at Cornell University, carrying a total appropriation of $43,710.

c. At the same meeting the commission recommended and adopted a resolution which stated: "We recognize the fact that the economic aspects of agriculture are now of predominating significance, and despite the handicaps of grossly inadequate physical facilities, the Department of Agricultural Economics at the State College of Agriculture has been and is making outstanding contributions to the present needs of agriculture, which it cannot continue without immediately improved physical facilities.

RESULT: I have just signed an act entitled: "AN ACT authorizing the construction of a building at Cornell University for agricultural economics, marketing and farm management, and making an appropriation therefore." (This bill carries an appropriation of $100,000.)

d. At a meeting of the Commission on February 21, 1929, they approved of the bills now before the Legislature which would provide additional state support for the county farm and home bureaus and junior extension work in the state. These bills failed of passage in the 1929 legislature.

RESULT: I have just signed as enacted by the 1930 Legislature, and it is now a law, an act entitled: "AN ACT to amend the county law, in relation to the state contributions toward the support of county farm and home bureaus, and junior extension work, and making an appropriation therefore." (This bill carries an appropriation of $40,500.)

e. At a meeting of the Agricultural Commission at Ithaca on August 2, 1929, the commission recommended and adopted the following resolution:

"THAT the State take immediate steps to survey the agricultural resources of New York in order to make plans for the most profitable use of each kind of land.

"RESULT: I have just signed, and it is now a law, an act entitled: "AN ACT making an appropriation for a survey of agricultural resources of the State by the New York

State College of Agriculture at Cornell University."
(This bill carries an appropriation of $20,000.)

I submit to the people of the State this record of accomplishment by my Agricultural Advisory Commission with a feeling of deep personal satisfaction in their work, and I wish to extend to the individual men and women who served on the Commission my congratulations and thanks for having performed such worthy, devoted and constructive public service.

The document bears in the lower-right-hand corner of its last page, the vintage signature of "Franklin D. Roosevelt." In the lower-left-hand corner are Roosevelt's handwritten words: "For Henry Himself." Although only at the beginning of the press release did Roosevelt refer to Morgenthau's role as chairman in facilitating the commission's work, setting up its meetings and notifying the members to come, guiding the adoption of the commission's resolutions, and seeing to the preparation of minutes to submit to the governor, still, Morgenthau took enormous satisfaction and pleasure in Roosevelt's personally written acknowledgment at the end of the document.

It is fairly certain that Morgenthau arranged with his editor Eastman to headline the issuance of the document in his rural newspaper the *American Agriculturist*. One may also assume that Roosevelt took great satisfaction and pleasure in seeing his press release prominently featured. And so, at no cost to himself, Roosevelt could know that his message was reaching perhaps as many as 100,000 rural households, whose members would go to the polls that year to vote in the coming gubernatorial election. What proved to be Roosevelt's enormous majority of 725,000 votes in the coming gubernatorial election included votes in rural counties of the state. A major cause of those upstate votes was that farmers and their wives knew about the information contained in the press release. For that, farm journals (and other local newspapers) played a vital role.

Roosevelt's three handwritten words, and especially the redundancy of the addition of the word "Himself," implied a very personal relationship and appreciation. That personal relationship is something that must have meant a great deal to Morgenthau. In a Social Darwinist world that engendered an insulting and personally hurtful prejudice against Jews, Morgenthau had broken through to a social connection with a most eminent member of the WASP Ascendancy.

However flattering Roosevelt's initial appointments may have been to Morgenthau and his wife, these were part-time, nonpaying positions. Then, in 1930, the position of commissioner in the Department of Conservation opened up. Roosevelt decided to give the job to Morgenthau. The Conservation Department then "had jurisdiction over [public] lands and forests, water power, fish, and game."[326] (The responsibilities of the Conservation Department have since been increased.) Henry III comments that it was "a job Morgenthau had coveted and was by experience and talent well qualified to execute."[327]

Morgenthau had revealed himself as clumsy and awkward in the management of his father's real estate business interests. He had no real "feel" for the nuances of the real estate market as had his father. In a bureaucratic setting, Morgenthau was able to show unanticipated administrative skills. Professor Blum writes, "His reorganization of his department revealed his talent in selecting expert advisors, his ability to take their advice." Blum goes on to list Morgenthau's "willingness to delegate the authority they needed to do their jobs." Now that Morgenthau was the Conservation commissioner, Professor Blum writes: "He began characteristically by appointing an advisory council of distinguished conservationists."[328]

Henry III comments that his father "was generous in crediting his subordinates with their share in his accomplishments."[329] Indeed, his mother frequently urged her husband "to be less modest."[330] Elinor Morgenthau's admonitions do not seem to have had any lasting effect. Harold Ickes later quotes John Nance Garner, then the vice president of the United States, as saying Morgenthau (by then Secretary of the Treasury) "comes up to [congressional] hearings with a retinue of experts from his Department and when he is asked the simplest kind of a question, he turns to one or another of his experts for an answer before he vouchsafes it himself."[331]

Freidel writes: "Roosevelt was particularly interested in rural electrification as part of his farm reforms, and had already worked out tentative plans with Henry Morgenthau, Jr., for a Rural Power Authority. Morgenthau [who earlier urged rural electrification in his weekly newspaper, the *American Agriculturist*], in turn had commissioned Professor George F. Warren of Cornell [University] to prepare a report on rural electricity rates, and apparently wanted to keep this firmly part of the agricultural program. [But] Roosevelt had a different master plan[332] [that would ultimately come to pass in legislation creating the State Power Authority]."

Professor Warren, a member of Morgenthau's advisory council on conservation, undertook "a pilot study of Tompkins County investigating the interdependence of soil, climate, population, the potential demand for various products, and the potential availability of hydroelectric power. His conclusions confirmed Morgenthau's personal enthusiasm for [the replanting of trees to replace those that had been cut down] for withdrawing marginal land from production, and for developing a long-range, regional plan for the use of land in New York [what urban planners now call a 'comprehensive general plan']."[333]

The advisory council developed a program for land reclamation and reforestation that required an amendment to the state constitution which Governor Roosevelt proceeded to implement. Following other of the advisory council's suggestions, Morgenthau established an independent bureau to employ scientific techniques for the preservation and increase of fish and game. Morgenthau also established a management section to introduce rational lines of responsibility to ensure staff accountability, and he also created a division of finance to rationalize the accounting practices of the department.[334] Morgenthau's own commitment to reforestation is illustrated by his order of trees from the Department of Conservation.

Notwithstanding Morgenthau's "technocratic" tendency to seek out the best possible people to staff his department, there are letters among his papers in the Roosevelt Library addressed to James A. Farley, the chairman of the state Democratic organization relating to patronage matters. Ed Flynn, the Democratic Party leader, said, "We had some difficulty with Morgenthau."[335] Morgenthau had been led to understand that a balance had to be achieved between the Party's needs and "good government" requirements. The balance that Morgenthau followed would lead many years later to the comment made by President Truman's biographer in connection with the scandals in the Bureau of Internal Revenue, revealed by the congressional investigations of the King subcommittee in the House of Representatives in the last years of the Truman administration. McCullough wrote: "In Truman's defense, it was stressed that the tax collectors [in the field] under fire were holdovers from the Roosevelt administration."[336] What is relevant is that those local, politically appointed tax collectors understood that Morgenthau would not have tolerated for one moment the conduct that later came under investigation, and those appointees knew it. Unfortunately, the standards to which Morgenthau adhered were allowed to fall into disuse later.

Morgenthau's letter to his parents dated July 10, 1930, reads:

I thought that you would be interested in knowing of the catastrophy [*sic*] which struck us last Sunday night. About 7 o'clock it started to hail and in twenty minutes it pretty well ruined our lovely apple crop. Some of the hail stones measured five inches in circumference, and that is no Jules Ehrich story either. I think it will cost us around $10,000. For a couple of days it really made me feel awfully blue and undermined my morale because I really had been looking forward with great satisfaction to the best apple crop we had ever had—and incidentally, taking some real money out of the farm. However, I have completely recovered my equilibrium and am again my optimistic self.

Fortunately, the *American Agriculturist* figures are looking a little better and that has helped to encourage me.

Mr. Mansbach of Lachman and Goldsmith advised me that the London Shoe Co. would like us to turn over to them the rent security of Lowey Horowitz & Fischer and the Wise Shoe Co. . . . I told Mr. Mansbach that we would be willing to pay them this money on the 1st of August. [Like the scion of wealth he was, Morgenthau then proceeds to write:] I would appreciate it if you would advance the money for Henry Morgenthau and Son, and sometime before January 1st I will refund my half to you.

He then goes on to write: "Elinor and I are looking forward with great pleasure to our trip next week with the Roosevelts. I think it will be lots of fun and will do us both a lot of good, especially Elinor who needs a change and rest."

By letter to his father dated July 23, 1930, Morgenthau has reconsidered the rent security repayment: "On thinking the matter over, I have decided to put up my rent deposit money due the London Shoe Co. Therefore, it will only be necessary for you to send me a check for $4,646.88 made payable to the London Shoe Co.

"I was awfully sorry that I was not able to come up to see you in Albany. The trip with Franklin was most interesting but a most exhausting one and the heat on Monday and Tuesday left me fairly tired. I want to give as much time to my business this week as possible as I will be gone for the month of August."

Henry III writes: "On the whole, although not entirely consistently the Morgenthaus avoided accepting token hospitality where other Jews would be unable to follow . . . [yet] in August 1930 my parents were extended a warm welcome from the Ausable Club."[337] It was an Adirondacks Mountain summer retreat comparable to the Eagle's Nest camp of Morgenthau's childhood, the only difference being it was Gentile and not Jewish. As Henry III describes it, "The Ausable regulars were a group of congenial families . . . They thought of themselves as a true cross-section of the establishment—businessmen, professionals, intellectuals, and clergy. They had no conscious policy of exclusion; they were simply disinclined to reach out beyond their accustomed social boundaries."

In 1930, in some fashion, in a Social Darwinist era, the members deemed Morgenthau suitable when he was conservation commissioner involved with the land and the natural world. A guiding spirit of the Ausable Club was Henry Stimson. In 1906, he had been appointed United States Attorney for the Southern District of New York, and among his six assistant attorneys, he had included the Jewish Felix Frankfurter (later, a confidential advisor to Roosevelt, and in 1939, the successor to Justice Louis Brandeis on the United States Supreme Court). Henry

III adds: "I can remember my parents talking about the arrival of Stimson, a regular at the club during one of the summers we were there. Awestruck, they kept their distance. But by 1940 they were friends in need in a very divided nation . . ."[338]

By letter dated September 2, 1930, Morgenthau writes to his father about the effects of the Great Depression on their real estate business:

I took out your old friend, Charles Noyes, for lunch and had a very interesting time with him. He tells me that there are not many bargains around because so many people were hit badly in the stock market and are now turning to real estate for safety. Evidently a great many people are in the same frame of mind as I am—that I would like to get out of the stock market and get into a safe investment in land. I asked him whether there were chances in other cities and he said that there are organizations who [sic] are looking all over the United States for good investments in real estate, and that other cities did not offer any better purchases than New York City. He tells me that there has been no deflation in real estate and that organizations like Bing and others have millions of dollars to invest in good properties.

When he got finished with this rather pessimistic talk, he tried to interest us in the Butterick Building. I told him that I doubted very much whether either of us would be interested in this proposition . . .

Mr. Noyes is going to look around and will get in touch with me next week and let me know what other properties he has to offer us.

I received your letter about your going to the State [Democratic Party] convention. I cannot advise you, as I think the only reason for going would be if you felt you would enjoy it. The convention is, of course, a cut and dried affair, and I doubt you would find it worthwhile.

I have your suggestion in regard to Mr. [Charles?] Michelson. I doubt very much if the [Democratic] National Committee would spare Mr. Michelson for a month, and even if they would, I think it would be a great mistake for Franklin to take him on at this time as everybody would say, "Aha, Roosevelt is getting ready for '32," and we know that that is the one thing that Franklin does not want to be spread around more than is absolutely necessary. However, I will follow your suggestion and will show Kent's article on Michelson to Franklin. [Charlie Michelson, a former newspaperman, would become one of Roosevelt's assistants in the White House.]

We returned to the farm Sunday night and everybody got home safe and sound after a splendid month at Nantucket. Talking for myself, I have gotten as fat as a pig and I believe that I weigh more right now than I did at any time since I came back from Turkey in 1926.

I think that you and I could have a lot of fun looking at various pieces of property and I feel sure that we could find something that would be worthwhile.

He uses almost the same language as he used twenty years earlier when he wrote to his father as a teenager at boarding school, inviting his father to join him in selecting a musical to see when his father next came to Boston.

This letter shows that Morgenthau is aware he has not mastered his parent's understanding of the real estate investment market, as the last paragraph of the letter reveals.

By letter dated February 4, 1931, Morgenthau gives his impressions about his new job as conservation commissioner. He writes: "Things are progressing quite well in my work here in Albany.

The combination of trying to keep track of new legislation and also trying to learn my job [as conservation commissioner] keeps me busy every minute. The part of my work which bothers me mostly is the many requests I get for political favors. I hope that after a while these will die down. I am certainly getting a liberal education in holding public office and I am glad to have it while I am still comparatively young, as I might have thought in later years that I missed something by not holding public office. What I like least about my job is being in Albany so many nights alone and away from my family."

Morgenthau goes on: "I have nothing to tell you about National Politics as whenever I see Franklin we only discuss agriculture and conservation questions."

Morgenthau then goes on to comment about the state of the economy: "There seems to be a trifle more optimistic feeling in the air in regard to business. Whether or not this is justifiable [justified?], time only will tell."

He then goes on to comment about a contemporaneous business scandal: "I have been reading the last few days the testimony that they are taking in regard to the officials of the Bank of United States, and the methods used in conducting the business of the bank was undoubtedly most disgusting and outrageous. The fact that all of these officials are Jews makes it all the more regrettable. I am delighted that you did not accept the position to represent the stockholders because I believe it would have drained your vitality, and in the long run, you or anybody else could do nothing to help the poor depositors."

Some background as to the closure of the Bank of United States is given by Allan Meltzer in his monograph on the Federal Reserve System:[339]

On December 11 [1930] the New York State superintendent of banking closed the Bank of the United States . . .

More than half a million depositors found their deposits unavailable. [Two smaller banks closed also.] The proximate reason for closing the bank was failure to merge the bank with two others—The Public National Bank and the Manufacturers' Trust Company. . . . All three banks had Jewish owners, and each lent to small- and medium-sized clothing and textile manufacturers. . . .

After two weeks of late-night meetings, a group including J. Herbert Case, chairman of the New York reserve bank, Leslie Rounds, Federal Reserve officer responsible for banking, and Mortimer Buckner, head of the New York Trust Company and chairman of the relevant [New York] clearinghouse committee, agreed to merge the three banks with Case as chairman of the new board. The Agreement required the clearinghouse banks to advance $20 million: "The Public was in fine shape, the Manufacturers' was in good shape, and the Bank of the United States was generally supposed to be in pretty poor shape."

. . . The governor, Franklin Roosevelt, "sent [Lt. Governor] Lehman down to plead that the consolidation should go through." [Although for this purpose, Roosevelt probably would have been better advised in this instance to have sought out the most eminent member of the WASP Ascendancy in either the banking or its legal community.] Meltzer continues "deadpan," "One of the distinguished bankers [a clearinghouse member] shook his head and said 'let it fail, draw a ring around it, so that the infection will not spread.' Obviously any such idea was impossible [citing Case, chairman of the Federal Reserve Bank of New York].[340]

Meltzer also comments:

Rounds [the Federal Reserve Bank of New York officer focusing on banks] had looked over the bank's records for several days and nights. He claimed the bank was solvent at the time it closed. "We had discounted the doubtful items very heavily. They had a pretty good bond account, they had $35 or $40 million of capital to be exhausted before they became insolvent" . . . Friedman and Schwartz [historians] report that the Bank of the United States paid out 83.5 percent of its adjusted liabilities despite declining asset prices in the following two years.[341]

To ease the burden of the closing of a medium-sized member bank and to slow the currency drain, the New York clearinghouse admitted the Manufacturers' Trust and the Public National Bank to membership. The owners of the Manufacturers' Trust sold controlling shares to a non-Jewish banker.[342]

Metzer then cites Rounds, the Federal Reserve officer as giving the explanation: "The feeling of the Clearinghouse was that the bank could not survive as a Jewish bank."[343] Rounds also commented: "I do think that in the public mind there was a strong aversion to Jewish banks . . ."[344] Apparently, the new, "mixed" ownership kept the bank's prior legal counsel, a firm of predominantly Jewish partners. Some thirty years later, after the last of the Bank of the United States' outstanding loans was finally satisfied, it would appear that all of the bank's own obligations were able to be repaid in full. The negative attitudes of the New York clearinghouse members and the opprobrium cast on what turned out to be the unwise business practices of the officers of the Bank of the United States, may be compared to what Black describes as President Hoover's Reconstruction Finance Corporation's "squandered investment of $90 million in Charles G. Dawes' Central Republic Bank, which sunk without a ripple."[345]

Perhaps one other dimension to the collapse of the Bank of the United States that may be spelled out is beyond Meltzer's focus on the functioning of the Federal Reserve System in a time of economic crisis. That is the fact that the owners of, and the borrowers from, the three New York City banks were without question largely of relatively recent Eastern European, immigrant origin.[346] Charles G. Dawes, a former vice president of the United States and afterwards chairman of the Reconstruction Finance Corporation, was a most eminent member of the WASP Ascendancy. While Eugene Meyer—and, equally, Paul Warburg, a predecessor as a governor of the Federal Reserve Board—was of (German) Jewish origin, they had at once great wealth (together with, at least for Meyer, the speech and manner of the native he was). So they could be accepted by their peers on the Federal Reserve Board. But the WASP Ascendancy members of the New York clearinghouse could look down on persons whose speech and dress probably stereotyped them not only as Jews, but as Jews of decidedly and very unfashionable Eastern European origin.

In 1930, it was the application of these Social Darwinist attitudes that caused people to be repelled by—and thus, to reject—those "others" deemed to be alien (and who were thereby considered threatening). In this same period, the United States Congress enacted the National Origins Act of 1929 that regulated immigration into the United States on the basis of the proportion of countries of origin among citizens of the country by the census of 1890—forty years earlier—rather than contemporaneously. With the same frame of mind, Chinese and Japanese immigrants were totally excluded as altogether beyond the pale.

Within the ambit of Roosevelt's presidential ambitions, shortly after the preceding letter was written by Morgenthau, professing ignorance of Roosevelt's plans, Roosevelt himself was in touch with Henry Sr. Henry III writes: "In March, 1931 FDR agreed to have Louis Howe set up a small office in New York City to raise funds and organize. He started with contributions of five thousand dollars each from . . . the senior Henry Morgenthau, Frank C. Walker, a Roosevelt friend, and William H. Woodin, a wealthy industrialist, destined to become the New Deal's first secretary of the treasury."[347]

After a lapse of some four months, Morgenthau writes to his father by letter, dated June 12, 1931: "If you would mail me a check for $1,000 towards payment of the Tennis Court, same would be greatly appreciated by me. This will make a total of $1,500 which you have advanced towards payment of the Tennis Court." Morgenthau was still seeking financial support from his father. In this instance, the justification was probably that the tennis court was for the benefit of Henry Sr.'s teenage grandchildren.

Morgenthau then goes on with a tidbit of political gossip: "I was greatly amused on picking up the *New York American* [newspaper] today to see that there apparently had been a leak in Franklin's plans to meet with Governor Pinchot [of Pennsylvania, a noted conservationist and political associate of Theodore Roosevelt's]. I would be willing to bet dollars to doughnuts that the leak was from the Chief Executive himself, as often he finds it very difficult to keep as good a story as this [under wraps] . . ."

Morgenthau now reveals that the effects of the Depression were reaching the Morgenthaus' properties. He writes: "I had a very unpleasant call [visit] from Mr. Weingarten of the London Shoe Co. [a commercial tenant] today. [Evidently, the tenant was unable to pay that month's rent and asked for more time in which to pay; he may have also asked to renegotiate the amount of rent that was due each month.] I told him I was very sorry but there was nothing that I could do for him. After he left, I wrote him a letter asking him for the June rent. I said that I wanted it by Monday, June 15th. I then got Mr. Ridley of Sullivan & Cromwell [Alfred Jaretzki's law firm] on the telephone and told him about our troubles. He told me that this was going on all over the city and not to let it worry me too much. I sent him our lease with the London Shoe Co. and he is going to read it over the weekend so that if the London Shoe people do not pay us on Monday, we can begin [an eviction] action against them."

The reference to Sullivan and Cromwell, Alfred Jaretzki's law firm, is a clear indication that Morgenthau was seriously upset. Here, Morgenthau was dealing with a summary dispossess proceeding that should not have required the legal services of a corporate law office. He referred ordinary legal matters to Henry Sr.'s old law firm, now Lachman and Goldsmith (such as signing a new lease with Lerner Stores). Only major legal matters were referred to Jaretzki (as in the case of the British corporation, Photomaton). And the lawyer to whom he spoke, Mr. Ridley, sought to calm him by telling him that things were "tough" all over the city. This would suggest that the Morgenthau properties up to that point in time had not been affected by the Depression. Apparently, most of their tenants had managed to continue to pay the rent on time. It was only the relatively minor investments by Morgenthau and his father in the stock market (as compared to their real estate holdings) that had suffered a sharp decrease in value.

Henry III wrote that as he was growing up during the Depression years in the 1930s, his immediate family's standard of living did not seem to be affected by the general economic malaise from which the country was suffering.[348] Morgenthau, in a letter to his father dated September 2, 1930, recounted his conversation with Mr. Noyes, the real estate broker, in which the broker told him that many people wanted to get out of the stock market and into real estate (as Morgenthau himself was thinking of doing). Morgenthau seems almost naive in his lack of awareness of how the spreading Depression was affecting the country. Vice President Garner's thought (expressed to Harold Ickes) that Morgenthau's sympathies lay with Wall Street rather than with the liberal programs of Roosevelt's New Deal was not entirely wrong. Still, he was a committed Democratic Party member with a dedication to the welfare of the farming community. Black would say of him "though his instincts were fiscally conservative, he always gave way to the requirements for emergency relief . . ."[349] Morgenthau was essentially a technocrat committed to implementing the policies of the government official whom he served.

Morgenthau had grown up a rich man's son, a scion of wealth, subject to what were painful social disabilities. In the course of his younger days, he had worked in settlement houses and had taken an interest in summer camps intended to help the children of Jewish urban poor. But his intellectual passions lay in the direction of the land and the natural world rather than people. Unlike his father, he found people difficult and forbidding. His response to strangers tended to be stiff and awkward. He found public speaking to a group of strangers an ordeal. It was only after he became used to people that he could relax and enter into warm and positive relationships with them.

Nowhere is the arc of Morgenthau's response to new people more vivid than in the development of his relationship with his secretary, Henrietta Stein (later Mrs. Herman Klotz). Henry III quotes her as describing Morgenthau as "a gentleman" and "a wonderful human being." She also spoke of "his suspicious and mistrusting nature." Still, she added, "when he trusted you, it was forever." In some ways, his attitudes paralleled the stereotype of farmers living in isolated, hardscrabble districts engaged in subsistence farming, who would regard strangers suspiciously as malevolent intruders, responding accordingly and describing them disparagingly as thieves intent on robbing those poor souls of their meager possessions. In a social sense, Morgenthau was responding toward intruders as a victim of a Social Darwinist world.

Shortly after hiring her, Henrietta Klotz told Henry III, Morgenthau asked her to bring him a file. "As she opened it a five-dollar bill fell out. 'I gave him the money and thought nothing of it.' Two weeks later he asked her to bring in a . . . book. As she took it out of the bookcase a ten-dollar bill fell out. She again turned it over to her boss. That was the end of that kind of nonsense. [She recounted,] 'Later he gave me power of attorney and everything . . .'"[350]

In farm matters and when he sought information of one sort or another, a different dynamic applied than when he had to deal with persons whom he could think of as strangers. As the supervisor dealing with employees, there may have been a certain reticence or, possibly, diffidence in his manner of speaking that could be interpreted as courtesy by his listeners. Similarly, when he acted as advance man for Roosevelt, he was, effectively, an employee doing a job. He was not acting on his own.

Henry III writes that in the spring of 1932, "Roosevelt dispatched Morgenthau on a swing through the Middle West and Southern farm belt to gather opinions on the causes and cures for the agricultural depression and on the Roosevelt candidacy. 'My trip is going fine,' he reported to the boss. '[In the Midwest,] I am meeting a lot of interesting farm leaders. Most are Republicans but are ready to vote for you, if given the opportunity. Our New York story on agriculture has reached them and they all admit New York has done more for the farms than any other state."[351]

Freidel notes, "In August [1932] Morgenthau did persuade a notable maverick Republican farm leader to come to Hyde Park. This was the Iowa farm editor Henry A. Wallace, who had supported Smith in 1928 but was a registered Republican and the son of [President] Harding's Secretary of Agriculture."[352]

This meant that Roosevelt, through Morgenthau's efforts, "had secured an influential editor of the Farm Bureau [organization] persuasion who was ready to work for [Roosevelt's] cause. He immediately drew upon Wallace for aid on the farm speech" he was preparing to give nationally.[353]

During that period, Roosevelt also used Morgenthau, whom Freidel describes as "his roving ambassador on farm matters," to circumvent the adverse publicity that could have accrued from Roosevelt's direct conversations with the conservative Board of Trade; he sent Morgenthau in his place.[354]

In July 1932, Roosevelt was invited by the governor of Kansas to give a major farm address at Topeka that had to include specific programs for farm relief to capture that state's voters. Roosevelt invited the governor's thoughts on the matter, then turned to his battery of experts, including Morgenthau, to craft the speech. Morgenthau and his assistant, Herbert E. Gaston, previously "a member of the radical Non Partisan League," then prepared language commenting on "the farm debt, oppressive farm taxation and planned use of land."[355]

When he acted as advance man for Roosevelt, Morgenthau was an employee doing a job, securing information for a person who was, clearly, one of the WASP Ascendancy. The psychological dynamics were different than when he was acting on his own. At the same time, it was useful that Morgenthau could speak from the position that accrued to him as the longtime publisher of a respectable farm weekly—someone who was knowledgeable about farm problems and, not least, an owner who actively managed a large, working farm.

In 1933, after Roosevelt had entered the White House, when there was talk of Morgenthau becoming the secretary of agriculture, "there were a number of strikes against him. On the national scene the image of Wall Street obscured the fact that upstate New York was in fact one of the country's major farm regions. Furthermore, with a New York governor moving into the White House, the notion of a Jewish secretary of agriculture from New York State was anathema in the Midwest and the Southern farm belt."[356]

The persons included under the heading "the Midwest and the Southern farm belt" were acting in a typical Social Darwinist mode. They regarded the land and farming as the special province of a group of people who could be described as overwhelmingly "good Christian folk," and a New York Jew was not one of their kind.

Henry Wallace, who was given the position of secretary of agriculture in Roosevelt's Cabinet, aside from a WASP ethnic identification, was otherwise remarkably similar to Morgenthau. He was the beneficiary of a very profitable business—that of selling the hybrid corn he had developed to farmers in the Midwest. He did not depend on the produce of his farm for his living any more than did Morgenthau (or Roosevelt, for that matter). And he also published a farm journal. Nor could it be said that his personality was more outgoing than was Morgenthau's. But in a Social Darwinist world, Midwestern and Southern farmers could identify Wallace as one of their own.

CHAPTER 6

Washington, D.C.

O n March 4, 1933, their grandfather shepherded Henry III and his siblings to sit directly in front of the very grand if temporary wooden structure in front of the Capitol. They were there to witness the inauguration of Franklin Delano Roosevelt as president of the United States. His parents sat above them in the section for family and distinguished guests, behind the podium at which the new president would deliver his inaugural address.[357] For Morgenthau and Elinor, his wife, the question was what he could expect by way of an appointment in the new administration. He had been active in the informal discussions concerning possible farm policies and legislation that had taken place at Roosevelt's request in the months prior to the inauguration.

Schlesinger describes him, for example, in conversations: "In December 1932 . . . about forty farm representatives met with Morgenthau and [Rexford] Tugwell in Washington, [and] it became apparent that [farm] opinion was flowing more powerfully than ever toward domestic allotment."[358] Freidel speaks of "Roosevelt's representatives like Tugwell and Morgenthau, who need not distinctively bear the label of envoy but could be identified respectively as an expert on agricultural economics and the editor [sic] of the *American Agriculturist* . . ."[359]

Freidel explains: "In time those who worked for Roosevelt came to understand his technique, sometimes sloppy and confused, and sometimes effective. It could easily generate animus among contenders. Morgenthau left [Raymond] Moley sputtering, and both Moley and Tugwell suspected him of being overambitious to become secretary of agriculture . . . It was Morgenthau who drew up with Representative Jones Title II of the farm bill, dealing with agricultural credit. Also it was Morgenthau who in January 1933 quietly acted as Roosevelt's envoy to Prime Minister Richard B. Bennett of Canada, preparing the way for an international wheat agreement."

Freidel goes on to say: "Roosevelt found each of his agricultural experts useful and continued to utilize them all."[360]

In truth, Morgenthau had set his heart on the position as secretary of agriculture. It was a job for which his experience made him particularly qualified: He actively managed a 2,000-acre farm; he had published a New York State farm journal since 1922; he had suggested, then chaired Governor Roosevelt's Agricultural Advisory Commission for four years, from which had come a remarkable assortment of farm legislation. That had contributed to an unprecedented 725,000 voter majority in Roosevelt's successful bid for a second gubernatorial term. Democratic political leaders across the country had concluded that Roosevelt had a nationwide appeal for both urban and rural voters. In 1932, Roosevelt had not hesitated to send Morgenthau across the country to ascertain farmer sentiment across the political spectrum.

Henry Sr. conducted political negotiations on Morgenthau's behalf, since his son did not have the nerve to ask Roosevelt for the job, whatever their personal friendship. Henry Sr. had been one of the chief fund-raisers for Roosevelt in 1930, and one of the three contributors to cover the costs of opening the office that heralded Roosevelt's efforts to seek the Democratic Party's nomination for president in 1932. He was also one of fifteen persons who had initially "bankrolled" the presidential campaign.[361]

Morgenthau was visiting his sons at boarding school in Massachusetts. Henry III writes: "At a pre-arranged time my father called his father from a pay phone in Deerfield to get the news . . . It was not long before the door squeaked open again and my father stepped out pale and crestfallen." Morgenthau sounded especially glum as was his habit when he was devastated.[362]

In a Social Darwinist world, Morgenthau was not to reach his goal.

Freidel writes: "[B]y early January [1933] Roosevelt was planning to appoint" Henry Wallace as secretary of agriculture. There was "Roosevelt's dear friend Henry Morgenthau, Jr. . . . Roosevelt . . . asked Thomas Beck of *Collier's* magazine to telegraph representative farm agencies and spokesmen on their preference: Wallace or Morgenthau. Out of two hundred replies, only one [had] favored Morgenthau."[363]

Farmers in New York State were a small component of the total farm population of the United States. Farm leaders in the Midwest, the South, and the Southwest expected one of their own to occupy that seat.[364] Henry III writes: "[T]he notion of a Jewish secretary of agriculture from New York State was anathema in the Midwest and the Southern farm belt."[365] Presidents starting their term of office have a common instinct to seek to avoid controversy. Roosevelt followed true to form.

Henry Sr. shared his son's disappointment. There had been only one prior Jewish cabinet member. In a Social Darwinist world, this felt like one more anti-Semitic exclusion.

Still, Henry Sr. reported, Roosevelt wanted Morgenthau to close Hoover's Farm Board and become governor of a successor agency. Freidel says Hoover's Farm Board was "unpopular."[366] It failed to perform effectively to help farmers unable to make their mortgage loan payments. The result had been an unconscionable number of farm foreclosures throughout the Midwest, the

South, and the Southwest. "Roosevelt proposed to reorganize the hodgepodge of federal agricultural credit instrumentalities into a single . . . Farm Credit Administration."[367] The reorganization followed Title II of the farm bill Morgenthau had earlier assisted Representative Jones in drafting.

The bill was effective May 27, 1933. Morgenthau's appointment ran from that date. He had the advantage of inheriting fully staffed bureaucracies, with established forms and experienced government personnel. The requirements for collateral by the farmers had been liberalized. As Schlesinger describes it,

> Under the fast-moving direction of Morgenthau and his deputy, William I. Myers of Cornell [University], the new agency took quick action to stave off the sheriff [from presiding over mortgage foreclosure auctions]. Its powers confirmed by the Emergency Farm Mortgage Act and supplemented in June [1933] by the Farm Credit Act, F[arm] C[redit] A[dministration] refinanced farm mortgages, inaugurated a series of "rescue" loans for second mortgages, developed techniques for persuading creditors to make reasonable settlements, set up local farm debt adjustment committees, and eventually established a system of regional banks to make mortgage, production, and marketing loans and to provide credits to cooperatives. It loaned more than $100 million in its first seven months—nearly four times as much as the total of mortgage loans to farmers from the entire land-bank system the year before. At the same time it beat down the interest rate in all areas of farm credit. . . . Though anger still rumbled in the farm belt, FCA gave every evidence of getting at least the emergency debt problems under control.[368]

In fiscal year 2006 the FCA would describe itself in its annual report (under the E-Government Act of 2002) as functioning to "regulate and examine a nationwide network of banks, associations, and related institutions chartered under the Act. The institutions of the Farm Credit System furnish credit and related services to farmers, ranchers, and producers or harvesters of aquatic products, their cooperatives and farm-related businesses."

The loss of rural credit across the United States after the stock market crash in October, 1929, is given in Meltzer's monograph on the Federal Reserve System.[369] He writes: "Before December [1930], most failed banks were rural. Despite the decline in nominal rates on short-term loans, real [interest] rates continued to rise. Wholesale prices had fallen at an annualized rate of nearly 25 percent in two months and a 20 percent annual rate since the start of the year [1931]. Farm prices had fallen faster. In response to the high real [interest] rates and the declining [activity in the business] economy, bank lending fell at an annualized 20 percent rate in the first six months of 1931."

Meltzer expresses astonishment seventy-five years later, commenting that,

> there is a remarkable difference between the flurry of activity set off by the foreign exchange crisis [involving European central banks] and the continuing failure to respond to the domestic crisis. [Its president, George L.] Harrison was willing to risk having some of the New York [Federal Reserve] bank's assets "frozen" in Central Europe to maintain the prevailing [foreign] exchange rates and the gold exchange standard [for paper money circulated in the United States], but he had been unwilling to offer assistance to prevent bank failures at home. In the fall [of 1931], he refused to offer rediscounts to banks that were willing to participate in a lending pool designed to

prevent the spread of domestic bank failures. The [staff] memo prepared for the August 11 [1931] meeting [of the Federal Reserve Board] refers to 166 bank failures in the country in June, the largest number since January. . . . The [staff] memo concluded, however, that financial difficulties abroad were more severe than the difficulties at home.

Apparently,

[fellow Federal Reserve] Governor [Eugene] Meyer went before the Federal Reserve Board's executive committee for 2 hours [without success], explaining that under existing conditions nothing but a major stroke would help the situation [the financial crisis resulting in the deep business depression in which the United States was finding itself] . . . perhaps [while such a gesture on the part of the Federal Reserve Board] would not [have any appreciable effect] . . . it was vitally important that the [Federal Reserve] System should make a bold stroke . . . .

Meltzer sums up the causes of the Great Depression in the 1930s in the following, technical terms:

In the previous deflation, 1920–21, falling prices raised real balances [i.e., money on hand in banks] and stimulated spending despite relatively high real interest rates. Falling prices also attracted gold, [thereby] increasing money balances.

The principle difference in 1929–33 is that the falling money stock [that was available to the general public] more than offset the expansive effect of falling prices . . . If the Federal Reserve [System] had prevented the decline in money, falling prices would have raised real balances, created an excess supply of money, stimulated spending, and limited or ended the decline when the economy began to recover in spring 1930 . . .[370]

By the beginning of the year 1933, private banks were charging higher interest rates and required far greater security than farmers were then able to offer. In effect, the Farm Credit Administration was providing a species of mortgage loan insurance to the lenders in its system to encourage the issuance of loans to farmers at a time when the banking industry was prepared to make few farm loans.

As Schlesinger describes the scene, " 'Damn you, old moneybags,'" [Vice President] John Garner, the Uvalde [Texas] banker, growled to Morgenthau one day at cabinet. . . . 'Until you came along, Mrs. Garner and I averaged 16 percent on our money, and now we can't get better than 5.'"[371] Henry III writes that "[a]fter his initial disappointment in failing to win a cabinet post, Morgenthau came to realize that he had been handed an assignment in the Farm Credit Administration at least as challenging as heading the Department of Agriculture." He adds: "This was Henry Jr.'s first venture into public finance and it was conspicuously successful. Even some of his closest and most loyal associates were surprised."[372]

Following the pattern Morgenthau had established during his years in Albany, Henry III reports that during their first year in Washington, his "parents resided in a three-room suite in the Shoreham Hotel overlooking Rock Creek Park." Henry III and his younger brother Robert were in boarding school, so that aside from a sitting room, only one other bedroom was needed, for his sister Joan.[373] Home for Morgenthau in a Social Darwinist world remained, very profoundly, the farm in Dutchess County.

So life might have gone along. Morgenthau had accomplished the task he was given—to set up a consolidated agency and realize its purpose of effectively providing a source for borrowing by the farming community across the country. He could also take great satisfaction in knowing his close friend was the president of the United States, although he and Elinor could feel "they had no personal base of power, no constituency" (where that was the true coin of the realm). "If they strayed behind—perhaps only for a moment—the sidelines were crowded with those ready to step in and replace them. Along with the excitement," Henry III continues, "I could feel their insecurity."[374]

Put into the larger context of the Social Darwinist ethos of the period, one may describe Henry III's parents' psychological sense of insecurity in the nation's capital as derived from an awareness that they carried with them throughout their lives: In a Social Darwinist world, Jews were thought of as outsiders, odd and peculiar, strangers among Gentiles, who made up the vast majority of the population. Without thinking about it, the latter could regard themselves as the true and authentic Americans who discriminated against the social acceptance of Jews as a matter of course.

In Germany, it may be said, Hitler was then carrying that discrimination to vulgar lengths; but within the Social Darwinist ethos of the period, the "inauthenticity" of Jews as a social group was derived from the same source on both sides of the Atlantic Ocean—a Social Darwinist concept of the true and authentic nature of human society that, by the very animalistic nature of human beings, for their safety and well-being, required the separation of one's own group from "others."

As with the choice of a New York State Democratic Party gubernatorial nominee in 1928, events were taking place in Washington of which Morgenthau was only dimly aware.

Roosevelt had solved the most immediate farm problem in 1933 by providing rural borrowing power through the creation and operation of the Farm Credit Administration. But, there remained other facets to the difficulties that beset farmers. They faced the prospect of unmanageable excess production and having to sell their produce at less than the cost of growing the crops. The Agricultural Adjustment Act (AAA) was one effort to attack that fundamental obstacle to profitable farming. Black writes: "Under the AAA plan, the secretary of agriculture would rent excess acreage and the farmer would be contracted to destroy or otherwise than commercially dispose of the surplus [estimated at 300 million bushels of wheat, 30 million hogs, and 8 million bales of cotton]. It was only with great difficulty that one-tenth of what was proposed to be destroyed, was set aside (through the efforts of Jerome Frank, then general counsel of the AAA) for distribution by Harry Hopkins as emergency relief.[375]

"Frank, Tugwell and [Harry] Hopkins worked out a plan for a federal Surplus Relief Corporation and presented it to Roosevelt," who approved the concept and authorized $75 million by executive order on September 21, 1933. (Roosevelt added surplus clothing to the list of surplus commodities.) This concept served as a model for the later-created Commodity Credit Corporation, which lent money to farmers without any personal obligation on their part, on the value of their farm produce when it was ready for marketing, valuing the produce at a little above its anticipated market price and charging the borrower interest of 4 percent. If the market price of the produce, when the commodity was actually ready to be sold, exceeded its valuation when the loan was taken, the farmer was free to sell on the open market and repay the government loan. Otherwise, the government was the effective owner of the commodity.[376]

Henry III tells of a minor diplomatic assignment Roosevelt gave to Morgenthau in the early spring of 1933. Soon after his inauguration Roosevelt determined to establish diplomatic relations with the Soviet Union. Secretary of State Cordell Hull and the members of the State Department were unsympathetic to the idea, so Roosevelt turned to Morgenthau to explore the possibilities—to Morgenthau's large discomfort. Henry III quotes his father as saying to Roosevelt, "If the deal worked out well . . . [I] would be a hero, but if it flopped, [I] would have to leave Washington." To which Roosevelt replied, "Well, of course, you know that I stand back of you in these negotiations . . . and if you have to leave Washington I will leave with you."[377]

The pretext was to initiate negotiations with Amtorg, the Soviet state trading corporation, for the purchase of American agricultural surpluses (this some two years after widespread famine in Ukraine, the result of Stalin's campaign against the so-called "kulaks," the more-prosperous, land-owning farmers who actively opposed Stalin's drive to collectivize privately owned farms). Morgenthau undertook wide-ranging, preliminary, and informal diplomatic discussions with Maxim Litvinov (who would escape the purge trials of the "Old Bolsheviks" that Stalin commenced within a few years, which eliminated most of Lenin's pre-revolutionary Communist party associates). Still, to his relief, Morgenthau was relieved of the assignment when it was given to William Bullitt, the State Department's Soviet expert.[378]

The negotiations culminating in the recognition of the Soviet Union no doubt facilitated communication with the Soviet government during World War II.

An incidental benefit to Morgenthau was his presence at a White House luncheon Roosevelt gave in honor of Maxim Litvinov, then Soviet commissar of foreign affairs. Morgenthau mentioned to Constantin Oumansky, the Soviet embassy's press officer (and later ambassador), that Ickes was a stamp collector, whereupon Oumansky whipped out of his pocket booklets of Soviet stamps that he presented to Ickes and Morgenthau (the latter for his son Robert, who also collected stamps), while the guest of honor did the same for the president.[379]

Morgenthau found the time to write to his father by letter dated March 30, 1933: "If you are the 'Setting Sun' you certainly have the satisfaction that, literally, hundreds of thousands of people have basked in the warmth of the rays of love and helpfulness that have emanated from you during your lifetime. Being your son is one of the greatest assets I have here in Washington, and not a day passes but what someone remarks about some kind thing that you have done for them at one time or another."

Morgenthau informs his father of a small favor he is providing him: "Steve Earley tells me that you will receive an invitation from the Gridiron Club." This was the newspaper reporters' organization in the nation's capital that threw an annual dinner at which the reporters performed skits, more or less wittily satirizing the prominent members of the national government, including the chief executive, all of whom attended. Morgenthau adds the caveat: "if you have not already received it."

In midsummer 1933, solutions to the farm problem were still evolving. Though Morgenthau's Farm Credit Administration had markedly reduced the number of farm mortgage foreclosures, the Agricultural Adjustment Act program had only temporarily raised farm commodity prices. Farmers were still forced to sell their produce below their production costs. A delegation from a radical Midwestern farmers' organization, the Farmers Holiday Association, came to Washington to demand government action on threat of a farm strike.[380] They were received by Roosevelt, Secretary of Agriculture Wallace, Peek, the AAA administrator, and Morgenthau, the governor of the Farm Credit Administration. (Government officials meet citizen groups as a body, although only one individual may do the talking.) Afterwards, Roosevelt commented to Morgenthau, "I don't like to have anybody hold a gun to my head and demand I do something."[381]

Still, the problem of low commodity prices existed and promised not to go away. Meltzer records that in 1913, 30 percent of the American labor force worked in agriculture. That percentage had not changed appreciably in the 1920s. (By 1951, the percentage had fallen to only 11 percent.[382]) The farm population in 1933 represented an important segment of the voting population of the United States—aside from any Social Darwinist respect Roosevelt might have for them.

Earlier that summer, one group of Roosevelt's economic advisors took the position that further monetary depreciation was undesirable. The economy required an orthodox adherence to the gold standard: American dollars must be freely convertible to gold. " 'I do not like or approve the report,' the President curtly told Woodin, adding, 'I wish our banking and economist friends would realize the seriousness of the situation from the point of view of the debtor classes, i.e., 90 percent of the human beings in this country—and think less from the point of view of the 10 percent who constitute the creditor classes.' He had a final word: 'Tell the committee that commodity prices must go up, especially agricultural prices. I suggest that the committee let you and me have the recommendation of how to obtain that objective and that objective only.'"[383]

Except Roosevelt's direction was not the last word. Merely speaking did not make it so. Senior federal employees take seriously the constitutional concept that the federal government (and each of its three separate branches) is one of limited powers. It is necessary to find sanction in the Constitution and statutes for executive action to proceed.

Earlier in the year, Roosevelt spoke to Morgenthau and others about the problem of the unconscionably low farm commodity prices received by farmers for their produce. Morgenthau, through his contacts in the academic community at Cornell University (from whence he secured his deputy while he was the New York State conservation commissioner, and now at the FCA), brought to Roosevelt's attention an obscure economic theory propounded by George Warren and Frank Pearson, having to do with a means of raising commodity prices by the expedient of creating a so-called "commodity dollar." This would happen by having the government purchase gold at a price above the then-current market price of the metal. Roosevelt had been sufficiently intrigued with the whole idea to ask Morgenthau to give him an amplified explanation of it.

The occasion was a cruise Roosevelt planned to take from Massachusetts to Campobello, New Brunswick, his summer home in Canada, last seen as he was painfully removed after the onset of infantile paralysis in 1921.

Before Morgenthau left with the president for the cruise on the *Amberjack II*, he wrote a handwritten letter to his parents dated June 9, 1933:

> I am writing this to you on the hottest day of the year.
>
> I was glad to see Dr. Haas and hear firsthand how you ran the whole show in Geneva. Haas is certainly crazy about you. I can not understand why the President [no longer "Franklin"] did not make you a delegate, but I am sure that with your ability you will come out on top of the heap.
>
> I have one more bill to get thru Congress. It should come up today or Saturday. I think it will pass . . .
>
> The stock market continues to boil as the dollar goes down. We have done very well.
>
> Just as soon as Congress adjourns we are taking the 3 children and ourselves to Chester, Nova Scotia for 2 weeks vacation.

The tension here is terrific on account of the patronage question. Senators and Congressmen [are] clamoring for jobs and we [are] withholding them until our bill passes.

On the "patronage question," Freidel comments:

Humid summer heat had returned to Washington [weather-wise, Washington is a Southern city, and air-conditioning—now taken for granted—was still several decades into the future], adding to the discomfort of fatigued congressmen; their tempers grew short. With impatient political lieu-tenants plaguing them for jobs, they became increasingly irritated over Roosevelt's tactic of withholding most patronage until the session was over . . . Further, in filling some major positions, Roosevelt had not consulted senators from the appointee's state. "Cotton Ed" Smith complained to Morgenthau that Hoover had treated him better than Roosevelt. "Mark you, Morgenthau," he stormed, "if they do not change their method of distributing patronage the President will soon have a revolution on his hands."[384]

Roosevelt's difficulties with the Congress would continue into the middle of June.[385]

On June 17, 1933, Roosevelt left Washington by train on the way to Marion, Massachusetts, where he planned to board the forty-five-foot, chartered schooner *Amberjack II*. His guests included Louis Howe, his political advisor; Morgenthau; and Missy LeHand, his secretary, besides Mrs. Roosevelt.[386]

Morgenthau received from Professor Warren, and prepared on his own, charts and graphs to illustrate what he proposed to discuss.[387] He gave his lecture one evening after dinner at the house at Campobello. Except for Roosevelt himself, the other listeners were "bored to tears." In any case, the talk was interrupted by an urgent telegram from Raymond Moley, one of Roosevelt's "Brain Trust" (who had tangled with Morgenthau in connection with forging agrarian legislation in the days prior to Roosevelt's inauguration), who was attending the International Monetary and Economic Conference then in session at London, where Secretary of State Cordell Hull led the American delegation.[388] The Economic Conference had as its purpose finding ways and means to alleviate what was, by then, a worldwide Depression.

Roosevelt was impressed with what Morgenthau was trying to say. Warren had written to the president, "A rise in prices is essential. The only way in which a rise can be brought and held is by reducing the gold value of the dollar. . . ."[389]

Schlesinger writes:

As early as August 16 [1933] Roosevelt had mentioned to Morgenthau that he would like the Treasury to buy gold in the open market. . . . The question remained whether the government had the legal authority. Dean Acheson declared for the Treasury that the President lacked the power to purchase gold at a price above that fixed by statute, which was currently $20.67 per fine ounce. The Attorney-General supported Acheson.[390]

On September 26 [1933] Morgenthau told [the President] that his lawyers in the Farm Credit Administration thought he could buy gold. . . . A few days later Morgenthau showed Roosevelt a longhand memorandum from his general counsel Herman Oliphant suggesting various ways by which the President might buy gold through his executive powers.

Roosevelt then proposed the formation of a subsidiary under the Reconstruction Finance Corporation to actually buy the gold. The subsidiary corporation would then use the gold purchased as collateral against money loaned to it by the Treasury Department to make the purchase.

Morgenthau referred the matter back to Herman Oliphant, his general counsel. "Oliphant, digging into the recesses of his memory, recalled a Civil War statute which permitted the government to buy gold at changing prices; combined with the RFA Act, this seemed to give the President the power he needed." Stanley Reed, general counsel of the Reconstruction Finance Corporation (later elevated by Roosevelt to a seat on the Supreme Court), agreed with Oliphant's position.[391]

Acheson was adamant in his belief that Oliphant's legal theory was rubbish, both as a matter of law and sound public policy.

The president was faced with what he called "agrarian revolt." He displayed increasing resentment at Acheson's intransigence and that of his more-conservative advisors. Finally, on October 19, 1933, there was a decisive meeting at the White House. After a heated recap of the arguments on both sides, the President announced: "I say it is legal." Acheson asked for a written order from the President authorizing the Treasury Department to lend the money to the RFC to purchase gold bullion, going so far as to say to Roosevelt that it was he, Acheson, who was placing his name to the order and not the President. "That will do!" was the presidential response, and the meeting broke up.[392] As Schlesinger describes it, "Later that day, Acheson arrived at the meeting of the RFC Board, his mustaches bristling, his face scarlet, his jaws clamped together, looking (according to Morgenthau) like a thunder cloud. He said, 'Gentlemen, I have just come from the President. You know that I am opposed to our buying gold. The President has ordered me to do it. I will carry out his orders.'"[393] Three days later Roosevelt, in a "fireside chat" over the radio, publicly announced his decision.

Implementation of the gold-buying program started out on October 25, 1933. Ready to set the price of gold purchases for that day, Morgenthau and Jesse Jones, the self-made Houston banker who was head of the Reconstruction Finance Corporation, appeared in the president's bedroom each morning, where they would find Roosevelt in bed eating his breakfast. Jones was there because he headed the agency doing the actual gold purchasing. Schlesinger suggests Morgenthau's presence was due to his recent experience in helping maintain wheat prices through a government purchase program. An equally likely consideration is that Jones was known to be a self-made Texas banker who never failed to express any opinion he might have.[394]

Roosevelt wanted someone else present who he knew would back him up, should Jones choose to express disagreement with the president's decision on any given morning. Schlesinger writes: "While Roosevelt ate his eggs and drank his coffee, the group discussed what the day's price was to be . . . One day Morgenthau came in, more worried than usual, and suggested an increase from 19 to 22 cents. Roosevelt took one look at Morgenthau's anxious face and proposed 21 cents [for that day's bid increase]. 'It's a lucky number,' he said with a laugh, 'because it's three times seven.' Morgenthau, never sure when his leg was being pulled, later made the literal-minded notation in his diary, 'If anybody ever knew how we really set the gold price through a combination of lucky numbers, etc., I think they would really be frightened.'"

Schlesinger comments: "As Jones pointed out, the rate of increase had to be unpredictable lest speculators figure out what was going on."[395]

Schlesinger does not believe Roosevelt thought much of Warren's theory of raising the prices for farm produce by raising the price of gold.

" 'I don't believe that Roosevelt ever accepted at face value the Warren theory,' Ernest K. Lindley later wrote. 'I heard him laugh over Warren's charts more than once while he was supposed to be under Warren's spell.' [James] Warburg [another of Roosevelt's conservative economists] agreed. What carried the day with Roosevelt, he always felt, was not conviction that the Warren theory was right so much as the fact that Warren offered a program of action at a time when the demand for action seemed irresistible."[396]

Schlesinger adds: "[I]t freed him from the intolerable necessity of sitting by and doing nothing while prices fell."[397]

Black's opinion of the gold-buying program is that, "despite its trivial results, [it] had been another Rooseveltian masterstroke for taking the wind out of the sails of Milo Reno and his radical Farm Holiday [farmers] at a critical moment." [398]

There was an important side effect to the inflationary program of increasing the price of gold: The Treasury Department was provided with a windfall profit amounting to several billions of dollars on its stock of gold reposing at Fort Knox in Kentucky. It would prove extremely useful to Morgenthau in succeeding years in the form of the Exchange Stabilization Fund that provided the financial wherewithal to support the Treasury Department's fiscal programs both domestically and in Europe.

Acheson was placed in an intolerable position. He was the acting secretary of the Treasury who had clashed with his political superior. There was always a partnership waiting for him at his old law firm. If he remained on the job, it was to seek to temper the worst misjudgments by the Chief Executive—who obviously did not appreciate Acheson's concern.

It was an unstable situation, but like the state of affairs of the Union in 1861 in the last months of Buchanan's presidency, as one after another of the Southern state legislatures passed resolutions rescinding their earlier adherence to the Federal Constitution, circumstances were allowed to drift. Then, as Schlesinger writes: "Unfortunately stories began to appear in the press hinting that some in the administration regarded the [gold-buying] program as unconstitutional . . ." The obvious culprit was Acheson. The newspaper insinuations were brought to Roosevelt's attention on October 27, 1933. Roosevelt said to Morgenthau, "I guess this boil has about come to a head, and you know me, Henry, I am slow to get mad, but when I do, I get good and mad."[399]

Two days later, all the officials involved in the gold-buying operation were summoned to the White House. Roosevelt reminded them it was administration policy and continued, "We are all in the same boat. If anybody does not like the boat, he can get out of it."

Schlesinger writes: "Before long another series of stories broke in the newspaper. Roosevelt, furious, immediately wrote to Acheson requesting his resignation. Before Acheson received the letter, the President informed the press that the Undersecretary of the Treasury had resigned. Acheson, hearing the news from newspapermen, took it philosophically."[400] Black comments: "Acheson's letter of resignation was civil and respectful [he had long wanted to leave the Administration], and at Woodin's insistence he came to the ceremony for [his successor's] swearing-in."[401] He was as "urbane and imperturbable as ever. . . . The Acheson gallantry made a deep impression."[402]

In due course, later on, the information came to the White House that Acheson had been blameless in the matter and that it was probably Lewis Douglas, the Arizona banker, then the Director of the Budget, who was the guilty party.[403] (Douglas would subsequently resign on August 30, 1934.[404])

It is apparent that Roosevelt had given some thought to a choice of successor to Acheson. He had found the latter's challenges distasteful. He wanted a successor who would be at once respectful of presidential authority and competent enough to do the job. Schlesinger writes: "On the day [November 13, 1933[405]] that Roosevelt decided to fire Acheson, he asked Morgenthau to stay a moment after the bedside meeting [that set that day's gold-purchase bid price]. Woodin, he said, was too sick to come back; therefore he was appointing a new Acting Secretary of the Treasury. He paused. Then he said, 'I have decided that that person is Henry Morgenthau, Jr. You made good for me in Albany, and you are one of the two or three people who have made an outstanding success here in Washington, so let's you and I go on to bigger and better things. . . . We will have lots of fun doing it together.'"[406]

Roosevelt's words suggest a bit of a bad conscience. In truth, he had treated Morgenthau a trifle shabbily, disappointing him initially when it came to a cabinet post. Now Roosevelt had come to the conclusion that he needed Morgenthau. How Roosevelt may have come to that conclusion can be gleaned from the following comments taken from Ickes' *Secret Diary*, for Tuesday, October 17, 1933:

The President . . . asked the members of the Cabinet to remain, together with General [Hugh] Johnson, George Peek [the AAA Administrator], Harry L. Hopkins, and Henry Morgenthau, Jr. The President first touched on the commodity market. Henry Morgenthau, Jr., [had been] instructed to place orders for wheat in the market today and he did buy on behalf of the Federal Government about $1.5 million worth, putting prices up three cents over the close last night. This wheat will be turned over to the Federal Surplus Relief Corporation for food for the unemployed. Then he [Roosevelt] went on to say that the bankers of the country were in a conspiracy to block the Administration program. He said the banks were not lending any money even on good security and that they were seriously hampering the business recovery. Reports have come to him from a number of sources as evidence of the unwillingness of the bankers to help out in this situation. He is quite clear in his own mind that a conspiracy existed, and he spoke of the possibility of extending Federal credit to businessmen who could not secure loans on good security at the banks. [In the fullness of time, Meltzer puts a rather less-melodramatic cast on the motivation of the bankers without changing the consequences of their inaction.] He said one thing that was hurting commodity prices was the belief engendered in the minds of the bankers that the dollar is to be stabilized and no further effort made to advance commodity prices. Two or three of those present, especially Lewis Douglas [the conservative Arizona banker, then Director of the Budget], defended the attitude of the bankers. Morgenthau made a suggestion that some of the big bankers be talked with to see if they would organize a pool of credit out of which loans could be made. The President approved this plan . . .[407]

The foregoing quoted excerpt from Ickes suggests that Roosevelt was using Morgenthau in matters beyond the narrow confines of rural credit problems within the ambit of the Farm Credit Administration. He was using him for the larger problem that centered around the inability to secure credit by urban commercial and industrial businesses. In that sense, Morgenthau was already operating as an unofficial "minister without portfolio"—a "troubleshooter."

Henry III reports his father's reaction to Roosevelt's announcement that he was being promoted: Morgenthau "was completely 'dumfounded' and 'broke out in a cold sweat.'"[408] Well he might, since he was painfully aware he knew little about the effects of currency flow or banking. In a real sense, he was largely unequipped for the job he was being offered—except for two considerations. As Henry III describes these, Roosevelt "knew from their days together in Albany that my father combined the virtue of absolute loyalty with an uncanny ability to get things done, sometimes in extremely unorthodox ways, using aides who were themselves idiosyncratic in their approach to problems."[409] Put another way, Morgenthau had an astonishing ability to choose extremely competent assistants.

Schlesinger puts the matter in this fashion: "Morgenthau's inarticulateness, as well as the penchant for worry which so often darkened his face with apprehension, caused people to underrate him. In a succession of tough assignments he had shown solid administrative gifts. He chose good people, used them effectively, ran tight organizations, got results, and kept his mouth shut. . . . Above all, his highest ambition was plainly not for himself. It was to serve Franklin Roosevelt."[410]

As to Morgenthau's "penchant for worry which so often darkened his face with apprehension," Henry III writes, "he seemed to have a great many things on his mind that bothered him. He suffered frequent migraine attacks. 'Your father has one of his sick headaches,' Mother would inform us once or twice a week 'Try to be very quiet.' Daddy meanwhile would be stretched out on a couch in his darkened dressing room, quietly or not so quietly suffering."[411] Yet, it must be noted, his ailments do not appear to have materially interfered with an active life. His headaches may be said to have added a grace note of mortality to the rhythm of his days.

Morgenthau assumed the position of Undersecretary of the Treasury on November 17, 1933. Roosevelt accepted Woodin's resignation very shortly thereafter, no longer having any reason to delay Woodin's formal departure from the scene. Roosevelt then submitted Morgenthau's name for confirmation by the Senate. Morgenthau was sworn in as secretary of the Treasury on January 1, 1934, recognizing that Roosevelt (as in diplomatic and other matters) retained control of policy in the areas of currency, banking, and the well-being of the national economy.

After Morgenthau entered the cabinet, nothing better illustrates the change in relationship with his father than the following two letters. The first, dated January 9, 1934, is one that Henry Sr. sent to Henrietta Klotz, the new cabinet member's longtime secretary and administrative assistant:

My dear Mrs. Klotz:

Mr. Wilfred Heck, who has had the ticket office concession at Carnegie Hall for thirteen years, and is now forty-six years of age, thinks that he could do a good job in supervising the collecting of taxes in the Internal Revenue Amusement Tax office, and I wonder who has charge of appointing a man for that purpose. I personally have known him a great many years, and can vouch for him.

I did not want to bother Henry himself, so I want you to let me know to whom I should send him.

Mrs. Klotz referred the letter to her boss, who handwrote a response across the top of the page: "Dear Pa: a request from the father of the Secretary is almost like an order, so you would be doing me a great favor if you did not give this man a letter."

On February 15, 1934, Morgenthau wrote a hurried note to his father on the secretary's official stationery: "Dear Pa: I had expected you to have lunch with me, but I have just received a wire that David Stern of Philadelphia is going to meet you here at 1:15. As I have several newspaper men lunching with me, I think it would be better for you to take David Stern across the street to the Hotel Washington. Please talk to me for a few minutes before you talk to David Stern."

Morgenthau now realized that the anonymity he had enjoyed as publisher of the *American Agriculturist* vanished after he became secretary of the Treasury. The publication could now be scrutinized for clues as to possible administration policy, so he made arrangements in 1934 to sell the *American Agriculturist* to the Gannett newspaper chain.[412] At least he had a good reason for knowing that one drain on his income was being eliminated (the annual subsidy the publication of his farm journal had entailed, which his father had grumpily noticed several years earlier).

If a losing investment financially, ownership of the journal had enabled Morgenthau to become familiar with the ideas and identities of the faculty farm experts at the Cornell University School of Agriculture. Those ideas gave substance to the opinions expressed in the journal's editorial columns, and allowed Morgenthau to suggest to Roosevelt the creation and membership of his Agricultural Advisory Commission after the gubernatorial election in 1928, which had led to Roosevelt's current eminence.

On the national scene, the administration faced the reality that in 1934, the country was in the midst of a severe and prolonged depression. Preceding recessions had averaged only nineteen months at a time. Meltzer writes that there were 113 months of recession from December 1895 through January 1912, some 55 percent of the time. He notes that several of the recessions were severe ones, amounting to financial panics, when interest rates rose to 100 percent and more, and financial failures and bankruptcies were, as he writes, "much too frequent." Meltzer goes on to say that in the 1920s, the Federal Reserve System "received credit for improving economic performance," since extreme "old-style financial panics did not return in the three recessions from 1920 through 1927."[413]

All that changed with the onset of the economic reverses that began with the stock market crash on October 29, 1929. Unlike the Panic of 1907, when leading bankers and insurance company executives recognized the need for immediate and decisive action to counteract the panicked reaction of businessmen and the general public (that led to "runs" on banks because the depositors lost confidence in the ability of banks to "make good" on deposits). In that instance they asked John Pierpont Morgan to take charge of efforts to staunch the panic. He accepted the challenge, directing bankers, insurance company executives, and finally, even the secretary of the Treasury to come up with millions of dollars in cash to allow those banks, under siege, to continue to pay out all demands for withdrawals by lines of waiting depositors—until those depositors decided the banks were in fact able to satisfy all requests for withdrawals. (It goes without saying that such loans were based, at Morgan's direction, on emergency reviews of the banks' assets by trusted auditors of the creditworthiness of the amount of debt written in the ledgers in the banks' vaults.)

Savings banks keep on hand only a small percentage of funds deposited, to satisfy anticipated daily withdrawals by customers' needs for cash. That percentage is determined by the bank's experience in everyday banking operations. The remainder and moneys borrowed from a central bank (like the Federal Reserve regional banks) is used to lend out money. Beginning with the enactment of the National Housing Act through the 1990s, savings banks lent money to borrowers on a self-liquidating basis, and the borrowers provided security for the loans in the form of liens on real property, homes, and the like. Commercial banks traditionally lend money to businesses, which provide security in the form of bills or notes acknowledging indebtedness.

Currently, federal bank regulating policies set the ratio of actual cash on hand to deposits. Since most all bank deposits are now insured by the Federal Deposit Insurance Corporation with the concomitant requirement under the Banking Act of 1935 mandating Federal regulation, the federal standard is universal. Toward the close of each banking day, banks not meeting the cash requirement look to borrow the funds from banks with a surplus for the day. Interest on such daily borrowing between banks is called the "federal funds" rate, and it is quoted in the business section of newspapers. (In practice, the transaction is conducted through a federal funds broker operating in the New York money market.[414]) Since the creation of the Federal Deposit Insurance Corporation early in Roosevelt's tenure, to guarantee repayment of deposits by insolvent banks,[415] "runs on banks" have become a thing of the past.

In the period after the stock market crash at the end of October 1929, the most important consideration was the lack of recognition by leading members of the business community in the United States of the need for someone to take command, like Morgan, who had been so instrumental in staunching the Panic of 1907. Perhaps there was a sense in the business community that such activity would be provided by the Federal Reserve Board, created in 1913 to deal with just such emergencies. (The Federal Reserve System had been given credit for the relative shallowness of the three recessions from 1920 through 1927.) Perhaps, also, the Social Darwinist ethos of the late 1920s had eroded the larger vision that animated the business community during the Panic of 1907 to seek Morgan's assistance.

In any case, the stock market crash would lead to a general loss of confidence in the economy. Businesses found that the bank loans on which they had depended for their operations had dried up, or, when offered, involved prohibitive interest rates. Businesses were starting to sell less of the products they produced. This led to workers being laid off in large numbers. Demand lessened in the retail trade. This in turn was reflected in the prices paid to farmers by processors of agricultural products.

The decline in prices received by farmers for their produce was piggybacked onto the low prices already in effect as a result of the agrarian recession, which began in 1920. (The concept of *parity*, developed in the New Deal years to justify programs involving payments to farmers, had reference to farmers' incomes in an earlier generation.)

Land values in rural areas plummeted. With the decline in the prices farmers received for their produce, they were unable to make the payments on their mortgage debt. Additionally, rural banks discovered, in turn, that state government regulatory agencies were determining that the current value of the bonds that had been signed by farmers when they took the loans, and the security they gave (that is, the mortgages on their farmland that underlay the rural banks' outstanding loans), did not meet the monetary standards the state regulatory agencies required, resulting in rural bank failures. This in turn closed off borrowing money by farmers who depended on the banks in their communities for funds to purchase seed and fertilizer to plant a new crop. [416]

In Keynesian theory, in these circumstances, it is the function of the central bank to inject funds into the local banking industry to "jump-start" business activity by making money available to local banks to lend at reasonable rates to encourage borrowing by businesses (and farmers). This would cause businesses to rehire workers, who would receive wages to allow them to purchase food, clothing, etc. This in turn would serve to reestablish normal economic activity. An incidental (and anticipated) effect would be a very minor degree of inflation, but inflation was a very real concern in the later 1920s after the ruinous inflation that had been allowed to happen in Germany in 1923. [417]

In any case, Keynesian theory was not applied in the period after the stock market crash. In 1929 and the early 1930s, Keynesian economic theory was all but unknown in the United States. (Keynes's seminal work would only be published in

1936.) In a real sense, Keynesian theory was antithetical to the Social Darwinist ethos of the period that thought in terms of a more-rigid and narrow-minded "neo-mercantilist" formulation that was analogous to the economic theory that had been the dominant government philosophy in the eighteenth century. It had held (in a sense, comparable to Thomas Malthus's contemporaneous ideas with respect to effects of population growth on starvation) that there was a finite amount of assets in the world, and if province or country was profligate and wasted its share on frivolities, it would be beggared as much as if it was conquered and had its assets seized as booty by conquering armies. It behooved governments to acquire and retain as much gold as each possibly could. Meltzer speaks of a "core principle of the gold standard [that was] accepted as basic at the start of the Federal Reserve System . . . [T]he central bank must raise and lower the discount rate [the cost of borrowing money] as required *to protect the gold stock* and the exchange rate [for foreign currencies to facilitate foreign purchases of American agricultural commodities and manufactured goods]"[418] (italics added).

Of course, the Bourbon governments of France and Spain in the Age of Enlightenment during the eighteenth century did not apply mercantilist theory in practice, but more closely followed the adage of parents to their children—*Do what I say, not what I do*. Spanish governments, during the course of the eighteenth century, tended to go bankrupt in every generation, while the royal government of France was insolvent by 1788, the result of its wars during that century, in addition to lending out vast sums of money—most notably to the nascent revolutionary government of the British colonies in North America in rebellion against the British Crown.

It would appear that the governors of the Federal Reserve System, after the stock market crash in 1929, were very much

Social Darwinist in their attitudes with respect to the national economy, which translated into a very negative-minded, contractive, "neo-mercantilist" monetary inaction. Such Social Darwinist ways of thinking paralleled the attitudes that had led to the restrictive immigration provisions of the contemporaneous National Origins Act of 1929, and the punitive charges embedded in the Smoot-Hawley Tariff Act in the same period.

Meltzer explains:

> Between February 1 [1933] and March 4 [1933], the demand for Federal Reserve notes and gold increased $1.43 billion and $320 million respectively. . . . [M]ost of the gold purchases were made by foreigners, including foreign central banks. . . . Bagehot (1962) describes the remedy for an internal and external drain as lending freely at a high rate. The Federal Reserve [System] continued to ignore this advice. Banks therefore could not meet demands for currency and gold. In the four months between [the November 1932] election and [the March 4, 1933] inauguration, the Hoover administration tried unsuccessfully both to activate the Federal Reserve [System] and to cooperate with the incoming administration.
>
> Burdened by its history of financial crises, a lame duck administration, Federal Reserve [Board] inaction, and Roosevelt's silence, the [American] financial system collapsed [in the beginning months of 1933].[419]

In this respect, after Roosevelt's inauguration, Harold Ickes wrote in his *Secret Diary* for Tuesday, April 11, 1933: "We had a long and interesting Cabinet meeting. The main subjects of discussion were the banking and currency situation, a proposed popular bond issue in small denominations in order to bring money out of hoarding, and a major program of public works to relieve unemployment and try to restore purchasing power."[420]

Meltzer adds to his discussion of the monetary crisis the nation faced: "In the middle and late thirties, just as in the early thirties, the Federal Reserve [System] did next to nothing to foster [the nation's economic] recovery. In a period of prolonged and widespread unemployment, the Federal Reserve System's principal policy action was the 1937–38 series of deflationary and contractive increases in reserve requirement ratios taken to forestall a possible future inflation."[421]

This, then, with some amelioration during the months since March 4, 1933, was the economic picture that Roosevelt faced on January 1, 1934, when Morgenthau was sworn in as Secretary of the Treasury. With an effectively nonfunctioning central bank, and millions of people still out of work, the business economy was a market looking for nonexistent customers. The effect was deflationary. Prices tended to drift downwards.

Morgenthau was presented with an extraordinary responsibility (subject to Roosevelt's overview). It was the "Treasury [that] controlled most decisions until after World War II . . . Congress and the Treasury made the important decisions about gold, silver, and banking legislation."[422]

Meltzer comments that the president's "April 18 [1933] order took the country off the gold standard . . . This was followed on June 5 [1933] by a joint resolution abrogating the gold clause in all public and private contracts. Payments could be made only in legal tender." [423]

Morgenthau's first significant Treasury Department action occurred when "Congress passed the Gold Reserve Act on January 30 [1934] . . . The following day the president [pursuant to the provisions of the Thomas Amendment] fixed the price of gold at $35 an ounce, a 59.06 percent devaluation [of the dollar] against gold. [Secretary] Morgenthau announced that the New

York Federal Reserve bank would buy gold for the Treasury at $34.75 and sell at $35.25 an ounce, but purchases and sales were restricted to transactions with central banks and governments. The nominal gold price remained fixed for more than thirty-seven years until President Nixon stopped gold sales and purchases on August 15, 1971."[424]

Meltzer goes on to explain the immediate benefits that accrued to the Treasury Department as a result of the upward revaluation of gold: "The Treasury used $2 billion of the profits from devaluation [of the dollar] to establish the Exchange Stabilization Fund [the name was probably taken from the existing British Exchange Equalization Account[425]], $650 million to retire national banknotes, and $27 million to finance industrial loans by reserve banks."[426]

Meltzer writes: "Gold and exchange rate policies, culminating in the 1934 devaluation, provided the main stimulus to domestic recovery in the first two years of the Roosevelt administration." Exports of American goods to European countries benefited.[427] "The [Exchange Stabilization] fund gave [Morgenthau and] the Treasury a strong hand in setting policy toward interest rates, money, and debt, and [Morgenthau and the Treasury Department] used [that] power. The Treasury remained the dominant partner [vis-à-vis the Federal Reserve Board] for the next fifteen years . . ."[428]

With respect to the state of the national economy, Meltzer comments, "Until 1937, recovery from the depression proceeded rapidly. In the four years following the trough in March 1933 . . . real GNP [Gross National Product] rose at a compound annual rate of almost 12 percent." He explains: "Prices rose during recovery, in part a result of [Roosevelt's] deliberate policy to devalue the dollar so as to raise agricultural and commodity prices."[429]

Lewis Douglas, the conservative banker from Arizona, then director of the Bureau of the Budget, apparently became disillusioned by the drift of affairs in Washington: the departure from the gold standard, the increase in the price of gold, the unbalanced budget with no foreseeable possibility of its rectification. His efforts at anonymously leaking information to the press about Roosevelt's intention to increase the price of gold had no practical effect other than to cause the resignation of Dean Acheson and his replacement by Morgenthau, whom Douglas would appear to think unsuited for the job—on the whole, a turn for the worse.

On August 30, 1934, Douglas came to Roosevelt's home at Hyde Park to announce his resignation as budget director. Although he might not take Douglas's advice, Roosevelt would appear to have found his presence in the government desirable. Douglas apparently had physical "presence"—a distinguished appearance—that added a certain dignity to the mass of persons who were the public face of Roosevelt's administration. Playing for time, apparently, Roosevelt asked Douglas to delay his resignation until after the forthcoming election in November. Douglas refused, and Roosevelt was faced with an important government position without an occupant.

It would appear that Roosevelt was nonplussed. As he had after his election as governor in 1928, Roosevelt again turned to Morgenthau, with whom he could think out loud. Roosevelt threw out the name Tommy Corcoran as Douglas's successor. The ebullient Corcoran (working with the scholarly Ben Cohen) was one of Roosevelt's not-so-anonymous administrative assistants and congressional lobbyists. Horrified, Morgenthau countered with the suggestion of Daniel Bell, then the Treasury Department's commissioner of accounts, competent, sober-sided, and colorless—adding up to a lack of good newspaper copy. Roosevelt immediately recognized Bell's more perfect "fit" for the job. The announcement of Douglas's departure and Bell's appointment was then made public over the Labor Day weekend, with no noticeable newspaper interest or public response.[430]

On October 24, 1934, Morgenthau wrote to his father from his private residence: "Thanks for your letter of October 23rd. I am very much interested in what you say about the Heckscher Building. That certainly has been an old favorite of yours for many years and perhaps it will fall into your lap. It is highly complimentary to me to see the class of people that they select to succeed me. Two weeks ago it was Jim Perkins, and now you say Tom Lamont [a partner in J. P. Morgan & Co.]. I will only really be flattered if the rumors say it will be J. P. Morgan—or maybe I should be insulted."

During this period, Roosevelt had Morgenthau take care of one more political chore for him. Roosevelt had been invited to address an American Bankers Association meeting on October 24, 1934. He was to be introduced by an old Columbia professor of his, Jackson Reynolds, now leading the First National Bank of New York. Reynolds was so kind as to send a copy of his introductory remarks to Roosevelt. Those included reference to Roosevelt's "limitations as a law student" and other statements Roosevelt found unflattering. Roosevelt left it to Morgenthau to convince Reynolds to revise his comments.[431]

Marriner Eccles had impressed Rexford Tugwell as a witness at a congressional hearing. He was a conservative Mormon banker from Utah. Tugwell introduced Eccles to Morgenthau, who hired him in February 1934 as an assistant for banking and monetary problems,[432] although Morgenthau disapproved of Eccles's version of what is generally thought of as Keynesian economic theory. Meltzer writes that both men were of very different "background, personality and beliefs. Eccles described himself as blunt," and Meltzer notes that his biographer describes their relationship as "deeply troubled." Meltzer goes on to say "Morgenthau saw Eccles as talented and energetic but also as confident, assertive, and ambitious, with 'an insatiable drive to personal power.'" Meltzer describes Morgenthau as "cautious, rarely willing to make a decision without the president's approval. He distrusted bankers [as did Roosevelt] and opposed 'bigness' and government deficits"[433] in principle, although in practice accepted Roosevelt's unbalanced budgets that were in large part the result of appropriations for extensive public assistance to the unemployed. "Eccles attributed many of his [later] disputes to the 'quirks of Morgenthau's personality,'" a polite way of phrasing a Social Darwinist incompatibility. Meltzer goes on to write that "[b]oth men tended to see substantive issues as personal, a fact that Eccles realized after Morgenthau resigned and his disputes and differences continued, and intensified, with Secretaries Fred M. Vinson and John W. Snyder, who followed."[434]

Notwithstanding their early disagreements, in September 1934, Morgenthau recommended Eccles's nomination to Roosevelt to fill a vacancy on the Federal Reserve Board of Governors. In 1936, he would become the chairman, remaining in the position until 1948.

When Roosevelt spoke to him, Eccles told Roosevelt the Federal Reserve Board governorship was not worth having unless the Federal Reserve Board was turned into a real central bank with the autonomous powers of the regional Federal Reserve banks curbed and transferred to the Board and its chairman. It was his thought that the regional banks, especially the one in New York, served "private interests" that ended up controlling the entire Federal Reserve System.[435] The result, following Eccles's suggestions, was the Banking Act of 1935, which centralized what had been the semiautonomous Federal Reserve System, leading to the independent Federal Reserve Board we know today.

Morgenthau was in favor of the provisions of the law because he foresaw continued budgetary deficits and looked to share the responsibility for any dire consequences that deficit financing threatened. More important, he wanted an agency with the authority to keep interest rates low in order to reduce the costs of continued government borrowing. Black speaks of Morgenthau's "frugality" in this respect.[436]

A factor that served to inhibit action by the Federal Reserve Board after Eccles became its chairman in 1936, but had been present prior to his accession to a seat on the Board, is that "Eccles believed monetary policy could do nothing in the 1930s when short-term interest rates were low, so he did nothing to lift the economy from the depression."[437]

Under the date of Sunday, February 17, 1935, Ickes records in his *Secret Diary* that Huey Long, the eccentric senator from Louisiana, had introduced a resolution calling for an investigation of Interior Department reports concerning the connection of a building supply company owned by James Farley, the postmaster general and national Democratic leader, with the construction of a post office annex in New York City. Joseph Robinson, the Senate Democratic majority leader, had asked the president whether there was anything embarrassing that might warrant squelching Long's resolution. Roosevelt had reviewed the documentation and thought it was harmless. However, the files indicated that a letter (and carbon copy) sent by an assistant secretary of the Post Office Department to his counterpart at the Treasury Division of Procurement had been destroyed by each. Ickes noted that destruction of official documents was a criminal offense, and described the destruction of the letter and carbon copy as "a highly improper act" that could "give Long an occasion for quite a beating of the tom-toms." Morgenthau then asked Ickes to look at the file and sent several of his assistants to review it.

Ickes' investigator, as late as the preceding December, had requested information from the Treasury Department as to why there had been so many cancellations of bids and repeated notices for new bids on this project. Morgenthau took umbrage at Interior's presumption in seeking to investigate the Treasury's handling of the matter. What was more, Morgenthau brought the matter up at a cabinet meeting. Ickes writes: "His tone and manner were quite belligerent." Ickes in turn bristled at any criticism of his operation, writing: "Looking him straight in the eye, I said that I took exception both to what he had just said and to the tone in which he had said it. But he was mad clear through."[438] There were further words, and the president had to intervene to quiet them. Both men were very sensitive and thin-skinned. Ickes spends three full pages and then some justifying his role and assuring his *Diary* that there could be no imputation of impropriety on the part of Farley in the matter, although he cannot resist repeating that Morgenthau should have picked up on the destruction of the letter to his subordinate.[439] Ickes then records how at a subsequent White House reception, he went and shook Morgenthau's hand "in a perfectly normal manner, not because I wanted to, but because it is necessary for Cabinet members to preserve amenities in public."[440]

Meltzer writes that by 1935 agricultural prices had increased in fact and in relation to the prices of other goods. Still, these were below the 1926 average (and below the relative return on agricultural commodities a generation earlier in the decade, at the beginning of the twentieth century).[441]

Meltzer believes Roosevelt had not abandoned the chimera of a balanced budget, but he recognized that the relatively low level of current business activity and the costs of relief expenditures prevented the realization of a balanced budget. For his part, Morgenthau financed the deficit the government was incurring through the periodic sale of government bond issues,

August 8, 1918.

Dear Colonel Austin:-

    It gives me great pleasure to say that
I know Mr. Henry Morgenthau, Jr., very well
and am only to glad to commend him to you with
the statement that he is a young man of highest integrity, sterling character and unusual
ability.

    Mr. Morgenthau desires to be appointed to
the Labor Battalion, and any consideration you
can show his application will be appreciated
by me.

        Yours very sincerely,

Lieut-Colonel W.A. Austin,

    Camp Lee,

        Virginia.

Letter from Assistant Secretary of State Breckenridge Long to Lieutenant-Colonel W. A. Austin recommending Henry Morgenthau, Jr., for the Labor Battalion. (Reproduced from the holdings of the FDR Presidential Library, Hyde Park, New York)

Before I assumed the office of Governor ~~in~~ ~~1928~~,
in *November 1928*
I organized the Agricultural Advisory Commission for the
specific purpose of a cooperative study of the outstanding
needs of the rural population of New York State. This commission, non-partisan in its every aspect, has now completed
its work so far as the two Legislative sessions of the present
administration are concerned, and I consider it advisable to
draw the attention of the people of the State, particularly
those toward whose requirements the work of the commission
was directed, to the accomplishments which have followed the
commission's work.

The first recommendations of the Commission were made
available to the public on November 24, 1928, by Henry Morgenthau, Jr., the commission's chairman. I feel that the most
graphic means of presenting the results of ~~the commission~~ *its*
efforts in cooperation with the Legislature, is to state,
chronologically and in sequence, the recommendations made
before I assumed office, together with the final result that
has followed each individual recommendation. This record
stands as follows:

1. THAT the counties be relieved of their 35% contribution
    to the state for the construction of new highways.

    RESULT: This was accomplished in 1939.

2. THAT the state assume the cost of removing snow from the
    state highways.

    RESULT: In 1930 the legislature passed a bill
              authorizing the state to aid the counties
              for snow removal from state and county
              highways and requesting that such snow
              removal be accomplished at the joint
              expense of the state and county. This
              bill is now a law by my signature.

3. THAT the state assume the cost of elimination of grade
    crossings.

    RESULT: In 1929 the counties' share of the cost
              of eliminating grade crossings was

to the present day needs of agriculture, which it cannot continue without immediately improved physical facilities.

> RESULT: I have just signed an act entitled: "An act authorizing the construction of a building at Cornell University for agricultural economics, marketing and farm management, and making an appropriation therefor." (This bill carries an appropriation of $100,000.)

d. At a meeting of the Commission on February 21, 1929, they approved of the bills now before the Legislature which would provide additional state support for the county farm and home bureaus /and junior extension work in the state. These bills failed 'of passage in the 1929 legislature.

> RESULT: I have just signed as enacted by the 1930 Legislature, and it is now a law, an act entitled:* "An act to amend the county law, in relation to the state contributions toward the support of county farm and home bureaus, and junior extension work, and making an appropriation therefor." (This bill carries an appropriation of $40,500.)

e. At a meeting of the Agricultural Commission at Ithaca on August 2, 1929, the commission recommended and adopted the following resolution:

> THAT the State take immediate steps to survey the agricultural resources of New York in order to make plans for the most profitable use of each kind of land.

> RESULT: I have just signed, and it is now a law, an act entitled:"AN ACT making an appropriation for a survey of agricultural resources of the State by the New York State College of Agriculture at Cornell University." (This bill carries an appropriation of $20,000.)

I submit to the people of the State this record of accomplishment by my Agricultural Advisory Commission with a feeling of deep personal satisfaction in their work, and I wish to extend to the individual men and women who served on the Commission my congratulations and thanks for having performed such worthy, devoted and constructive public service.

for Henry Himself   *Franklin D Roosevelt*

Undated draft of pages 1 and 4 of the letter read by Franklin D. Roosevelt at the public signing ceremony after receiving the recommendations of the Agricultural Advisory Commission. Note Roosevelt's corrections and signature. (Reproduced from the holdings of the FDR Presidential Library, Hyde Park, New York)

Portrait of Elinor Morgenthau, née Fatman, in her bridal gown with a large bouquet. 1916. (Library of Congress, Prints & Photographs Division, LC-USZ62-118080)

Eleanor Roosevelt and Elinor Morgenthau in Washington, D.C., in the spring of 1933. (Courtesy of the FDR Presidential Library, Hyde Park, New York)

In early 1934, Henry Morgenthau, Jr., visited Roosevelt in Warm Springs, Georgia. The note reads, "For Elinor from one of two of a kind." (Courtesy of the FDR Presidential Library, Hyde Park, New York)

Secretary of the Treasury Henry Morgenthau and Undersecretary Roswell Magill, appearing before the Joint Congressional Tax Committee, urge passage of legislation to close tax law loopholes. June 17, 1937. (Library of Congress, Prints & Photographs Division, photograph by Harris & Ewing, LC-DIG-hec-22882)

Morgenthau conversing with Herman Oliphant (left), General Counsel for the U.S. Treasury. September 21, 1937. (Library of Congress, Prints & Photographs Division, photograph by Harris & Ewing, LC-DIG-hec-23399)

Carter Glass, Henry Morgenthau, Jr., and Henry Morgenthau, Sr., March 7, 1939. (Library of Congress, Prints & Photographs Division, photograph by Harris & Ewing, LC-DIG-hec-26227)

Secretary of the Treasury Henry Morgenthau, Jr., with his father Henry Morgenthau, Sr., as they arrive at the Willard Hotel for the Gridiron Club Dinner. December 13, 1937. (Library of Congress, Prints & Photographs Division, photograph by Harris & Ewing, LC-DIG-hec-23763)

Secretary of the Treasury Henry Morgenthau with Secretary of Agriculture Henry Wallace and wife Ilo Brown Wallace, ca. 1937. (Library of Congress, Prints & Photographs Division, photograph by Harris & Ewing, LC-DIG-hec-24048)

while maintaining the market for such issues through the periodic purchase of government bonds, using the moneys that were available to him from his new Exchange Stabilization Fund and the existing trust funds the Treasury Department administered for the Postal Savings program, the Railroad Retirement Funds, and others. [442]

In 1935, the Supreme Court was considering an appeal on the question of whether government bonds payable by their terms in gold then suffered a measurable loss of value because of the Roosevelt administration's change of the law to limit payment solely to "legal tender." The administration's successful, inflationary program to increase the price of gold now made payment in gold very attractive because of the price differential. But the Supreme Court had to so rule.[443] While the appeal was pending before the Supreme Court, Morgenthau noted that gold bonds were commanding a premium on the open market, and he directed that such bonds in the Treasury's possession be sold and legal tender payment bonds bought in their stead.

The administration also prepared for an adverse decision from the Supreme Court. Morgenthau directed President Harrison of the New York Federal Reserve Bank to stabilize foreign exchange and gold markets by keeping the French franc—France was still on the gold standard—within acceptable foreign exchange limits. This was to be accomplished by selling British pounds and buying French francs, whatever the cost to the Treasury such a fiscal operation might incur. As it happened, the Supreme Court's ruling accepted the government's position that no actual loss had occurred.[444]

Harold Ickes includes in his *Secret Diary* Roosevelt's comments at a cabinet meeting held on December 13, 1935, about "the attempt on the part of Great Britain and France to dismember Ethiopia in order to bring about peace with Italy. The President thinks this is an outrageous proceeding . . . Secretary Hull had a map showing just how serious this proposed dismemberment would be."[445] Whatever Roosevelt's sympathies for the beleaguered Ethiopians, he effectively could do nothing to help them. (This was the period of the adoption by the Congress of the Neutrality Act of 1935, signed into law by Roosevelt on August 31, 1935.[446]) The British and French governments did no more about the subsequent Italian invasion and conquest of the country than to allow the Ethiopian emperor Haile Selassie to address the League of Nations on June 30, 1936[447]—an occasion that was notable for revealing nothing so much as the ineptitude of democratic countries in the face of Social Darwinist totalitarian determination, a bad precedent for Hitler to follow the next year with the remilitarization of the Rhineland.

As the British pound slid in value in 1935 against the dollar and franc, the French got into the act. The Bank of France offered support for the pound provided the British were serious about setting firm exchange rates and would indicate the level at which they would try to hold their currency on the international market. The French then sought support from the New York Federal Reserve Bank, the American financial institution most involved with foreign exchange transactions. Apprised of the French initiative, Morgenthau brought it to the president's attention. Roosevelt, who was not a professional economist, probably found the idea of French interest in the British currency problems confusing, and he was ambivalent. Officially, the American government gave "sympathetic support" and looked to the exchange rate for the pound remaining at $4.86. But the pound slid on average during March to $4.776 for the month.[448]

Later that spring, the Bank of France asked to sell gold to the United States. Morgenthau agreed to purchase up to 150 million dollars' worth on May 31, 1935, and to make the dollar funds available immediately in Paris or New York. Meltzer comments that the French government understood Morgenthau's action as indicative that the American government was sympathetic to France's currency problems due to its desire to remain on the gold standard.

Morgenthau continued conversations with the French and British focused on foreign exchange rate stabilization through the remainder of the year 1935, although Roosevelt's mistrust of the British government—and, more particularly, of Neville Chamberlain, then Chancellor of the Exchequer—prevented any real progress. Stabilization of foreign exchange rates promised improvement in the economic recovery of each of the countries involved. That in turn would slow the inflow of gold from Europe to the United States.[449] The continuing receipt of gold in the United States from foreign sources (perhaps due to apprehension over the threatening drift of European political events) caused the nation's "monetary base to rise at an 18 percent annual rate for the first three quarters of 1935 and at a 25 percent annual rate in the fourth quarter."[450]

The year 1935 also saw the Federal Reserve Board become concerned about the possible inflationary effects as member banks' excess monetary reserves increased along with worrisome rises in the prices of shares of public corporation stock on the nation's stock exchanges.[451] This could lead to another stock market bubble with results comparable to the economic and financial collapse in 1929.[452] There was a widely held belief that "the 1927–29 stock market boom had caused the economic and financial collapse" the nation had experienced.[453]

By November 1935, the Federal Reserve Board was ready to act to contain perceived inflationary forces in the nation's economy. On November 7, 1935, Eccles briefed Morgenthau as to the Board's intention to raise loan reserve requirements for member banks. Morgenthau, as always, was concerned with financing the 1936 fiscal year budget deficit with the lowest cost of interest payments. He urged at least a short-term, three- or four-month delay. Eccles was amenable. He saw no reason for immediate activity.[454]

The Federal Reserve Board shepherded by Chairman Eccles now concentrated on giving public warning of its dismal prognosis. Excess monetary reserves held by member banks rose in January 1936. Unable to restrain themselves further, the members of the Federal Reserve Board voted on January 24, 1936, to increase stock market margin requirements from 45 to 55 percent.[455] Then, in March 1936, the Board voted to increase the reserve ratio requirements for member banks' loans.[456]

Meltzer remarks that the gold stock held in the United States continued to increase during the winter and spring of 1936. Chairman Eccles at the Federal Reserve Board agreed with Morgenthau about holding off on any increase in loan reserve ratio requirements until after the Treasury Department completed its June 1936 budget deficit bond sale.[457]

Roosevelt, looking at the matter from a political vantage point—he was soon to begin a political campaign for reelection that fall—concluded that it was important to display a concern for possible inflationary pressures in the national economy. But in this instance, Morgenthau prevailed, and no immediate measures were taken in May 1936 to further increase banks' reserve ratios against outstanding loans.[458]

Toward the end of April 1936, the British pound fell slightly after Poland effectively went off the gold standard by instituting foreign exchange controls and embargoing the further export of gold that month. Morgenthau then was able to secure Roosevelt's consent to engage in talks with the British government, centered on stabilizing foreign exchange rates.[459]

The results of French elections in May 1936 (that brought the Popular Front into office) provided an impetus to the talks between Morgenthau and the British conservative government. The Popular Front was led by Socialist premier Léon Blum, and included Communist Party ministers. Their primary concern was a domestic agenda: reducing the work week to forty hours and raising French workers' wages (all at the same time, without regard to any effect on prices, whether domestic or for export). They were uninterested in international monetary problems. (The Blum government, in very civilized fashion, would appear to have offered to hold harmless the cost of increased wages through 3 percent government-guaranteed loans to affected employers.) While Blum, when faced with the negative effects of his domestic agenda on French exports, was willing to accept a devaluation of the French franc, the Communists of all parties objected. (Meltzer is not interested in exploring what nationalist sentiments impelled the French Communists to defend the gold franc.)

By June 1936, Morgenthau accepted the idea of a 15 percent devaluation of the French franc. Several of his advisors suggested the need for a 25 percent devaluation. The president accepted the idea of Morgenthau's raising the question with the British of both their countries allowing a French devaluation of 25 percent without any negative response by either Britain or the United States.[460]

Morgenthau succeeded in May 1936 against opposition from the State Department, in getting a decision by the solicitor general that the Nazi government of Germany had violated the Smoot-Hawley Tariff Act of 1930 by using currency manipulation to increase exports. On June 4, 1936, the United States then imposed punitive import duties on German-made products. This action helped convince the French Popular Front ministers of Morgenthau's goodwill and led to Franco-American talks in Washington focused on foreign exchange problems.[461]

Morgenthau's fundamental rule of conduct was the recognition that he was Roosevelt's adjutant, there to implement policy as set by the president. There is no question that Roosevelt appreciated and was grateful for Morgenthau's loyalty; still, Roosevelt was no economist, and problems of foreign exchange and government bond interest rates would appear to have been almost beyond his comprehension or interest. On rare occasion Roosevelt could express his annoyance at being presented by Morgenthau with what seemed to be picayune and obscure details of interest rate expectations or currency disparities (that might relate to exports and foreign trade). So the following excerpt from Ickes' *Secret Diary*, dated Saturday, May 16, 1936, ". . . the President made a statement which came nearer to being a criticism of Morgenthau than any I have ever heard. He said that Henry had to get in to see him at least four times a week to tell him what francs were selling at or how he believed the next bond issue would go, and that on the other days of the week he had to call him by telephone to give him the same information."[462]

What is significant about the president's comment about Morgenthau is that even if Roosevelt on occasion found his information trivial and ultimately incomprehensible, he never discouraged Morgenthau's efforts. Having to placate Ickes, who was threatening to resign, Roosevelt would appear to have expressed his own feelings that could serve to mollify Ickes.

Roosevelt had accommodated Morgenthau in the matter of holding off on any action by the Federal Reserve Board that could affect the June 1936 sale of Treasury bonds to cover government deficits in the current fiscal year. That short delay had been accomplished, and now the Federal Reserve Board was free to act on further increases in reserve loan ratio requirements. On July 14, 1936, the Board voted "to increase reserve requirement ratios by 50 percent." These increases were to take effect August 15, 1936.[463]

To Morgenthau's consternation, government bond prices fell in the week following the announcement of loan reserve rate ratio increases. In addition, Morgenthau was outraged that Eccles had not given him notice of the Board's intention to raise the reserve rate requirements. It appears that Morgenthau did not accept Eccles's assurance that Roosevelt himself had agreed to the rate increases in a conversation Eccles had had with him the preceding week.[464]

Notwithstanding Morgenthau's concern over the decline in government bond prices, Meltzer reports that the increase in bank loan reserve ratio requirements "had no perceptible effect on the [nation's business] economy in the remainder of 1936," or on the presidential election results. Landon, the Republican candidate, won only two states.[465]

Typically, Morgenthau's irritation at what he might describe as Eccles's bad faith evaporated, and he made efforts at restoring some semblance of cordiality in the relationship. Eccles complained that Morgenthau was secretive about his gold operations. Morgenthau then agreed to release weekly data to the FOMC on net purchases and sales by his Exchange Stabilization Fund. In turn, Morgenthau asked for help from Eccles to stabilize the domestic market for Treasury bond issues. The Treasury Department had undertaken extensive market purchases of recent bond issues to keep prices above par. Morgenthau and Eccles between them proposed a tentative arrangement whereby the Treasury Department would itself make market purchases instead of having the New York Federal Reserve Bank act as the Treasury's agent. Then (just as local banks are in touch with the federal funds broker to borrow or lend money to meet the requirement for an actual cash reserve at the close of each business day), the Morgenthau-Eccles joint proposal provided that the Board's Open Market Committee could decide to take half the amount of the bonds the Treasury may have purchased that day. Eccles then checked with the Federal Open Market Committee's members, who agreed to ratify the new arrangement. Morgenthau could think the result made the Federal Reserve Board the Treasury's partner. Meltzer uses the somewhat stronger term "adjunct" to describe the relationship.[466]

The year 1936 saw excess bank reserves rise to more than $2 billion by the end of October 1936, a large amount for the period. These were almost equal to the amount of the debt carried in the Federal Open Market Committee portfolio. The gold inflow into the United States, when added to bank reserves and base money, caused increases in the prices of goods offered for sale in the country. Still, inflation remained low. In fact, consumer prices increased only 1 percent in 1936.[467] (It is evident that a Depression mentality continued to retain its hold on Americans—especially when one takes into account the 5 million persons who remained out of work.)

Roosevelt was alarmed about the effects on the American economy of continuing gold inflows into the United States, especially in the event of irresponsible actions by European nations.[468] If one took into account the contemporaneous reality of Mussolini's invasion of Ethiopia, the Spanish Civil War, and Hitler's remilitarization of the Rhineland, in violation of the provisions of the Versailles Treaty and the Locarno Pact of 1925, along with the bombast that accompanied each of these actions, there was a real possibility that a general European war would be ignited. World War I, bloody as it was, had not changed people's Social Darwinist ideas. War was a concomitant of that view. As with the Italian Fascists, the Nazi government in Germany encouraged the gamut of militarist gestures—uniforms, marching, flags, public mass singing.

If war came, Roosevelt concluded, European governments would take control of their citizens' American assets and proceed to sell such assets to finance their war effort. This, in turn, he believed, would lead to a removal of gold from the United States with untoward and negative effects on the American economy.[469]

(Things turned out rather differently when war erupted in 1939. The British and the French—until the French surrender in 1940—having sequestered their citizens' American assets, then used those assets to purchase American war materiel, while the Nazi regime in Germany financed its war effort largely by seizing the gold of the governments of the European nations it conquered,[470] as well as the assets of European Jews incident to murdering them in the death camps in Poland.)

Eccles told Morgenthau that he wanted the Federal Open Market Committee at its November 1936 meeting to authorize the sale of $300 to $400 million in debt holdings to offset the increase in excess bank reserves during the period from August to November 1936.[471] Eccles then modified his approach "to favor a second 50 percent increase in required reserve ratios." Morgenthau looked to his staff for an alternative. They proposed continuing to accept gold, for which the Treasury would issue gold receipts. But rather than affecting the country's bank reserves, the Treasury could pay for the gold it received by "selling debt"—that is, by selling United States bonds it held in its various fund accounts.

Should foreigners later decide to sell American securities and demand payment in gold, the Treasury Department could repurchase government bonds, feeding dollars into the banking system and the American economy, nullifying any deflationary effect from the loss of gold. Meltzer notes that the Treasury proposal had the same effect as a Federal Open Market Committee sale of Treasury bonds to private individuals, except that "the responsibility for the conduct of the operation remained with the Treasury."[472]

(As this is written, something of the same principle operates with the vast adverse trade balances currently [the first decade of the twenty-first century] incurred by the United States in favor of the People's Republic of China, amounting cumulatively to hundreds of billions of dollars. The latter requires its local banks to surrender to the Chinese government American dollars deposited by its entrepreneurs that they receive from American buyers. In exchange, Chinese domestic banks receive Chinese government local currency [RMB or yuan] bonds, while the Chinese government "sterilizes" the foreign currency by returning it to the United States through the purchase of United States government bonds that the American government issues to cover its budget deficits, resulting mostly from the costs arising from its military involvement in Afghanistan and Iraq. The term *sterilize*—as in the phrase "sterilizing gold"—is jargon, i.e., a word beloved by persons in the banking industry, and means "to neutralize the possible adverse effects of gold or money" [the latter the abstract concept that in the material world exists as gold or other metallic coins or as paper currency, e.g., dollar bills].)

Eccles was indecisive at that moment in 1936 on the question of whether the Treasury proposal could effectively avoid increasing monetary reserves, or whether it would merely shift responsibility for monetary policy from the Federal Reserve Board to the Treasury Department. Finally, Eccles wrote to Morgenthau saying the Treasury's proposal, if adopted, should work automatically; that is, the Treasury should not be left with independent discretion to modify the operation and, in effect, to determine monetary policy.[473]

Morgenthau took offense at any hint of limitation of his authority. According to Meltzer, this "led to another in the series of disputes that frequently disturbed their relationship."[474] Ultimately, the matter was referred to the president. Curiously, Eccles then agreed to Morgenthau's plan for the Treasury Department to accept the influx of foreign gold by selling government bonds owned by the Treasury's trust funds.[475] Hearing unanimity, Roosevelt directed the commencement of the Treasury Department program to accept foreign gold and sell government bonds owned by one or another of the trust funds administered by the Treasury.[476] Eccles appears to have been overwhelmed by the magnetism of Roosevelt's personality. While he argued regularly with Morgenthau, Eccles does not appear to have had the will to cross Roosevelt. (In that sense, we are a world away from Roosevelt's status a decade earlier, when Al Smith was governor of New York State and Roosevelt, then still a private citizen, was protesting Smith's condescension to him.[477])

In due course, the FOMC executive committee sat down with Morgenthau and agreed to renew its partnership with the Treasury Department to maintain the market price of Treasury.[478]

Black comments that:

> [u]nemployment had continued to decline steadily through 1936 at the average rate of about 150,000 jobs per month. It now stood at about 60 percent of the total that had greeted Roosevelt at his inauguration. The number of employed people had increased by about 6 million, from 38 to over 44 million. And the number of unemployed had declined by over 5 million in the same period, from about 13 million to about 8 million. . . . In the spring of 1936, the *New York Times* business index had risen again to 100 for the first time since 1930. Corporate America, which had run a $2 billion deficit in 1933, showed a $5 billion dollar profit in 1936. In the same period, net farm income quadrupled.[479]

Meltzer notes that in the last months of 1936, short- and long-term interest rates were at their lowest recorded levels, while both the economy and the stock market kept improving. Gold accumulations had never been greater.[480]

Morgenthau thought many bondholders believed interest rates on government bonds must soon rise. For Morgenthau, rising interest rates would increase the cost to the Treasury of financing the government's deficit. He felt the economy would suffer because less money would then be available for corporate investment. Nevertheless, he went along with what was being proposed. At the very end of the month, Morgenthau and Eccles then discussed the proposed reserve requirement increase with the president. It does not appear that Roosevelt had any great comprehension of the factors involved; it was a technical matter, and he left the decision to the members of the Federal Reserve Board.[481]

The Board's resolution on January 30, 1937, approved the increase in loan reserve requirements by 33 1/3 percent of then current limits.[482] Meltzer writes: "Neither the Federal Reserve [Board members] nor the Treasury [Morgenthau and his staff] anticipated the break in the [government] bond market on March 12 [1937]. Rates rose on March 12 and March 13, ending at 2.52 percent on March 13."[483]

Once more, Morgenthau was outraged at the collapse of his efforts to hold down interest rates on government bonds. George Harrison, longtime president of the Federal Reserve Bank of New York, and member of the Federal Open Market Committee, disagreed with him, saying government bond rates were at their lowest ebb since records had been kept. Morgenthau was so incensed, he broke off the conversation. He insisted the Federal Reserve Board and its Federal Open Market Committee proceed to make net purchases to support government bond prices. The Treasury Department had committed $75 million for this purpose in only three days. Morgenthau needed help from the Federal Reserve.

Eccles might not have entirely agreed with Morgenthau, yet he had to agree that a problem existed, which the Federal Reserve Board had gone on record to discount.

To acknowledge the seriousness with which Morgenthau viewed the situation, the members of the executive committee of the Federal Reserve Board went to Morgenthau's office. Eccles told Morgenthau the members of the committee had declined to commit themselves to stabilize the price of government bonds specifically at par (the bonds carried an interest rate of 2.5 percent). Still, they were amenable otherwise to cooperating with the Treasury Department.

Morgenthau proposed in turn to end his policy of gold sterilization with respect to the continuing inflow of gold into the country from Europe. (This would have the effect of "nullifying" the Federal Reserve Board's objective to stifle any threat of inflation.)

Threatened by Morgenthau's "end run," the FOMC's executive committee members were reduced to reminding him that his proposed action would "transfer responsibility for monetary policy to the Treasury"—in theory inconsistent with the mandate of the Banking Act of 1935.

An effort was then made to find a suitable compromise; they agreed to maintain the status quo.[484] Unfortunately, the agreement between Morgenthau and the governors of the Federal Reserve Board did not stabilize the market price of government bonds. Government bonds continued to decline on the open market. Morgenthau could foresee the cost of government borrowing increase.[485]

Roosevelt, in a conversation with Morgenthau, saw no serious problem. Government bond prices continued to fall, reaching an interest rate of 2.72 percent in the week ending March 27, 1937.[486] A week later the interest rate on government bonds reached 2.78 percent. Morgenthau was waiting impatiently for some Federal Reserve Board action. He had committed himself to Sunday, April 4, 1937, to learn what decision the FOMC would take at its meeting the preceding day. Then, the FOMC decided its executive committee should meet with Morgenthau at his home that Saturday evening.[487]

The afternoon before the meeting occurred, the president saw Eccles and Morgenthau. Hearing them out, Roosevelt suggested Morgenthau could tell the members of the FOMC executive committee that should they fail to act to fulfill the duties given them by law, Roosevelt would act himself. The meeting Saturday evening at Morgenthau's home then proceeded, ending indecisively with Morgenthau repeating the President's warning. However, the next day, the Federal Open Market Committee voted to begin purchases of government bonds—as Morgenthau and Eccles had agreed earlier.

Notwithstanding FOMC intervention that involved purchases aggregating $2.525 billion by the end of April 1937, the interest rate on government bonds reached a peak of 2.80 percent before starting to decline. Meltzer comments: "In all, rates increased 0.34 (14 percent) from the January low."[488]

The meeting at Morgenthau's home on Saturday evening, April 3, 1937, is interesting to the extent that it reveals that Morgenthau and the members of the FOMC executive committee were at cross-purposes. Morgenthau was focused on keeping government debt costs as low as possible. At the beginning of the twenty-first-century, interest rates on government bonds in the 1930s have an element of fantasy. But money as a commodity in its own right, relative to other commodities and services, had far greater value in 1937 than it does today. The author remembers spaghetti costing three cents a pound. A standard, 80-horsepower, four-door, Chevrolet automobile could be bought for $800. One could buy a used Model A Ford sedan with glass vases and artificial flowers on the post between the front and back doors for $25 in June 1937, and sell it back to the used-car dealer in September for $15. Black writes: "In 1936, 47 percent of American families made less than $1,000 per year."[489] For Morgenthau in the economic world of 1937, increases of two- or three-hundredths of a percent represented a significant, cumulative increase in the federal budget, and created a "crisis."

In a Social Darwinist world, where struggle and insecurity were viewed as a constant, inflation, uncontrolled, promised chaos—the obliteration of any value for money as a commodity. The members of the FOMC executive committee tried to focus on what they understood to be fundamental concerns. Measured against the Social Darwinist vantage point of the members of the FOMC, Morgenthau's concern with two- or even three-tenths of a percent increase in the interest rate for government bonds was minutiae in the face of a threatening chaos.

As the meeting at his home dragged on, Morgenthau finally dropped all pretense of professional courtesy and told his guests: "You people just don't want to admit that . . . you monkeyed with the carburetor and you got the mixture too thin."[490]

That rather melodramatic imagery was probably dismissed out of hand by the sober-sided gentlemen who sat in Morgenthau's living room. At that moment they were looking to avoid blame for unsettling financial markets, while their primary concern was to respond to perceived threats of inflation that promised, if once allowed to start, to be uncontainable.

Meltzer some three generations later can be mildly astonished at their lack of understanding that reducing the money supply available to the business community would cause not only an increase in the interest rates paid by borrowers (because the relative scarcity of money had made the available money more valuable), but also result in a slowdown in a business economy that depended on bank loans to finance business operations.[491] Meltzer concludes: "The policy . . . did not achieve what the Federal Reserve [Board] set out to accomplish. It not only contributed to the recession [of 1937–38] but also failed to reduce the [Federal Reserve] System's fear it could not prevent future inflation."[492]

By August 1936, the French franc was losing value. The French government in just nine months had given up 25 percent of its gold reserves. Devaluation promised a bonus to the French. With the surplus funds, the government could look forward to actually balancing its budget that fiscal year. They were ready to work out some agreement with Morgenthau. What was offered to them was a simple understanding that there would be no retaliation because of a French devaluation.[493] At the same time, the British agreed to refrain from unilateral devaluation. The French, the British, and the Americans indicated each was to seek to stabilize currency exchange rates for gold every day. The French franc and the dollar were for the moment in a more-realistic monetary relationship in line with the 1929 exchange rate.[494]

Just after the Tripartite Agreement was finalized, the pound began to fall against the dollar. The Russian State Bank had put in an order with the Chase National Bank to sell 1.2 million pounds for dollars. Morgenthau was incensed. This was a blatant attempt to subvert his agreement.[495] Afterward, on September 28, 1936, Winthrop Aldrich, president of the Chase National Bank, telephoned Morgenthau to say that the Russian order was purely a commercial dealing that had no sinister motives. The Russian State Bank needed the dollars to repay a Swedish loan that was falling due. Blum writes: "Talking later with his friend Arthur Sulzberger, the publisher of the *New York Times*, Morgenthau mentioned his 'particular satisfaction' in breaking 'this idea that there was any relationship between us and Russia.'"[496]

The financial problems encountered by the French government go far to explain the ostrich-head-in-the-sand attitude in that period by the French government toward Hitler's military reoccupation of the Rhineland in 1936, although it represented a potential military threat and was a violation of the Versailles Treaty and the Locarno Pact of 1925. The French government, facing the difficult fiscal consequences of the domestic issues upon which it was focused, did not need the additional financial headache of a general military mobilization. For France, there was also the unsatisfactory precedent of the 1920s occupation of the Ruhr Valley.

There may also have been a latent problem for Blum and his colleagues with his Jewish ethnic identification. It would not do for a government he headed to seek to restrain the anti-Semitic Nazi regime of Germany. For French conservatives in a Social Darwinist world, it would smack too much of "special pleading."

Likewise, the British government's fiscal difficulties encouraged the insular "Little England" attitudes of Conservative Prime Minister Stanley Baldwin, which put a damper on an active British response to Hitler's provocative actions. In a Social Darwinist world, "provocative" gestures were to be expected from foreign countries. The great thing was to take these in stride as mere bombast that was part of the background noise. Inaction by both Britain and France provided an excuse and a justification for the like failure of the other.

According to Blum "[T]he French began to respond to German rearmament by increasing military spending . . . By February [1937] the franc was under pressure."[497] At a Cabinet session held February 26, 1937, Ickes writes: the French "franc broke badly . . . and Henry Morgenthau reported a flight of capital from France to [the United States]."[498]

At the same cabinet session, Morgenthau, to Ickes' surprise, defended a government, public housing, slum-clearance program, saying "the government had spent a billion dollars helping out the farmers with nothing comparable" for low-income urban wage earners, and he "pointed out the building trades craftsmen had been the hardest hit of all and that they were still to a large extent unemployed."[499] The president was undecided at that moment. The matter would be resolved with the introduction in the Congress later that year and the enactment into law of what became the United States Housing Act of 1937. The federal government provided annual contributions to cover interest and amortization payments by local housing authorities (public corporations organized under state law) to pay the long-term costs incurred in building public housing projects. The reduced rents received from low-income, working tenants need be applied solely to the costs of management and maintenance.

Facing problems, the French government suggested palliative measures, including an American purchase of some $5 million to $10 million worth of French francs without conversion into gold until the end of the summer tourist season. Meltzer describes Morgenthau as "shocked" by the suggestion, as it probably would have violated the Johnson Act, adopted in 1934, which prohibited loans to foreign governments that had defaulted on their World War I debt.[500]

The pattern of ebb and flow of French fiscal crises had been established. Meltzer ascribes the difficulties of the recurrent French fiscal crises to the unrecognized misalignment of foreign exchange rates with "wholesale prices in the principal countries."[501] Finally, in June 1937, the Blum cabinet lost a vote of confidence and resigned. A new government then devalued the French franc by an additional 15 percent.[502]

Meltzer finds the Tripartite Agreement had flaws. Nevertheless, Meltzer finds political benefits accruing from the effort involved in creating the understanding between the Americans, the British, and the French. Morgenthau wanted to establish that the democratic countries could cooperate "toward a common goal," and in the process, Roosevelt lost many of his suspicions about British policies, so that he was less hesitant when it came to developing a wartime partnership with Churchill.[503]

At a Cabinet session held May 14, 1937, Ickes writes:

Under Secretary [Roswell] Magill, according to the Secretary of the Treasury, has been to New York and has made
some valuable discoveries of loopholes through which
income taxes of the rich are evaded. He said that in one
instance it was discovered that a man had incorporated
his private yacht and put into that fund enough to keep
the yacht going. Naturally no profit would show here.
The President said that in Texas he had heard of a rich oil
operator who sold his oil abroad and received payment
in a Nova Scotia bank. He draws out of the Nova Scotia
bank only enough to pay his expenses and he pays practically no income taxes. Morgenthau said that we would
be surprised when Magill brought in his report. The
President said that the names ought to be published and
Morgenthau said that the President knew most of them
personally.[504]

Ickes provides a second chapter to the tale of income tax
evaders in the 1930s: "The President was all for making the list
public, but Morgenthau was opposed, and so was Magill. The
President told me that the marriage of Franklin Jr. to Ethel du
Pont would be a happy affair because some of the du Ponts were
involved in these tax matters. He also told me that Robert R.
McCormick [a conservative Republican political opponent of
Roosevelt and the publisher of the *Chicago*] *Tribune* . . . had set
up a personal trust. The President said that some of his friends
were caught and he mentioned Vincent Astor as probably being
in the net."[505]

During the summer of 1937, Morgenthau took his family on
vacation to Hawaii. On August 4, 1937, he wrote to his father:

Everyone has been very nice to us. The President wrote a letter to Harold . . . Dillingham [and his wife]. [Dillingham was one of the "five families" who ran the Hawaiian economy in the 1930s] . . . they met us at the dock and have entertained us. They say they know you. In fact many people always ask after you and tell me stories of kind things you and Ma had done for them at one time or another.

Saturday and Sunday we sailed in the races at Pearl Harbor and it was lots of fun. . . .

[H]aving an ocean between me and Washington tends to soften everything. So many things that seemed so important at the time when one is in the midst of the fight, seem at this distance just small and unimportant. I wonder if we will ever have real peace in this world? [The latter sentence, seemingly out of nowhere, gives a fascinating glimpse into Morgenthau's very private awareness of the Social Darwinist world in which he was living, and, more specifically, what his fate might be were he living in Central Europe at that moment.]

Our family has certainly every reason to be thankful for so many reasons. I am always thankful to you for the many opportunities you gave me, and I hope that you realize that I appreciate what you have done for me.

Writing that his "family has certainly every reason to be thankful for so many reasons" suggests that Morgenthau realizes what their situation might have been were they living in Central Europe. Many times when Morgenthau speaks about truly serious concerns, he is never able to articulate the precise contours of the problem. Like any beginning Freudian analysand (one who is undergoing psychoanalysis), he only hints at what he meant. The same could be said about the prior sentence in the letter, regarding "real peace in the world."

Morgenthau was profoundly affected by the Nazi persecution of German Jews. His father had been born in Germany and probably spoke German with a better accent than English. (Henry Sr. found German useful while serving as ambassador to the Ottoman Empire,[506] and in his conversations with Pilsudski in Poland. He always retained the German pronunciation of the last syllable of the family name as "tow" rather than his children's "thaw.") Morgenthau himself could be described as a second-generation American, although it was his grandfather who had brought his family to the United States. He was still bilingual, and quite familiar with a German-speaking environment with his family of origin. In a Social Darwinist world, overwhelmingly Gentile, he was limited in how he could voice his concern about the deteriorating situation for German Jews in Nazi Germany.

As a government official, Morgenthau was circumscribed in what he could do without compromising the administration and, more particularly, the president, whom he served and to whom he owed an unconditional obligation of loyalty, aside from any personal bond between them. If he attempted to express his concern about Nazi persecution, he ran the real risk in a Gentile world that he would be dismissed with the phrase *special pleading*. He was left with one more private anxiety over which he could only agonize in silence. The one gesture left to him was a charitable donation. Blum writes: "Long before the [Second World] war, [Morgenthau was] a regular and generous contributor to the American Jewish Joint Distribution Committee, whose agents were working for the removal of Jews from Germany to the United States and other havens."[507]

To return to Morgenthau's family vacation in Hawaii—by letter dated August 14, 1937, still at the Royal Hawaiian Hotel, Morgenthau writes to his father:

We were delighted to receive your letter and learn that you are having such a good summer. I know you are a good housekeeper from my stay at Constantinople.

We have just returned from a week's visit to the island of Hawaii. At the Volcano House we ran into a great admirer of yours, George Lycurgus, a Greek who runs the Hotel there. He gave us a swell party and would not let us pay for a thing, all thanks to you. He says the Greeks will never forget what you did for them.

This place certainly offers a lot for everybody. The children are having a grand time. Lots of young people their own age. Henry 3d is getting so he likes golf and plays every day. The Arthur Murray Dance Studio has just sent four teachers here and all of my children are taking lessons.

Joan went out to a dance at night with a beau, for the first time.

I really have relaxed for the first time. Monday I am calling Washington for the first time as I want to get the feel of the bond market. We do our next financing on the day after Labor Day. I only expect to get back to Washington Sept. 4th, so I will have very little time to get ready.

The situation in Japan and China certainly looks black. One gets very little idea from read[in]g the papers what is really going on there. I do hope Congress will be out of the way before Labor Day. It would help my financing a lot to have Congress go home.

Well, here is hoping that you and Ma continue to have a good summer.

Best wishes from your devoted son,
Henry

Morgenthau has occasion to write once more from Hawaii. This time the date is August 22, 1937, and the letter is addressed to both of his parents:

Dear Pa & Ma:

Your nice letters of Aug, 10th & 11th arrived by Clipper [Pan American Airways seaplane] on Aug. 20th. The Clipper left one day late for some reason.

Your friend Crommwell [?] invited us for dinner last Sunday night but we could not go. I suppose he asked us on account of knowing you.

I suppose by the time this letter reaches you, Ma will be back. What made you [and] Ma come home so much earlier than you intended? I hope you are feeling well.

The 75th Congress is come and gone and we now have time to sit back and see what, if anything, has been accomplished in the eight months [the Congress was in session]. It is certainly a break for me to have it out of the way. I would have to have been thrown into that mess on my return. We will be able to go on with our financing in an orderly way knowing fairly well how large the Federal bill will be. I have just learned how they rushed through a sixty million [dollar] appropriation to pay the cotton farmers a bonus. I think it one of the worst steals I have ever seen. Ten cents a pound for cotton is good money, but it does not taste so sweet when they have been receiving 13 [cents].

If I was on the American continent I would be rushing back to Washington to try and get the President to veto the cotton appropriation bill, but at this distance I can't do much but go on a nice drive with Elinor and forget about it.

Ickes writes that the subject of "possible immigrants from Austria and perhaps from other European countries" came up at a cabinet session after Hitler's seizure of Austria early in 1937. The president was sympathetic to the idea that political refugees should be allowed to come into the country without reference to permanent residence. Ickes could say it would be "a fine gesture,"[508] making reference to "a fine class of citizens, similar to the type we got after the abortive revolution of 1848 [in Germany]." To which Vice President Garner responded: If left to a secret vote of the Congress, "all immigration would be stopped." Ickes might be appalled (and Morgenthau privately horrified), but there the matter ended.[509] There was a strong isolationist sentiment in the United States at this time; America wanted nothing to do with the problems of the outside world.

In November 1938, after the Munich Pact had dismembered Czechoslovakia, Morgenthau could confess his apprehension to Ickes about the future, "not only in Europe but in South America."[510]

At a Cabinet meeting held on March 10, 1939, Roosevelt brought up the matter of German continued "dumping" of exports (i.e., giving government subsidies to exporters to reduce the wholesale price of German-manufactured goods sold in the United States). Ickes writes that the State Department had kept urging Morgenthau to defer the application of the provisions of the Smoot-Hawley Tariff Act, which required punitive tariffs be attached to the German-made products. The president remarked that the provisions of the law were "mandatory" and left no discretion to Morgenthau, who could go to jail "for failing to carry out this law." Neither Morgenthau nor the president was ready to ignore the law any longer. The president requested Frank Murphy, then the attorney general, to prepare a legal opinion within two weeks, and for Sumner

Welles to inform the German chargé d'affaires that the American government lacked the legal authority to defer penalties.

It was decided that Morgenthau would proceed to act upon receipt of the legal opinion. Ickes writes that Morgenthau sent him a note across the table that read: "Dear Harold: Two weeks from Monday I think they will hang my picture next to yours in Germany. I will consider it a compliment."[511] In this way, Morgenthau showed his gratitude to Ickes. Ickes, more than anyone else among Cabinet members, was unceasing in his principled stand against the acceptance of Nazi government actions—on this occasion, that meant one more instance of the latter's carrying the amorality of Social Darwinist objectives to an unacceptable degree. Roosevelt and Ickes, as Gentiles, could object, where in Morgenthau's case, he had the deep-seated suspicion it would take on the character of special pleading.

With respect to the economic picture of the United States at that time, Black comments:

> Throughout the autumn [of 1937] there were disturbing evidences of an economic downturn [in the United States]. Roosevelt in his electoral enthusiasm had represented and believed that the Depression was in inexorable retreat and that the recovery was now self-sustaining.[512] The result was a roll-back of the Federal relief system that resulted in tens of thousands of relief recipients going without emergency food and clothing.[513]
>
> Unemployment had descended by late spring [of 1937] to about 12 percent, barely a third of the March 1933 percentage, and only about 4 percent when the Hopkins and Ickes job-creation programs are taken into account. But unemployment started to jump in startling increments later in 1937. Although consumer and commodity prices held up well, business activity indices fell by about a

third from 1937 to 1938. Where in the spring of 1937 the country had pulled ahead of 1929 output levels, the *New York Times* Weekly Business Index plunged from 110 in August [1937] to 85 in December [1937] . . .

By then, March 1938, the ranks of the unemployed, which . . . had got down to about 6 million (2 million if the emergency relief workers are counted as employed persons) from a high of around 13 million in early 1933, had ballooned to about 10 million (6 million if the public works employees are deducted).[514]

Morgenthau discounted the role the Treasury Department itself played in contributing to the recession of 1937–38 by its program of sterilizing gold inflows from Europe as the Federal Reserve Board was increasing its requirements for loan reserves by member banks.[515] Morgenthau threatened to reverse the policy of sterilizing the inflow of gold, but he was using the threat merely as a ploy to induce the Federal Reserve Board and its Open Market Committee to reinstate its participation in the Treasury-support program for government bond price stability. No thought was given by Morgenthau to an independent program allowing the gold inflows to infect the banking system by creating inflationary pressures to staunch the incipient recession. In this, he may only have been following Roosevelt's lead, but there is no evidence the Treasury Department economists were aware of or considered the consequences of the Federal Reserve Board's contractive policy decision for several months.

Meltzer also ascribes two other contractive and reductive considerations as causes contributing to the recession of 1937–38—aside from the action of the Federal Reserve Board to increase its requirements for member banks' loan reserve ratios. These were "the reduction of [World War I veterans'] bonus *payments* [by the end of 1936] and the passage of the undistributed profits taxes." Veterans' bonus bonds, aggregating $1.7 billion, were authorized (over the President's veto) and issued in the summer of 1936.[516] "By December [1936] veterans had cashed $1.4 billion of the bonds and spent the money." That temporary influx of money into the nation's economy had disappeared in 1937.[517]

The role of the undistributed profits tax was more psychological in nature. Meltzer explains: "The tax was based on the peculiar belief that corporations held funds idle instead of investing them. If these funds, like the excess reserves of banks, could be put to work, the economy would expand faster. The Treasury expected the tax to raise $620 million, about 5 percent of the prospective deficit."[518] That expectation was never realized and the tax was repealed after a relatively short existence on the statute books.

Meltzer reports that "[t]he National Bureau of Economic Research ranks the 1937–38 recession as the third most severe in the years after World War I." He assesses "[t]he two more severe recessions [to be] 1929–33 and 1920–21."[519]

In November 1937, Morgenthau first suggested ending the gold sterilization program. Eccles (whom Roosevelt apparently consulted on the matter) objected because he thought "Roosevelt might grab the idea as a panacea for solving all economic problems. He considered excess [bank] reserves plentiful and contended that neither desterilization nor loosening of reserve requirements would actually ease credit."[520] Morgenthau persevered, having now recognized the severity of the recession.

On Saturday night, December 11, 1937, the Washington newspapermen held their annual Gridiron Dinner. Morgenthau was the subject of one of the skits. Ickes writes: "[I]t was rougher, in my opinion, than good taste or fair play could justify . . . They had Morgenthau and Oliphant, his Chief Counsel, before them for a discussion of the tax situation. One or the other of them would ask a question directed to 'Mr. Secretary.' Morgenthau would stand dumb while Oliphant would give the answer and then Morgenthau would repeat word for word what Oliphant had already said, with occasional promptings from Oliphant . . .

"Henry Morgenthau . . . had been cut pretty deeply. I can sympathize with his feelings. This was going altogether too far. After all, Morgenthau is a member of the Cabinet and no one can doubt his sincerity or his loyalty. He is doing the best that he knows how and such lampooning as he had to submit to last night is altogether unjustified as I see it."[521]

Ickes' insertion under the date of Sunday, December 12, 1937, also includes a summary of an off-the-record meeting he had on the preceding Saturday morning with correspondents from the liberal news magazines *The Nation* and the *New Republic*. The reporters were interested in Nathan Strauss Jr.'s experience as head of the semiautonomous public housing unit in the Department of the Interior.[522] As Ickes made clear in earlier entries, he had no great regard for Strauss's abilities, and thought of him as a political dilettante whose appointment had been imposed on Ickes against his better judgment. Ickes reports that Morgenthau had spoken to Jonathan Mitchell, the correspondent of the *New Republic*, to suggest to Ickes that he get together with Morgenthau to actively assist Strauss to "prevent a failure." Elinor Morgenthau's uncle, Irving Lehman, a member of New York State's highest court (and who would shortly become its chief judge), was married to Nathan Strauss Jr.'s sister, Sissie.[523] The Morgenthaus and the Irving Lehmans were on cordial terms with each other, so it's not strange that Morgenthau would be approached and would seek to intercede to help someone (who was a quasi-relative) to find his bearings in the federal bureaucracy. Since Ickes had made up his mind to leave Strauss to his fate, Morgenthau's initiative came to nothing (although

Morgenthau himself may have given Strauss private and unofficial advice). Strauss's tenure involved no noticeable incompetence or scandal.[524]

Henry III recounts an event which conveys some sense of the social relationship and friendship that the Morgenthaus enjoyed with Franklin and Eleanor Roosevelt. Henry III writes that on New Year's Eve, 1938, he and his brother Robert escorted their "dates," Mrs. Roosevelt's niece Eleanor and a local post-debutante, Eleanor Flood, to the White House, "to join our parents before midnight to see the old year out." At the main entrance, they were questioned "by a Secret Service guard much more closely than [Henry III could] recall on similar occasions." They were then allowed to proceed to the Roosevelt family quarters upstairs where they were met by their father in a state of high agitation. It turned out that earlier that evening some teenagers on a dare had gone to the White House to get the autographs of the president and Mrs. Roosevelt. Confused with the Morgenthau sons, the teenagers were allowed by the Secret Service guard on duty to enter and were ushered into the Roosevelts' presence.[525]

Morgenthau met with Roosevelt on February 8, 1938, to speak about the economic picture. Although Morgenthau retained his dislike of deficit spending, he was now more upset over the effects of the recession that the United States was suffering. He proposed an additional $250 million appropriation to allow increased Works Progress Administration (WPA) employment for 650,000 men in the remaining months of the fiscal year.[526] Since in his view, "falling prices encouraged delays in private spending," he wanted to do away with further gold sterilization. Roosevelt agreed to what Morgenthau was proposing.[527] Meltzer comments, "Morgenthau's diary explains that Morgenthau ended [gold] sterilization, in part, to prevent more government spending." If nothing was done, they "would get a transcontinental highway or $8 billion of extraordinary expenses."[528] (The reader will remember that a generation later Dwight Eisenhower, when president, proposed just such a highway system as a defense measure.)

While Eccles and the Federal Reserve Board went along reluctantly with abandonment of the gold sterilization program, they did not go so far as to reduce their bank loan reserve ratio requirements or to increase the purchase by the FOMC of outstanding debt for its open market account.[529] Nevertheless, by early March Eccles had given Roosevelt a written statement "warning of 'a severe depression' and urged the President to 'provide the democratic leadership that will make our system function.'"[530]

The stock market suffered a sharp loss on March 25, 1938, and in April 1938 the administration took further steps to encourage an increase in economic activity. Those whom Meltzer describes as "the proponents of spending within the administration" argued that the national economy required more spending, as did the Democratic Party. Roosevelt announced at a cabinet meeting held on April 4, 1938: "The situation was bad not only for the country but also for the Democratic Party, which might lose the fall election if conditions continued as they were."[531]

On April 11, 1938, Roosevelt had had a meeting with congressional leaders at which Morgenthau sat on the administration side of the table. Black notes that Roosevelt announced details of a proposed supplementary budget amounting to $1.55 billion to cover expenditures by the WPA, CCC, and Morgenthau's old agency, the Farm Security Administration. Much of the supplementary budget expenditures could be expected to intrude into the fiscal year 1939 deficit.

Morgenthau understood perfectly that his role was purely ornamental and his presence was limited to providing psychological support to the president. Still, he felt compelled to announce that the supplementary costs would increase the 1939 fiscal year deficit to $3.5 billion. It was a breach of the etiquette expected of subordinate figures on the executive branch's side of the table. Roosevelt was irritated, and after the meeting ended, Roosevelt told Morgenthau he had been "mischievous and obstructionist." Morgenthau apparently realized that he'd misspoken, and responded, "No use yelling at me."[532]

As if to do penance for speaking out of turn, Morgenthau came up with a new package of proposals at a White House staff meeting the next day. Roosevelt figuratively patted him on the head by commending him on his "ingenuity," and proposed to add his list of suggestions to those already being considered.[533] Morgenthau, wounded, concluded it was time for him to leave the scene with good grace. On April 13, 1938, Morgenthau offered his resignation to the president, who would appear to have been taken aback. Contrary to what Morgenthau had come to think, Roosevelt continued to regard him as a valued player on his presidential team, and the president sought to reassure him. Roosevelt spoke to Morgenthau of "his 'grand' performance," asked him to rise above "pique," and not to "quit under fire." The president told him he would not accept the proffered resignation. By the end of the day Morgenthau had calmed down to the point where he withdrew his resignation.[534]

Shortly thereafter Roosevelt announced his decision on April 18, 1938. It included increased expenditures for construction and public assistance that added roughly $2 billion to the federal budget for that fiscal year. The Treasury Department then desterilized some $1.4 billion of gold—all that remained of the gold inflow since December 1936.[535]

The Federal Open Market Committee at its earlier meeting on September 11, 1937, had concluded that "while the [Federal Reserve] System could act alone . . . the most desirable action would be the suggested joint action."[536] Now, the Federal Reserve Board fell into line with the President and reduced loan reserve ratio requirements for member banks, doing away with its May 1, 1937, increases.[537]

Meltzer notes the "president's announcement of the new program sparked a rally in the Treasury [bond] market."[538] Yields on long-term bonds dropped from 2.62 percent in April 1938 to 2.56 percent in May and June 1938.[539] Morgenthau could take a large satisfaction in the decline in the interest rates, even if secured at the cost of increased federal debt. Meltzer concludes: "Desterilization [of gold] and the reduction in reserve requirements appear to dominate any effect of a larger deficit; the market viewed the monetary ease as more than sufficient to absorb any additional debt resulting from the deficit or increased private spending and borrowing."[540]

Midsummer 1938, Morgenthau and his family started their August vacation schedule by boarding the Holland-American liner, *Statendam*. On their way to the French Riviera, they first stopped in Paris.[541] American ambassador William Bullitt invited them for Sunday lunch at his country retreat at Chantilly so that Morgenthau could satisfy his desire to meet Léon Blum, the former Popular Front premier[542] whose efforts Morgenthau had supported in connection with the Tripartite Agreement. Part of Morgenthau's curiosity with Blum's personality would appear to be the fact that while he shared upper bourgeois status and Jewish antecedents with Morgenthau (and, for that matter, with novelist Marcel Proust through the latter's mother), Blum also had a magnetic personality and strong political instincts, like Roosevelt—a combination that seemed to fascinate Morgenthau. In a few short years, Morgenthau would read in the newspapers that Blum, charged with treason, was fighting for his life in a criminal trial concocted by Pierre Laval, Blum's former fellow parliamentarian, who was the French premier during the Vichy government interlude after the French military defeat in 1940.

Henry III reports that after Ambassador Bullitt's Sunday luncheon, "the minister of national economy, Patenôtre, was selected to give [Morgenthau] a lavish official dinner to which the family was invited." After the dinner was over, Mme. Patenôtre and her sister invited Henry III and his younger brother Robert to "go out on the town." Parental acquiescence was given without enthusiasm. When the young men arrived back at the American embassy (where they were staying), they found their parents, like the good bourgeois they were, anxiously waiting up for them to return from their escapade with older women who were moreover French sophisticates.[543]

Morgenthau wrote by letter dated August 2, 1938, from Antibes on the Riviera, that they had a "perfect crossing" on the *Statendam*, and that "she was just as nice a ship as Ma said she was." He found Antibes "very beautiful," with every comfort and pleasure at their disposal. He reports that his family was leading a "very lazy existence and swim[ming] and sleep[ing] a lot. Of course the food is the best." He goes on to say that he is not worrying about anything and his office has not bothered him. He regards the last as "a good sign."

He admits to a cloud overhead: "I get a great many letters for appeal from [German Jewish] refugees but can not nothing [sic] to help the poor things." The incoherent sentence structure would appear to reflect an inner turmoil and anguish. Some months later the Hamburg-Amerika liner *St. Louis* sailed from Hamburg, Germany, in mid-May, 1939, bound for Havana. On board were some 930 German-Jewish passengers with Cuban entry visas that the president of Cuba, Laredo Bru, had invalidated shortly before the ship was due to sail. Near Havana, Cuban authorities duly informed the ship's captain, Gustav Schroeder, of the visas' invalidity. Schroeder did his best for the passengers. The American charity, the Joint Distribution Committee, upon learning that a more-expensive visa could be obtained that would allow the passengers to land, provided the money. Tragically, the JDC's representative in Havana bungled his interview with Bru, who revoked his offer to provide the more-expensive, acceptable Cuban visas. Schroeder was then required to quit Cuban waters.

At that point Morgenthau tried to get Secretary of State Cordell Hull and Undersecretary Sumner Welles to allow the passengers to land in the United States Virgin Islands. Hull determined Morgenthau's suggestion would be in violation of existing law and would need an act of Congress to be allowed. Black writes: "Morgenthau had the *St. Louis* shadowed by a Coast Guard cutter, not as was alleged at the time, to keep the ship's passengers out of the United States, but to be sure of the ship's whereabouts in the event of a breakthrough on admission of its passengers." Unfortunately, there was no breakthrough in the Western Hemisphere, and so the ship returned to Europe, where the Belgian government gave an asylum that proved illusory with the Wehrmacht attack and German occupation less than a year later. Many of the passengers were later seized and deported, eventually perishing in the gas chambers at Auschwitz.[544]

Black then allows himself the rare occasion to make an adverse comment about Roosevelt, although his volume is otherwise a paean to Roosevelt's sagacity and brilliance: "It is hard to understand why Roosevelt did not simply muscle the Cuban president on the issue. Even if his lack of enthusiasm for admitting the *St. Louis*'s passengers to the United States could be understood (with difficulty), he could surely have insisted that Berenson [the JDC representative in Cuba] pay up and Bru admit those who embarked for Cuba in good faith in Hamburg, visas at hand. It must also be said that in the circumstances, the onus was on the JDC to sort it out with the Cuban government when it had the opportunity to do so. The whole episode is a rending human tragedy that reflects no credit on anyone except Captain Schoeder."[545]

The year 1939 was a period when the American economy was well into recovery. Meltzer writes: "By early 1939, real GNP rose above its pre-recession [1937] peak, with prices slowly falling. Falling prices and economic recovery, plus the threat of a European war, increased the gold flow from $113 million in the first half of 1938 to $1.3 billion in the second half. More than $3 billion followed in 1939."[546] In the fall of 1939, as the national economy recovered, long-term Treasury bond interest rates started to increase. The Treasury Department, assisted by the Federal Open Market Committee, bought government securities to bring down the interest rate, although the sense of urgency to do so seemed to wane in the autumn of 1938 after the Munich crisis (that ended with the dismemberment of Czechoslovakia).[547]

Once more disagreement erupted between the Federal Open Market Committee and Morgenthau. The FOMC would have liked the Treasury Department to increase the quantity of its weekly Treasury bill auction. The FOMC theory was that an increase in the supply of short-term Treasury bills would give rise to the idea of a tendency toward a more-unrestricted printing of "greenbacks," which, in turn, would suggest an inflationary policy, causing bidders to ask for a higher interest rate to cover the risk of inflation. The FOMC was concerned with both increasing its income (to pay the costs of the Federal Reserve System's operation), and, at the same time, reducing the risk that long-term securities entailed, namely, that future inflation could erode the real value of its portfolio by locking in fixed interest rates.

Morgenthau's objective was to keep the government's interest costs on its outstanding debt as low as possible, so he declined to go along with that FOMC request.

In February 1940, Morgenthau spent a short vacation near Tucson, Arizona, at the home of his old friend, Harold Hochschild.

He knew Hochschild from their Eagle's Nest summer vacation days when they were both growing up. Hochschild was now the president of the American Metals Climax Corporation. (Hochschild would invite Morgenthau again a year later to vacation with him.[548]) Morgenthau writes to his parents by letter dated February 18, 1940:

> I have had a very pleasant time here . . . I have kept off the telephone all but twice and don't even listen to the radio. The Finns certainly seem to be up against an impossible situation. Once the Russians break through to the Atlantic we will curse ourselves for not having given the Finns some real help. [Morgenthau was no misty-eyed "fellow traveler," and could regard the Soviet Union as a potential enemy of the United States.] The cost of one new battleship given <u>now</u> [underlining in original] to the Finns would be the best investment we could make.
>
> When I am away like this for a short vacation, I realize how damn lucky our family is an[d] how much we have to be thankful [for]; you certainly gave us a wonderful start, and I for one appreciate it. I will telephone you when I get back to Washington.

The letter was written after the German invasion of Poland on September 1, 1939, and the division of that country between the Germans and Soviet Russia. Concerned with the effect of a European war on the government bond market, the Treasury Department called upon the Federal Reserve Board to enunciate a policy to deal with possible bond market "disorder." The executive committee of the FOMC "agreed to share purchases [of government bonds] equally with the Treasury until the Treasury had invested all of the balances in the [Treasury's] trust accounts, approximately $100 million. After that, the [Federal Reserve]

System would purchase on its own up to $500 million. [This would represent] a 20 percent increase in its portfolio." Eccles explained that should the Treasury continue to buy government bonds beyond the $100 million figure, the money must come from its Exchange Stabilization Fund. This would result in a sizable Treasury open market portfolio of government bonds and that would be "undesirable" from the FOMC executive committee's point of view. They preferred to be the sole government agency holding sizable quantities of government bonds.[549]

Bureau of the Census figures for the fall of 1940 show about 5.5 million persons still unemployed, or 11 percent of the workforce. If one separates out those holding relief-project jobs, the unemployed numbered 3 million, or under 6 percent of the workforce. Conscription—the drafting of young men into the armed forces of the United States—was in the process of being enacted into law during those months, and it would have the effect of further reducing the ranks of the unemployed.[550]

During the year 1940, the president sent messages to the Congress requesting successive, increasing military appropriations aggregating billions of dollars: $1.84 billion on January 4, $5 billion on July 10, and $9 billion on October 8, because of the continuous victories of the Wehrmacht, conquering Denmark, Norway, Holland, Belgium, and finally, proud France, with only Britain left to fight on alone. There was increasing alarm that in a world at war, hostilities could spread to the shores of the United States; the country needed to be prepared for any eventuality—notwithstanding a substantial and vocal isolationist sentiment that sought to argue Germany represented no threat to the United States.[551]

Although Morgenthau recognized that at all times he was there to implement policy as Roosevelt might declare it, he was nevertheless able to act as a "minister without portfolio" and a troubleshooter. An example was his reaction to the Nazi invasion of Holland, Belgium, and Luxembourg on May 10, 1940, which began with the destructive bombing of the Dutch port of Rotterdam and the airborne capture of the seemingly impregnable Belgian fortress at Liège.

The message Roosevelt sent to Congress on January 4, 1940, was intended "to support the Army's program for expansion."[552] Still, it seemed to Morgenthau, after the events on May 10, that a comprehensive picture of the nation's military needs was not being given to Congress by the War Department. In ordinary circumstances, Morgenthau had vehemently objected to the Interior Department putting its nose into matters within the ambit of Treasury authority (as in the case of the construction of a post office building in New York City involving a supply company owned by Postmaster General James Farley). But these were no longer "ordinary times." Morgenthau regarded the Wehrmacht invasion of adjacent, neutral countries as a threat ultimately to the security of the United States. It was imperative for the United States to respond quickly to the dangers the German action portended. For Morgenthau the feud between the secretary of war, Harry Woodring, and his immediate subordinate, Assistant Secretary Louis Johnson, prevented the War Department from acting with the necessary dispatch. (Black describes them as being "at each other's throats."[553])

The first step to take was to speak to General Marshall to secure a comprehensive understanding of the army's real needs for the creation of an exponential expansion of the nation's armed forces. Morgenthau asked General Marshall to see him on May 11, 1940, and Marshall complied, deferring to the civilian government supremacy over the military. Morgenthau started by apologizing for his ignorance of military logistical problems and asked for Marshall's patience. Marshall then explained that the army "needed funds for mechanization, for paying troops, for their travel, subsistence, shelter, clothing, medical facilities, and signal equipment. It needed modern machinery, indeed even shovels, to build barracks . . . rifles, field guns, anti-aircraft guns, ammunition, training planes, fighting planes and bombers." Marshall added that there would be greater needs in the future. It was important for Congress to understand the difference between the needs necessary for total mobilization—a possible future contingency—and the current needs to equip a new citizen army. Morgenthau urged Marshall to make that distinction very clearly to the president. Morgenthau then suggested to his guest that he was the administration's best witness before the Congress.[554]

Alone, Morgenthau called "Pa" Watson, the president's military aide, who arranged for an appointment with Roosevelt on May 13, 1940. Present besides Morgenthau were Marshall, Woodring, Johnson, and Budget Director Harold Smith. Morgenthau wrote in his diary, "At first, the President was entirely opposed to Marshall's program, and when I put up a strong argument for it, he said, with a sort of smile and sneer, 'I am not asking you. I am telling you.' And my reply was, 'Well, I still think you are wrong.' He said, 'Well, you filed your protest.'" Continuing to play with fire, at the end of the meeting Morgenthau also suggested that Marshall testify before the Congress, to which Roosevelt responded, "I am going to have a message. Don't go up and tell them anything."[555]

Morgenthau came dangerously close to outright insubordination. Still, if we are to accept that Roosevelt had long recognized the need to contain Nazi aggression, he could not disagree with Morgenthau. So he expressed his irritation but accepted the memorandum Marshall had prepared. Morgenthau in his diary rationalizes the unpleasantness he experienced by saying that Roosevelt was caught unawares, and he flared out at the messenger. In due course, Roosevelt sent a message to Congress that embodied almost everything recommended to him at the meeting held on May 13, 1940, adding, "I ask the Congress not to take any action which would in any way hamper or delay the delivery of American-made planes to foreign nations which have ordered them, or to seek to purchase more planes. That, from the point of view of our national defense, would be extremely shortsighted."[556] His *envoi* was, "I should like to see this nation geared up to the ability to turn out at least 50,000 planes a year."[557]

Morgenthau tells of an extraordinary accolade he received upon leaving the president's office: "[F]irst Woodring and then Johnson said would I please call them together. So did Harold Smith. Johnson then saddled [sic] up to me and said, 'You had better do this, because after all you are really the assistant President,' and I vehemently told him if he wanted to ruin my usefulness all he had to do was to say it out loud."[558]

The increasing federal appropriations for defense spending created demands for more workers during 1940 that increased exponentially until these job openings measured in the hundreds of thousands of newly employed workers each month. Those continuous demands for more new workers in industry were wiping out the remaining vestiges of unemployment in the United States.[559]

As 1940 ended, the gold inflow into the United States continued. The Treasury Department was holding 80 percent of the world's gold supply. Continued unabated, the United States might have ended up with 100 percent of the world's gold supply. This did not happen (although the gold possession of the United States was sufficient for the American dollar to displace the British pound as the world's reserve currency by the end of World War II). Leaving aside Soviet gold holdings and British government gold assets, the remaining official gold holdings of the occupied nations of Europe were deposited in the vaults of the Federal Reserve Bank of New York.

British monetary reserves were starting to scrape the bottom of the barrel. Britain had already purchased large quantities of military supplies in the United States, using some $2.5 billion derived from sequestering its citizens' holdings of gold and American stock shares and other securities. Roosevelt was faced with a large Social Darwinist, isolationist sentiment in the country, which wanted to have nothing to do with European problems. At that point in time, this meant the plight of the British, who were standing virtually alone against the might of the Wehrmacht, which had overrun a vast part of the European continent.

In March 1941 Roosevelt secured the adoption by the American Congress of the Lend-Lease Act (HR 1776), which allowed for military supplies to be "lent" to the British without the need for payment "on the barrelhead." To assist the passage of the legislation, Morgenthau said he would make sure that the British sold every last American asset they possessed before they could get the benefits of lend-lease.[560]

Black writes: "Morgenthau . . . had been concerned that his testimony [on January 15, 1941, before the House Foreign Relations Committee] would be discounted as emanating from a Jew preoccupied with Nazi anti-Semitism." He "revealed the figures the British Treasury had given him to justify waiving the long-standing cash-and-carry rules in the sale of armaments to belligerents . . . [Secretary of State Cordell] Hull was opposed to Morgenthau's revealing so much of Britain's needful condition for fear it would give comfort to Britain's enemies. Morgenthau emphasized that never before had the government of one country authorized such a revelation of its accounts in the legislature of another country. He was quite effective in defending the financial implications of the proposed arrangements."[561] Meltzer writes: "Lend-lease substituted United States government debt for gold as payment for war material."[562]

CHAPTER 7

The War Years and Beyond

Morgenthau and his family were eating lunch at a "posh" New York City restaurant, Voisins, on December 7, 1941. They had come to the city to attend a special radio broadcast of a concert conducted by Arturo Toscanini with the NBC Symphony Orchestra, to promote the sale of Defense Savings Bonds.[563] (The National Broadcasting Company employed the symphony orchestra to meet the Federal Communications Commission's public service requirement in those years to justify its radio band licenses.)

The reference to the sale of Defense Savings Bonds merits some elaboration. Anticipating the entrance of the United States into a war economy, the president's successive messages to the Congress in 1940—requesting multibillion-dollar appropriations for defense expenditures—promised growing budget deficits. Morgenthau understood that this would result in mind-boggling debt for the country[564] that had to be financed by federal government borrowing. Meltzer notes that the deficit resulted "despite the larger share of [income] taxes and faster share [i.e., increase] of base money."[565] While the public bought Defense Savings Bonds, the largest part of the federal government debt would be financed by the Federal Open Market Committee's purchases of government bonds on behalf of the Federal Reserve System, i.e., the government central bank.[566]

After the Morgenthaus had finished their meal and returned to their limousine, the chauffeur told them he'd heard a report on the radio of the Japanese air attack on the naval ships at Pearl Harbor in the Hawaiian Islands.[567] This is where Morgenthau, on vacation, had sailed in boat races four years earlier. At their hotel was a telephone message from the White House. Responding to the president's call, Morgenthau told him he would fly back to Washington at once. In response to Morgenthau's grim tone of voice, Roosevelt "quipped cheerfully, 'Be careful you don't get shot down, Henry.'"[568]

The Treasury Building is adjacent to the grounds of the White House, and from Morgenthau's office on December 8, 1941, it was possible to see the flashbulbs going off in the Oval Office, signaling that the president was signing the declaration of war against Japan.[569] Speaking of his father at that point in his life, Morgenthau's older son described him as a "grim observer of the puritanical code that the Roosevelts in their personal conduct found so easy to abridge, [while Morgenthau] sternly adhered to the straight and narrow path."[570] In a Social Darwinist world, the Roosevelts were part of the WASP Ascendancy, and thus had a margin for error that Morgenthau was denied. As an outsider, Morgenthau had no birthright inclusion in the world in which he found himself. He had to try harder to prove he could belong, and no matter how hard he might try, there were always those who would cast him into outer darkness. As a Jew, Morgenthau was a member of a group presumed guilty until individually proven innocent.

Later in the same week declarations of war issued from the Congress against Germany and Italy—after Hitler and Mussolini quixotically honored their treaty obligations with Japan, and, as the expression of what proved to be a Social Darwinist death wish, declared war against the United States.[571]

Disputes between Morgenthau and the Federal Reserve Board ceased. The governors of the Federal Reserve Board patriotically recognized that the war effort was the unquestioned responsibility of the executive branch of the government. The Federal Reserve Board issued a public statement "that it was 'prepared to use its powers to assure that an ample supply of funds is available at all times for financing the war effort and maintaining conditions in the United States Government security market that are satisfactory from the standpoint of the Government's requirements.'"[572]

When long-term Treasury bond interest rates increased in December 1940, from 1.88 percent to 1.97 percent, Morgenthau had cast responsibility onto Eccles. Morgenthau concluded that the interest increase was "unwarranted."[573] Still, long-term Treasury bond interest rates remained between 1.9 percent and 2.0 percent.[574] Morgenthau was able to maintain his goal of low interest rates on long-term government bonds.

Wartime conditions did not curb Marriner Eccles's appetite for commenting on policy matters to Roosevelt, who would appear to have remained receptive to Eccles's visits. Eccles "strongly urged higher taxes and interest rates to finance defense and wartime spending." By the same token, Morgenthau took an opposite position, favoring lower interest rates on government securities. Eccles advocated smaller deficits and higher taxes, while Morgenthau, the former proponent of balancing the federal budget, now urged deficits as an inexpensive means of carrying defense and wartime costs—keeping interest rates low. (Congress turned out to have its own ideas on the extent of taxation.)[575]

It does not appear that prior to the emergence of the war economy in the United States, Roosevelt ever came up with a satisfactory answer to the problem of unemployment other than the Works Progress Administration (WPA) and the Public Works Administration (PWA). Morgenthau thought "the best way to stimulate building was to knock down building costs"—that meant the most directly controlling variable in the construction equation: labor costs incurred for carpenters, masons, plumbers, electricians, plasterers, roofers. Meltzer writes that for a change, Eccles agreed.[576] (Morgenthau, although he may not have considered it, was taking a very conservative position. It is no wonder that a conservative banker was in agreement.)

Selective service—the induction of millions of young men into the armed forces of the United States—and the need for manpower in defense plants would finally solve the persistent and seemingly unsolvable problem of wide-scale unemployment. Yet, as late as the year 1940, more than 8 million persons, aggregating some 14.6 percent of the population, remained unemployed. Meltzer writes that while the labor force increased by 7 million persons by 1940, the actual number of employed individuals was no greater than in 1929. The country had not been able to integrate the numbers of new entrants looking for work into the business economy. Morgenthau recognized the problem. One possible explanation is that business executives took some time before they accepted the reality that market demand for goods and services was not a momentary blip in an otherwise sluggish economic picture. During that lag in time such executives continued to rely on overtime by their existing workforce rather than hiring new workers—until the point was reached when they finally recognized they were falling too far behind in producing sufficient quantities of their products to fill accumulating orders.[577]

Despite "the mutual antipathy between Eccles and Morgenthau, the Treasury [Department] usually led and the Federal Reserve [Board] followed."[578] Meltzer attributes this to Morgenthau's access to his Exchange Stabilization Fund to which most of the profit from the devaluation of the dollar had gone. (The Treasury Department's windfall resulted from the vast amount of gold stored at Fort Knox in Kentucky. Increasing the dollar price of gold had the consequence of reducing the gold content of the dollar, thereby making the metal more valuable in terms of its dollar equivalent. The Treasury Department's accounting ledgers recorded a dollar increase in the value of the major commodity it held: gold.[579]) An additional cause of Federal Reserve Board inactivity, as noted, was that Eccles, George Harrison, the president of the Federal Reserve Bank of New York, and other governors of the Federal Reserve Board did not believe, given the context of the low interest rates prevailing in the 1930s, that the Board had the means to affect the country's business economy. So they did nothing to try to stimulate business activities, i.e., the private sector of the nation's economy.

Viewing the economy within the parameters of a Social Darwinist, neo-mercantilist, narrowly focused lens, any imaginable Federal Reserve Board initiative was no match for Roosevelt's (and Morgenthau's) expansive view of their governmental mandate. Morgenthau's access to his Exchange Stabilization Fund always threatened to usurp the Federal Reserve Board's responsibility relating to monetary policy by taking over the FOMC's function of buying and selling the nation's business debt and government securities on the open market (although, as Meltzer notes, in the New Deal years, the portfolio of the FOMC rarely changed). By the same token, Morgenthau's view of the power that came with his command of the Exchange Stabilization Fund was limited almost exclusively to keeping the interest rate on government securities low. Beyond that purpose was a *terra incognita* in which there was only Morgenthau's basic distrust of Eccles's ideas and Roosevelt's feeling that Federal Reserve officials were mostly Republican Party–affiliated bankers with questionable loyalty to the Roosevelt administration's agenda.[580]

Morgenthau was not able to convince the Congress to go along with his tax policies during World War II, although there was a Democratic Party majority in both the Senate and the House of Representatives. By 1944, notwithstanding the serious losses of lives and materiel entailed by the Allied invasion of the European continent in June of that year, the divergence between the legislative and executive branches of the government was so wide that the Congress "overrode the president's veto of a tax bill for the first time in United States history."[581]

The difficulty centered on the level of surcharge rates, and, more generally, on which economic level of American society the tax burden should fall. Many members of Congress wanted a sales tax (much as the European Union currently imposes a Value Added Tax [VAT] at the wholesale level of the production and sales process). Morgenthau objected to a sales tax as an unfair burden on the poorer wage earners—those least able to bear the levy. Roosevelt wanted to limit annual incomes to $25,000 for individuals and $50,000 for families. Congress did not seriously consider Roosevelt's idea.[582]

Beardsley Ruml, an executive with New York City's R. H. Macy's Department Store, came up with a truly revolutionary tax collection procedure: pay-as-you-go tax collection (i.e., income tax payments would be deducted from the taxpayer's regular pay). This was incorporated in the 1943 tax legislation. This simplified income tax collection by the federal government.[583]

Morgenthau found difficulties with the mechanics of putting the concept into practice. Initially, the proposal was to forego the tax on 1942 incomes and start withholding in 1943. But Morgenthau felt that would benefit mostly "high-income tax payers (and wartime profiteers)" when one took into consideration the high wartime tax rates and progressively higher tax bracket surcharges. The compromise that evolved forgave "$50, or 75 percent of the lower of 1942 or 1943 tax liabilities. Withholding would start on July 1, 1943."[584]

Morgenthau thought inflation was equivalent to an additional tax on households because inflation eroded the value of savings. He could identify with the virtues of hardworking, law-abiding families who put away a few dollars each payday to meet unforeseen future difficulties. His preference was for direct taxation rather than inflation during the war period. But at the same time his primary concern was to achieve low interest rates on government debt.

One of his proposals would have increased Social Security deductions on employees' incomes while the war went on, with the excess payments returned after the war ended. This in turn implies that he believed there would be a recession after the conclusion of hostilities. Historically, that had been the usual consequence of a termination of hostilities. Blum writes, "The heart of his policy . . . was an immediate, substantial increase in Social Security rates, calculated to yield $5.5 billion in new revenue. That increase . . . followed after the war with a broad expansion of Social Security benefits, would accomplish the purpose of compulsory lending while at the same time strengthening the fabric of American society."[585] The proposal was accepted by Roosevelt, only to go down to defeat in February 1944, when the Congress overrode the presidential veto of the tax bill.[586] Meltzer comments that Morgenthau, probably without his realizing it, "had become a proponent of [Keynesian] countercyclical fiscal policy."[587]

Morgenthau recognized that the full mobilization of the American economy would necessitate a degree of government borrowing never before experienced by the United States. Morgenthau's insistence on voluntary borrowing from its citizenry—as opposed to the British program of forced savings (which Eccles preferred)—had curious results. Morgenthau went to great efforts to sell as many bonds as possible to the civilian population of the country. Well-known entertainment and Hollywood personalities were enlisted in the effort. (*Reader's Digest* told the story during World War II of how famed comedian Groucho Marx, volunteering on a bond-drive train, took a walk when the train reached Chicago. Returning to the station platform where the train was parked, the soldier guarding the train refused Groucho reentrance, not recognizing him without his makeup.)

Once the United States actually entered World War II, production of civilian goods was curtailed. Spending by civilians was restricted by the severe lack of goods on which to spend the money now available. In addition to the excess supply of money, there was an excess demand for the limited supply of goods—the reverse of the state of the American economy in the years 1930–39. Only in part did savings increase,[588] leaving huge amounts of money in the hands of the American civilian population.

Morgenthau hoped to finance the war years' government budget deficits—first, by taxation that would cover 50 percent of the military expenditures, and second, by the voluntary civilian purchase of government bonds. Morgenthau came close to his 50 percent goal for tax receipts; he kept interest rates on government bonds to the previous years' 2.5 percent; and he avoided a compulsory bond-buying program. Hence the successive defense and war bond drives.[589] There were eight bond drives in all.[590]

Although the money supply increased, there was a much smaller increase in individuals' share of the federal debt. The reason given is that while "Morgenthau's Treasury [Department] urged individuals to purchase [government] debt [in the form of government bonds] , , , he was unwilling to pay them to do so."[591] The Treasury Department tried to encourage private persons to buy government bonds by issuing wartime E-bonds in denominations as little as $18.75. Savings stamps to be accumulated to purchase E-bonds were issued for 10 cents apiece. Corporations, schools, and other organizations were asked to sell such bonds and stamps by payroll deduction plans and by urging purchases as a patriotic duty. But although corporations and individuals succumbed to government appeals to buy defense—and later, war—bonds, retention of the bonds was another matter.

With the low interest rates the bonds offered, many of the bonds that were purchased during the government's bond campaigns were "cashed in" at banks soon after the bond drives were over. Knowledgeable individuals and banks could sell shorter-term securities for higher-yield, long-term government bonds. Also, intent on meeting the sales quotas it had set, the Treasury Department allowed banks to lend people the money to buy defense savings bonds at an interest rate below the defense bond interest rate. After the bond drive was over, the banks would agree to buy the bonds from their borrowers, resulting in a profit to the purchasers from the difference in interest rates. The consequence was that while the Treasury Department could show a successful bond drive that was oversubscribed, the reality was not so much public participation as bank-supported financing. Meltzer writes that while non-bank purchasers bought $147 billion of non-marketable war bond issues and other Treasury securities, only some $93 billion of the issues were actually retained. Corporations bought some $60 billion in government bonds, but only increased their holdings of the bonds by $19 billion.[592]

The slack was taken up by the banking system, which financed the war effort without the government having to resort to unrestricted inflationary printing of paper money or the payment of unconscionable rates of interest. Morgenthau's objective of financing the war effort with minimal interest rates on government debt was achieved. But there was a price to be paid.

With virtually full employment, more money became available to the civilian population. Meltzer comments that "the monetary base doubled in the four years ending fourth quarter 1945, [with] an 18 percent compound average annual rate of increase. Purchases of Treasury securities account for almost all of the $18 billion increase in the base."[593]

Morgenthau blamed "speculative practices" for the sales by non-bank investors. Eccles's conclusion was that the Treasury Department's lid on interest rates was the ultimate cause of the sales. Morgenthau's response was that any rise in interest rates would primarily benefit private bankers and the Federal Reserve System, to the detriment of the government.[594]

Seeking to resolve the problem of resale of government bonds that were purchased during the Treasury Department's bond drives, the executive committee of the FOMC sent a recommendation to the Treasury Department, proposing: (1) tap issues to absorb surplus funds of non-bank corporations; (2) a 2.5 percent rate on securities with fifteen or more years to maturity; and (3) flexible rates on shorter maturities, ranging between 0.25 percent and 0.5 percent for Treasury bills. The Treasury Department "was not interested in a long-term plan. Morgenthau preferred to remain [what Meltzer refers to as] opportunistic, and he was not tempted by rate flexibility or higher interest rates. He accepted the fixed 2.5 percent maximum rate. . . . [H]e was proud of his achievement—financing more than $200 billion at an average cost of 1.94 percent."[595]

Nevertheless, the psychological effects of participation in bond purchases should not be disregarded. Though commercial banks held 40 percent of the federal debt, after the government itself and the Federal Reserve System,[596] an individual pledging to buy a Treasury war bond made a personal commitment to be a part of the American war effort. In the simplest of terms, it meant it was that individual's war.[597]

With the vast increase in defense appropriations voted by the Congress in the year 1940, the problem of how to generate moneys for payment by the government still loomed large. The initial response of the Congress to the need for government income to meet the extraordinary expenditures it had voted resembled nothing so much as a hesitant swimmer reluctantly lowering a toe into an oncoming wave at the beach. Blum writes: "The First Revenue Act of 1940, little more than a gesture toward what was needed that year, increased individual income taxes in most brackets, lightly increased corporate rates, and set a 'defense' supertax of about 10 percent on most other existing internal revenue taxes." The act also reduced personal exemptions.[598]

Morgenthau found the bill inadequate to meet his goal of using income taxes to cover 50 percent of the government's war expenditures. In his view, old-fashioned patriotism called for real excess profits legislation. While Roosevelt recognized the need for quick action, other pressing problems had a higher priority on his attention, and he left the matter to Morgenthau with the admonition to "make it rough." Roosevelt met with congressional leaders who presumably agreed on the need for action. On July 16, Morgenthau told his staff to go ahead with drafting a bill. "I don't care how steep it is," he said. Except congressional conservatives managed to sit on the administration's bill in committee.[599] On August 5, as Morgenthau told his staff, the President was sitting in a rocking chair on his back porch. "[H]e says, 'I can tell you very simply how I feel . . . I want a tax bill; I want one damned quick; I don't care what is in it; I don't want to know . . . The [war plant construction] contracts are being held up and I want a tax bill [to allow the construction work to proceed].'"[600]

Morgenthau thought the legislation, passed by the Congress, was terrible—"a lousy bill" in his words, full of the kind of loopholes he thought disgraceful. "The new legislation, Morgenthau wrote Roosevelt on October 21, 1940, sponsored the very kinds of discrimination that the president and the Treasury had for so many years opposed."[601] The president was less concerned with excess profits than with covering his political flank on the question of securing some excess profit legislation. The latter purpose had been formally accomplished.[602] As Morgenthau told his staff on August 5, 1940, "I am not President and I am not running for President, and he is."[603]

The enormous amounts of money floating through the American economy taken together with the limited production of civilian goods once the United States entered World War II, promised uncontrollable inflation. Minor price controls proving ineffective, Congress wasted no time in adopting the Emergency Price Control Act in January 1942, authorizing further selective price controls, but prices rose by 4.8 percent annually in the first nine months of the year. A committee reported to the president that selective controls were ineffective. Congress then adopted the Economic Stabilization Act of 1942,[604] which gave the president broad authority to control prices and wages.[605] Morgenthau was in favor of exempting wage controls, unrealistic since he also favored limiting profits to 6 percent of invested capital. The opportunity to demand wage increases would make a mockery of price limits on finished products. (Included was the introduction of rationing; people were given ration stamps that allowed only specified amounts of food, clothing, and gasoline to the civilian population.)

Controls were set at the levels in effect in the preceding March for all wages, prices, rents, and services. Everyone could agree those earlier price levels were honest and fair—before any "war profiteering" had begun to come into the picture. The Act created the Office of Economic Stabilization. Roosevelt appointed Jimmy Byrnes, a former senator from South Carolina, and most recently a justice of the United States Supreme Court, to run the agency. The legislation gave Byrnes powers that on paper made him the assistant president.

The legislation included provisions out of which came the Office of Price Administration, to enforce the purposes of the statute through criminal sanctions. The author was told the story of how the OPA director in New York City paid a call on then–chief judge John Knox of the United States District Court for the Southern District of New York, to whom he explained that enforcement required prosecution in the Federal District Court. Judge Knox agreed, and the august precincts of the federal courthouse were soon filled with complaints of wholesale overcharges of 2 cents on this item, 10 cents on that item. Very soon federal courtrooms took on the character of a marketplace, with the courtroom and the adjacent hallways overfilled with alleged price-control violators and their lawyers. The federal judges endured the assault on their dignity for a year. Then, Judge Knox called in the OPA director and told him that with procedures having been established, future overcharge violations belonged in the local criminal courts.

Toward the last months of 1940, Morgenthau became concerned with the need to freeze the American assets of citizens of European countries, with exemptions for nationals of friendly countries. The State Department held back, saying international law did not provide for freezing of assets of private citizens of countries with which the United States was not at war. The State Department only agreed to freeze assets of citizens of countries that had been invaded by the Wehrmacht. By 1941 the Wehrmacht had covered a great deal of ground in Europe. On February 26, 1941, Roosevelt sent a memorandum to Hull, Morgenthau, and Attorney General Robert Jackson, appointing them to a Cabinet committee to oversee Treasury Department proposals. The committee secretary was to come from Treasury.

Although it had the appearance of movement, nothing changed since the State Department retained its veto.[606]

On April 30, 1941, Acheson spoke to Morgenthau, urging him once more to seek consent from Secretary of State Hull to a general order of control over the American assets of citizens of European countries, subject to waiver in the case of nationals of countries deemed friendly to the United States. Morgenthau was reluctant, saying, "I don't want to read in the newspapers that this is another plan of the Treasury bright boys." Acheson suggested the situation had changed in the State Department.[607] On June 12, 1941, Hull agreed to recommend freezing the funds of all European countries, with discretion to exempt Switzerland, Sweden, Spain, Portugal, and Russia. Finally, Hull agreed to a recommendation to be given to Roosevelt for a "proclaimed list of certain blocked individuals" deemed to be acting for Germany and Italy, barring exports to such persons as against the national interest. Blum writes that it "gave the Treasury substantially the authority which Morgenthau had been seeking for more than a year."[608]

Edward Bernstein, who worked in the Treasury Department as an economist beginning in 1940, commented that "work on [the] Bretton Woods [Agreement] began in December, 1941, just after [the Japanese attack on] Pearl Harbor, with a short memorandum by Harry White."[609] Meltzer suggests that a week after the attack on Pearl Harbor, Morgenthau asked White, then director of monetary research, to "prepare a memorandum on the establishment of an inter-Allied stabilization fund" that could be used for "postwar international monetary arrangements." White developed the idea of a permanent fund that could lend to debtor countries.[610]

The State Department determined that a meeting of foreign ministers of the Latin American countries was useful to secure a declaration of support. The conference met in Rio de Janeiro beginning January 20, 1942. Sumner Welles, the undersecretary of state, and leading the American delegation, wanted a resolution the foreign ministers could support. Harry White, representing the Treasury Department among the United States delegates, proposed a resolution that the American Republics recommend an International Stabilization Fund be undertaken after the war. Bernstein comments that Morgenthau's Exchange Stabilization Fund already was exchanging Latin American currencies as security for American-lent dollars "under [short-term] repurchase agreements." The idea of making the transaction available on a global scale through an international banking institution was novel. He writes that this is "the way the International Monetary Fund operates today [using drawing rights]."[611]

Meltzer writes that the negotiations by Morgenthau's Treasury Department, with a British delegation led by Lord Keynes in connection with lend-lease agreements, included shifting postwar planning from trade issues (Hull's original focus) to finance and exchange rates (more congenial to economic technocrats). By September 1941, Keynes had put together the concept of an "international clearing union" that could issue an international currency that would be available to resolve foreign exchange imbalances between nations. But it is White's version rather than Keynes's that provided the basis for the Bretton Woods Agreement.[612]

What is fascinating about the bleakness of the war news after the attack at Pearl Harbor is that there was never any doubt among American officials that the Western Allies would ultimately prevail over Germany, Italy, and Japan.

It was not merely White's five-page memorandum prepared in December 1941 and the resolution adopted at Rio de Janeiro that became the basis for the Bretton Woods Agreement, but rather the elaboration of the concept that White had developed in the course of 1942, which came to include the contours of the World Bank. When he was finished, White had written a book that was reduced to a ten- or twelve-page report entitled, "The Treasury's Proposal for an International Stabilization Fund."[613] Morgenthau, who at first had suggested a nebulous concept to White, initially understood no more than what White created might involve "expanding the prewar Tripartite Agreement to avoid competitive devaluation."[614] Later, he came to understand the larger dimensions of what was contemplated.

Bernstein reports that around that time the Treasury Department was presented with the Keynes proposal. From the American point of view, the Keynes proposal was inadequate in two ways: First, the United States would have a potential liability encompassing "twenty-six billion dollars in reserve credit if all other countries drew dollars." Second, the proposal did not provide for much discipline by any country except the United States. Other countries could continue to draw dollars indefinitely.[615] (It was Henry Wallace's concept of the "ever-flowing granary" transposed into monetary terms—based on the theory that the United States had just about "cornered" the international gold market.)

Persons in the American banking world, including the Federal Reserve System, were nostalgic about a return to the gold standard now that the United States held most of the world's supply of gold, and prosperity had returned. (It was only a little more than ten years since the halcyon days of the gold standard of the 1920s.) White had to remind the Federal Open Market Committee in 1945: "There isn't the slightest chance of getting other countries to return to the gold standard." White explained that the "only chance for agreement was to combine stability of exchange rates with flexibility to change them with the fund's approval. Other countries would agree to this mixture of stability and flexibility if it was part of an agreement that gave each country some assurance that it could borrow in an emergency: 'We must give them time to balance their payments in such a way that they will not hurt the rest of the world.' Adjustment might take two, three, five, or even ten years."[616]

By 1943 the Treasury Department had determined that [the future International Monetary] "Fund would give each country the currency it needed to meet its [balance of payments] deficit and the country would give its currency to the Fund. But then it would be obligated to repay the money it drew and it had to begin to correct its balance of payments." (Keynes had wanted no requirement to repay unless and until a country acquired a positive balance of payments. If no positive balance of payments was ever achieved, Keynes would never require repayment.) The Treasury plan required a limit on how much money the United States would advance to countries with a negative balance of payments. The United States obligation was limited to its initial subscription. Countries drawing on funds had to have an obligation both to repay what was borrowed and to correct the cause of the deficit that required the draw.[617] The United States plan also required that part of each country's subscription to the Fund must be paid in gold (as well as local currency)—a sticking point for the British. The Treasury's thought was that this way, the Fund would have increased liquidity.[618]

Eventually, at a meeting in Washington in 1943, the British delegation, chaired by Lord Keynes, recognized the United States was financially stronger than a Britain facing bankruptcy by the end of the war.[619] Keynes made a last effort to retrieve the glory that was Britain's, proposing to rewrite the proposal in his more-elegant Cambridge style, but Edward Bernstein, representing the Treasury, responded that "Cherokee," as Keynes dismissively characterized the American bureaucratic style, was the language understood by "the braves of Wall Street," whose support the Treasury needed. Bernstein comments: "Keynes became nasty to me at this meeting."[620] The Treasury did make a few later changes, following British suggestions.[621]

There were two more inclusive meetings with representatives of other nations. Agreement was achieved on the World Bank, but not on the International Monetary Fund. The first meeting in 1943 involved eighteen countries in Washington; the second was in Atlantic City, preliminary to the final conference at Bretton Woods, where forty-four nations were represented. At Atlantic City, it was agreed the final conference could decide organizational details for the International Monetary Fund. Bernstein suggests there was not much difference between the different versions—American, British, and, in some cases, suggestions from governments in exile. He explains: "The purpose in Atlantic City was to agree on a series of proposals so that the Conference would know the general shape of what it was to do, but would have . . . the right to choose among alternatives."[622]

While the preliminary discussions were proceeding with respect to the contours of a system for a grand postwar stabilization of international monetary relationships (foreign exchange rates), the British faced a more-specific problem relating to their financial needs immediately after hostilities ceased, during the period of reconversion to a civilian economy. In 1938, British gold and dollar reserves amounted to more than $4 billion. Roosevelt's fertile imagination had conceived the idea of Lend-Lease, when the British revealed they were running out of money to pay for the ordnance they needed. Faced with strong isolationist sentiment in the Congress, Morgenthau, while testifying at committee hearings on the Lend-Lease bill, had made a commitment that the British exhaust their dollar assets in the United States before Lend-Lease shipments began.

The Treasury Department interpreted that commitment to mean that Britain's wartime American reserves should not go much beyond $1 billion. Richard Gardner believes that Harry

White was also interested in keeping British assets as low as possible, to increase British dependence on American assistance to create "leverage" to induce the British to more easily acquiesce with State Department ideas on postwar multilateral trade (abolition of "Empire preferences" and the like).[623]

In December 1943, Morgenthau and White "made strong representations that those reserves had grown too high and that the British would now have to pay in cash for some of the goods being supplied on Lend-Lease account." British Exchequer bureaucrats, faced with a horrifyingly uncertain postwar future, looked longingly back at the lost $4 billion in American equities and "pleaded the need to maintain adequate reserves for the post-war period . . ." Morgenthau's response, made in all sincerity knowing Roosevelt's concern for British survival, was that the British needed to trust in America's good intentions "that British needs would be met by special measures at a later date."[624]

That was enough to make a British civil servant's blood run cold. As Gardner describes it in stiff-upper-lip fashion, "Sir David Waley . . . took a dim view of this approach, remarking that Britain could not afford to deplete its dollar balances in reliance on 'a promise that the American Government could make available through one means or another substantial sums after the war.'" The comment is taken from Harry White's minutes of a luncheon meeting that included Morgenthau, White, Lord Halifax, the British ambassador, and Waley, held on November 26, 1943.[625] Eventually, the British would recognize that Morgenthau's commitment to Congress was political in nature. Churchill broached the problem with Roosevelt and, eventually, at the second Quebec conference in September 1944, it was agreed between them that Britain's American reserves could rise.[626]

In the denouement, Morgenthau's assurance would come to pass. But by then, Roosevelt was dead and Morgenthau was no longer the secretary. The British Loan Agreement was signed by

Fred Vinson, his successor, on December 6, 1945. Congress then approved the loan because the illusion of postwar amity with Stalin had faded into the beginnings of the Cold War. Democratic nations had to be strengthened as a bulwark against the Communist threat.

As Morgenthau's letters to his father reveal, during the 1930s he reacted with private anguish to the systematic degradation of German Jews by the Nazi regime. Unlike Jacob Schiff and the Warburgs, equally members of *Our Crowd*, Morgenthau and his father had neither family nor business connections in Germany. Morgenthau knew of his immediate family's origin in southwest Germany, while his parents were both bilingual, as was he. In a Social Darwinist world, Morgenthau identified with German Jews and their fate.

Morgenthau had forged a social connection with the Roosevelts almost by accident. While Roosevelt thought of Morgenthau as a neighbor and friend, there were unacknowledged but rigid parameters in which their friendship existed, dictated by an unspoken understanding that they lived in a Gentile society which set the pattern of their lives. The families exchanged Christmas gifts, and Morgenthau would throw an annual New England "clambake" for the members of the White House press corps at his farm in East Fishkill.[627]

The unspoken Social Darwinist anti-Semitism of the United States in the 1920s and '30s had cost Morgenthau any chance of an appointment as secretary of agriculture in 1933. Although Morgenthau had achieved an astonishing political eminence when Roosevelt nominated him to be secretary of the Treasury, there were clear limits as to how far the Semitic element could be carried. Too many Americans thought there were too many Jews in the upper reaches of the federal government in Washington. At one point, Ickes, who had a great respect for the professional abilities of the scholarly Ben Cohen, one of the president's administrative assistants, suggested to Roosevelt that the president consider Cohen for the position of undersecretary of the Treasury, as "there will soon be a vacancy on account of the resignation of Roswell Magill. The President said that he would be a good man but he questioned the wisdom of appointing a Jew under Morgenthau."[628] There were Jewish appointees in the Treasury Department—Harry Dexter White would be appointed as an assistant secretary (if after some hesitation), and Edward Bernstein worked under him, and there were others—but the position as undersecretary was altogether too public and too prominent to permit to a Jewish occupant.

Once Hitler and the Nazis were allowed to take control of the German government and institute anti-Jewish measures, some memory of Victorian decency caused democratic countries to officially respond by convening conferences, first at Evian-les-Bains in 1938, and then, the Bermuda Conference in 1941. But while the representatives of democratic countries at those conferences might have adopted resolutions deploring discriminatory and anti-Semitic governmental measures, in a Social Darwinist world, no meaningful, alleviating action would be forthcoming. Essentially what happened at these conferences was a replay of the hand-wringing that had accompanied Haile Selassie's address to the League of Nations assembly after Mussolini's conquest of Ethiopia.

David Wyman, in his searing indictment of the failure of democratic governments to act, wrote: "The Intergovernmental Committee, the ineffectual creation of the Evian Conference on refugees in 1938, had been moribund since the war began. Its twenty-nine member nations had never supported it; it had seldom been possible even to convene representatives of the few states that composed its executive committee. While the Nazis methodically murdered thousands of Jews each day, America's leaders offered a 'preliminary exploration' of ways to revive a proven failure."[629] Wyman's publisher felt it necessary to include on the last page of the book, and on the book jacket, the fact that he was "the grandson of two Protestant ministers."

The general attitude of Gentiles in a Social Darwinist world was that native Jews were to be tolerated, and certain foreigners, including Asians and European Jews, were highly suspect. Upton Sinclair, in one of his Lanny Budd novels (which surveyed the history of the first half of the twentieth century) has his hero present in the year 1934 at a gathering in Paris of a German Jewish family of the *haute bourgeoisie*, the Hellsteins, to discuss the plight of a family member, Uncle Solomon, who had not escaped from Germany and was now in a Nazi concentration camp. The family conclave met to discuss what means could be found to help him. The author writes that Olivie, a daughter, was married to a French aristocrat who had not deemed it necessary to join his in-laws.

Although Morgenthau occupied a government position of great importance, he was subject to unspoken restraints. Acutely conscious of his German Jewish heritage, he was horrified by the war, and identified strongly with the Jewish victims of Nazi persecution, even if the latter was of small interest to the general community. Three incidents served to pierce through the defenses Morgenthau had erected to keep his silent anguish hidden within him.

Henry III writes: "[T]he initial breakthrough to my father's conscience was achieved by three zealous Christian Treasury lawyers he trusted and respected. The senior member of the triumvirate was Randolph Paul, whom my father had brought to the Treasury to draft tax reform legislation. The two junior members were John Pehle, then thirty-five, director of the Foreign Funds Control Board (and subsequently director of the War Refugee Board), and Josiah DuBois, the thirty-two-year-old assistant to the general counsel. Their smoldering moral indignation caught fire when Pehle became aware that the State Department was actively blocking the transfer of funds from private Jewish organizations intended for refugee rescue. Moreover, they discovered that the State Department was suppressing critical information from its own official sources."[630]

Beschloss comments that they "informed Morgenthau that Assistant Secretary of State Breckenridge Long, hostile to foreigners, especially Jews, had been deliberately obstructing the flow of money, information and passports [i.e., visas] that might save Jews from Hitler." Additionally, the State Department "had also blocked efforts to find refuge for Jews in the United States, Turkey, Switzerland and Palestine."[631]

Henry III quotes Pehle: "[Morgenthau] valued above everything else his relationship with the President, and to get him to act in this area took a bit of doing. But . . . once he saw what was really going on, he was very supportive all the way through . . . He didn't want to stand out as a Jew. He wanted to stand out as secretary of the Treasury. It was doubly hard, I would think, for him, but he did it."[632]

The second factor that caused Morgenthau to come to his decision that he could no longer evade Jewish refugee problems involved Rabbi Stephen Wise, who had officiated at Morgenthau's marriage to Elinor Fatman in 1916.

Wise, in addition to his religious duties, had a wide-ranging interest in public affairs in New York City and elsewhere. Consulted by Henry Sr. when he was considering the acceptance of the ambassadorship in Istanbul (and while Henry Sr. was still the president of the Free Synagogue founded by Rabbi Wise), Wise was eloquent in urging him to accept the post. Having recently visited the area, Wise had been passionately concerned with the welfare of those Jews living in the Holy Land, then under the suzerainty of the Turkish sultan. It would have been astonishing if Wise had not been concerned about the Nazi persecution of German Jews. Indeed, in 1933, Wise had been at the forefront of those who urged a boycott of German-made products once Hitler and the Nazis had seized control of the German government. When the first evidences of genocide leaked out of occupied Europe, Wise issued notice in a publication of the American Jewish Congress, an organization he headed. Wyman writes "*Congress Weekly* brought out its December 4, 1942, issue in a funereal black cover, while the magazine itself was given over largely to documentary evidence of the mass killing."[633]

Rabbi Wise considered how he could reach Roosevelt. Without any real choice, his best and only approach lay with Morgenthau, whom he had known relatively well, however attenuated the connection had become once Henry Sr. became aware of the rabbi's commitment to Zionism with its ideology of a Jewish return to its ancient biblical homeland. Wise asked for an appointment with Morgenthau. Henry III quotes Henrietta Klotz: " 'Stephen Wise . . . came into the Treasury and told your father what was going on in Germany.' . . . Klotz remembers her boss imploring, 'Please, Stephen, don't give me the gory details.' Of course, [Wise] went into their making soap [from murdered Jewish victims], and your father was just getting paler and paler, and I thought he was going to keel over.' "[634] Beschloss adds: "Morgenthau cried out: 'I cannot take anymore.' "[635]

Morgenthau's response does not suggest a matter of first impression. Rather, it appears more the pouring of salt on an existing, festering wound.

Then, there was the response of Supreme Court Justice Frankfurter in 1943 to Jan Karski's story. Karski related the horrors of the Warsaw ghetto and the death camp into which he had been smuggled, and from which he had escaped and gone on secretly to the United States. (Karski spent his later years on the faculty at Georgetown University in Washington.[636] He was interviewed in Claude Lanzmann's documentary film on the

Holocaust, *Shoah*.) The Polish ambassador knew Frankfurter and asked him to hear Karski. Wood and Jankowski write that Karski was meeting Oscar Cox and Ben Cohen at the same evening dinner at the Polish Embassy on July 5, 1943.[637] The dinner lasted until nearly 1:00 AM. Karski gave "an objective description of the persecution of Jews in Poland. Over dinner, he referred only in passing to what he himself had witnessed—but the stories were still enough to 'make your hair stand on end,' as Cox wrote to Harry Hopkins."[638]

"Frankfurter remained after the two other guests departed. Frankfurter then asked Karski whether he knew Frankfurter was a Jew. Karski nodded. Frankfurter then asked Karski to tell him exactly what was happening to the Jews of Poland, which Karski explained for half an hour 'in gruesome detail.' Frankfurter asked . . . how Karski got into the Ghetto and the death camp [at Belzec]. Karski answered . . . Frankfurter stood up and paced the floor for a few moments, after which he sat down again."[639]

He finally spoke. " 'A man like me talking to a man like you must be totally honest. So I am. So I say: I do not believe you.' The ambassador rejoined, 'Felix, how can you say such a thing? You know he is saying the truth. He was checked and rechecked in London and here. Felix, what are you saying?' Frankfurter answered, 'I did not say that he's lying. I said I don't believe him. There is a difference. My mind, my heart they are made in such a way that I cannot conceive it.'"[640]

Leonard Baker adds that Frankfurter was "stretching out his arms and crying, 'No! No! No!'"[641]

One can only imagine the vast dimensions of shock that Frankfurter underwent. His world was falling apart. For a moment, at least, he had to imagine in his mind Nazi soldiers entering the quiet precincts of his chambers at the Supreme Court and roughly ordering him out to a collection point where, anonymous, he would be transported to a nameless death camp from whence there was no return. He was unable to face that reality.

Then, there was Roosevelt's reaction. The Polish ambassador with Karski had an appointment with Roosevelt on July 28, 1943, at 10:30 AM.[642] (The ambassador would have acted again as the interpreter or translator.) Beschloss writes: "In July 1943, at the White House, Lieutenant Jan Karski of the Polish underground army told Roosevelt about the mass murder of Jews he had witnessed taking place in a concentration camp: 'Our underground authorities are absolutely sure that the Germans are out to exterminate the entire Jewish population of Europe.' The President listened intently, but when Karski implored Roosevelt to get the Allies to intervene, the President replied [speaking more to the ambassador than to Karski], 'Tell your nation we shall win the war.'"[643]

Although he could envision the dimensions of a glorious democratic future shared on a global basis (as in the "Four Freedoms" Declaration), Roosevelt was not immune on other occasions to the narrowness of a Social Darwinist outlook.

Did Roosevelt speak as Beschloss reports—after a direct plea for an effective response to Nazi genocide? Walter Laqueur in 1980 agrees with Beschloss.[644]

A different version is given in Polish ambassador Jan Ciechanowski's report published in 1947. Ciechanowski explains: "The quotations in my conversations with President Roosevelt . . . are not verbatim minutes. They are reconstructed from comprehensive personal notes of these conversations, as recorded by me immediately after they took place and while they were still fresh in my mind."

Ciechanowski records that Karski did tell the president of his experience in the Warsaw ghetto and in the Belzec death camp, where he entered disguised in the uniform of a Latvian guard. He also said that the Polish Underground authorities were "absolutely sure that the Germans are out to exterminate the entire Jewish population of Europe."[645] Ciechanowski quotes the president as replying: "Tell the Polish Underground authorities . . . that their indomitable attitude has been duly appreciated. Tell them that they will never have cause to regret their brave decision to reject any collaboration with the enemy, and that Poland will live to reap the reward of her heroism and sacrifice." Roosevelt added: "I thank you, my friend, I thank you very much. . . . What you have told me [especially details about the Polish Underground's activities] is very important . . ."

The ambassador also adds that Roosevelt continued, "I am really thrilled, Mr. Ambassador. Thank you for having given me this opportunity of hearing Karski's report on the wonderful resistance and spirit of Poland."[646]

Wood and Jankowski write that "Karski long believed that his attempt to move Roosevelt to action on behalf of Europe's Jews had been a failure, and it may have been. But John Pehle [one of Morgenthau's Treasury staff] . . . later insisted that Karski had made a difference. Roosevelt's willingness to set up the [War] Refugee Board on January 22, 1944 in an attempt to help those Jews who were still alive—a mission in which it succeeded to some extent—resulted from his deeply moving encounter with Karski . . ."[647]

It does not matter whether Roosevelt actually said what Beschloss and Laqueur attribute to him. (In that sense, Ciechanowski's report is nearest in time to the actual event and, therefore, the most believable version of what transpired.) The words, most probably, accurately reflect Roosevelt's thinking at the time.

Aside from Morgenthau's visceral reaction to the information Rabbi Wise conveyed to him, there was probably a third factor that led to Morgenthau's active involvement in Jewish refugee problems. This was the special vantage point that came to Morgenthau as an important figure in the government bureaucracy. It is impossible to convey to those on the outside exactly what that particular sense of involvement means. (Morgenthau himself would tell his new daughter-in-law on the occasion of her marriage to Henry III in 1962 "that she should have known him when he 'was somebody.'"[648])

Edward Bernstein conveys some of that sense of belonging and the concomitant authority that flows from it in a comment made by Harry Dexter White. After Bernstein had paid a visit to the office of the British Treasury representative in the Willard Hotel, a short distance along Pennsylvania Avenue from the Treasury building, White told him: "Remember that when you are representing the Treasury, it doesn't matter who it is who wants to see you, he comes to your office, not you to his office." Bernstein adds: "That's the last time I ever left the Treasury to talk to the British or any other foreigners. White had a very strong sense of what was proper. The dignity of the U.S. Treasury was at stake here and I oughtn't to have gone over there."[649] In the eyes of a member of the president's cabinet (and under then-existing law, third in line to succeed to the presidency), it was an underling, a mere assistant secretary, who was acting totally out of bounds. That Morgenthau had known the man casually for many years did not help the matter. It is that sense of bureaucratic authority, of belonging, of knowing where he fitted in the structure of government that, in part, explains the familiarity Morgenthau used when Breckenridge Long came to talk with him, face-to-face.

Rabbi Wise had a representative in Switzerland. That person, Gerhart Riegner, was a Jewish refugee with contacts to one or more German Gentiles (*Aryans* in the official Nazi terminology) who had business dealings in Switzerland. They passed on information that might be of interest to him. With the difficulties wartime conditions imposed on ordinary mail, Riegner had the assistance of the American minister to Switzerland, Leland Harrison, who routinely transmitted cables addressed to Rabbi Wise through the State Department. This practice allowed the American government another window into areas of Europe controlled by the Third Reich before delivery to its intended recipient.

On January 21, 1943, the American minister, Harrison, sent his 482nd cable to the State Department in Washington. The cable was from Riegner and was intended for Rabbi Wise. Its contents detailed the herding of Polish Jews into ghettos and their murder in death camps. It reported deportations of Romanian Jews to "Transnistria," the eastern area of Bessarabia (then a part of Romania bordering on Ukraine), an agricultural region unprepared to receive numbers of people without the means to support themselves. It reported the starvation of local Jews in Germany, Austria, and Czechoslovakia; and lastly it reported the organized murder of Jews in lands occupied by German armies.

The organizational chart of the State Department had the cable pass to the desk of Assistant Secretary Breckenridge Long prior to its transmission to Rabbi Wise. Long occupied a high-enough organizational level in the State Department so that he also supervised the section that issued visas to foreigners to enter the United States.

During the years of the Wilson administration, Long had occupied the position of third assistant secretary of state. In those years he came to know Roosevelt, who was then the assistant secretary of the navy. It would appear they were members of a group of young officials occupying second- and third-tier positions in the government, who socialized together. Henry III confirms Roosevelt and Long were friends since the Wilson administration.[650]

The Morgenthau archives at Hyde Park contain a copy of a letter written on the letterhead stationery of the third assistant secretary of state. It is dated August 8, 1918, during World War I, and is addressed to "Lieut-Colonel W. A. Austin, Camp Lee, Virginia." It reads:

> Dear Colonel Austin:
>
> It gives me great pleasure to say that I know Mr. Henry Morgenthau, Jr., very well and am only to[o] glad to commend him to you with the statement that he is a young man of highest integrity, sterling character and unusual ability.
>
> Mr. Morgenthau desires to be appointed to the Labor Battalion, and any consideration you can show his application will be appreciated by me.
>
> Yours very sincerely,
> Breckenridge Long

(The reason Morgenthau wanted to be connected with a labor battalion is that—as he wrote in a letter to his father, dated November 24, 1913[651]—he had spent a day at Hampton Institute in Virginia, attended by black students. He was offered a trusteeship of the school which he was much inclined to accept. Labor battalions were then manned by black soldiers with whom he would thus have had a connection, assuming he followed through and became a trustee.)

If one would speculate further, it would appear that Morgenthau made known to Roosevelt his desire to receive an officer's commission. In the succeeding September he was commissioned a lieutenant junior grade in the United States Navy, and received notice of his commission by a letter from Louis Howe, Roosevelt's secretary (and afterwards his political confidant). Roosevelt wanted to cultivate Morgenthau for political reasons, and it would appear that Roosevelt went to some effort to accommodate Morgenthau in the matter of a commission in the armed forces during the war. It would also appear that Morgenthau was aware of Roosevelt's efforts on his behalf and was appreciative. (With Roosevelt's political career later seemingly as shriveled as his leg muscles, that sense of gratitude could explain in large part one of the reasons why Morgenthau came, a few years later, to devote so much of his time to Roosevelt after Roosevelt was confined to his bed, crippled by infantile paralysis. "[D]uring the dreary months . . . Morgenthau drank without relish or complaint the gin and orange juice his host insisted upon serving and played Parcheesi with him hour after hour."[652])

Both Roosevelt and Long had held political appointments in 1918 at the pleasure of the chief executive. This suggests both were active politically. Henry III writes that, later, Long had been quite helpful at the Democratic National Convention in Chicago in 1932, lining up "significant" delegate support for Roosevelt's presidential nomination.[653] Long, though a Democrat above the Mason-Dixon Line, was a Southern conservative.[654]

In a Social Darwinist era, the conservative Long most probably was a firm believer in the efficacy of the National Origins Act of 1929. He probably thought the law should have been more stringent, more severely restricting the entrance into the United States of undesirable foreigners, a category that included Southern and Eastern Europeans, and Jews. From Long's Social Darwinist vantage point, they were, most probably, untrustworthy, unscrupulous degenerates. As Wyman writes: "Callousness prevailed in the State Department. Its officers, mostly old-stock Protestants, tended strongly towards [Social Darwinist] nativism. Little sympathy was wasted on East Europeans, especially Jews."[655] One suspects Long's attitude was not dissimilar to Neville Chamberlain's dismissal of Czechoslovakia during the Munich crisis in 1938 as a far distant country.

One can imagine Long's Social Darwinist reaction to Minister Harrison's 482nd cable. Strictly speaking, the cable was none of his business, since it was clearly intended for Rabbi Wise. There was Henry Stimson's reported comment when he was a member of President Hoover's Cabinet: *Gentlemen do not read other people's mail.* Except that the State Department was custodian of national security concerns and reserved the right to evaluate and use whatever information came its way. But Long did not merely forward a copy of the cable to those persons in the department detailed to evaluate the information contained in the communication for its value as background data for the secretary's use. Long would appear to have dismissed the contents of the cable with something resembling the sense of exasperation and outrage of a conscientious housewife seeing muddy shoeprints on a newly scrubbed kitchen floor. For a conservative Southern gentleman with aspirations to acting rationally, the communication had to be unbelievable. He must have found the contents of the cable so much absurd claptrap—an amateurish, melodramatic concoction by unscrupulous foreigners designed to swindle money from unsuspecting Americans.

It was no doubt with a sense of righteous indignation that Long dictated State Department cable #354 addressed to Harrison. It directed him to cease sending any more such cables to Washington. In good diplomatic and Social Darwinist fashion, the real reason for the directive was not given. Long's explanation for the directive was that such cables would violate neutral countries' censorship regulations. Retrospectively, Long's cable must appear callous when one considers the reality of what was then happening in Europe.

In any case, the explanation Long gave Harrison for the cable he was sending is preposterous. The gathering of local information and impressions is one of the traditional and accepted functions for diplomatic personnel (provided a diplomat does not cross the line and seek to subvert local officials by offers of monetary gain, sexual favors, and the like—in which case, once the conduct becomes known, a diplomat will be declared persona non grata and "invited to leave," i.e., expelled). Such information sent by diplomats is recognized as privileged communication, a courtesy that sovereign governments extend to each other. By common agreement, diplomatic pouches are not searched. Diplomatic personnel are expected to pass along what is considered "raw data." Taken together with other material, it is there to be evaluated and given whatever weight is called for.

Long was officious and exceeded his official responsibilities. Unfortunately, Long's action was consistent with the attitudes of his fellow State Department members. In other circumstances, Long's conduct might be taken as high comedy—the diplomat as busybody—except in this instance, the effect on people's lives was tragic.

There is only the phrase sung before the long orchestral interlude near the end of Mahler's symphonic work, *Das Lied von der Erde*: *Trunk'ne Welt*—drunken world.

In some fashion, Morgenthau's assistant Josiah DuBois became aware of what was happening and advised Morgenthau of what he had come to know. Morgenthau asked him to get the whole story. Henry III then quotes DuBois: "I had good relations with Donald Hiss, the head of the Foreign Funds Control Division in the State Department [who] gave me copies of the original cables, which was crucial because, when the Treasury asked for them, they were supplied with paraphrased cables . . ." [656]

The deletions and paraphrasing suggest that Long probably felt there was something to hide (which would tend to corroborate the thought, suggested above, as to the context of his motivation for his response to Minister Harrison). The secretary of the Treasury was now taking Harrison's cable seriously. That put a different light on the cable dispatched from Bern.

In the loneliness of his soul, Morgenthau came to understand there was no one else. With the energy of despair, Morgenthau then pursued a meeting with Secretary of State Hull. It took place on December 20, 1943, and Assistant Secretary Long was present.[657] The meeting occurred after congressional action. A resolution had been introduced in both houses of Congress on November 9, 1943, urging the creation of a presidential commission to formulate a plan "to save the surviving Jewish people of Europe from extinction at the hands of Nazi Germany."[658] Five days of testimony were taken before the House Foreign Affairs Committee.[659] (The same resolution later in December, 1943, would be approved at a meeting of the Senate Foreign Relations Committee and referred to the Senate for adoption after the Christmas recess.[660])

The fourth day of hearings before the House Foreign Relations Committee, November 26, 1943, Assistant Secretary of State Long testified at a closed session. Wyman writes: "He insisted on secrecy because, he claimed, the Germans might block projected refugee-aid operations if they found out what he was about to reveal." Long testified for some three and a half hours. His position was that "the United States and the Intergovernmental [Refugee] Committee were already doing everything humanly possible to save Jews. He greatly exaggerated the little that had been attempted since Hitler's rise to power, assigned most of the credit to the State Department, . . . and turned the inert Intergovernmental Committee into an effective mechanism for rescue."[661] When one member suggested the committee disapprove the pending resolution, Long diplomatically replied, "I think it would be very dangerous to vote it down, very unwise, in a way."[662] Long made an impressive witness.

Apparently, the committee members concluded some action was necessary. The solution appeared to be publication of "the still-secret mandate of the supposedly revived Intergovernmental Committee." Long was happy to secure the agreement of the British and the ICR committee members to make public the secret Intergovernmental Committee authorization document.[663]

Wyman writes: ". . . the favorable response from the congressmen, who were generally ignorant about the refugee situation, misled Long and [committee chairman Sol] Bloom. They concluded that release of the entire transcript of Long's remarks, rather than the ICR mandate alone, would prove even more effective in quieting Jewish pressures. Vanished was the need for strict secrecy . . . On December 10 [1943] Long's testimony was made public."[664]

Once Long's secret testimony was publicly available, those persons who could recite in their sleep the background data to which Long alluded were able to review in minute detail each statement he gave. It turned out that he was guilty of grave misstatements.[665] Public misstatements by government officials are unpardonable, all the more so when such misstatements are made to an official body.

During Morgenthau's meeting with Hull on December 20, 1943, Long asked to meet in a separate room with Morgenthau. The only possible explanation for Long's request is that he had come to realize he was in an awkward position. Desperate, he could only identify Morgenthau as a friend of Roosevelt's, someone who could relate to Long as a member of the same social class. Confidentially, Long could tell Morgenthau the source of the difficulty was his assistant Bernard Meltzer, one of the few Jewish State Department employees, hoping that Morgenthau would then sympathize with Long, who was finding himself in a politically difficult spot. Long claimed his assistant had been "raising technical difficulties."[666] However Morgenthau may have responded to Long's overtures if the year were 1918, it was now a generation later in a vastly different world.

Morgenthau said: "Breck, we might be a little frank . . . The impression is all around that you are particularly anti-Semitic."

Long admitted he was aware of the accusation, "and hoped Morgenthau would use his 'good offices' to correct the impression." Long explained that he did not think of himself as anti-Semitic.[667] In a Social Darwinist world, no doubt, there were individual Jews for whom he had the highest respect. Morgenthau, in his capacity as a cabinet officer (and twenty-five years earlier, as a friend of Assistant Naval Secretary Franklin Roosevelt, who needed a letter of recommendation to accompany an application for a commission as an army officer), may well have been included. But those individuals had nothing to do with Long's general, impersonal, Social Darwinist attitudes.

Wyman writes: "At the State Department conference, Morgenthau managed, offhandedly and without revealing his purpose, to get Hull to tell Long to send a copy of [Long's] cable 354 [which he sent to American Minister Harrison in Bern] to the Treasury. But the line in the cablegram that referred to [Harrison's own cablegram] 482 had been deleted. . . . Only because DuBois had already seen a true copy of [Long's cable] 354 did the Treasury realize what happened. Morgenthau immediately sent one of his staff to look at Long's [own] copy of [his cable] 354. Noticing the reference to [Harrison's cable] 482, the Treasury official told Long that Morgenthau would also want a copy of [cable] 482. The next day, [a copy of cable] 482 reached the Treasury, confirming DuBois's disclosure."[668]

Wyman suggests that even the evidence of Social Darwinist subterfuge did not initially convince Morgenthau of Long's distaste for assisting refugee relief efforts to the point of sabotage, or the need to remove supervision of such activities from Long's grasp if any effective relief effort was to be realized. Moreover, there was the public airing of the congressional resolution that had to be considered. Still, Morgenthau hesitated to bring the matter of Jewish refugees to Roosevelt's attention. It was a difficult course of action for him to pursue, although, as Beschloss writes: "Since the start of the war, Morgenthau had quietly and cautiously tried to help Jewish refugees."[669]

Oscar Cox tried without success through the remainder of December 1943 to get Morgenthau to speak to Roosevelt, to urge him to create a new agency (as the proposed congressional resolution directed) before the pending resolution was officially adopted by Congress.[670] By January 1943, Morgenthau's other staff members accepted Cox's suggestion. On January 13, 1944, DuBois's Foreign Funds Control section presented to Morgenthau a copy of an eighteen-page document titled "Report to the Secretary on the Acquiescence of This Government in the Murder of the Jews."[671] The Report began: "One of the greatest crimes in history, the slaughter of the Jewish people, is continuing unabated."[672] Randolph Paul "particularly condemned State Department restrictions on visas. Under pretext of concern for national security . . . Long and his associates had held immigration below available quotas."[673] The Report concluded that the State Department was "guilty not only of gross procrastination and willful failure to act, but even of willful attempts to prevent action from being taken to rescue Jews from Hitler." Another passage spoke of officials in the State Department "kicking the rescue matter around for over a year without producing results."[674] In the face of civilians being murdered on an almost unimaginable scale, traditional courtesies between cabinet-level departments were being left behind.

Beschloss quotes Henry III as saying that neither Henry Sr. nor Elinor Morgenthau was enthusiastic about Morgenthau's involving himself in Jewish refugee affairs. It threatened the quietude of the life they had carved out for themselves. "But Henry Sr. was slowing down—he was now eighty-eight years of age, while Elinor Morgenthau was afflicted by the onset of severe cardiovascular disease."[675] (The development of blood chemistry analysis, heart-regulating pharmaceuticals, and ameliorating surgical techniques was unfortunately decades into the future.) Morgenthau was left with only his secretary, Henrietta Klotz, who had an intense ethnically Jewish identification. Morgenthau was aware of her feelings about genocide and how it was disregarded by Social Darwinist, Gentile society.[676]

Morgenthau pointed out during one of his staff meetings that there was "the imminence of Congress doing something" first. Since the Rescue Resolution's sponsors included several Republicans, they could seek to take credit for any congressional action. Morgenthau had commented during one of his staff conferences (as much to himself as to his listeners): "Really, when you get down to the point, this is a boiling pot on the Hill. You can't hold it; it is going to pop, and you have either got to move very fast, or the Congress of the United States will do it for you."[677]

After mulling over the Report for two days, Morgenthau realized there was no one else in a Social Darwinist world to whom he could pass the responsibility for attempting to break through what was an unspeakable disregard by the United States government for the sanctity of human life on the European continent. He must act without thinking about the personal consequences. The appointment with the president was for the next day, a Sunday afternoon.[678]

"As Randolph Paul recalled, his boss was 'taking his political life in his hands.'"[679] And, as Beschloss puts it, "If going to Roosevelt made the President think of him as a special petitioner for his fellow Jews, so it would have to be. If his boldness jeopardized his treasured presidential friendship, so be that too."[680] On his way to go from the Treasury building next door to the White House, Morgenthau was heartened to hear his young assistant Josiah DuBois, who was not joining him, say, "If it means anything, and if you want to, you can tell the President that if he doesn't take any action on this report, I'm going to resign and release the report to the press."[681]

Morgenthau, Paul, and Pehle met with the president for twenty minutes and presented a shortened version of the Treasury's report to Roosevelt. Oscar Cox had prepared an executive order that provided for the creation of a rescue committee to be headed by Morgenthau, Hull, and Leo Crowley, now the director of the Foreign Economic Administration.[682] The president listened while his callers summarized the contents of the report they had handed to him. Beschloss writes: "The report warned that a 'growing number of Americans' saw 'plain anti-Semitism' behind the State Department's actions, which 'could explode into a nasty scandal . . . Rescuing the Jews from extermination is a trust too great to remain in the hands of men who are indifferent, callous and perhaps even hostile.'"[683]

Roosevelt made a pro forma defense of the State Department. His friend Breckenridge Long was " 'somewhat soured' on the refugees after Rabbi Wise persuaded him to admit a long list of them, 'many of whom turned out to be bad people.' Morgenthau retorted Attorney General Francis Biddle had assured the Cabinet that only three Jewish refugees admitted during World War II had been found undesirable."[684]

Roosevelt studied the proposed order, suggested Stimson be substituted for Crowley, and agreed to sign and issue the executive order. Wyman suggests that Roosevelt's quick agreement to what his callers were recommending indicates he was aware of the publicity about the pending Rescue Resolution in the Senate and knew he needed to act before Congress did.[685] Roosevelt's executive order creating the War Refugee Board, consisting of Morgenthau, Hull, and Stimson, was issued January 22, 1944. The Rescue Resolution had been placed on the calendar for a Senate vote on January 24.[686]

Morgenthau would later comment modestly to his staff: "After all, the thing that made it possible to get the president really to act on this thing—we are talking here among ourselves—was the thing that—the resolution . . . to form this kind of a War Refugee Committee . . ."[687]

Wyman allows himself to wonder why it had taken fourteen months between the moment Rabbi Wise had publicly decried the genocide taking place in Europe until the president issued his executive order. Wyman gives three reasons: First was the State Department's disinclination to act, its attempt at suppression of information forwarded to it, and its attempt to use the 1941 Bermuda Conference to suggest something was being done when the State Department was doing nothing (and, in fact, impeding rescue efforts); second, there was the indifference of most Christian leaders, both secular and religious, and also of the media, to the information that filtered out of Europe; and finally, there was the inability of the American Jewish community to unite and provide a sustained demand for some action.[688]

In the abstract, Roosevelt understood that Nazi political amorality represented a fundamental menace to simple human decency and democratic governance, but he also recognized that in the particulars, Social Darwinist prejudice in the United States could create difficulties that would impede his ultimate objective. He understood that he led a coalition of disparate groups in American society, many mutually antagonistic. Just as in the early years of his administration he had bested the radical farm organizations, later, although the isolationists represented a substantial proportion of the American electorate, he had succeeded in his efforts to give aid and assistance to the British short of war, even to legislation authorizing Lend-Lease. Ultimately and tragically, he could not imagine, any more than did his friend Breckenridge Long, the urgency of the menace of Nazi genocide.

Roosevelt's experience in World War I and its aftermath conditioned him to understand that war was productive of horror. That awareness rested on the assumption that however savage and cruel wartime circumstances were, those circumstances were a by-product of military actions. He could not imagine, although he was conditioned by Social Darwinist thought, that Hitler would be so mad as to interfere with his own war effort and "aggravate a severe labor shortage" to divert equipment and manpower to sheer nihilistic civilian death, destruction, and pillage.[689] If Roosevelt's response to Jan Karski's plea to do something to save people's lives makes any sense, Roosevelt's response was predicated on the premise that however severe wartime conditions might be, most people would survive. While most people in Europe during World War II did survive, most of the subgroup of European Jews did not, due to a sustained program of Nazi genocide on the European continent. This was beyond the imaginative powers of a Social Darwinist world that predisposed people to think primarily in narrow terms, limited to the threat of harm to their own ethnic kin.

Roosevelt could relate to the problems that farmers experienced in the United States. He managed a farm that cost him money each year. He could understand the problems of farmers who had to depend on the produce of their farms to earn money to buy necessities their farms did not grow. And Roosevelt could think of Morgenthau as a fellow farm owner, a member of Roosevelt's own social class in Dutchess County, and a friend who had given freely of his time and effort to help Roosevelt at crucial points in Roosevelt's own life. Morgenthau's Jewish ethnic identity probably had a piquancy of no more importance to Roosevelt than the circumstance that his mother's maiden name, given to him for his own middle name, generations back had probably been some variant of the Huguenot De la Noye or De la Noire.

In the aftermath of the meeting that afternoon, Morgenthau was concerned that he may have offended Roosevelt in some way. He telephoned the president that evening to ask his opinion on a speech he intended to give. Roosevelt suggested he add the adjective "proven" before the phrase "ringleaders of hate." Morgenthau wrote in his diary, "He joked and kidded with me and seemed to be in a grand humor." He concluded that Roosevelt appeared to show "no unfavorable reaction in his mind about myself, which is encouraging . . . I hope he will see the thing through that I went to see him about."[690]

Breckenridge Long had his hour on the public stage and he mishandled it. In a Social Darwinist vein, he understood his fundamental views could not be aired publicly, even though there might be substantial agreement among members of Congress. The need to dissimulate led him into compromises with the truth that could be accepted by those same members of Congress, who were not knowledgeable about his subject matter. But there were those outsiders who were letter-perfect about the factual details, who knew precisely what it was he was talking about, who could and did refute his details, and had access to magazines and news-papers, as well as members of Congress. Long had embarrassed the administration.

"Publicity about his remarks crested in late December [1943], at the same time as the Treasury Department's showdown with him . . ."[691] Blum quotes Edward R. Stettinius, the recently appointed undersecretary of state, as telling Morgenthau that he was "not surprised about Breckenridge Long since Long had fallen just as badly and in an equally shocking way in the handling of the exchange of prisoners. Stettinius was very frank in his views on Long's failures and pointed out that in the reorganization of the State Department which he had worked out, the only remaining function assigned to Breckenridge Long is Congressional rela-tions." Blum has Stettinius adding that "he found Long, no longer a young and perhaps never a vigorous executive, inefficient in everything he handled." Reviewing the proposed executive order, Stettinius said: "I think it's wonderful."[692] Left with his job title, Long retired a year later.[693] It is probable that by then he had accumulated the requisite time in government service to ensure a decent government pension with which to live out his years.

Roosevelt's Executive Order 9417 had been drawn up by dedicated hands in the Treasury Department, and Roosevelt signed it with only one change: the substitution of Stimson for Leo Crowley as the third member of the War Refugee Board. Although Roosevelt signed the executive order presented to him, it is not clear that his basic ideas had changed in the sense that he had really come to a full realization of the cruelty, horror, and sadism of Nazi mass murder. There was the usual jumble of circumstances: a need to dominate political action in the Congress involving matters in which Republican members were taking an interest; the number of public figures who gave testimony at the House Foreign Affairs Committee hearings; Morgenthau's concern; and possibly also some irritation at Breckenridge Long's ineptness and lack of understanding about how to manage the public aspect of his official responsibilities. But there is no evidence that Roosevelt felt ready to challenge the latent anti-Semitism in the American electorate by too elaborate and public an effort to assist European Jews. Roosevelt's purpose was to keep the effort within discrete bounds (notwithstanding the very broad language of the executive order[694]).

Wyman comments that of all the divisions of the federal government, "[o]nly the Treasury Department met its full responsibilities," giving space and most of the personnel to the War Refugee Board, while "Morgenthau himself kept in close touch with the board." The middle levels of the State Department experienced no conversion to philo-Semitism, while McCloy, acting for Stimson and the War Department, retained his skepticism about atrocity stories and felt refugee relief efforts were not a primary military concern.[695]

Morgenthau had wanted John Pehle as the Board's director and got the agreement of Stimson and Hull. For some reason,

Roosevelt wanted to make the announcement himself at his press conference, then failed to do so. One has the sense that the whole idea of the War Refugee Board had been imposed on Roosevelt, and while he had recognized intellectually the need for creating the Board, there was a latent irritation on his part that he had been forced to do something he would rather have "kept on a back burner."[696]

Wyman comments: "The War Refugee Board staff, which never numbered more than thirty, revolved around a dozen people, mostly non-Jewish and mostly veterans of the Treasury's battles with the State Department over the rescue issue. They were, as one observer remarked, 'young, dynamic, bold, clear and a bit brash.'"[697] Representatives were assigned to neutral countries on the perimeters of Wehrmacht-occupied Europe, although the effort failed with Russia, Spain, and Egypt.[698] Stalin's not-so-latent anti-Semitism precluded singling out Jews for separate rescue efforts. Within a few years he would murder the members of the (Communist) Yiddish cultural committee and later commence newspaper agitation about the so-called Kremlin "Doctors' Plot"—cut short only by his fortuitous death in 1953. The British government was not interested in Jewish rescue efforts in Egypt, so close to Palestine, while the American ambassador to Spain, Carlton J. H. Hayes, was personally opposed to the idea of board representatives on his diplomatic staff.

Wyman comments that the board was severely underfunded. Most of its funding came from private Jewish philanthropic organizations and not the government. Apparently, John Pehle was afraid of the general anti-Semitism of the period that could be stirred up if approaches were made to the Congress for funding of the Board's activities in Europe.[699] It would appear he was concerned with the possibility of charges that Jews were seeking "special" benefits (as if Nazi genocide activities were not focused overwhelmingly on the destruction of European Jews). "Morgenthau soon realized that his influence with the President on rescue matters was very limited, and he lessened pressures in that direction."[700]

At one point in 1944, Pehle sought Eleanor Roosevelt's assistance to speak to the president about the failure of Ambassador Hayes in Madrid to support the mission of the War Refugee Board. She reported that the president responded "wearily, 'Well, the complaints are mounting.'"[701] Apparently, Ambassador Hayes, an academic by profession, felt any intrusion by any other government operation, whether the War Refugee Board, the Office of Strategic Services, or the Office of War Information, would represent a fatal interference with his diplomatic efforts to cut off Spanish exports of tungsten ore to Germany.[702] In a Social Darwinist world, while Hayes had small interest in foreign Jewish refugees, at home he was apparently proud to be the Catholic co-chairman of the National Conference of Christians and Jews, a position he retained while ambassador in Madrid.[703]

After Eleanor Roosevelt's appeal to her husband, Morgenthau felt emboldened, and he urged Roosevelt to appoint Wendell Wilkie to go to Madrid and speak to Hayes about cooperating with other government agency representatives, but to no avail. Roosevelt merely referred him to speak to Secretary of State Hull.[704] Roosevelt apparently felt that Hayes was doing a good job in weaning Francisco Franco, then the ruler of Spain, from cooperating with the Germans. Roosevelt's thoughts on the plight of European Jews would appear to remain centered on the idea that however hard their current plight, *most* would survive the war. It seems that Roosevelt never understood the magnitude of Nazi genocide, and he never lived long enough to finally come to understand its dimensions.

Still, Beschloss writes:

[O]n Friday, March 24, 1944, [prodded again by Morgenthau] during an Oval Office session with reporters, he made the most direct proclamation of his life about the Final Solution. . . . From a script, Roosevelt read out, "In one of the blackest crimes of all history—begun by the Nazis in the day of peace and multiplied by them a hundred times in time of war—the wholesale, systematic murder of the Jews of Europe goes on unabated every hour. . . . None who participate in these acts of savagery shall go unpunished. . . . All who knowingly take part in the deportation of Jews to their death in Poland or Norwegians and French to their death in Germany are equally guilty with the executioner himself.

Hitler is committing these crimes against humanity in the name of the German people. I am asking every German and every person . . . everywhere under German domination to show the world by his action that in his heart he does not share these insane criminal desires. Let him hide these pursued victims, help them to get over their borders and do what he can to save them from the Nazi hangman.[705]

Those were noble words—even if they were prepared by Pehle and his staff—and Roosevelt read them.[706] But there is no evidence that he had changed his belief in the survivability of the majority of the European Jews. Indeed, the proclamation was made in an effort to cause a new cabinet in Budapest to resist Nazi pressures and inhibit action against Jewish Hungarians.[707] With the Wehrmacht ready to occupy the country, there is no evidence Roosevelt's words had any effect (although in the end the Wehrmacht did occupy the country). The point to be made is that Roosevelt was moved to act to maintain the status quo in Hungary. Although he spoke generally of deportation and murder, there is no evidence of any continuity of focus on his part. If McCloy is to be believed, it was Roosevelt's decision *not* to interdict the rail lines leading to Auschwitz. That decision can only be explained in terms of a failure to comprehend the actual dimensions of Nazi genocide.

He had spoken words that had been prepared by other hands without any true awareness of the meaning of those words. That he consented to read the words is to his credit. The tragedy is that he lacked the ability to relate to what he was saying. In that sense, his thinking was bounded by—and he saw the world through the prism of—the Social Darwinism of his day. His experience led him to be sympathetic with the problems faced by American farmers in a time of agrarian recession—among whom he could count himself—and he could have a Social Darwinist identification as an Anglophile, which led him to conceive of the idea of Lend-Lease at a time when the British were fighting alone against the Nazi juggernaut and in the process rapidly beggaring themselves. He was intellectually sophisticated enough to recognize the menace that Hitler represented to a civilized society (as Anne Morrow Lindbergh wrote with poignant regret looking to a seemingly inescapable totalitarian future). Tragically, Roosevelt lacked the imagination in a Social Darwinist world to relate to the poor souls who were being delivered in boxcars to the portals of Auschwitz. He was unable to recognize that what was needed, pure and simple, was to help European Jews to escape from the snares of Nazi genocide.

When a reporter asked Roosevelt after he had finished his statement whether that meant the United States was prepared to take in refugees, the president replied, "No, not yet," and feeling the need to give some explanation, he added, "because there aren't enough to come." He was unable to understand the scale, the magnitude, of Nazi genocide. He was thinking in terms of the proposition that *most would survive*. In a Social

Darwinist world that premised struggle and strife as the human fate, Roosevelt could not conceive that millions of European Jews had already fallen victim to Nazi genocide. In his "Four Freedoms" pronouncement, he could speak of humanity in the whole, but in his ordinary thinking, while his Social Darwinist identification could go so far as to include the British Isles, it did not extend to anonymous European Jews in places like Poland, Russia, Slovakia, Slovenia, Croatia, Romania, or Ukraine.

On June 24, 1944, Pehle (as had others) asked McCloy to explore the possibility of bombing the five separate rail lines to Auschwitz.[708] Beschloss suggests Pehle's request was probably at Morgenthau's urging.[709] In three weeks the Nazis had deported one-third of Hungary's Jewish population to Auschwitz.[710] Beschloss quotes Roosevelt as telling McCloy "that bombing Auschwitz 'wouldn't have done any good' and that 'we would have been accused of destroying Auschwitz [by] bombing these innocent people.'" McCloy is then quoted as saying Roosevelt added, "Why the idea! They'll say we bombed these people, and they'll only move it down the road a little way and [we'll] bomb them all the more. If it's successful, it'll be more provocative, and I won't have anything to do [with it] . . . We'll be accused of participating in this horrible business."[711]

McCloy near the end of his life admitted to Henry III that he had not wanted to bomb Auschwitz either.[712] (The Allied advance into southern Italy had secured airfields which made that option feasible.) Perhaps it was only those who could identify in a Social Darwinist sense with the unfortunate souls in the boxcars lurching slowly to the death camp at Auschwitz, those whom McCloy would characterize as "a bunch of fanatic Jews,"[713] who could be desperate enough to advocate bombing the rail lines. In roughly the same period as the bombing of Auschwitz caught Morgenthau's attention, he also was concerned that the United States make some symbolic gesture toward giving refuge to a small group of mostly dispossessed Jews then in southern Italy. He asked Pehle to find a small unutilized army base or other available facility to house them temporarily. On June 1, 1944, Josiah DuBois mentioned it to McCloy on the telephone. McCloy's response was that refugees were not the army's concern.

Morgenthau thought McCloy's answer out of bounds and brought a transcript of the conversation to a cabinet meeting that afternoon. Stimson agreed that refugees were not the concern of the army. While Roosevelt on another occasion might have reacted the same way, he apparently felt it was inappropriate for Stimson to voice those sentiments and said, "Under no circumstances must these people be turned back." In his office, Stimson dictated a memorandum to his secretary that said "someone" at the cabinet meeting that afternoon had criticized McCloy as an "oppressor of the Jews." The memorandum, when prepared, appeared on McCloy's desk. In a Social Darwinist world, such thoughts might be held but were not to be spoken in polite society. McCloy felt insulted and outraged. Word got back to Morgenthau, who realized he had to work with McCloy, whom he then invited to see him at home early the next morning.[714]

Morgenthau acknowledged he had spoken at the cabinet meeting of McCloy's disinclination to act on the request for a haven in the United States for war refugees in southern Italy. He added that Stimson was "annoyed" that he had not been briefed on the matter. McCloy could be upset at the thought his boss criticized him in public. Morgenthau then pointed out that the United States must give some example to the rest of the world if others were to be expected to take some action on refugees. The Germans were gleefully pointing out American hypocrisy.

In the last analysis, the president had spoken. McCloy could not seriously expect to disobey a presidential direction. Making the best of an awkward situation, McCloy offered to house 1,800 refugees at Fort Ontario in Oswego, New York, and he promised the army would transport them. But he drew the line at meeting their needs once they arrived.

Morgenthau was delighted he had gotten McCloy's commitment, but the interview had exhausted his nervous energies. At his desk at 9:15 AM, he admitted at his staff meeting that he was "ready to go [back] to bed."[715]

Perhaps the last word was said by Henry III, who wrote: "In August [1944] 982 refugees (89 percent of them Jewish) arrived at Fort Ontario . . . having been transported by an army troop ship returning otherwise empty from Italy. As things turned out, this 'token payment to decency' was the sum total of the American safe haven."[716] Of the War Refugee Board and Morgenthau's efforts on its behalf, he writes: "In the end some 200,000 lives [in Europe] had been saved—a not insignificant, yet heartrendingly disappointing number."[717]

Since life continues on multiple levels at one and the same time, it is not unusual that during the spring months of 1944, Morgenthau's staff at the Treasury Department were busy making the final choice on the participant nations, issuing formal invitations, deciding on a site, and arranging the logistical requirements to house the delegates for what became the Bretton Woods Conference. It was intended to settle the parameters for international financial cooperation and provide for the stability of foreign exchange ratios and the maintenance of individual nations' economic equilibrium in the postwar world—no small goal. The objective was to avoid the international monetary difficulties and the recurrent national and international fiscal crises during the preceding decade.

In a world before air-conditioning was commonplace, the closest site to Washington with bearable summer weather was New England.

Forty-four governments were invited to Bretton Woods,[718] each with multiple staff members expected. The United States delegation numbered twelve aside from the Treasury Department aides: Harry White; Edward Bernstein, given the title Executive Secretary and Chief Technical Advisor; and Ansel Luxford, designated Chief Legal Advisor.[719] Among the American delegates were United States senators—Senator Fred Vinson (who would be Morgenthau's successor and later a chief justice of the United States) was designated vice-chairman under Morgenthau; congressmen; and several distinguished university professors.[720] Roosevelt was careful to avoid Wilson's fatal error (of not including members of the Senate and House of Representatives in the American delegation to the conference at Versailles in 1919), which had led to the United States Senate's rejection of Wilson's peace treaty ending World War I and his cherished League of Nations.

There were the usual auxiliary conference personnel— shorthand reporters, typists, interpreters, and the like for whom sleeping, dining, plenum, and committee meeting space was also needed. Once the summer resort hotel at Bretton Woods, New Hampshire, was chosen—it had been closed during the war years—arrangements had to be made to have it reopened, temporary hotel staff hired, the quarters made ready for guests, food and beverages bought, and timely delivery arranged.

The Bretton Woods conference opened on July 1, 1944.[721] It represented the emergence of the United States on the world stage as the leader of the free world.

Eccles, a member of the American delegation, described the agreements that resulted as "the most important in the international field from a monetary standpoint."[722] Gardner writes that at "Bretton Woods final agreement was reached on a[n International Monetary] Fund with resources of $8.8 billion, with an American contribution of $3.175 billion."[723] Harry White explained: "[T]he [International Monetary] Fund is the means for establishing and maintaining stability, order and freedom in [foreign] exchange transactions."[724] Gardner writes: "The Treasury stated . . . that the establishment of the Fund 'would [com]mit 44 countries to an international agreement to maintain stable [foreign] exchange rates and to remove exchange controls.' On the subject of [foreign] exchange stability, White declared that under the Fund Articles 'whatever changes are made in [foreign] exchange rates will be made solely for the purpose of correcting a balance of payments which cannot be satisfactorily corrected in any other way . . .'"[725] There would be effective limits on "drawing rights" by individual countries as a result of the preliminary Anglo-American negotiations conducted principally by White and Keynes in Washington over a period of some two years. What is remarkable is that the configuration of ideas that coalesced into the Fund would succeed, whereas less than a decade earlier, the Tripartite Agreement of 1936, with roughly the same objectives, had failed ignominiously.

It was Morgenthau's finest hour as Treasury secretary, and he executed it flawlessly. Edward Bernstein commented: "It was a very smooth conference, because everything of importance had been discussed and settled in the two years of discussion before the Conference."[726] Morgenthau's great accomplishment as Treasury secretary in connection with the Bretton Woods Conference had been to find extremely competent subordinates and then allow them complete discretion to do their job. As host, Morgenthau welcomed the delegates at the initial plenum session. Then, he had the sense to stay out of the way. Edward Bernstein writes, "The conference was organized into two main commissions, I on the [International Monetary] Fund and II on the [International] Bank [for Reconstruction and Development]. Morgenthau was chairman of the general conference. White was chairman of Commission I; Keynes was chairman of Commission II."[727]

Both institutions would have their headquarters in Washington. The British for one might have expected the site to be more naturally New York rather than Washington (for the same reasons that it was the Federal Reserve Bank of New York which dealt with international financial transactions as agent of the United States Treasury). Morgenthau and White preferred Washington, thinking distance from the large banks in New York would insulate the new international financial organizations (in the hands of international bureaucrats) from what Gardner describes as Morgenthau's and White's idea of "the intrigues of vested interests," i.e., the neo-mercantilist attitudes of private bankers that had led to the collapse of the American banking system in the years preceding Roosevelt's inauguration in 1933. Gardner suggests that proximity to the leaders of the United States government led to a different set of political imperatives. In this respect, Gardner wrote: "[T]he transfer of decision-making from New York to Washington . . . might actually increase the nationalistic and political components of international financial policy."[728] (Those issues are necessarily beyond the scope of this study.)

Bernstein gives an example of Morgenthau's role at Bretton Woods. The Russians protested to him that the committee on quotas had not given them the Fund quota they felt they had been assured would be theirs. The secretary went with Bernstein and a State Department Russian expert (to act as their interpreter as required) to talk with the Russian delegates, and the Russians' quota was adjusted more to their liking.[729] Other nations also had objections to aspects of the preliminary decisions. The Belgian government-in-exile objected to the provisions for liquidation of the International Monetary Fund. They felt they would never have need to exercise their drawing rights, in which case, they did not want to be held liable for part of any losses. The Treasury representatives arranged to modify the liquidation and withdrawal provisions more to their liking. They provided the first managing director of the Fund[730]—setting the precedent that the president of the World Bank (as it is popularly known) is an American, and the managing director of the Fund, a European. Bernstein writes that Morgenthau and the American delegates wanted everyone to understand that the United States looked to be fair to all.[731] The final period of the conference was left mostly to the Committee on Unsettled Questions relating to the International Monetary Fund that necessarily involved arcane, monetary issues.[732] By then, Morgenthau temporarily had gone back to Washington.

Gardner explains that the International (or "World") Bank could make loans from its original resources (the initial payments of the original subscribing countries), but its principal function was intended to provide guarantees of private loans. Twenty years later, "the Bank was now a respectable and conservative financial institution."[733]

Once the agreements at Bretton Woods had been signed, it was Morgenthau's responsibility to assist in the creation of favorable public opinion so that Congress would ratify those agreements. To this purpose, Morgenthau addressed a group of industrialists in Detroit. He assured them that "if the Bretton Woods agreements were adopted, world trade would be 'freed from restrictive [foreign] exchange controls and depreciating [foreign] exchange rates' and the American automobile industry could look forward to a standing export market for more than a million cars a year."[734]

For those—like Senator Robert Taft of Ohio—concerned that the transition period from war- to peacetime national economies might place unbearable strains on the resources of the International Monetary Fund, Harry White explained that ". . . this country assumes no moral responsibility for a scarcity of dollars. The technical representatives of the United States have made it very clear to other countries in a number of memoranda that a scarcity of dollars cannot be accepted as evidence of our responsibility for the distortion of the balance of payments."[735]

Gardner writes: "To gain approval for the Fund the Administration had found it necessary to allay Congressional fears that the institution might become a sieve for the outpouring of American dollars. The Bretton Woods Agreements Act subjected the American Executive Directors to close control by the American Government." The members of Congress did not want the resources of the Fund to be used to rebuild either ruined buildings or commercial arrangements in Europe.[736] (That would be the function of the Marshall Plan, several years hence.)

In July 1945, public opinion had swung in favor of Bretton Woods. A majority of Republican members of Congress were prepared to vote in favor of joining the Fund and the Bank. The vote in the House of Representatives was overwhelmingly in favor, and on July 18, 1945, the Senate followed. By then, Morgenthau was no longer Treasury secretary.[737]

If the measure of success is longevity, then the continued existence of both the World Bank and the International Monetary Fund is evidence of their success. Gardner would suggest that with the rise of the Cold War, the original conception of the functioning of both organizations changed. That is perhaps inevitable with the passage of time, new generations, and unanticipated problems. Morgenthau and his staff, most notably Harry White, configured the contours of both organizations with "good bones" (as architects are wont to say), making both able to adjust to changed circumstances. On July 6, 1944, Morgenthau was temporarily back in Washington for a meeting with the president on plans for civil administration in the liberated areas of France.[738] The Treasury Department had an interest in the currency made available to the local population, but its input on that issue was settled a long while before. McCloy had written a memorandum to Roosevelt on June 1, 1944, denying press reports that Churchill would soon be discussing French fiscal matters with Charles de Gaulle. Asking "Pa" Watson to give the memo to the president, McCloy requested that he emphasize: "special currency for the invasion forces had been decided [upon] 'many months ago . . . with rates of exchange agreed.'"[739] Eisenhower issued a proclamation validating the occupation currency in France on June 10, 1944.[740]

Black makes the interesting point that around this time the president's wife had been lobbying him to renominate Henry Wallace for vice president. At a private talk with Morgenthau on July 6, 1944, the president recounted this information. Black writes: "Morgenthau strenuously counseled the President otherwise."[741] Roosevelt was again using Morgenthau as a sounding board. Morgenthau responded as a technocrat evaluating Wallace's limitations. Roosevelt would be looking at the matter from a political vantage point. As a reaction to Garner's obstructionism, Roosevelt had swung the pendulum sharply. Now, in a world where domestic considerations were no longer paramount, he had come to realize Wallace was no longer adequate. Morgenthau could be expected, with his focus sharply fixed both on wartime conditions in Europe and postwar international financial concerns, to reinforce Roosevelt's judgment.

Morgenthau's meeting with the president took place shortly after the Allied forces had established a beachhead on the European continent, where they would be preparing to end a three-week stalemate. They were looking to close the so-called Falaise Gap in Normandy to allow the Allies to spring a trap to capture the forward German divisions. Although the western-invasion armies would not complete their objective, allowing a partial

German withdrawal to occur, the Allied forces' tactical advances permitted General Patton's tank units to fan out eastward to cut German supply lines across France—requiring a major German military retreat to the Rhine River—and, optimistically, victory by Christmas.[742]

As of July 6, 1944, there was still only a small beachfront area in Normandy no more than twenty miles in depth in which to actually distribute "occupation" currency. The meeting could serve to decide the projected volume of currency that would be needed eventually, and to ascertain the currency then available.

What would have been a subject of the private talk Morgenthau had with Roosevelt afterwards would be a report by Morgenthau on how superbly the conference had gone at Bretton Woods. The participation of congressional leaders promised to ease approval of the agreements. Roosevelt could be satisfied that he had corrected Woodrow Wilson's fatal mistake of ignoring the members of Congress at the Versailles Peace Conference in 1919. It is in that context that Morgenthau asked for a special reward. He wanted to go to England and have Roosevelt's permission to visit what was still essentially the beachhead in Normandy.

Roosevelt could remember how eager Morgenthau had been to join the army in 1918 and how he had abetted Morgenthau's ambition by getting Breckenridge Long to write a letter of recommendation, and how, in the end, he had gotten his boss, Secretary of the Navy Josephus Daniels, to agree to give Morgenthau a naval commission.

"That would be fine," Roosevelt told him.[743] Morgenthau could "play soldier" and renew his acquaintance with Churchill and Anthony Eden, the British foreign secretary. Henry III said, "He got a great kick out of getting into the war zone and getting the . . . sounds and smells of war." He had already visited the North African battle area.[744]

Morgenthau asked Roosevelt if he could take along McCloy and if he could have letters authorizing his trip to generals in charge. Roosevelt agreed and wrote out a note to General Marshall endorsing the trip. Beschloss writes that Morgenthau *knew* "it would strengthen his hand in Europe" to include McCloy[745] (whatever the quoted words might mean). More likely, knowing Morgenthau, he knew he had offended McCloy and felt he wanted "to make it up" to McCloy by giving him a chance to see on the ground what it was he was dealing with in the reports that flowed over his desk.

McCloy did not see things the same way as Morgenthau, and declined the offer. Eisenhower was outraged at what he regarded as an imposition on field officers. The trip to the European bridgehead was reduced to an overnight visit.[746] After a relatively short summary by General Omar Bradley, outlining the battlefield tactical situation focused on Allied troops occupying the area between the towns of Falaise and Argentan in Normandy (and capturing German solders and Panzer units west of the "gap"),[747] Morgenthau was taken to visit a military evacuation hospital area, and most of his time—"a wonderful 31 hours"—was spent with his son Henry III, then in uniform.[748]

Henry III writes that "[t]he climax of Morgenthau's visit was two hours spent with the prime minister. . . . Churchill kept returning to the point that England 'was broke.'" Morgenthau was convinced.[749] That was the message Churchill conveyed to Roosevelt virtually from the moment he had become the prime minister.

As it turned out, events did not proceed as anticipated. Morgenthau faced problems of which he had not been aware. Once the airplane carrying Morgenthau and his assistants White, Smith, and DuBois had taken off, White gave him a copy of a State Department memorandum covering German postwar reparations with which Morgenthau sharply disagreed.[750] In England,

Morgenthau met with a former Treasury subordinate, Bernard Bernstein, then a colonel attached to the Civil Affairs division of SHAEF (Supreme Headquarters, Allied Expeditionary Forces).[751] Bernstein gave Morgenthau a copy of a proposed *Handbook for Military Government* intended to instruct army personnel serving in a future military government of an occupied Germany during continued military operations.[752] Military government personnel would be told their "main and immediate task" was to preserve the existing functioning of German civilian government to see that local government "works efficiently," to avoid a "morass of economic wreckage."[753] The local German industrial plants were to continue on an "even keel." German civilians would be fed 2,000 calories a day. Beschloss quotes Morgenthau as suggesting the proposed *Handbook* operation looked like one of Harry Hopkins's WPA jobs.[754]

Written by military bureaucrats, the proposed *Handbook* was entirely consistent with the War Department's idea that the army must concentrate solely on the military means necessary to defeat the enemy's soldiers, thereby winning the war. Beschloss notes in a footnote that the Anglo-American Combined Chiefs of Staff (CCSW-551) directed that while Nazism must be removed, "normal German life should be restored 'as soon as possible, insofar as conditions will not *interfere with military operations*'" (italics added). Although limited to the period of continued military operations, the point was not emphasized. As Beschloss notes, "[T]he proposed *Handbook* was likely to influence those planning the postwar occupation of Germany." [755]

It was written in terms appropriate to eighteenth-century dynastic territorial aggrandizement—comparable to the Prussian seizure in 1740 of the Hapsburg province of Silesia to allow customs duties, along with government monopolies like the salt tax (the major sources of eighteenth-century government income) to flow to the Hohenzollern dynasty in place of the

Habsburgs. Absent from that context was any real thought given to the *political* objectives of the contemporaneous war against the Nazi rulers of Germany.

Morgenthau was undoubtedly disturbed by what he read.

Courtesy required Eisenhower to invite Secretary of the Treasury Morgenthau and his assistants to lunch in his mess tent. Eisenhower writes that Morgenthau suggested that once Germany was occupied, the value of the German mark should be set at a foreign exchange level to prevent giving German industry any economic advantage. In response, Eisenhower explained he was then far too busy with military problems to give any thought to future economic problems. He explained he had an able staff working on that.[756] Morgenthau nodded to White to raise the question of their host's general view of Allied military government operation once Germany was occupied after active combat was finished.[757]

Eisenhower writes that he expressed himself in the following words: "These things are for someone else to decide, but . . . there must be no room for doubt as to who won the war. . . . the German people must not be allowed to escape a sense of guilt, of complicity in the tragedy that has engulfed the world. Prominent Nazis, along with certain industrialists, must be tried and punished. Membership in the Gestapo and in the SS should be taken as *prima facie* evidence of guilt. . . . The war-making power of the country should be eliminated. . . ."[758]

Morgenthau would comment, "I never saw Eisenhower in such good shape. . . . He made the best impression he has ever made on me."[759]

On August 14, 1944, marshalling support for his views on preventing a recurrence of German military aggression, Morgenthau invited the American ambassador, John Winant, and his advisors on the European Advisory Commission to lunch at the country house where he was billeted. After expressing his view on the need for containment of German military aggressiveness, Morgenthau learned that Winant and his advisors basically followed Stimson's idea that a German economy had to be maintained as a bulwark against dependency on Soviet assistance. Ambassador Winant and his group wanted to keep Russian influence out of Germany.[760] Still, the European Advisory Group, Mogenthau concluded, was not "doing very much . . . because it lacked clear authority and instructions."[761]

Lastly, Morgenthau saw Anthony Eden, then British Foreign Secretary. When Morgenthau spoke of Winant's European Advisory Commission's lack of instructions, Eden ". . . exclaimed that this had all been settled at Tehran. To prove his point he sent for the minutes of the Tehran Conference."

Morgenthau was astonished to learn "the Big Three had already specifically instructed the EAC to study the problem of partitioning Germany. Stalin, determined that Germany should never again disturb the peace of Europe, strongly favored its dismemberment. Roosevelt backed him wholeheartedly, and Churchill reluctantly agreed that the European Advisory Commission consider the proposal."

Morgenthau and Eden "were both amazed to learn that the EAC was . . . drawing its plans on the basis not of German dismemberment but of German unity. Winant had been at Tehran. But with no instructions from the State Department, he felt that they might not know of the Big Three decision and that it was not his business to inform his superiors on such matters."[762]

Roosevelt wanted to be his own foreign minister. So Hull, the secretary of state, was not a staff member brought to the Tehran talks with Stalin and Churchill. Aside from any discourtesy to Hull, Roosevelt was denying the State Department the knowledge to operate effectively. Keeping State Department personnel ignorant boded trouble.

Starting with his presidential election in 1932, Roosevelt's favorite mode of operation had been a version of Mao Zedong's (Tse-tung) ephemeral dictum, *Let a Hundred Flowers Bloom*. Roosevelt's staff put forward conflicting policies. He could listen and read, accepting whatever information he found useful until he was able to formulate a decision. It was a mode of operation that was rough on the losing advocate.

In July 1946, out of office and talking with the staff of a national magazine in connection with an article that would bear his name, almost in spite of himself, Morgenthau described Roosevelt: "... if we are going to be completely truthful, he never let anybody around him have complete assurance that he would have the job tomorrow. That gave you a sense of uneasiness, of insecurity, of his playing one person off against another . . . The thing that Roosevelt prided himself the most about was, 'I have a happy ship.' But he never had a happy ship. Just the opposite . . . I don't know why I said all this . . ."[763]

That mode of operation—allowing staff members to put forth differing policies and modes of approach to problems—rested on two prerequisites: the need for knowledgeable staff members, and the ability to keep abreast of the separate strands of conflicting arguments. Roosevelt at that point in his life was rapidly losing the physical energies necessary to stay on top of the arguments for competing ideas. By 1944, he was not that old in years, but the demands of coping with his physical infirmity had worn him out. He was starting to cut corners.[764]

Stalin's paranoia did not permit him to stray far from the borders of the police state he had created, so Roosevelt had gone to Tehran. The trip and the encounter with Stalin proved to be a severe strain on Roosevelt's constitution, after which Roosevelt "failed to regain his usual vigor." He spoke of "undue fatigue." His cardiologist, Dr. Bruenn, diagnosed "cardiac failure," a "grossly enlarged heart" with a "tortuous" aorta, the major artery in the body.[765] Apparently the president's personal physician had not advised his patient to be examined by a cardiologist. Dr. Bruenn was simply added to the president's medical staff and the president accepted the addition without any concern.

On March 28, 1944, Roosevelt was examined by Bruenn in the Electrocardiograph Department at Bethesda Naval Hospital. As Bruenn and his staff assisted Roosevelt onto the examining table, Bruenn discovered to his horror that the president was short of breath during the maneuver. During the doctor's examination, his patient's prior medical records arrived. These "showed a steady rise in systolic and diastolic blood pressures." Bruenn's own blood pressure readings were "clearly dangerous, 186/106." His diagnosis was "hypertension, hypertensive heart disease, cardiac failure (left ventricular) and acute bronchitis." Dr. Bruenn thought the president's health was "God-awful."[766] At that point, Dr. Bruenn was able to effectuate remedial action.

The president knew he had a problem with his blood pressure,[767] but apparently he did not fully understand the gravity of his situation, nor was he curious to find out. It does not appear that Dr. Bruenn made any attempt to convey the import of his findings. That he left to the president's personal physician, Admiral McIntyre, who was disinclined to discuss such matters with his patient.[768]

Morgenthau returned to Washington on August 17, 1944. Before talking to Roosevelt about the disturbing information he had received in England, Morgenthau went to see Hull the day after he came home. Hull explained that although he had appealed to the president to allow him to review the minutes of the Tehran conference, his request had not received a response.[769] Morgenthau then spoke with Roosevelt the next day. He reported Churchill's concerns about Britain's financial prospects after the termination of military operations in Europe. There was an outstanding question about the need for continuation of

Lend-Lease deliveries once hostilities ceased. Roosevelt scoffed at Churchill's fears about his country's postwar solvency.

Morgenthau next turned to the unsettled state of policies for the governance of Germany once hostilities ended, and pointed out "that planning [at SHAEF] for postwar Germany was in disarray." The European Advisory Commission was doing postwar planning in ignorance of what had been agreed upon at Tehran.[770]

Whatever Roosevelt may have said at the Tehran conference to Stalin about future German boundaries, governance, reparations, etc., had been said in the context of securing postwar cooperation from Stalin with respect to participation in a "united nations" international organization, trade arrangements, the economic recovery of Europe, and issues of that ilk. Roosevelt did not connect such talk with practical concerns such as military government policies once SHAEF troops entered Germany proper.[771]

Paris was liberated a week later on August 25, 1944.[772] General Patton's Third Army's forward units were advancing toward the approaches to the Rhine River and the German frontier. Black writes: "Starting in the last week in February 1944, the Royal and U.S. Air Forces had been sending almost 4,000 bombers over Germany on clear days, pounding German defense plants [still remaining above ground]. At night they bombed German cities indiscriminately, with devastating effect. . . . Churchill and Roosevelt had promised severe punishment to the civilian populations of both [Germany and Japan]."[773]

Roosevelt no longer had the physical strength to think of the implications of what Stalin could consider as commitments on Roosevelt's part with respect to postwar Germany. Roosevelt's habit of putting off decisions to the last possible moment had now been overtaken by his physical decline.[774] Still, Roosevelt played for time, past the hour policy should have been set for the governance of postwar, occupied Germany. He arranged for Stimson to have a talk with Morgenthau, well knowing there was a divergence of views between them. Their conflicting views would leave Roosevelt without any immediate need to consider the problem himself.[775]

A week later, Morgenthau saw the president again. Morgenthau proposed a cabinet committee to settle the matter of postwar military government policy for an occupied Germany. Roosevelt was uninterested. He wanted to retain responsibility for that and he was not ready to entertain the problem.[776] Morgenthau raised the matter of the exchange rate for dollars and marks about which there were conflicting opinions among the State and Treasury Departments and the British government. Here Roosevelt had an opinion: Let American troops make their own arrangements. (Eventually, the British prevailed on Roosevelt to set an exchange rate.)[777]

Next, Morgenthau brought up the matter of the SHAEF *Handbook for Military Government*, giving Roosevelt the copy he had received in England and making a list of the more-provocative excerpts copied from it. The president said he would read it that night and return it. Lastly, Morgenthau felt compelled to bring up the subject of a possible postwar recession. Roosevelt was clearly uninterested.[778] Morgenthau at this meeting for the first time noticed Roosevelt's gaunt and haggard appearance—in large measure due to his cardiologist's insistence on the president's losing weight to bring down his high blood pressure.[779] The president clearly had no energies to consider possible future eventualities.

In any case, Edward Bernstein was correct when he did not expect a postwar recession. In his monetarist analysis, historical postwar recessions were due to the efforts of governments to return prematurely to the gold standard for monetary value. He writes that he once told Lord Keynes "that it was the interaction of wartime inflation and the return to the gold standard, at historical parities, and the consequent deflation that caused great postwar depressions." He also explained, "War inflation exhausted the money-creating power of gold standard countries and the return to the gold standard led to overvaluation and undervaluation of currencies." He did not think the same mistake would be made by the United States at the end of World War II.[780]

Roosevelt had read the statements Morgenthau had given him from the SHAEF *Handbook*. The president found the quoted excerpts disagreeable, and he read some of them at a cabinet session on August 25, 1944.[781] Beschloss writes,

> Roosevelt was especially repelled by the *Handbook*'s insistence that . . . the Allies "restore as quickly as possible" the "regular German civil service" and the "highly centralized German administrative system" and "import needed commodities" to feed the Germans. He was incensed to the point he dictated "what McCloy called a 'spanking letter' to Stimson . . . This so-called *Handbook* is pretty bad . . . It gives me the impression that Germany is to be restored just as much as the Netherlands or Belgium, and the people of Germany brought back as quickly as possible to their prewar estate . . . I do not want them to starve to death, but . . . if they need food to keep body and soul together . . . they should be fed three times a day from Army soup kitchens . . . They will remember that experience all their lives.'"[782]

Beschloss goes on: "The President wrote that he would not accept the view of those who said that 'the German people as a whole are not responsible for what has taken place, that only a few Nazi leaders are.' The Germans must have it 'driven home' that they were 'a defeated nation' so that they would 'hesitate to start any new war.' The Allies must make the Germans understand that their 'whole nation' had been waging 'a lawless conspiracy against the decencies of modern civilization.'"[783]

The foregoing quotations are remarkable. Their eloquence equals the statement Roosevelt read at his press conference on March 24, 1944. Roosevelt understood, as did Morgenthau, that the German polity was Social Darwinism run amuck. Beschloss writes that Roosevelt "reported [to Morgenthau] that he had written to Stimson and McCloy about the SHAEF *Handbook*, quoting 'directly from your memorandum' . . ."[784]

In a Social Darwinist world, and as a loyal deputy to Stimson, McCloy would not consider the *Handbook* "as bad as the President did." Stimson (whatever his private beliefs), as a meticulously correct subordinate, agreed with Roosevelt that the proposed manual was "unduly solicitous of the future welfare of Germany."[785] Morgenthau would settle for a stiffly worded insert that it would be operational only until surrender.[786]

The first meeting of the president's cabinet committee on a future occupied Germany took place on September 5, 1944, in Hull's office. Unexpectedly, to Stimson's dismay, "Hull sounded 'as bitter as Morgenthau against the Germans.'"[787]

Stimson had been a superb trial lawyer in his day, and trial lawyers play to win. The thought that the cabinet committee would submit a recommendation for a military government antithetical to what Stimson believed was right "made the Secretary of War depressed and angry." That afternoon, McCloy recognized that his superior was feeling he was in a hopeless situation. If so, the next step was to submit his resignation. At 5:45, McCloy telephoned Hopkins to pass word to the president of an impending crisis.[788]

Stimson's resignation would be final since it involved a fundamental issue of principle. Roosevelt had sought out Stimson, and he had entered the cabinet as an independent Republican who might have large reservations about New Deal programs. (Roosevelt tolerated and even deferred to comments from Stimson that would bring down presidential wrath on other members of the cabinet.)

In a moment of international crisis, Stimson represented political unity. As a former secretary of state in Republican president Hoover's cabinet, Republican leaders of Congress like senators Taft and Vandenberg had enormous respect for his sense of probity. Although they represented Midwest constituents with isolationist political views, they appreciated the importance of Stimson's positions on international problems. For example, Vandenberg's turnabout from isolationist to internationalist is incomprehensible without factoring in the weight attached to Stimson's very conservative opinions. A resignation by Stimson would upset Roosevelt's carefully constructed national unity on international affairs and the continuing war effort in Europe. Roosevelt was not about to run any risk of Stimson's defection.

The very next morning, September 6, 1944 (after McCloy had alerted Roosevelt to Stimson's unhappiness with the thought he would be outvoted as to recommendations because of what he had heard from Hull at the first meeting of the president's committee on Germany), Roosevelt met with his cabinet committee members. Stimson emphasized his opposition to any destruction of the Ruhr and Saar valleys' industrial sites. "I cannot treat as realistic," he said, "the suggestion that such an area in the present economic condition of the world can be turned into a nonproductive ghost territory." He was willing to concede to "endeavoring to meet the misuse which Germany has recently made of this production by wise systems of control or trusteeship or even transfer of ownership to other nations."[789] (Morgenthau would finally agree to a trusteeship solution in his book, *Germany Is Our Problem.*)

Though Roosevelt reiterated his opinion that Germans could be fed from "soup kitchens," he readily agreed with Stimson's position that the future operation of the industries in the Ruhr valley was needed for Europe's postwar recovery. He hazarded the guess that the Ruhr coal mines could supply fuel for British steel foundries. He then went on to modify what he had just said by returning to his preferred thought that there was no need to decide the matter "right away."[790] Seemingly heartlessly throwing a bone to Morgenthau, he said, "The Germans are very wonderful in agriculture, aren't they, Henry? With their methods, they could take care of another million people, couldn't they?"[791]

Morgenthau was devastated by Roosevelt's turnabout. He could only feel betrayed by the inscrutable whims of an all-powerful *imperator*. He might think that Roosevelt's appointment of Stimson and Frank Knox in 1940 was a "nice" gesture in the face of an international crisis. Roosevelt, going back to his Albany days, was always trying to co-opt liberal Republicans. (So, for example, in Morgenthau's letter to his father, dated April 8, 1930, he had written: "Franklin is desperately looking for an independent Republican to appoint as Public Service Commissioner."[792]) And Ickes had been a Teddy Roosevelt "Bull Moose" Republican. Morgenthau himself had helped corral nominal Republican Henry Wallace. But Morgenthau had no understanding of the political dimensions that Stimson's appointment represented, so Morgenthau could tell his staff and others, "he was just 'heartbroken.'"[793]

To add to Morgenthau's misery, McCloy sent the president's son-in-law, John Boettiger, then an assistant in the War Department, to talk to Morgenthau about agreeing to the *Handbook for Military Governance*. Boettiger apparently lacked finesse. There was urgency, he said. The *Handbook* had already been printed. There would be a special flyleaf attached to the cover limiting its duration. The army needed to have the matter settled. Morgenthau reminded Boettiger that the president had wanted it rewritten. Boettiger acknowledged that, adding there would be time to rewrite the directive for a postwar military government. Then again, there was already a draft of a revision in their office. So Morgenthau agreed to what he considered an unsatisfactory compromise, reserving the right to review the revised *Handbook*.[794]

Roosevelt understood that he had dealt Morgenthau a cruel blow. And he had been harsher to Stimson than perhaps he may have wanted to be. The unintended consequence required immediate correction. (Whether he had expressed his real feelings to Stimson is an interesting question. Eleanor Roosevelt said he probably had not made up his mind yet.[795] The proposed SHAEF *Handbook* undoubtedly irritated him because it showed an utter lack of any real understanding of the purpose of the war in Europe.)

Having tilted too far in the first place, Roosevelt's recoil had unintentionally wounded Morgenthau. So one day later, on September 7, 1944, Roosevelt invited Morgenthau to walk over from the Treasury building to see him. "Don't be discouraged about yesterday's meeting," said Roosevelt. Cast in the negative, it really offered no certainty. What had seemed settled, was now undone. Balm had been applied to the wounds of both cabinet members. They were now less apt to make any rash moves. While Roosevelt had achieved his desire to put off the matter of the direction of military government, the wounds remained.

That afternoon, Morgenthau was so upset, he was rude to a British civil servant who had an appointment to see him in connection with setting the military occupation dollar exchange rate for German marks. (Apparently, Morgenthau's quite unsuspected temper tantrum convinced the British the matter was getting out of hand, and the next day they agreed on a rate of exchange.[796])

Stimson expressed his unhappiness by telling General Marshall that Morgenthau would shoot Nazi war criminals instead of putting them on trial first[797]—contrary to the way any lawyer would expect to proceed. Apparently, a few days later, and possibly aware of Stimson's private opinion, Roosevelt told Robert Murphy, a diplomat who was leaving to join Eisenhower's staff in London, that "German war criminals should be 'dealt with summarily.' No 'long, drawn-out procedure.' After proper identification, they should simply be executed."[798]

On Saturday, September 9, 1944, at noon, Roosevelt met once more with his cabinet committee. Morgenthau passed out loose-leaf copies of the report prepared by his staff, entitled: *Program to Prevent Germany from Starting a World War III*. (It would provide the basis for his later book, *Germany Is Our Problem*.) The recipients in the room professed ignorance of its contents. Roosevelt picked out one talking point: "It is a Fallacy that Europe Needs a Strong Industrial Germany." He commented: ". . . I agree . . . Furthermore, I believe in an agricultural Germany." Beschloss writes: "Hull and Stimson continued their schoolyard bickering." Stimson did not hide the fact that he considered the Treasury effort rubbish. Roosevelt allowed that he was in favor of a trusteeship over the Ruhr and Saar areas, and included the Kiel Canal as well. He also favored the division of Germany into three separate political areas.[799] Stimson stated his opposition to any "permanent" division of Germany. Roosevelt then announced that he expected to meet Churchill in Quebec shortly, and said that if the question of Britain's insolvency came up, he would want Morgenthau present. Morgenthau would afterwards tell his aide Harry White that he thought Roosevelt had definitely resolved the matter of Germany's future. White remained skeptical. And Stimson was discouraged by the week's recurrent turn of events.[800]

Roosevelt had not affixed his signature to a formal written document that included the Soviet Union, so all remained in flux. The combatants could look forward to returning to the fray another day. That evening Roosevelt and his wife left on his special train for an overnight journey to Highland, New York, a few miles from Hyde Park. Morgenthau and his wife Elinor were invited to join the Roosevelts on the train. On arrival the next morning, both couples would be driven to their respective homes.[801] Roosevelt would tell his confidant Margaret Suckley, at his newly constructed Hyde Park presidential library on the family land close by his home, "the last four days had been 'awful.'"[802]

The next week was consumed with the president's conference with Churchill at Quebec. Roosevelt had asked Morgenthau to be present.[803] The conference ended with Churchill and his wife being the houseguests of the Roosevelts at Hyde Park. On Monday, September 18, 1944, Roosevelt took Churchill to visit the Morgenthau farm, where its proud owner showed the British visitor his ripe apples weighing down the branches of the apple trees on which they were growing.[804] Blum earlier quoted the herd manager as saying, "Mr. Morgenthau knows his cows," and, Blum added, Morgenthau also knew his apples.[805]

The month of October 1944 was consumed for Roosevelt primarily with his fourth presidential campaign. The early part of the month included a public airing of the Morgenthau Plan, to public displeasure. Roosevelt, ever sensitive to public opinion, realized he had to backtrack. He wanted to hear no *cri de coeur* from Morgenthau to argue his position over again—the president had heard it all. The practical effect was that he simply refused to see the anguished Morgenthau, and had his daughter Anna lead him away from a closed door.[806]

Still, at the very end of the campaign, although the weather was cold and damp, the president insisted on making a sentimental tour of the Hudson River area, centered on his old state senate district, where he had begun his public career. Morgenthau accompanied him in the open auto as he had so often earlier in Roosevelt's life. It was almost as if the president wanted to push away the impairments, the deterioration, the ravages of time, and return to those happy days of years past when life seemed to be filled with promise. Morgenthau's presence was evidence that some part of that earlier world remained constant. Mindful of the passing years, Morgenthau included a roadside diner stop for sandwiches and hot coffee.[807]

Stimson thought any overt activity on Morgenthau's part was unseemly.[808] In a Social Darwinist world where Jews were merely tolerated, there was a preference that they remain inconspicuous. Matters such as "the German settlement" were best left to Gentiles, who could be objective and not subject to racial instinct that would distort their viewpoint. Ickes told Anna Roosevelt, the president's daughter, "the less Henry has to do with the German settlement, the better." Although he was truly sympathetic to the plight of victims of Nazi prejudice and aggression, Ickes thought that too great a Jewish interest in postwar plans for Germany could only lead to rising anti-Semitism.[809]

True to the president's directive, Stimson and McCloy instructed their staff to prepare a judicious and comprehensive policy statement covering military government in a future occupied Germany. It embodied Roosevelt's statements but left room for governing personnel to use their best judgment as circumstances might arise in the field. Within the ambit of Roosevelt's general directions, JCS 1067 sought to cover all possible contingencies—as is a lawyer's professional ideal in preparing a document intended to cover conduct in the future.

The one contingency that would appear to not be covered in JCS 1067 was the effect of any declaration the three heads of government might agree to thereafter that would overrule any of JCS 1067's particular provisions. The cause of the omission was that Stimson, as with Hull, was not privy to the minutes of the meeting of the heads of government at Tehran. The only Cabinet member who had had a glimpse was Morgenthau during his conversation with Anthony Eden in London concerning the seemingly rudderless course of the European Advisory Commission. It would have needed someone more sophisticated than Morgenthau to divine that Roosevelt was *deliberately* keeping the Tehran Conference minutes from the prying eyes of his Cabinet members.

At a cabinet meeting held on January 19, 1945, Roosevelt divulged that he was proposing to attend another meeting with Stalin and Churchill. In his absence he specifically authorized Morgenthau as the ranking cabinet officer in Washington (the new secretary of state, Edward Stettinius, would be joining Roosevelt) to assemble a cabinet session during Roosevelt's absence if he thought it appropriate. (Significantly, the new vice president did not figure in the equation.) Morgenthau wrote to his sons that he did not look forward to such an eventuality "because it does place considerable responsibility on my shoulders, but frankly it rather thrills me."[810] In the event, Morgenthau never had occasion to do so.

The new secretary of state secured Roosevelt's consent to appoint James Dunn, a civil service employee, as the number-three official in the State Department. (Stettinius probably felt that Dunn had "institutional memory" that had accrued over his years of service, which could prove of great value to the understanding of future problems with which the department might be presented during Stettinius's tenure.) Dunn presented Secretary Stettinius with a memorandum dated March 10, 1945, entitled *Draft Directive for the Treatment of Germany*.

Whereas the Yalta Conference had focused on decentralizing German political authority and reducing the responsibility of the occupying countries for the German economy, Dunn wanted Allied economic controls over the German economy that "would be 'paramount throughout Germany.'"[811]

Dunn claimed it was a summary of the notes on the Yalta conference (although it varied radically from what the heads of government had agreed on). Stettinius accepted Dunn's assurance and a few days later asked Roosevelt to sign it. Misled, Stettinius added that Stimson had read it with approval. Knowing Stimson approved nothing without full review, Roosevelt initialed the document.[812]

With underhanded, Social Darwinist cunning, Dunn could now feel the State Department's position on German governance had prevailed over the efforts of Morgenthau and the War Department's JCS 1067. Exultant, Dunn telephoned McCloy on March 15, 1945, to suggest McCloy revise JCS 1067 "at the earliest possible moment." It would appear that Dunn lost no time in dispatching a courier to hand-deliver a copy of the *Draft Directive* to McCloy to assist him in proceeding with the task.

JCS 1067 had been, in good part, McCloy's own work product. He was not about to see it upended. As McCloy understood the *Draft Directive*, it required "very close control of German prices and wages," and seriously reduced the legal powers of the American zone military governor.[813] He telephoned Morgenthau and asked him to "raise hell" with Stettinius. Morgenthau might have agreed that something had to be done; he was not about to be the War Department's point man. He reminded McCloy the War Department must take the lead. Still, once an appointment had been made for that afternoon for a visit by Stimson and McCloy to the secretary of state, Morgenthau joined them. The dispute was whether an occupied Germany would be governed by a four-power allied control council in Berlin, implementing economic control of the German economy, or by four autonomous zonal military governments with *limited* responsibility for the German economy.[814]

Now it was Stettinius's turn to say the offending *Draft Directive* was only an "interim document." At the same time, he promised to explain to Morgenthau what had been decided by the three heads of state in their meetings at Yalta. Stimson does not appear to have taken an active participation in the discussion, and McCloy would afterwards tell Morgenthau that he had not had a chance to brief Stimson.[815]

The next day Stimson spoke to Roosevelt, who apologized, saying he had initialed the state department *Draft Directive* without really considering the matter. Roosevelt mentioned the matter to Stettinius, who apologized to Morgenthau the next day, Saturday, March 17, 1945, saying his subordinate had misled him.[816]

On Tuesday, March 20, 1945, Morgenthau lunched with the president, presenting him with a memorandum in which Morgenthau wrote: "I am confident that this Directive goes absolutely contrary to your views." He thought it encouraged "a strong central German government and [would] maintain and even strengthen the German economy."[817]

Apparently, Morgenthau conceded during the presidential lunch that it was probable Europe would need coal from the Ruhr and Saar valley coal mines, but said that it would be unwise for American officials to supervise the operation. It appears the president was uninterested in coal mining in the Rhineland at that moment, because he responded rather flippantly that he would appoint three German businessmen to supervise the operation and monitor them from Washington. If they failed to perform, they would be shot.

Morgenthau was urging a low-key military government. In the last analysis, the technocrat in Morgenthau overrode the political advocate. Morgenthau might have been passionate, almost to a point of obsession, about the danger the German polity represented to international peace. But when it came to how government—especially a military occupation—should operate, his innate understanding of how government should work took precedence. And Roosevelt, who knew Morgenthau better than Morgenthau did himself, could appreciate the joke and go along with Morgenthau's wholly unconscious inconsistency.[818] (Roosevelt could agree to Morgenthau's plan to publish a book *after* the end of hostilities in Europe, setting forth how an occupied Germany should be treated so as to nullify the dangers to peace the German polity represented.[819])

After the presidential luncheon, Morgenthau was upset and incensed by the president's son-in-law John Boettiger interjecting himself into the matter of an occupied Germany and heavy-handedly requesting Morgenthau to "change his recommendations on Germany . . ."[820]

On March 23, 1945, a new directive was presented to Roosevelt by Morgenthau and Joseph Grew, an assistant secretary of state. It revoked the *Draft Directive* and reinstated JCS 1067.[821] Meeting Roosevelt's requirement for unanimity of opinion by the members of the Cabinet Committee on Germany, Morgenthau, McCloy, and Will Clayton, another assistant secretary of state, signed off on it.[822]

One can understand why McCloy was irritated by what Dunn had done, but it is not clear why Morgenthau need have been concerned. Any unified Allied council at that point necessarily involved the Soviet Union. Retrospectively, knowing the Soviet Union's approach to the subject of German reparations, the political subdivision of Germany, and their approach to German governance, Morgenthau's fears were groundless. The only explanation is that Morgenthau was ignorant of all that. Eden's pointing out a few lines of a transcript of the minutes of the Tehran Conference was insufficient to enlighten Morgenthau as to the whole of the transcript. Dunn had no conception of the mischief he was proposing by requiring a four-power council to oversee the whole of the governance of the German nation. The actual Allied Control Commission that was officially set in place in Berlin was inoperable in practice. As it was, at Potsdam, in July 1945, Stalin secured Truman's written agreement to *consider* reparations to the Soviet Union from the occupation zones allotted to the Western Allies. McCloy succeeded in involving Morgenthau in retrieving McCloy's "chestnuts out of the fire." But then, Morgenthau was impressed by McCloy. McCloy apparently had a quietly persuasive presence. In this he was much like Stimson, except for being younger; he had far more energy than Stimson and was capable of carrying a far heavier workload, relieving Stimson of a great deal of detail.

After Harry Truman's swearing in as the vice president on January 20, 1945, he was entitled to the use of an official chauffeur-driven Mercury limousine to take him from his residence to his office at the Capitol and back again. One morning he noticed a strange young man sitting next to the driver in the front seat. Modestly, he assumed the driver was giving a lift to a friend, another government employee, except that the stranger appeared in the same place at the end of the day.

Bemused, the vice president mentioned the circumstance to his friend and military aide, Harry Vaughan. Vaughan explained to Truman that he thought the vice president merited Secret Service protection. He had asked to see the secretary of the Treasury (who for budgetary purposes was the cabinet member to whom the director of the Secret Service reported). Morgenthau agreed and called the director of the Secret Service to suggest that an agent accompany the vice president. This was the first time that Secret Service protection had been given to a vice president.[823] Vaughan considered this protection a perquisite of office comparable to the use of an official limousine.

While Truman, Morgenthau, and others noticed Roosevelt's increasing frailty, no one apparently drew a serious inference that such frailty could portend a terminal event. The practical consequence is that the vice president did not express any curiosity about the operations of the executive branch of the government, and cabinet members did not extend an offer to the vice president to spend an afternoon becoming acquainted with the current problems with which a department might be dealing. The vice president appeared content to devote his time to presiding over the Senate and to the official and unofficial activities of Congress. Perhaps all might have considered too intense an interest in acquainting the vice president with the operations of the executive branch of the government an unpardonable species of *lese majesté*. Whatever the frailties Roosevelt may have exhibited, on those occasions that required it, Roosevelt could still muster his energies to project his usual persona. No one can predict the date of a natural, terminal event to which we are all subject, and, in any case, such matters are generally left to doctors. That said, the president's attending physician, Admiral McIntire, had declared the president fit to serve an additional, four-year term of office.

Elinor Morgenthau was not well, and the Morgenthaus decided a vacation in Florida might do her some good. With the matter of the *Draft Directive* settled, they entrained the next evening, March 24, 1945, for Daytona Beach, where they had reservations at the Sheridan Plaza Hotel. It did not ordinarily accept Jewish guests, but Elinor Morgenthau enjoyed breaking such taboos, and Morgenthau's cabinet position facilitated such gestures.[824] With Morgenthau's presence in the city noted, he was asked to come to a Passover Seder arranged for Jewish servicemen in the Daytona Beach City Hall. Since it involved members of the Armed Forces, he felt compelled to accept the invitation.[825] At some point in the religious readings that accompany the occasion, the officiating rabbi asked Morgenthau to say a few words. He declined because he felt too ignorant to say anything appropriate.[826] It was Morgenthau's first experience of a Passover Seder.[827] (It would appear that after Henry Sr. resigned the presidency of Rabbi Wise's Free Synagogue because of the latter's allegiance to the concept of Zionism, neither Henry Sr. or his son ever joined another congregation. Elinor Morgenthau herself was quite irreligious, so there was no encouragement from that quarter.)

In the first week of April 1945, Elinor Morgenthau suffered a serious heart attack that put her in an oxygen tent. By April 11, doctors advised Morgenthau that she was well enough so that she could be expected to survive and he could go back to Washington. Roosevelt had left for Warm Springs, Georgia, on March 29, 1945. Morgenthau—no doubt after making arrangements with Roosevelt—had his military flight stop in Georgia where he had dinner with Roosevelt and the latter's houseguests.[828] After dinner, Morgenthau spent some time alone with the president, during which he repeated his vision for a postwar Germany.[829] The subject of the book Morgenthau hoped to write—which would go into detail about the reconstitution of Germany—came up, and Roosevelt agreed that Morgenthau should take on the project.[830]

The ladies returned and Morgenthau excused himself to call his wife to find out how she was faring. He came back to the party to say good-bye. H would remember that Roosevelt and his houseguests "were sitting around, laughing and chatting . . . the President seemed to be happy and enjoying himself."[831] Morgenthau left for the airport. He arrived in Washington in the wee hours of the morning, allowing for a few hours of sleep.

The next morning, April 12, 1945, Morgenthau was irritated by reading an article in the *Washington Post* that implied he had improperly used his influence to secure a reversal of the *Draft Directive* prepared by the State Department. The author of the article ignored the fact that the subject was a War Department document, and that the War Department had taken the initiative to have the *Draft Directive* reversed; Morgenthau merely supported that initiative. Morgenthau was outraged at the tone of the article. Stettinius called Morgenthau that afternoon. Stettinius was shocked and embarrassed at the publication of the article but defended his staff against any responsibility for the event. Morgenthau rejoined that it was unlikely the leak came from Treasury. While Stettinius assured Morgenthau that he had "read the riot act to his staff members," it does not appear that he offered to issue a press release correcting any misinterpretations. It might seem at this remove in time that all that was needed was a simple press release stating the matter involved a War Department document, and that Morgenthau participated only because he had the obligation to do so as a member of the Cabinet Committee on Germany. The consensus of Morgenthau's staff was that this information should be leaked to the press.[832] It was an unpleasant beginning for Morgenthau's workday.

Late in the afternoon Eleanor Roosevelt called Morgenthau to tell him of Roosevelt's death a few hours earlier. He was greatly touched when she suggested he come to the White House while she called his wife Elinor at the hospital in Florida.[833] (The new president had very generously urged Mrs. Roosevelt to remain at the White House as long as she needed.) Morgenthau issued a press release in which he said simply that he had lost his best friend.[834]

Morgenthau was present with the other cabinet members to watch Harry Truman sworn in as Roosevelt's successor at 7:00 PM that evening; Truman then called his first cabinet meeting. He asked each member of the cabinet to continue what he or she had been doing without interruption, "just the way President Roosevelt wanted it."[835] Morgenthau recollected there was a pause, and he looked to Stettinius as the senior cabinet officer to say something. He was the senior cabinet member (measured by dates of creation of each department). Stettinius told the new president that the cabinet members were "all behind him." Each cabinet member in turn assured the new president of his and her intention to give him complete loyalty and diligence. Morgenthau started his remarks with a slight breach of etiquette, addressing the new president as "Mr. Truman," instead of "Mr. President." He continued, "I will do all I can to help, but I want you to be free to call on anyone else in my place."[836] In the stress of the moment, the slip may not have been noticed.

Two days later, on a Saturday morning, Morgenthau was given the president's first appointment of the day.[837] Morgenthau was in a state of shock. It seems absurd to say that Morgenthau, now middle-aged, had never had occasion to confront death in a personal relationship. There had been the death of his mother. But the important parental relationship had been with his father, who was still alive, although close to his ninetieth year. Morgenthau's relationship with Roosevelt had been very personal, complex, and on many levels. Morgenthau was lost in an emotional wasteland of grief with no clue as to how to proceed. He was reacting to Truman with his lifelong shyness with strangers. In a Social Darwinist world, Morgenthau could have been aware subconsciously that Truman came from that Midwest, where people often harbored prejudice against Eastern Jews (sufficiently so that he had been denied the position of secretary of agriculture in 1933, for which he was eminently qualified).

The first conversation between Truman and Morgenthau that Saturday morning reveals the difficulties on both sides of the president's desk. Apparently, Truman recognized Morgenthau was in a great inner upheaval. (Beschloss writes, "Morgenthau was never very good at concealing his emotions."[838])

The president tried to ease the tensions by saying, "I think I admired Mr. Roosevelt as much as you did."[839] That was really a very generous effort on Truman's part to cope with Morgenthau's distress. In the circumstances, and if Morgenthau were in full command of his emotions, the appropriate response was to thank the president for his sympathy and continue with some innocuous remark, acknowledging that he was having a rough time coming to terms with what happened. That said, it would have been the president's gambit to lead the conversation in whatever direction he wished it to proceed.

But Morgenthau was not in command of his emotions; he was in a state of shock. Morgenthau responded to Truman's offer of sympathy out of his intense emotional sense of hurt by saying, "I don't think that's possible." If Morgenthau's answer is understandable, the response was discourteous and disrespectful to the office of the presidency. It was also not in keeping with the basic, underlying generosity of spirit that Henrietta Klotz described of her longtime boss, who had provided the vice president with Secret Service protection when General Vaughan requested it, even though there was no precedent for doing so. But Morgenthau was now incapable of thinking outside of a narrow psychological, prison-like cage, or of recognizing the problems that Truman faced. Truman was on a vertiginously steep learning curve. With no preparation, he had been thrust into a maelstrom of decision-making without familiarity with the factual background necessary to knowledgeably meet his new responsibilities.[840]

Instead of Morgenthau's leading with his strong suit, by suggesting the president might want to hear a short summary of the problems with which the Treasury Department was dealing at the moment (which would have allowed the president to thank him for the suggestion without committing either of them to anything), Morgenthau marched on to disaster by bringing up the topic of Roosevelt's use of Morgenthau's talents to investigate special problems. At that moment Truman was desperately trying to pigeonhole a mass of information with which he had to become familiar. He did not need to think about ancillary matters. Finally, Morgenthau brought up his plan for the reconstitution of Germany. At that point it would appear that Truman wanted to end an unsatisfactory interview without further difficulty, and so he said, "I would like to know about it."

Morgenthau then said that financial interests wanted to get rid of him, and without the president's support "he would not last two minutes." Truman must have had a reservoir of respect for Morgenthau's direction of the Treasury Department because he responded, "I want you to stay with me." (The scandals in the Bureau of Internal Revenue that developed after Morgenthau left, which would subsequently come to light in the investigations of the King subcommittee in a few short years, warranted such respect.) Morgenthau replied sensibly that he would stay "just so long as I think I can serve you." To which Truman added, "When the time comes that you can't, you will hear from me first. Direct."[841] (That would not prove to be the case.)

That Saturday night Morgenthau felt very much alone on the train that carried Roosevelt's body, his family members, the new president, and important political figures to Hyde Park for the burial in a garden near the family home. In his misery Morgenthau forgot he had a daughter studying at Vassar College close by Hyde Park. He finally was able to remember and invite her to keep him company at the funeral ceremony. Her presence proved comforting to him.[842]

Morgenthau's difficulties with Truman were exacerbated by Truman's choice of Jimmy Byrnes as his secretary of state. Byrnes had been appointed in 1942 as the czar of the civilian economy. Byrnes thought that ought to include tax policy. Morgenthau regarded tax policy as a traditional area of Treasury concern.

The matter finally required Roosevelt's attention. Morgenthau suggested they could probably work out some modus vivendi, to which Byrnes rather nastily responded, "I wouldn't agree with you on anything."

Truman felt comfortable with Byrnes, a Southerner, a former Senator from South Carolina, and a United States Supreme Court Justice who had resigned to become the wartime economic czar. From Truman's vantage point, he also understood that Roosevelt had taken Byrnes to the Yalta conference; Byrnes had actually sat in on one of Roosevelt's sessions with Stalin and Churchill.[843] At least Morgenthau had the satisfaction of telling Roosevelt he thought little of Byrnes's possible nomination to succeed Hull as secretary of state.[844]

Morgenthau's relationship with the new president had begun dismally. It would appear that Truman recognized Morgenthau's competence in supervising the programs over which the Treasury Department had jurisdiction. In the first ninety days of his administration, while he was trying to assimilate a mass of seemingly endless factual data, Truman would appear to believe he needed to keep Morgenthau in place. So he could tell Morgenthau, "I have complete confidence in you and if I ever haven't, I will tell you." To which Morgenthau could reply, "I hope that day will never come." In one sense, perfectly honestly, Truman could respond, "I am sure it never will."[845]

Whether, beyond the possible menace Germany promised to the peace of the world, there would be other aspects of governance that promised to be bear traps to snare a positive interpersonal relationship between Morgenthau and Truman, is an interesting question. Morgenthau applied a rigid governmental morality, which had been consistent with Roosevelt's absolute determination to prohibit scandal and political corruption in his administration. Once he was in a position to ignore machine politicians, he was merciless with political wrongdoing.

Truman came out of a different background. He owed his eminence in the world to the recognition he had been given by Pendergast's Kansas City Democratic political machine. While no one could question Truman's personal probity, as a matter of simple decency, he felt he could not repudiate the debt he owed machine politics. He had to give James Hannegan leave to put onto the public payroll persons whose sole qualification for public employment was their connection with influential political bosses.

Andrew J. Dunar writes,

> One of Truman's defenses against the charges stemming from the Bureau of Internal Revenue scandal was that the four disgraced collectors had been appointed before he assumed the presidency. This defense, however, overlooks two aspects of these appointments. First, it was Truman's backing that initiated Hannegan's rapid political rise and gave him responsibilities that allowed him to change appointment policy. Second, Truman implicitly endorsed the policy himself. Frank Pace, the bright budget director, once asked Truman why he continued to allow machine politicians to influence the administration: Truman chuckled and gently admonished Pace, "Frank, you make a splendid Director of the Budget, but a lousy politician."[846]

Explaining the effect of Hannegan's influence, Dunar writes: "Hannegan's tenure as commissioner [of Internal Revenue] was brief—less than six months—but several observers have attributed to his leadership a change in approach that led to the later scandals. Hannegan's predecessor had been conservative and exacting, and the new commissioner set out to change what he saw as a stodgy bureau. He relied on patronage for appointment of [local] collectors."[847]

Morgenthau urged Truman to reauthorize JCS 1067, overseeing the military government of occupied Germany, and Truman did so on May 12, 1945. This was McCloy's handiwork, and no doubt Stimson on McCloy's account was intent on seeing the document reauthorized by Truman. Accepting that the document was elastic, Morgenthau was convinced that if it were applied properly, it would ensure the peace of the world for the next fifty years.[848]

The French government unknowingly created problems for Morgenthau's relations with Truman by deciding to hold an American War Bonds Exhibit in Paris in the first weeks of July 1945. The war bonds program was Morgenthau's idea, and they invited him. Morgenthau spoke to the president on May 16, 1945, seeking permission to go to Paris.[849] By itself this was an innocuous request. Truman probably had thought of the successive war bond drives as a very successful home-front public relations gesture. Unfortunately, Morgenthau was blind to the fact that Truman wanted to separate into its own box the separate areas of responsibility each federal department entertained. Beyond that, he probably believed, in a Social Darwinist world, that Jews could not be expected to be objective about what would come to be called *genocide*. Truman could not blame them for that. For that reason, Truman felt (along with Stimson, Ickes, and others) that Morgenthau should not concern himself with the reconstitution of Germany.

Morgenthau's next comment was like a lighted match applied to dry tinder. Morgenthau said he "wanted 'to go up the Ruhr and the Saar and see what was going on.'" Rather than risk a possibly ugly scene, the President simply agreed, even to giving Morgenthau a government plane for the trip.[850] But no letters to the War Department directing arrangements be made for Morgenthau's trip nor authorization for a military plane were forthcoming from Truman, though Morgenthau kept referring to it. Finally, it appears that Truman came up with a diplomatic formula to finesse Morgenthau's projected trip.

On Monday, June 18, 1945, Truman "called in Morgenthau and said, 'You know, I feel like a brother to you, and I wish you could feel that way towards me.'" Truman explained he thought about Morgenthau's proposed trip " 'all day Sunday,' [and] he had concluded that since Morgenthau was the next-ranking Cabinet member after the Secretary of State, he shouldn't be out of Washington while the President and Secretary of State were in Europe."[851]

What is remarkable about the foregoing language is the lengths to which Truman was going to conciliate Morgenthau. At that point in time, Morgenthau and his connection to a well-run Treasury Department would appear to be important to Truman, enough so that while Truman might deny Morgenthau permission to accept the French invitation, he did not want to alienate or irritate him unduly. Yet very shortly thereafter, Truman decided to dispense with Morgenthau's services and appoint Fred Vinson in his stead. There is no question that Truman felt more comfortable with his Midwestern, border-state senatorial friend.

If Morgenthau was unqualified initially to head the Treasury Department when Roosevelt gave him the job, Vinson could be said to be even more unqualified. Morgenthau had shown administrative ability as the New York State commissioner of conservation, and later, as governor of the Farm Credit Administration. Vinson's forte had been that he was a superb legislator. He was shrewd, easygoing, affable. He fitted in with his senatorial colleagues. He understood the compromises necessary to secure the passage of bills before Congress when it was important to enact laws. He came out of the same milieu as Truman, those Midwest border states where the South merged into the Midwest. For these reasons he had been named the vice-chairman of the Bretton Woods Conference, and had presided on June 6, 1945, when Morgenthau was absent. Morgenthau, if he had little personal understanding of international monetary problems, did have an instinctive respect for those who did. Vinson in his conversations with Keynes could drive Keynes to distraction. (Gardner writes, "Vinson showed little interest in the refinements of economic analysis [and] he showed even less appreciation of the shafts of wit which Keynes . . . broke about his brows." Gardner reports, " '[M]ebbe so,' Vinson would say after hearing some particularly brilliant contribution, 'but down where I come from, folks don't look at things that way.'"[852]) Still, Vinson recognized Harry White's abilities and kept him on as an assistant secretary.

In the last days of June 1945, Morgenthau started to hear that Truman might be thinking of replacing him with Vinson. Morgenthau knew he was relating badly to the president, and he had no understanding of how the situation could be corrected. If he left the Treasury Department, he hoped the moment would be his to decide. Finally, in desperation, on July 5, 1945, Morgenthau secured an interview with the president (who was leaving the next day to attend the Potsdam Conference with Stalin and Churchill).

Morgenthau began, "The last time I was here, you said you felt like a brother to me. . . . I would like to reciprocate that feeling and have an official family talk. You are leaving, and there is all this gossip about my being through."

Truman responded, "Oh, I am going to say you are the man in charge while I am gone."

Truman's answer did not answer Morgenthau's concern, and Morgenthau posed the issue more directly: "I would like to know now whether you want me to stay until VJ-Day."

In the words that follow, there is a reluctance on the president's part to come right out and cut his ties with Morgenthau. He said: "I don't know. . . . I may want a new Secretary of the Treasury."

If the president's words were a curious evasion of the issue, Morgenthau failed to catch any hesitancy. All he heard was the reference to a "*new* Secretary."

Cut to the quick, Morgenthau went on: "Well, Mr. President, if you have any doubts in your mind—after my record of twelve years here, and after several months with you, when I have given my loyal support—you ought to know your mind now. And if you don't know it, I want out now."

Again there was the odd expression by the president of a disinclination to cut the bonds: "Let me think this over."[853]

Morgenthau's reaction was in the Social Darwinist context of being an outsider who was being treated with scant ceremony; in his mind, this had all started for him with his father's mad idea to send him to Phillips Exeter Academy in 1905, where he had been exposed to the adolescent cruelty of anti-Semitic snobbery from the other students there. Morgenthau said, "Either you want me to stay until VJ-Day or you don't!"

Morgenthau then forgot himself to the point of being extremely indiscreet: "I don't think it is conceited to say that I am at least as good or better as some of the five new people you appointed in the Cabinet, and on one of them, I think you definitely made a mistake. . . . I am going to write you a letter of resignation. Would you like me to stay while you are abroad, or would you like me to have it take place immediately?"

Again, there was reluctance on Truman's part to terminate the relationship. He said: "You are rushing it," ignoring the discourtesy that Morgenthau was showing.

The president went on to express his wish to publicly announce Morgenthau's continuing presence in the cabinet with the understanding that only upon Truman's return from the conference with Stalin would Morgenthau's resignation be made public. Heedless of the consequences of what he was saying, Morgenthau insisted that though he agreed to remain as

Treasury secretary, his resignation must be published without delay—otherwise Morgenthau would issue his own press release. The president deferred to Morgenthau's insistence.[854]

Beschloss suggests that only then did Morgenthau bring up his vision of the reconstitution of Germany and offer the president a copy of the plan. The president demurred by saying he knew of its contents and thought it was "very good."[855]

In 1954, apparently off the record, Truman would give his recollection of Morgenthau's final interview with him: "When the trip to Potsdam was being arranged, Morgenthau came to see me and said he had to go along." (At that point, Truman may have been confusing Stimson's verbal request on July 3; 1945, with Morgenthau [after McCloy, Stimson's deputy, had been invited to join Truman at Potsdam but not Stimson himself].) Truman continued: "I said, 'I don't need you and it's none of your business.' . . . He said, 'If I can't go to Potsdam, what's going to happen to the Morgenthau Plan?' I said they could throw it out the window. He pouted and said he would quit. 'All right,' I said, 'I accept your resignation right now.'" Truman then apparently went on to say Morgenthau's plan "wasn't worth a hoot."[856] Truman added that he thought Morgenthau a "nut" and a "blockhead," someone who didn't "know shit from apple butter."[857]

One of Truman's biographers, McCullough, accepts Truman's recollection of the July 5, 1945, interview as authentic.[858] Henry III writes, "When he realized that he was about to be dumped, Morgenthau insisted on resigning immediately. At the last minute, as the presidential party was setting sail for Potsdam, Vinson was literally yanked off the boat and sworn in. Truman did not tell Morgenthau about his intentions as he himself had promised. He designated Sam Rosenman, a holdover from the Roosevelt White House and a Jew, as his messenger."[859]

McCullough adds, "In his own diary account of the breakup Morgenthau made no mention of the Potsdam issue, only that

Truman seemed 'very weak and indecisive' about whether he wanted Morgenthau to stay on the job until the [Japanese phase of] the war ended."[860]

At least superficially, one has several *Rashomon* narratives relating to what transpired at Morgenthau's last interview with Truman.[861] Where does the truth lie?

It is useful to start with two aspects of Truman's recollection of the event: (a) He told Morgenthau the meeting with Stalin "is none of your business," and (b) he went on to make rather nasty remarks (if colorful in a Southern manner) about Morgenthau. Also, it was after General Vaughan, Truman's friend and military aide, and four local Bureau of Internal Revenue collectors were found to have committed criminal acts on Truman's presidential watch.

Truman's understanding of governance and his method of operation rested on the proposition that his cabinet members had separate and distinct areas of responsibilities. Morgenthau's near-obsession with the menace the German polity represented to the future peace of the world violated Truman's fundamental division of cabinet responsibilities. It is not too far-fetched to infer that Truman wanted Morgenthau to understand and accept his theory of governance, and for Morgenthau to be able to say: "Mr. President, I have come to understand how you want the cabinet to operate and how you want cabinet members to act. I want you to know that while I have strong feelings about the danger Germany holds for the future peace of the world, how Germany should be treated and how military government should proceed, I recognize that as long as I remain a part of your administration, I must not concern myself with such matters."

Except that Morgenthau was emotionally unable to either make such a commitment or to keep it. If Morgenthau had been able to do that, (a) he would have been a different person than he was, and (b) there is at least the possibility that Truman might have kept putting off a rupture between them.

It has been said that Truman was always right when it came to the major decisions. It was only in small matters that he made mistakes. In making that distinction, there is always the problem: How do you differentiate the one from the other; where do you draw the line?

Truman had a deep and abiding respect for the integrity of the national government. His wartime Senate committee investigations of rot in defense contracts and shoddy production of military ordnance illustrates that. The man who performed that service for the nation was the man chosen as the Democratic Party's candidate for vice president.

Still, Truman had a fundamental sense of gratitude for the opportunities for government office given to him by the Democratic Party machine in Kansas City, starting with his election as county judge.[862] As a county judge (or executive), while his personal probity was unquestioned, he had no problem giving local jobs to party stalwarts. But when it came to the integrity and security of the United States, Truman had no problem putting aside political organization connections and recognizing the talents of Dean Acheson or General Marshall.

In that respect, it is probable that the Treasury Department and its functions—in terms of the integrity of American currency, national debt, and the value of the dollar—came within the ambit of Truman's understanding of the need for governmental integrity. Certainly, Fred Vinson, appointed vice-chairman of the Bretton Woods Conference, must have been impressed with the important purposes of the gathering, its flawless execution, the numbers of foreign delegates, and the results. In the informal after-hours sessions of his senatorial friends—including Truman—there can be no question that Vinson must have waxed enthusiastically over the efforts of Morgenthau and his Treasury staff. It is probable that most of the discussions he heard were beyond his comprehension. Economists speak a jargon incomprehensible to everyone else, and White, Keynes, and their staffs compounded the difficulties. That Morgenthau seemed to stay on top of what was going on at Bretton Woods was impressive.

It is evident from Truman's comment to Frank Pace, his budget director, that when it came to the lesser levels of government, Truman regarded it as fitting and proper that political organization connections be recognized and rewarded.

If Beschloss's version of the successive conversations between Truman and Morgenthau is valid, what is curious is the length to which Truman went to accommodate Morgenthau. Truman was trying to establish a real personal connection with his Treasury secretary. At one point, on May 9, 1945, Truman apparently did try to explain something of the stress he was under. Beschloss quotes: "I couldn't explain it to you fully," said Truman, "but you have put all your cards on the table and I will put all my cards on the table. I have got to see Stalin and Churchill, and when I do, I want all the bargaining power—all the cards in my hand—and the plan on Germany is one of them." Pulling out a map of German food production and population, Truman said, "I just wanted to show you that I am studying this myself."[863]

Truman was making an enormous effort to reach Morgenthau. Still, neither could find a common language between them that could ripen into the kind of trust that supersedes words. So Truman had said to Morgenthau on June 18, 1945, "You know I feel like a brother to you, and I wish you could feel that way towards me." One must believe Truman was completely sincere in what he is quoted as having said. (In this sense, early on, Morgenthau was not entirely wrong when he said he had "positive vibes" from Truman.) Except the language Truman used was artificial. Neither he nor Morgenthau ordinarily spoke that way. In the process, they each had an agenda that neither man succeeded in explaining to the other in words the other could understand and accept.

As spring was turning into summer, Morgenthau became aware through information provided by Chaim Weizmann's associate in the United States that Jewish displaced persons were ending up in former concentration camps in Europe. He felt that these survivors, homeless and starving, deserved better after all they had witnessed and undergone themselves. Several times he urged the president to put the matter in a cabinet meeting agenda. Truman ignored Morgenthau's requests. Morgenthau finally understood that he must find someone in the State Department hierarchy who would agree to recommend a survey of the conditions in DP camps, and he did.

The proposal to investigate the circumstances of Jewish displaced persons was made by an impeccably Gentile official without any apparent Jewish connection. Secretary of State Byrnes approved the proposal and referred it to the president. The investigator was appointed and came back with a devastating report for Truman in the last days of August, 1945. Henry III writes that the report "made a lasting impression on the President." Weizmann's associate could report a successful conclusion to his intervention with Morgenthau.[864]

The end to Morgenthau's term of office was rather sordid. Truman did announce Morgenthau's resignation effective upon the president's return from the Potsdam Conference with Stalin. Whereupon various and sundry persons discovered that if anything happened to both the president and his secretary of state while crossing the ocean or in Europe, the presidency would be left to a Jew with a draconian peace plan for Germany. Whether the outcry resulted from latent Social Darwinist anti-Semitism or a fear of the consequences of a possibly harsh occupation policy is left to the reader's judgment. Forgotten was that the same situation existed the preceding February, when Roosevelt left on his trip to Yalta, although in the interim the reality of presidential mortality had become very evident.

Truman apparently felt he had more pressing problems that required his attention than whether Morgenthau remained in office two weeks more or two weeks less. He had a choice as to what to do next: He could dismiss Morgenthau, or ask him to make his resignation effective immediately. Either choice meant going back on his original arrangement with Morgenthau. For whatever reason, Truman felt he could not appear so callous as to dismiss the secretary of the Treasury. The alternative was to ask Morgenthau to make his resignation effective immediately. Apparently, the president did not have the stomach to make the request himself. In a sense, it was demeaning to have to ask Morgenthau to speed up the effective date of his resignation. Although Truman assured Morgenthau that when he wanted Morgenthau to leave, he would tell him so himself, Truman delegated the chore to Samuel Rosenman, one of his holdover administrative assistants. Rosenman took it upon himself to say that if Morgenthau agreed to make his resignation effective at once, there stood a good chance that the president would appoint him the United States representative at the World Bank and the International Monetary Fund. The president himself proved not so inclined.[865]

Morgenthau ended up no more interested than Truman in whether he remained in office two weeks more, and so he submitted his letter of resignation effective immediately, together with drafts of letters of acceptance and an offer to be United States representative to the World Bank and the Fund. The latter draft was not used.

So ended Morgenthau's career in Washington.[866]

If Beschloss is correct in the statements he ascribes to Truman in the latter's interviews with Morgenthau, there is a curious—and glaring—dichotomy between the lengths to which Truman went to conciliate Morgenthau while Morgenthau was still a cabinet member and the very angry and vindictive opinions Truman kept expressing over the years about Morgenthau once Morgenthau was no longer in government.

The question that comes into focus is whether Truman was being hypocritical in what he said prior to July 5, 1945, and if so, why he felt the need. The answer to the question, one suspects, lies in the circumstance that, more than Morgenthau's administrative skills, there was his stubborn, unyielding sense of rectitude. His son had described him as "[a] grim observer of the puritanical code . . . [as] he sternly adhered to the straight and narrow path."[867] From his earliest days as New York State Commissioner of Conservation to his insistence that Harry White be promoted to the post of assistant secretary of the Treasury instead of an important Democratic Party contributor, Morgenthau reserved second- and third-tier positions to merit appointments.

There can be no question that if James Hannegan had been presented to Morgenthau as a candidate for the position of commissioner of Internal Revenue, Morgenthau would have been outraged and turned Hannegan down flat. He need never have made explicit a threat to resign over the issue. He would have drawn the line for the president and given him an unassailable reason to tell his political associates that the nomination was out of the question because Morgenthau objected, and the president could not run the risk that Morgenthau's objection might become public. But, by resigning, Morgenthau deprived Truman of an excuse to which he could point to avoid blurring the distinction between those positions involving the integrity of the United States and minor bureaucratic postings. In that sense, it could be said Truman was thinking possibly of using Morgenthau in the same way as Roosevelt.[868] Morgenthau could have been of invaluable assistance to Truman when Truman had to choose between his allegiance to the integrity of the United

States and his moral debt to the political organization that gave him his start in his political career.

Truman's vindictiveness toward Morgenthau could be said to be an expression of anger. Such anger (or however one chooses to characterize Truman's thoughts on the matter) could be derived from a feeling that Truman thought Morgenthau had failed him. In that sense, Morgenthau misstated the matter on July 5, 1945, when he told Truman he thought he had been loyal to him. He had neither accepted nor understood Truman's conception of Cabinet organization. The disappointment which Truman may be said to have felt, because Morgenthau proved incapable of understanding Truman's concept of government, could be one possible explanation for Truman's vindictiveness toward Morgenthau in later years.

Morgenthau courteously attended the swearing-in ceremony of his successor even though he was drained emotionally. As the saying goes, *Le roi est mort; vive le roi.* His longtime secretary Henrietta Klotz was present and felt his sense of isolation. He had none of the suavity of Dean Acheson at his own swearing-in as the undersecretary twelve years earlier. Klotz walked over to stand with him. Morgenthau was touched by her loyalty.[869]

At the end of 1945, Morgenthau relocated to New York City, staying at the farm on weekends as he had done twenty years earlier. Elinor Morgenthau was increasingly ill. Her husband was at loose ends and, as their son describes it, "somewhat drained financially." Earlier in the fall, Morgenthau had published his position on military government for post-surrender Germany in the book, *Germany Is Our Problem.* There were a series of newspaper and magazine articles, ghostwritten by Arthur Schlesinger Jr. He also gave weekly broadcasts over radio station WMCA, "owned and operated . . . by Nathan Strauss, Jr.,"[870] whom he helped when Strauss had assayed public office as the Public Housing Administrator for a short while seven or eight years earlier in Washington. None of the large financial institutions were ready to offer Morgenthau a job, and he was not ready to become what is currently called a lobbyist among his old subordinates. About the only offer that came to him was one from a small commercial bank in New York City with a grandiose name, The Modern Industrial Bank. He was invited to become the chairman of its board,[871] hardly a full-time position. His name now appeared in the bank's newspaper advertisements.

Henrietta Klotz recognized her old boss's malaise. Then again, apparently Fred Vinson had given her unwanted attention at the Bretton Woods Conference, going so far as to invite her to his room. (Political conventions and government conferences in places that are detached from the patterns of their lives may give some men a sense they are in a kind of "midsummer's night dream" that allows them to try to temporarily escape the ordinary constraints of their lives.)

Klotz found working under Vinson awkward. She had connections to persons in major Jewish charitable organizations, which she was able to use to bring their attention to Morgenthau's availability for charitable work. At the same time, if Morgenthau became involved in a Jewish charitable organization, it would enable her to leave an unpleasant work situation.[872]

During his Washington years, Morgenthau had gained a reputation for a lack of involvement in Jewish communal affairs. Neither his father nor his wife encouraged such involvement. Quite the reverse.[873] (For that matter, after he was sworn in as secretary of the Treasury, he had sold the farm weekly, the *American Agriculturist*, that he had acquired in 1922, because he thought it could provide an inadvertent window into administration deliberations.) Beyond his avoidance of any possible conflict of interest, he still could identify with the victims of Nazi persecution in Germany. If Polish ambassador Ciechanowski never pursued a meeting of Morgenthau with Jan Karski, it was probably because he did not think it promised a fruitful result. Rabbi Wise and Morgenthau's staff repaired the omission and led Morgenthau to successfully convince Roosevelt to create the War Refugee Board.

The war years had devastated Europe and Japan. Only the United States (and Canada), the "arsenals of democracy," were unscathed. The needs of war resulted in Keynesian "pump-priming" on a previously unimaginable scale of prosperity. Edward Bernstein assured Keynes that the economic pattern of depressions following the cessation of hostilities was unrelated to the devastation of war, but had been due to a hasty and premature return to the gold standard, resulting in deflation or inflation, purely monetarist phenomena. Any return to the gold standard in the United States was not possible politically, Harry White had told the banking community.[874] The United States experienced no recession after the cessation of hostilities in 1945. There was a continuance of an unparalleled prosperity. The Congress passed legislation that set a goal of a 6 percent unemployment rate. In a short while, that rate would come to be regarded as the beginnings of a recession.

The American Jewish community participated in the general flow of prosperity. On the one hand, the experience of the Depression years—the sense of economic malaise, the general insecurity, the feeling of just getting by, the idea that there was a very small margin between coming out in the black instead of finding oneself insolvent—these psychological pressures were still too recent, so that the prosperity people experienced seemed like "found money," something they were not entirely ready to accept or come to regard as the natural course of events. People wanted to share their newfound prosperity, to give to charity. (They would not come to discover the rather expensive fashion of becoming art collectors for perhaps two generations.)

Coupled with the sense of liberation from economic insecurity, the American Jewish community discovered the truth about Nazi genocide. The stories of concentration camps and genocide that had filtered out of Europe during the war years, which had been either ignored or relegated to the back pages of newspapers, now called for front-page news articles.

It was not that American Jews were unaware that Nazi persecutions were brutal. But during the war years, neither the government, the press, news magazines, nor radio commentators had given particular notice to, and thereby validated, Nazi atrocities. There had been Jan Valtin's memoir of Nazi tortures (published in 1938) and Arthur Koestler's novel, *Arrival and Departure*, published during the war years, the latter used psychoanalytic technique as a framework in which to tell its story of fascist torture practices in an unnamed middle European country. But both could be regarded as alien to American sensibilities. Though it might be admitted that Koestler wrote in English, it was thought to be a foreign-soured, inauthentic use of the language. In a Social Darwinist world, Koestler's use of English as the medium of communication was felt to be spurious, an intellectual trespass, an improper usurpation of a language that was the exclusive attribute of a special Anglo-American sensibility.

Morgenthau entered this Jewish ethnic community, with its odd combination of inchoate impulses toward generosity coupled with the psychological impact that resulted from realizing the true import of Nazi genocide. The latter was inescapably intertwined with the sense that it was only an accident, a momentary decision by parents or grandparents to emigrate to America a generation or two earlier, that had saved the present American Jewish generation from the horrors of Nazi gas chambers and death. Morgenthau himself was finished with government service, and liberated in his feelings from a Social Darwinist social order. With time on his hands, Morgenthau was ready to ask the American Jewish community to provide the wherewithal to rescue the tiny remnant of survivors.

The only question was where Morgenthau could best fit. Henrietta Klotz's suggestions bore fruit. Knowing Morgenthau was available, the leaders of the United Jewish Appeal invited Morgenthau to become a co-chairman of that organization. It was an amalgam of three separate organizations: one focused on providing assistance to impoverished foreign Jews, one focused on providing assistance to the Zionist enclaves in the British mandate area of Palestine, and one providing help to newly arrived Jewish immigrants in the United States.

Henry III suggests that his father occupied an executive function. This seems improbable. Major charitable organizations, whatever their denominational character, require a highly specialized bureaucracy in order to operate. A large donor may be given the post of president or chairman, with the role of soliciting more donations. In Morgenthau's case, he might have arranged to be briefed at morning meetings, but his briefings would have focused on luncheons, meetings, and dinners at which he would be expected to be introduced to prospective donors, make small talk there, and at large meetings, to give speeches. Additionally, he needed tutorials in the differences between the separate components within the umbrella organization, the important personnel setting policy in each component and in allied organizations. His mentor was Executive Vice President Henry Montor.

Those waiting for him to speak were usually self-made, rising out of early poverty. They were mostly of Tsarist Russian extraction—they or their parents or grandparents had come from present-day Russia, Ukraine, Poland, Belarus, the Baltic countries, Moldova, or Romania. As Chaim Weizmann would describe it in his autobiography, *Trial and Error*, they thought of themselves as coming from a warm, friendly, outgoing, unpretentious community, as compared with the cold, rigid, socially snobbish

German Jews with their Gentile-oriented Reform religious services.

In this context, Morgenthau's shyness, inarticulateness, social rigidity, wooden delivery (if in a firm baritone voice), put him in good stead. He was the very model of a German-Jewish stereotype to his audiences. That he would seek to make common cause with his audience legitimized his message and resonated with his listeners' instincts to identify with the beleaguered remnant of what were once vibrant ethnic Jewish communities in Eastern Europe. It authenticated their inchoate impulses toward extraordinary generosity for those they could identify as kinsmen.

To his audiences, Morgenthau also represented a connection with the magical aura that emanated from the recently deceased Franklin Roosevelt. Morgenthau had known Roosevelt personally; they were good friends. He could tell casual, intimate stories of sitting on Roosevelt's porch on a summer's evening, joining Roosevelt in a campaign swing, what being invited to lunch or dinner at the Roosevelt home was like; he could share these intimacies with those sitting or standing before him. If need be, he could feel relaxed enough to go up to men sitting or standing in front of him, put his arm around their shoulders, and ask them for money. In the six years between 1948 and 1953, he raised record amounts of donations, averaging $100 million a year,[875] when American dollars still had extraordinary value. Morgenthau would set a benchmark in charitable giving that elicited admiration and even envy in the American nonprofit sector for a generation.

In the post–World War II years, Britain's near-insolvency mandated a contraction of imperial obligations. The Palestinian mandate territory might have seemed a small-enough patch of land with a limited and affordable financial expenditure that promised to provide stability in nearby Arab countries for British investments in oil production. Ernest Bevin, the Labour

Party foreign secretary, certainly shared that point of view, and found Zionist imperatives a nuisance. The Zionist enclaves in the mandate territory had been settled on the premise of restoring an ancient biblical sovereignty that could provide refuge for beleaguered Jews (such as those in displaced persons camps in Germany). That dream faced the reality that the British Colonial Office in 1939, in an effort to remove Arab alarm over Zionist influxes of Jews, had limited further Jewish immigration to 75,000 persons, a number that was now filled. There was Zionist agitation to remove the bar to further Jewish immigration. This led in turn to a recurrence of the Arab violence that in 1939 had caused the 75,000-person limit to be imposed. By 1947, the British proposed to give up their mandate responsibilities on May 15, 1948, and referred the future of the mandate territory to the new United Nations General Assembly for resolution.

The result was an increasing emphasis for the United Jewish Appeal and Morgenthau to meet the needs of the Zionist enclaves in the mandated territory. During this period, the United Nations Assembly resolution called for the end to British sovereignty and partition of the area into six cantonments divided between two independent countries, one a Jewish-majority state and one an Arab-majority state. Unfortunately, the Arab leadership found the UN compromise distasteful and rejected it, seeking a martial conquest of the whole of the mandate area upon the end of the British administration. The projected Arab victory contemplated the forcible removal of the Zionist inhabitants of the former mandate area—much in the way of the precedent of Kemal Atatürk's expulsion of the Greek-speaking inhabitants from Turkey's Aegean littoral twenty-five years earlier.

Golda Meir might make a celebrated trip in January 1948 to a Jewish philanthropic conclave in Chicago that would produce some $25 million in donations on the spot. (The total for her three months in the United States would add up to $50 million in all.)[876] The needs of what would become the country of Israel were ongoing and required an institutional response.

There were two periods of open warfare during which Israel occupied western Galilee, and Trans-Jordan's Arab Legion won the Jewish Quarter of the old city of Jerusalem and the area now known as the West Bank. (The Gaza Strip would be administered by Egypt.)

The hostilities were separated by a short, initial armistice that was ineffective. The United Nations then sponsored what proved to be permanent armistice talks on the island of Cyprus under the aegis of American Ralph Bunche, then an assistant UN secretary-general. The expectation of the participants in the armistice talks apparently was that the resulting armistices would be succeeded by peace treaties between the member states of the Arab League and Israel.

The first peace treaty would not come about for some twenty-five years.

Henry III writes that his mother's health problems increased with each passing year. She was bedridden, beset with a painful illness. In New York Hospital she suffered a stroke, after which she did not regain consciousness. She died on September 21, 1949. She was only fifty-eight years old. In a span of three years, arguably the three most important persons in Morgenthau's life—Roosevelt, Henry Sr., and Elinor—all disappeared.[877]

The new Israeli government sought to realize the ideal of becoming a refuge for harried Jews who had been deported from their homes, wherever that may be on the face of the earth.

At a meeting held in the home of Israeli minister of finance, Eliezer Kaplan, on October 5, 1950[878] (which Morgenthau attended, along with Golda Meir [still identified as "Meyerson"], then minister of labor and social security, and David Horowitz, governor of the Bank of Israel), Kaplan said, "If America should receive Jews at the same rate [as they were then coming to Israel], the United States would receive 200,000,000 . . .[879] We appeal to you for destitute Jewry. But to settle these Jews is such a tremendous job."[880] and "Not only [Israeli] treasury people but others say we cannot continue our immigration. We are reaching the breaking point. We will have to stop—that will be decided for us. That is the dilemma. We are not masters of immigration. Every Sunday Romania dumps 1,500 newcomers."[881]

In addition to the costs immigration imposed on the Israeli government's budget (by the necessity to provide for the needs of the newcomers), the Israelis were slowly coming to realize the consequences resulting from the absence of peace treaties: low-grade, Arab, guerrilla warfare in its border areas that required continued defense expenditures, which distorted the Israeli budget. Kaplan explained: ". . . the military [budget] is unbalanced. We are trying to cover the deficit by internal loans. Our hope is that in two or three years we may reach a balanced budget. Our difficulty is that we are still afraid to give the figures of our military budget. I am afraid for security reasons and economic reasons. . . . If we can get the proper equipment and ammunition the situation will be better. We could have a smaller army if better equipped. . . . A three-year period may give us the opportunity to absorb six hundred thousand people."[882]

He could respond to Kaplan: "What looms biggest in your mind is the immigration problem. If left to yourself you will stop it. What is popular in the United States? They admire Israel because of its open-door policy. If, instead of constantly having it that immigration is your stumbling block, you would face the audience [in the United States] with an enthusiastic approach of the open-door policy, and that the stumbling block is caused by [the] army [budget costs], and then paint a picture where Israel would be if you were at peace with the six Arab countries."[883]

Henry Montor, the executive vice president of the UJA, had come up with the idea that direct donations might be supplemented by an Israeli bond program, allowing American sympathizers to buy Israeli bonds, just as they had bought defense and war bonds during World War II. Morgenthau was enthusiastic about the idea, and the Israeli minister of finance accepted the possibility as a feasible supplementary program of assistance. Kaplan explained that the Israeli prime minister, David Ben-Gurion, had proposed to find the source of funding for a $1,500,000,000 Israeli economic development program: one-third from local and "soft money" sources, one-third to come from United Jewish Appeal donations, and one-third from American buyers of Israeli bonds.[884] Kaplan hoped to invest such funds in a way that would improve the Israeli balance of payments.[885]

Morgenthau asked if Kaplan could explain the investment opportunities in detail. Kaplan responded that he could do so only generally, not in specific detail. He understood Montor to say he would get an exemption from the American Securities and Exchange Commission that would permit the Israeli bonds to be sold in the United States. Morgenthau rejoined: "That is impossible. I don't believe it can be done."[886]

At the end of the session Morgenthau returned to his initial thought: "I say, stress peace as against immigration." Golda Meir supported Morgenthau's position. Governor Horowitz of the Bank of Israel was concerned that "peace with the Arab states, with that pace of immigration, would not alter the situation. The first problem is the balance of payments. The reduction [in the size] of our army would rectify the problem." Morgenthau then brought up the possibility of another Arab war. Kaplan agreed it was "an important question." With that thought, they recessed for dinner.[887]

Afterwards, Morgenthau returned to his original theme: "I do not see why you cannot stress peace—maintaining a large army is expensive and a waste of manpower." Kaplan assented, adding, "Our ordinary budget we settled, [aside from the costs of integrating newcomers into the social and economic fabric of the country, although, maybe it was] not so good, and the telephone does not work so well, but it will work. We may need the know-how. We are trying our best to settle our defense problem, and if it is settled it will be a tremendous improvement." Referring to the costs of integrating newcomers into Israeli society, he said, "Let us be partners in this tremendous task." Morgenthau commented: "You are now making a UJA speech." Kaplan could understand he was being flattered. He replied: "I will tell them—to open our gates and prepare the absorption of 600,000 Jews, we need Israeli funds, UJP funds, borrowed money, international help, and then [I] will talk about private investments, and go into the projects which you spoke of."

Morgenthau summed up their discussion:

I wonder if you could do this—give your conclusions first—I do not care whether you use a five- or ten-year plan—and say, at the end of five years these are the different things that Israel has to do to make it a prosperous nation. What we need is so many hundreds of millions of dollars. Internally, we feel that with peace, at the end of five years we will be on a balanced budget, and we hope with surplus. On the export basis, once these projects get started, after so many years we will have a surplus of foreign exchange. Now, in order to accomplish this, we must do the things you suggest—we will have to sell bonds, gift dollars, private investment, etc., and if all of these things come in, then at the end of five or ten years I can assure American Jewry that Israel will become a prosperous nation.[888]

It appears that Minister Kaplan spoke English, but it was not his first language. Morgenthau's comments, coming as they did from an emissary of the American Jewish community from which survival funding must come, were too important to be misunderstood. Therefore, Kaplan arranged to have their conversation transcribed, so it could be studied afterwards—to make sure no thought was either missed, or, worse, misunderstood. For the same reason, Golda Meir, who was American-born, was asked to participate, although her ministry had no connection with the discussion. She could understand American idiomatic speech and catch the meanings in tones and overtones of words that a nonnative speaker could easily miss. Likewise, and as a courtesy to Morgenthau, he would receive a carbon copy of the transcript for his review and modification, should Morgenthau feel it necessary.

These tough-minded, first-generation Israeli leaders saw Morgenthau as a guru, and he could feel great satisfaction in his work. He had developed a large emotional concern for Israel's security and its future prosperity.

Yet, three years later, Morgenthau severed his connection with the charity and the Israeli bond campaign. Henry Montor, initially the executive vice president of the UJA, had been Morgenthau's mentor. He conceived the Israel bond campaign as a necessary supplement to charitable giving, to raise money to meet the gigantic fiscal needs of the new nation. Those who would be left with the responsibility for running the charity felt the bond campaign was in direct conflict. Montor disagreed. The disagreement led to acrimony. Henry III suggests that his father found the arguments between Montor and the charity leaders unpleasant. He thought these were unnecessary and even destructive. This led to Morgenthau's resignation effective early in 1954.[889] Henry III thinks his father might have rescinded his resignation, had it been asked. But for whatever reasons, the formal leadership of the charity never asked, nor did the Israeli government emissary.[890]

Morgenthau performed one more service for the state of Israel. In 1948, Senator Fulbright of Arkansas had questioned the tax-exemption status of the United Jewish Appeal on the theory it was a conduit for the transfer of money to a foreign country. For the one and only time, Morgenthau participated with others to explain to his former subordinates in the Bureau of Internal Revenue that the recipients of charitable largesse were destitute immigrants and not the government of Israel. (In that sense, the United Jewish Appeal was operating in like manner to the International Red Cross to alleviate individual distress in foreign countries.) The tax-exempt status was quietly restored.[891]

During the years Morgenthau was devoting himself to raising money to help meet the needs of the nascent nation of Israel, he had undertaken the adventure of a new, middle-aged marriage, acquiring a new wife on November 21, 1951. She was French and living in New York City. Although nominally Catholic, she had been married in France to a husband of Jewish origin from whom she was divorced.[892]

Morgenthau was returning to a path he had forsaken when he was a young man of twenty-two, then exploring a vocation as a farmer in the town of East Fishkill.[893] In a Social Darwinist world, he had given up the pursuit of a young lady, having come to the painful realization—as he implies in his letter to his father—that he could only feel comfortable with a wife who was from the same *race* as he.[894]

Now, in a different world, Morgenthau concluded he could cross the social divide. He did insist his wife-to-be convert to Judaism. Need it be added that Morgenthau's children regarded it as a misalliance? Eleanor Roosevelt would comment tartly to Henry III, "Your father could never have [just] a mistress. He had to marry his mistress."[895] It is apparent that his new wife, Marcelle, amused this most staid of men. He had reached the age when he could finally give himself over to frivolity. She asked to redecorate his New York City apartment, and he agreed. The result was that the old-fashioned, rather stiff furnishings were succeeded by what were described as "garish" replacements.[896] His wife took him to France frequently,[897] where he could feel he was discovering the reality of French life rather than the superficial tourist scrim to which visiting foreigners were exposed. It does not appear from Henry III's comments that the new Mrs. Morgenthau made much of an effort to become friends with her grown-up stepchildren.[898]

During those same years, the United States reacted with disillusionment to the failure of the Soviet Union to enlarge upon the friendship the Western allies offered during the war years. During World War II, the need to find allies where one would temporarily dampened any concern with Communist subversion. By 1948, a series of former Communist agents, including Whittaker Chambers and Elizabeth Bentley, came forward and testified before the House Un-American Activities Committee and Senator McCarran's Senate Internal Security Subcommittee, providing a long list of Communist sympathizers and spies in the federal government, the communications industry, and Hollywood during the 1930s and 1940s. Included in the list of names was that of Harry Dexter White.[899]

Morgenthau was horrified by the thought that a close associate of his could have been disloyal to the United States.[900] Eventually, in 1952, he wrote to J. Edgar Hoover, the head of the FBI, requesting to see the evidence.[901] Henry III would tell Beschloss that his father "was never able to resolve the question of White's Communist affiliations in his own mind."[902]

Beschloss writes: "Harry Dexter White had a close secret relationship with Soviet intelligence."[903] He goes on: "Along with the British economist John Maynard Keynes, he was an architect of the postwar world economic order that would be centered around an International Monetary Fund and World Bank."[904] Beschloss continues: "According to recently opened evidence, White was *also* secretly meeting with Soviet intelligence agents"[905] (italics added).

In any case, neither Edward Bernstein nor Gardner, who are quoted earlier, suggest that White's defense of a limitation on the American obligation to fund the IMF, was defective in any way. Bernstein states that the American position prevailed and Gardner does not disagree. With respect to White's position on the Morgenthau Plan, Beschloss himself observes: "In fact, White had actually questioned some of the more draconian measures of Morgenthau's plan . . ."[906] And Beschloss adds, "Morgenthau never relaxed his intense faith in his tough plan for postwar Germany."[907] It is clear that Morgenthau did not follow White's ideas.

Beschloss goes on to write: "According to Whittaker Chambers's public testimony, White in 1937 described for him a proposal he was writing on reform of the Soviet monetary system."[908] In 1937, Chambers was a lowly courier in the Soviet espionage network in Washington. Apparently, White's ambitions to do something intellectually important were reduced, at that point, to talking about his current conceptualization with a messenger-boy, Chambers, who led a threadbare existence. Apparently, Chambers survived because his wife Esther had entrée to a hall bedroom provided by her brother in his apartment in a two-story row house he owned on Rochester Avenue in a lower-middle-class neighborhood in Brooklyn, New York, to which both Chambers and his wife could retire for four or five weeks from time to time. Here, they could bathe, eat three meals a day, and rest—fatten up until their fancy took them back to their conspiratorial adventures.[909]

Beschloss relies on three volumes,[910] focusing on the so-called Venona files in Moscow that were made available to American scholars in the 1980s after the collapse of the government of the Soviet Union. The Venona files are the reports (necessarily written in Russian) sent back to Moscow by Soviet agents in the United States; these agents cultivated mid-level government bureaucrats in Washington to provide classified information and documents to the Soviet agents during the 1930s and 1940s. Chambers was the courier who periodically collected the documents and delivered them to successive Soviet agents—with one notable exception: the last collection of documents that are known today as the "pumpkin papers." Apparently it was after he made his last collection in 1938 and before he delivered it to his Soviet "handler" that he came to his momentous decision to opt out of the Soviet spy network. Though she had spent her years in a passionate embrace of the Communist cause, Chambers's wife Esther went along with him and dropped Communism. Her decision in itself was an old-fashioned example of a woman so enraptured with her husband that she had no hesitation in following him and cutting the ties that for years had made her life meaningful.

Did they then retreat to her brother's hall bedroom while they sorted out the options available to them? One does not know. What is known is that Chambers feared for his life. He knew the Soviet government could be pitiless when it came to those it considered traitors to the cause. Then, there was the packet of documents waiting to be delivered. Chambers, in his elegantly written autobiography, *Witness*, published twenty years later, obscures the details. (Chambers sums up the hall bedroom episodes in his life by writing that he maintained "cordial relations" with his wife's family through the years.)

Chambers was not prepared to go to the FBI himself, but as a safeguard, he wanted the packet of documents to get to FBI personnel, should anything violent happen to him. The number of persons in their acquaintance to whom they could entrust the documents was limited. The most reliable person they knew appeared to be Esther's nephew, Nathan Levine. If the Soviet agents realized the documents were undelivered, they could never connect those papers to Levine, who had nothing to do with his aunt's radicalism. Chambers explained to Levine that he was to put the packet in a safe place. In the event of a violent end to Chambers, Levine was instructed to deliver the oilskin-wrapped packet to the FBI. The conversation most likely took place in the apartment where the hall bedroom was located, because Levine then placed the packet in an unused, skylight-airshaft overlooking the tub in the apartment's bathroom, where it would lie forgotten for ten years. Apparently, it took the Soviet agents a while to realize that Chambers had defected, and by that time, nobody understood there were documents that remained undelivered. It turned out that Chambers was considered so unimportant that his defection was ignored and lost to memory.

In some lives there are sudden, unbelievable turns of fortune. In a few years Chambers would end up as an editor at *Time* magazine, with an income that enabled him to buy a farm outside of Baltimore, Maryland—one more Social Darwinist urge to connect with the land.

Haynes and Klehr write: "... White was not one of Chambers's most productive sources in the mid-1930s ..." They note: "Most of the [pumpkin papers'] material had come from Hiss, but it also included a long memo in Harry White's own handwriting."[911] If the memo was in White's own handwriting, it is probable that he was not the source of the document: (a) A handwritten document is most likely an initial draft. It must be typed out by a typist as a memorandum to a supervisor with the appropriate heading so addressed. In the process it will be reread and corrected before being handed back to the typist. Haynes and Klehr do not give any clue as to the contents of the memo. This suggests it was concerned with an obtuse, theoretical monetarist subject, written in monetarist jargon unintelligible to non-economists. It is not certain that White ever intended to put the document in final form or convey its contents to Morgenthau; (b) Earlier, the Soviet secret agent was told by White "that 'compromise' would bring 'political scandal' so he must 'be very cautious.'"[912] Given the circumstances, it follows that White would never give a Soviet agent a document in his own handwriting. It is not clear that White placed the document in a locked file cabinet, and it is entirely possible that one of the other members of the group, working in the Treasury Department,[913] for unknown reasons decided to pass a photostat copy to the Soviet secret agent.

More serious is the charge that White facilitated the employment of other Communist sympathizers.[914] Apparently, White was in charge of hiring economist personnel. Yet, Edward Bernstein, who was a conservative monetarist, was also hired by White. It is possible that White may have hired personnel primarily on the basis of professional competence, and in the process he may also have accepted recommendations from Communist acquaintances.

Haynes and Klehr write: "There are fifteen deciphered KGB messages during 1944 and 1945 in which White was discussed or which reported information he was providing Soviet intelligence officers. The KGB mentioned that White offered advice concerning how far the Soviets could push the United States on abandoning the Polish government-in-exile . . . and assured the Soviets that U.S. policy-makers, despite their public opposition, would acquiesce to the USSR's annexation of Latvia, Estonia and Lithuania."[915]

It must be noted that the foregoing paragraph involves State Department matters in which White had no direct input. He was repeating gossip—information received secondhand. With respect to the Polish government-in-exile, the United States did secure the inclusion of Stanislaw Mikolajczyk and two other members of the Polish Peasant Party in the initial postwar cabinet. The problem, among other considerations, was that the

Soviet army was occupying Poland while American troops were several hundreds of miles away. Although the London-based, Polish government-in-exile claimed to have an underground army in Poland, their August 1944 Warsaw revolt accomplished nothing (except for the destruction of the central section of Warsaw). The United States withdrew its recognition of the Polish government-in-exile on the promise of Stalin to amalgamate its members with the Stalinist provisional government initially organized in Lublin. Unfortunately, Stalin's promise in this matter was no more honored than in other situations. The Peasant Party most probably could have won an honest election except the Russians were able to prevent that from occurring. And the United States never officially recognized the Soviet occupation of the three Baltic states.[916]

Romerstein and Breindel write,

By November, 1941, as war drew nearer, the State Department was pushing for an agreement with Japan that might delay the outbreak of hostilities. Soviet agents in the [American] government . . . were concerned that if Japan did not go to war with the United States, it might go to war with the Soviet Union. The last thing Stalin needed was for Japan to open a second front in the Soviet Far East. Germany had attacked the Soviet Union in June [1941] . . . The Soviet agents in the U.S. government knew they had to do something. . . . White rewrote his hard-line memorandum for Morgenthau, who signed it and sent it to President Roosevelt and Secretary of State Cordell Hull. Hull used most of the harsh, demanding language in his ultimatum to the Japanese on November 26, 1941. It would strengthen the hand of the war party in Tokyo, which was already prepared to attack the United States. . . . [M]ost historians of World War II agree that the war party in Japan would have provoked hostilities with the United States sooner or later. What is certain is that Operation Snow was being carried out with Soviet, not American, interests in mind.[917]

Though one may accept the conclusion in the penultimate sentence in the preceding paragraph, the entire paragraph gives a greater effect to White's actions than is warranted.

One may observe, first, that there is a long history to American interest in Chinese territorial integrity. The United States never sought "treaty port" hegemony in China. And in 1908, the United States returned a portion of the indemnity—to be used for educational purposes—it received from the Chinese government as a result of the eight-nation, international occupation of then-Peking to stop the anarchy resulting from the waning Manchu dynasty's inability to contain the Boxer Rebellion at the turn of the twentieth century.

Secondly, as Black notes, "Japan was dependent on American oil for 75 percent of its needs. [The United States was once an oil-exporting country.] U.S. oil exports to Japan had been cut back in the summer of 1940 because of the irritation of Roosevelt and his more hard-line cabinet members, Stimson, Ickes, and Morgenthau, at the brutal Japanese aggression in China. Unknown to the President, [Assistant Secretary of State Dean Acheson] starting in July 1940, had denied Japan any export permits for oil. In fact, Roosevelt had wanted only to reduce the flow of oil to a trickle, not stop it."[918]

Stimson had been President Hoover's secretary of state in 1931 when Japan, by military force, occupied the Chinese province of Manchuria, turning it into a puppet state ruled nominally by Henry Pu Yi, the last Manchu emperor of China. Stimson strongly objected to the Japanese military seizure, and the United States never recognized it. It goes beyond the wildest imagination to think either Acheson or Stimson could be considered as Soviet agents. Black concludes, "Roosevelt and Churchill were concerned to deter Japan from joining in the [German] attack on Russia. The tide of war could turn against Hitler if Russia could survive the German onslaught."[919]

Accepting that White was concerned in 1941 about the survival of the Soviet Union after the apparent success of the Nazi invasion, that concern was shared by Roosevelt and Churchill. Their objective was to keep the Soviet Union fighting the Wehrmacht to preserve Britain. In that sense, there was a confluence of purpose. White's role was minor considering Roosevelt's and Churchill's concern. White prepared a memorandum in which not only was Morgenthau's purpose served, but also those of Stimson, Hull, and Roosevelt. In the last analysis, White was following instructions and prepared the memorandum at the direction of his supervisor. Unlike White's initiative in conceptualizing the World Bank, diplomatic relations with Japan were not a matter within Treasury concern, and appropriate for someone in White's position to initiate.

Similarly, Edward Bernstein describes how "when we issued the White Plan [for the International Monetary Fund and the World Bank] in 1943, White and I held a press conference at the Treasury. . . . White explained what we proposed to do and undertook to answer questions. One question was, what will the quotas be [in connection with drawing rights from the Fund] for the United States, the British, the Chinese and the Russians. Well, White said, having given what the United States would have, he said, "Well, maybe for the Russians we'll have 1 billion, and for the Chinese 800 million" . . . The minute White said this I knew it was a mistake. . . . I was afraid the Russians would take this as a commitment and try to bargain up from there."[920]

At the Bretton Woods Conference, the Russian delegation first complained to Morgenthau that the committee on quotas failed to assign them the quota on drawing rights they had been promised. (Bernstein thought it was $800 million.) Morgenthau spoke to the Soviet delegation and ultimately their drawing rights were increased to $1.2 billion.[921] Still, "the Russians placed a formal protest against Harry White on the quota question."[922]

That raises an interesting question. Was the Russian delegation going through an intricate and elaborate Sherlock Holmesian subterfuge to conceal White's Soviet sympathies, or was it simply that the KGB did not share its information with ordinary organs of the Soviet government? In any case, it does not appear that the initial quota assigned to the Soviet Union, nor the quota ultimately set, was abnormal in any way. The most likely explanation for White's refusal to qualify the quota he mentioned at the press conference in 1943 is that he was speaking hypothetically and stubbornly did not want to be corrected by his subordinate, a psychological quirk that had nothing to do with possible Communist sympathies, which were to be found in a different part of his brain. One does not know the answer.

In any case, in the early 1950s, when Morgenthau was faced with the possibility that White was guilty of espionage, Morgenthau was naturally chagrined and upset that he might have been taken advantage of. Still, White's conduct had always been impeccable, and White died before Morgenthau could confront him to search out the truth. Henry III concludes that his father was never able to satisfy himself on the question of whether White had committed espionage. He could console himself with the thought that beginning on September 3, 1939, when the British went to war, White "was ceaselessly doing his part to see that the United States would have a preparedness program . . . After we got into the war, [White] was most helpful in seeing that everything was done to wage war successfully against the enemy."[923]

One detail needs be added to the story of Morgenthau's life. By 1966, at the age of seventy-six years, Morgenthau appears to have developed peripheral arteriosclerosis. Henry III does not indicate whether the complications of diabetes mellitus entered the picture, whether the condition reached a point where non-healing ulceration or gangrene had occurred, or whether his doctors simply feared the latter conditions would develop in the near future. One may speculate about whether the cure prescribed by Morgenthau's doctors in this instance proved worse than the disease. Henry III writes that in "a desperate remedial effort, the doctor amputated one of his legs above the knee." He adds: "His mind fogged; still there were painful lucid moments. On one such occasion while I was sitting at his bedside, he asked me in that odd demanding way of his [or, possibly, in a postoperative state of physical exhaustion, and, in that sense, feeling utterly bereft], 'Was I a good father?'"[924]

CHAPTER 8

The Morgenthau Plan for the Reconstitution of Germany

L eaving aside Morgenthau's commitment to his life as a farmer, it may be said that only once did Morgenthau devote himself to the advocacy of a program without it being solely the implementation of some policy determination by a chief executive for whom Morgenthau was working. This was his solution to the problem of what to do with Germany after the ending of World War II—the so-called "Morgenthau Plan." His son Henry III expresses a species of astonishment and some embarrassment at the persistence—and even zeal—with which his father pursued the advocacy of that program.

Morgenthau started out with the premise, first, that his generation of Germans could not be trusted to prevent the seizure of governmental powers by a criminal element in the population that would again lead to war with a concomitant mass murder of civilian populations and an almost unquantifiable destruction of the artifacts of a civilized and operative human society. Morgenthau wrote in his forgotten book, *Germany Is Our Problem*,[925] ". . . Germany must be disarmed in her own mind as well as in reality. The most fertile soil for the seed of democracy would be those Germans who know it is useless to plot for dictatorships, war and conquest. There is no point in a dictatorship unless it be for war, and no incentive for Germans to fight unless they think they can win." Second, the concept of European collective security, once put to the test in the 1930s, had proven a dismal failure. A third factor is perhaps relevant. It is that Morgenthau defined "Germany" as it existed in the years 1941 and 1942. Those were the years German troops had occupied the whole of the western littoral of Europe to the Pyrenees, when they overran Ukraine to reach toward the Caucasus Mountains and came within perhaps twenty-five miles of Moscow; when, after the Wehrmacht crossed the eastern frontier and penetrated farther and farther into Russia Einsatzgruppen brigades, like hyenas skulking after a lion's kill, following the German armies into Soviet territory to murder the Jewish inhabitants of the conquered areas—the days when genocide became a reality.

Morgenthau's solution to the threat that Germany posed—starting with what he conceived as the strong possibility of a second Hitler seizing political power in Germany—was to move to interdict their ability to wage war by removing the means to do so. Morgenthau reasoned that modern warfare required the use of iron and steel in the construction and manufacture of guns, tanks, shells, bullets, airplanes, and bayonets. He wrote, "The elementary lesson for the German people [to learn] is that there is no use planning and working for war because they will not have the means to wage it."[926] Curiously, in this respect, George F. Kennan, in 1943, prepared a memorandum for the State Department (which he believed was never seen by the upper-level department officials) that included the words: "The best treatment for the present ruling class in Germany is . . . a grim demonstration that Germany is not strong enough to threaten the interests of the other great powers with impunity and that any unsuccessful attempt in this direction will inevitably lead to catastrophe. . . . Once they realize it, the realization will soon take the guts out of their own nationalism."[927] Morgenthau explained, "The only possible way to make the lesson effective is to make it true. As long as Germany has her heavy industries, it will not be true. For then there will always be the possibility of renewing the battle . . ."[928] He proposed to therefore remove the raw materials and the factories—iron and steel works—from within the geographic boundaries of a reconstituted Germany. The Ruhr Valley was to be turned over to France on a permanent basis. Then, "[t]he French steel mills, which for many years had to depend upon German coal supplies very largely, would be independent."[929]

(It must be noted that the foregoing represents a reconsideration and a retreat from Morgenthau's position in September 1944, when he argued for the destruction of the coal mines in the Ruhr and Saar territories by flooding. At that time Stimson was taking the position of acquiescence with the idea of "systems of control or trusteeship or even transfer of ownership to other nations."[930] Morgenthau had initially overruled Harry Dexter White's suggestion of a United Nations' trusteeship over the Ruhr Valley.[931])

Also, he proposed to further ensure against the re-creation of a unified German war machine by dividing Germany proper into three separate states—northern, southern, and international. The result would be a simplified replica of the politically decentralized Holy Roman Empire that nominally existed in eighteenth-century Germany—the world that had brought forth Beethoven, Mozart, Haydn, Kant, Goethe, Schiller, Lessing, and the latter's friend, Moses Mendelssohn, the grandfather of the composer Felix—in a word, the world of idealistic rationalists who believed in the achievement of societal perfection through the exercise of the powers of human reason.

Put in its best light, Morgenthau's conceptualization reflected a laudable purpose. In its own way, it was a tribute to the worlds of Morgenthau's German forebears.[932] In this latter respect, Henry III recounted the story of the visit of the Grand Duke and Duchess of Baden to the cigar factory of Morgenthau's great-grandfather in Mannheim. Henry III quotes from an article in the *Mannheimer Anzeiger* of May 25, 1860: "Their Excellencies spent half an hour in Morgenthau's cigar factory and inspected all rooms with the greatest interest . . . The illustrious visitors were surprised with an attractive scene from the factory owner's family life: His ten children were placed side by side in accordance with their age and made lovely curtseys before the illustrious pair of [sovereigns]."[933]

The Morgenthau Plan postulated that the iron and steel necessary for those civilian artifacts, such as irons and ironing boards, pots and pans, I-beams for building construction, piping for gas and sewer lines, screws and nails and tools such as hammers and saws, ice picks and eggbeaters, must needs be imported into Germany.[934] Morgenthau in his book presented a plethora of statistics to prove that iron and steel production represented no more than 2 percent of the German annual gross national product. By keeping tabs on the importation of iron and steel into Germany, any efforts to direct these metals into armaments could be pinpointed and interdicted. Additionally, these objectives were to be reinforced by the division of Germany into separate political entities.

Morgenthau wrote prophetically, as it turned out—considering the years between 1950 and 1990—"Two Germanys would be easier to deal with than one."[935] The map at page 160 of his book was intended to illustrate how the division of Germany might be effectuated. Something of his idea of separate geographic divisions came into being as the separate Allied countries' occupation zones and with the separate states that afterwards came to form the political subdivisions of the German Federal Republic. More particularly, it was realized by the separation of Germany into separate sovereign entities—the Federal Republic in the west and the "Democratic" Republic to the east, representing the separate spheres of influence of the Western Allies dominated by the United States and of the Communists controlled by the Soviet Union. (The psychological effect of a Russian-oriented, totalitarian East German polity on West German political thinking is worth extended comment unfortunately beyond the scope of this study.)

Although his text (written after the event) envisioned easterly boundaries of a postwar Germany measured by the Oder and Western Niesse rivers, the lesser, present-day boundaries of Germany were actually the result of Stalin's insistence, first at Tehran in 1943 (as George F. Kennan suggests in his *Memoirs 1925–1950*[936]) and then confirmed at Yalta in February, 1945—to which Roosevelt acquiesced—and lastly at Potsdam the following July, agreed to by President Truman. As Truman's biographer David McCullough puts it, ". . . it was the Western leaders who made the big concessions, because they had little choice—Russian occupation of Eastern Europe was indeed a fait accompli."[937] The Soviet Union was also given the right to take reparations in the form of whole factories and other material assets it found in the areas it was occupying. In that context, the references to a "pastoral" society—the word is not Morgenthau's, but actually appears in a memorandum Winston Churchill dictated—as the Morgenthau Plan objective came to be understood, make sense only as the word "pastoral" may be comprehended to imply a "peaceable" landscape.

Still, it must be emphasized that Morgenthau envisioned a transfer of workers from heavy industry to agrarian pursuits. By way of justification, Morgenthau wrote, "The transition from factory to farm will be much easier for Germans than for most urban dwellers. Even more than most of us, the present generation of industrial workers has been recruited from farms. An even greater number are the sons and daughters of farmers."[938]

A striking confirmation of Morgenthau's words is given by Kennan in his portrait of the immediate post–World War II president of the city of Bremen's senate: "He was a strong, simple, quiet man, with old-fashioned, drooping mustaches: a farmer by origin, and a member of the pre-1914 generation. After his original imprisonment by the Nazis, at the outset of the Hitler era, he had gone back to the country and had worked the land, silently and patiently, for twelve years, paying no attention whatsoever to politics. Called back to political life after the defeat, he had dropped his tools and returned, with equal simplicity and resolution, to take the top job in the Bremen enclave."[939]

That given, it must be recognized that the Morgenthau Plan for the reconstitution of the fabric of postwar West German social, political, and economic worlds—taking into account *as these came to exist after 1945*—did not comport with reality and, in that sense—retrospectively—was unfortunately naive.

By the same token, one may also say that the attitudes of Henry Stimson, and those who thought as he did, were equally the consequence of a priori reasoning and equally oblivious to the facts on the ground as these came to exist in Germany after 1945. It was those facts on the ground which were the basis for the political successes in post–World War II West Germany. So Stimson could write to President Truman on May 16, 1945, "A solution must be found for Germany's 'future peaceful existence,' and it was in America's and the world's interest that it 'should not be driven by stress of hardship into a non-democratic and necessarily predatory habit of life.'"[940] Communist East Germany was non-democratic, and its quality of life never met the standards of West German society, but whether that led to a "necessarily predatory habit of life"—whatever Stimson may have meant exactly by the use of that Social Darwinist language—is questionable.

Taking the analogy of an eighteenth-century society spread over the multitudinous political entities that could consider themselves as coming within a German ethnic identity, one must include the Kingdom of Prussia—a kingdom in name only since 1701. It was an appendage to the Holy Roman Empire, including territory both inside and beyond that nominal political empire headed by the Hapsburgs. It also contained a portion of those lands (from which the name *Prussia* was taken) that had been a part of the Teutonic Order, a medieval political confederation dissolved in 1525, as the untoward consequence of its great defeat at the hands of the Polish Republic, then at its political zenith, at the first battle of Tannenberg in 1410.

Something of the martial heritage of the Teutonic Order descended to the rulers of Prussia/Brandenburg. In the early eighteenth century, that king of Prussia, who was the progenitor of Frederick the Great, husbanded every *pfennig* he could get for the army he prized. He ruled a political entity that consisted of what was essentially—except for a few cities like Danzig, Berlin, and Königsberg, and small market towns—a relatively poor country of potato farmers ruled by a gentry that supplied the officer corps for his army and the personnel of his nascent bureaucracy. That army came as a legacy to his son Frederick, who, in his own way, may be compared with Prince Hal in Shakespeare's plays devoted to Hal's father, Henry IV—a matter of life imitating art. Papa was a stingy, stolid German burgher whose passion was his army, and whose son may be said to have been a sore trial to him.

His heir appeared frivolous and lacking any appreciation for that war machine. To his father's indignation, Frederick chose to play the flute, a seemingly effeminate music maker instead of a proper stringed instrument like a violin or a cello. And he liked boys. One can imagine how he used his status to entice young men to his bed. (Although, it would appear that during his adolescent years Frederick engaged in an intense, idealistic friendship with another young man. When his father discovered what he considered an improper connection, he promptly had the other young person hung and required Frederick to watch the hanging—one might call it a rather severe apprenticeship in cynicism.) Later, as a king, it might be simpler to suggest to the colonel of a regiment that the latter order a young soldier who caught his fancy to report to the king's tent or a room in a palace. Still, when the time came, Frederick did his duty and married, although without producing an heir to the Prussian throne. His nephew, who succeeded him, reverted to type.

Like Prince Hal, when Frederick became king, things were different. He might keep his predilection for boys and his flute, but he was determined to use the army that his father had so painfully financed and husbanded as if it were a collectible—as other royal personages might collect art in Dresden or, later, Fabergé eggs in St. Petersburg. Frederick had a keen intelligence; he had taste (as his palace at Potsdam attests); he was interested in ideas (inviting Voltaire as a royal houseguest); he had a nose for opportunity; and, not least, he turned out to be a military genius.

He won battles, invariably finding the means to turn an opposing army's flank, creating panic and causing its retreat from the battlefield.

In a political sense, Frederick was utterly unscrupulous. In 1740, the Hapsburg government was distracted by a constitutional crisis. Maria Theresa, the sole child of the deceased emperor, appeared unable to succeed to the vacant throne because of the Salic law that called for a male heir. Taking advantage of the situation, Frederick sent his father's army into the Austrian province of Silesia to add it to his own domain, precipitating the War of Austrian Succession.

Frederick was cynical. To pay for his wars, he summoned the Jewish bankers in Berlin, directing them to extract the interiors of gold coins and substitute lead to maintain their weight and seeming value. He used the extracted gold to mint new lead coins covered with a veneer of precious metal and then distributed the coins to pay his soldiers. In due course, the gold wore off, revealing the ruse. But rather than blaming Frederick for the deception, the populace named the counterfeit coins after the Jewish bankers.

Frederick was also lucky. The one time he found himself in a seemingly inescapable trap surrounded by an array of armies of Austria, Russia, and France, his soldiers threatened with starvation, the ruler of Russia unexpectedly died. The politics of tsarist succession caused the departure of the Russian army and the disintegration of the coalition against Frederick.

With the additional territorial accretions resulting from the successive partitions of Poland, Frederick brought Prussia to the level of a first-tier country—the equal of the Hapsburg Empire.

Frederick left a baleful example—a legacy of cynicism—that proved to be a disaster when it came to twentieth-century Germany. The latter was filled with Prussian technicians in both the military and civilian bureaucracies of government. But however competent and even brilliant they were, they lacked that "pinch of Attic salt" to measure up to Frederick's ability to come out on top. In an ultimate sense, they lacked the intuitive or intellectual capacity to understand the dimensions and limitations of the problems they faced, resulting in the political and moral disasters of twentieth-century Germany. They knew the cynicism that Frederick exhibited without in the least understanding how to use it effectively.

The last paragraph raises an interesting point that needs to be explored further.

With respect to the significance of the word *cynicism*, the habits of mind engendered in each instance—the Age of Enlightenment and a Social Darwinist world—were vastly different. The word might seemingly stay the same, but the frame of reference rendered understanding as poles apart. It is perhaps valid to say that "cynicism" in the context of eighteenth-century rationalism included a very clear-eyed awareness of the difference between what was right and what was wrong in a moral sense. In a rational world, one remained conscious always that the ideal to which one strived was a degree of human perfection in which one acted in accordance with the highest standards of *noblesse oblige*. In a word, cynicism in the eighteenth century referred to circumstances overriding the best of intentions.

In a Social Darwinist world, conversely, "cynicism" operated in the context of those biological "laws of life" that promised strife, lawlessness, and unending fear of dispossession by others as the evolutionary legacy. By the first half of the twentieth century, cynicism had come to mean that one not only needed—but there was also the evolutionary right, and indeed the necessity—to mislead, defraud, and prevail over others. In the simplest of terms, a gas chamber at Auschwitz designed to successively murder hundreds of thousands upon hundreds of thousands of human beings locked into an enclosed space through the use of poisonous fumes would have been incomprehensible in the world that existed in the eighteenth century, and Frederick would probably have dismissed General von Bernhardi's paean to war as rubbish.

(The other face of the Social Darwinist canon is revealed in the actions of the Nazi government of Germany during World War II, while German armies still ruled a vast part of the European continent. That government rewarded its ethnic kin, the civilian population of Germany, as their natural Social Darwinist right, with delicacies, trinkets, clothing, food, furs, and furniture taken from the nations the Wehrmacht conquered and the Jews it dispossessed and murdered. In the introductory passages to his book, *Hitler's Beneficiaries: Plunder, Racial War, and the Nazi Welfare State*,[941] Götz Aly tells that he inherited some beautiful antique furniture from his wife's parents whose house in Bremen had been destroyed in an Allied air raid. He writes that it is now known how the German government came to provide replacement furniture for the losses of bombed-out house owners in Bremen. He is haunted by the knowledge that those antiques came from the abandoned homes of unknown Dutch Jews—who were deported and killed by inhalation of poisonous fumes as they stood naked in the gas chambers of death camps in Poland.)

That, then—in foreshortened form—was a portion of the context in which Morgenthau and others in the United States government, notably Henry Stimson, considered the question of what to do with Germany after World War II finally ended. In truth, the participants in that debate had only the vaguest perception of the total context and its implications for a successful resolution in a reconstituted Germany.

At the crucial point—when the debate raged and a decision was required—Morgenthau was at a fatal disadvantage. Policies are decided not so much by what later proves to be successful as by the nature of the personalities of those engaged in the debate—the intuitive ability to convey the sense that proposition *X* rather than thesis *Y* must be right. In that crucial debate, Morgenthau lacked that subtleness of temperament—something that came naturally to his father—that might have allowed Morgenthau to prevail in the debate about the future of Germany. And, in Stimson, Morgenthau was dealing with an opponent quietly possessed of an extraordinarily charismatic and commanding personality.

As an example of how Stimson could command an issue and succeed in directing a result, his early biographer Elting E.

Morison comments how, after Stimson settled into the nation's capital with his appointment in 1940 as Secretary of War, Stimson found what he regarded as a "very singular situation."[942] Morison writes, "Many of the decisions affecting the defensive strength of the nation were in the hands of Henry Morgenthau [who] had been conducting most of the negotiations with the British Purchasing Commission. Since what was sent to the British determined what was left for the growing American army, Stimson believed the British negotiations should be placed in the control of the War Department."[943] What is more, Morison writes, Stimson "persuaded the President to place the British negotiations in his hands."[944]

In Stimson's maneuvering to acquire control of negotiations with the British Purchasing Commission from Morgenthau and the Treasury Department, Stimson, by profession an attorney, was raising an issue of national security and arguing a hypothetical future contingency stripped of the usual legal context of an actual, adversarial litigation. In a sense, his reasoning was analogous to the logic behind the legal doctrine of anticipatory breach of contract—the idea that once it is apparent a contractual agreement has broken down, a contracting party has been injured and is entitled to recompense even though the transaction that the agreement envisioned has yet to take place.[945]

To fully appreciate Stimson's accomplishment, one must be aware of other matters involving British government purchases and requests for logistical support.

Earlier Roosevelt had ruled against Stimson's predecessor, Secretary Woodring (and the latter's assistant secretary, Louis Johnson, later to become a secretary of defense in President Truman's Cabinet), who made the same objections to Morgenthau and the Treasury Department's Division of Procurement continuing to coordinate British and French war materiel purchasing.[946] Responding to their objections, Roosevelt wrote, by letter dated December 13, 1939:

> I think you fail to realize that the greater part of such purchases is not, in the strict sense of the word, munitions—probably well over 50 per cent of the purchases will consist of articles and raw or semi-raw materials which are primarily of civil use. . . . With all due deference to the Army and Navy Munitions Board, it is not as experienced in making purchases as is the Procurement Division [of the Treasury Department]. . . . In any event, the coordinating committee . . . will have representatives of the Army and Navy on it. . . . Finally, it must be remembered that we are not at war, that we are trying to keep prices in this country down, that the work of the committee deals with civilians, and that the general fiscal and purchasing policies of the Treasury are very definitely involved."[947]

In that respect, as Roosevelt had noted in his letter, the purchase of munitions and equipment by the British Purchasing Commission to replace what had been lost in France the preceding spring with the emergency evacuation of British troops from the French beaches at Dunkirk, involved payment and the transfer of funds—matters properly within the Treasury Department's sphere of authority. Nor was there any assertion that Treasury supervision of British purchasing transactions, in fact, had been adversely affecting national security in any way. Quite the reverse: Representatives of the War and Navy Departments reviewed the allocations for the British and French as members of the Liaison [Coordinating] Committee which Roosevelt had appointed at Morgenthau's suggestion.[948]

Thereafter, on the evening of May 16, 1940, Roosevelt reviewed a request for urgently needed supplies from Winston Churchill with Morgenthau, "whom he commissioned to see what he could get the army to release." Blum then quotes Morgenthau as telling General Marshall the next day, "If I [were] the President . . . I would make you make the decision [as to what equipment could possibly be diverted from intended army use to meet British needs]." Blum quotes Morgenthau as emphasizing, "There will be no pressure from me."[949]

An example of the way Morgenthau applied his responsibilities vis-à-vis British purchases of war materiel versus American military needs is a second, three-hour meeting held December 10, 1940 at his office. (An earlier, preliminary meeting was held on December 3, 1940, which included Hull, Stimson, Knox, Jesse Jones, and General Marshall, when Morgenthau first introduced the subject of looming British insolvency.[950])

The discussion revolved around the problem presented by the circumstance that the British ambassador, Lord Lothian, had let it be known that Britain would be unable to pay in full for a $600 million order for war materiel it proposed to buy. The proposed contract also involved the construction of factory buildings in which to manufacture the military ordnance to be purchased in part by the British. The largest part of the output of the projected factory buildings would be to meet American military needs, so the United States Army would join in the construction costs. The British share of the factory construction costs amounted to $57 million. Apparently, they were able to furnish their share of the construction costs of the factory buildings, and also the down payment of $200 million toward the total cost of $600 million for their segment of the factory output, but would be unable to pay the remainder of the cost of their proposed contract.

Present at the meeting in Morgenthau's office were Secretary Stimson, his aide John J. McCloy, General George Marshall,

Army Chief of Staff, acting Secretary of the Navy James Forrestal, Admiral Ingersoll, as well as Jesse Jones, head of the Reconstruction Finance Corporation, which would initially finance the costs of construction (a "bridge loan" subject to reimbursement by the Army and the British government), Undersecretary of State Sumner Welles, William Knudsen, formerly president of General Motors Corporation and now a "One Dollar a Year" Director-General of the Office of Production Management, and Harry Dexter White and other members of Morgenthau's Treasury staff.[951]

It was agreed by everyone present that the indiscretion of the British ambassador in revealing the British could not pay for the total cost of the military ordnance that would be produced, created problems because the federal government had no legal authority to pay for ordnance delivered to the British. Equally true is that the persons present were agreed that they were all there to assist the British war effort to the greatest possible extent short of war. There was an absolute necessity for the construction of the factories and production of war materiel. The problem was that Congress would have to adopt legislation to make this happen legally. The importance of the policy underlying the discussion—namely, the need to support the British war effort against Germany—required presidential involvement to bring the matter to the attention of Congress.

The point to be made here is that Morgenthau, in arranging for the meeting, was meticulous in showing regard for the concerns of the War Department where British purchases were involved.

Actually, that the British ambassador would give information to the American government about the looming British insolvency was not as foolish as it might seem at first blush—no matter what fiscal problems could result for American officials. The British had too much at stake to think of subterfuge with the American government. During that period, the isolationists were a substantial sector of the American electorate, strongly opposed to Roosevelt's policy of giving support to the British. In that sense, the Roosevelt administration "leaned over backwards" to avoid a public relations debacle. To avoid any possibility of that happening, the Treasury monitored British assets in the United States by means of monthly bank reports of the dollar holdings in foreign-owned accounts in American banks to keep on top of British assets in the United States—what Edward Bernstein called "capital movement figures."[952] And the British would have a good idea that the American government was monitoring British assets. (Sophisticated British Exchequer bureaucrats would expect to do the same themselves if they were in a similar position. And it is entirely possible that local bank officers in the United States could feel a fiduciary obligation in connection with substantial deposits to tell their depositors of Treasury Department requirements.)

Edward Bernstein tells how a problem arose because the British and French had transferred almost all sequestered dollar holdings to a Joint Purchasing Commission with a local American address. It was necessary for the Treasury Department to modify the bank reporting forms to include holdings of foreign diplomatic and trade missions with local United States addresses.[953]

In the course of the discussion in Morgenthau's office as to how to treat the looming British insolvency, Morgenthau indicated he must refer the matter to the president for his consideration as to how to proceed. He said he proposed to send a message to the president immediately after the meeting adjourned. The President was then vacationing on the USS *Tuscaloosa* in the Caribbean Sea, spending his "days fishing, taking the sun, and considering" another urgent letter from Winston Churchill, outlining British military materiel requirements and foreseen British insolvency.[954] The text of Morgenthau's message to the president,[955] sent that evening, reads in pertinent part:

At this meeting the Treasury presented the most up-to-date figures that we have received as to the financial status of the British. This shows that with the orders they would like to place now, plus the orders already placed, their total orders will amount to over $5,000,000,000. The British Treasury claims that their cash and other assets readily available amount to about a billion [and] eight [hundred million dollars]. They also have other assets about which we have not yet received full information. The War Department states that in case the British should stop fighting or run out of cash, our Army can make good use of substantially all of the output of the so-called "B" ordnance program of the British, which amounts to at least $600,000,000.

We have proposed tonight to the English, subject to your approval, that they make the usual advance payment to the manufacturers of $200,000,000, which is approximately one-third of the total order. The new facilities will cost approximately $150,000,000. Of this amount, the Army feels it cannot certify to as useful one-third of the facilities amounting to $50,000,000, which the British will, therefore, have to advance. The [Reconstruction Finance Corporation in the person of its Administrator, Jesse Jones, the Texas banker] is prepared to advance the balance of $100,000,000 for new ammunition plants upon certification of the War Department and the Defense Commission. If the English will accept this proposal, all of us feel that this will tide them over until Congress meets in January [1941], at which time it is the unanimous feeling of this group that we should present the entire matter to Congress, including the financial status of Great Britain which, in the light of their projected commitments and their claimed assets, seems inadequate. May I hear from you at an early date.

Aside from the light Morgenthau's meeting of December 10, 1940 (and the message he sent to the President immediately afterwards) casts on Morgenthau's concern for American military needs vis-à-vis the negotiations with the British Purchasing Commission, both activities are significant because these provided factual background out of which Roosevelt came to develop his concept of Lend-Lease. His idea was that the United States could forego payment from the British for war materiel on the theory that no sale was involved, but merely that equipment was being lent and that it would all be returned after the war ended. His public relations gesture—reducing what he was proposing to the dimensions of gardening tools lent to a neighbor, who would return them when he had no further use for them—was masterful.

Roosevelt urged the Congress to consider legislation authorizing Lend-Lease in his State of the Union address on January 6, 1941, and a bill was introduced as early as January 10, 1941, styled "HR 1776" by the Parliamentarian of the House of Representatives.[956]

"On 30 December 1940 Roosevelt assigned to the Treasury the drafting of the Lend-Lease bill," Morgenthau wrote in his diary. "He is definitely counting on the Treasury to do the drafting . . . and he definitely wants it in a blank check form."[957] Morgenthau then assigned the drafting to Edward Foley, his general counsel, and Oscar Cox, who would later become an assistant solicitor general. The financial aspects devolved on Harry Dexter White and his subordinates. Drafts of the proposed legislation were submitted for comment to cabinet officers and agency heads, and also to the Democratic Congressional leadership.[958] Roosevelt wanted control over allocations of prospective military equipment between American military needs for its new armed forces in creation and the British requirements. There was also a question of the mode of reimbursement. Foley and Cox reviewed their definitive draft with Ben Cohen (now in the State Department), who made some minor changes, including a specific presidential authorization to allow British ships to be repaired at American naval bases.

What would raise eyebrows today is that Foley then asked sitting Supreme Court Justice Frankfurter to review the proposed legislation, as well as the Parliamentarian of the House of Representatives. (Roosevelt wanted it to appear that the bill originated in that legislative body.) Morgenthau also directed that the draft be shown to Dean Acheson, then still a lawyer in private practice but publicly committed to supporting the British by every means short of war. Making sure that all bases were covered, Foley then showed the draft to Secretary of the Navy Knox and Secretary of State Hull. Only then did Foley and Cox prepare a memorandum for the president's eyes.[959] Roosevelt, in company with Morgenthau and Stimson, thereafter arranged with congressional leaders how the proposed bill would be handled legislatively. On January 10, 1941, a bill was introduced in both houses of Congress and given the symbolic number HR 1776.[960]

At Hyde Park, Morgenthau urged the president two days later to ask Secretary Hull to lead the congressional fight. Describing the episode in his diary, Morgenthau wrote: "The President did not take my suggestion too well. He said, 'Hull is going to testify,' and I said, 'I know that, but up to now in the Treasury we have done everything, even to preparing the statements for Barkley [the Democratic majority leader in the Senate] and Rayburn [the Speaker of the House of Representatives].' He said, 'I know that.' I said, 'We are perfectly willing to continue but I think seeing that it goes before Foreign Affairs [Committee], that Hull ought to do it.' The President said he would take it up the first thing . . . when he got back [to the capital]. The important thing is that I have planted a seed in his mind."[961]

In due course, Hull made an impressive statement at the committee hearing, part of which was the handiwork of the president.[962]

In point of fact, technical amendments were necessary, slightly modifying the president's discretion before congressional leaders felt the legislation could be adopted.[963] HR 1776 did become law. Lend-Lease is one of Roosevelt's greatest and most imaginative presidential achievements.

Blum quotes Acheson as saying Morgenthau "was entirely responsible for the fact that . . . between [the British soldiers' evacuation from the beaches at] Dunkirk and the first of the year [1941] . . . the English kept fighting."[964]

Morison writes that once Stimson secured control of the British purchasing approvals, this led to a survey of prospective needs of the Army, Navy, and the British taken together[965]—something that ought to have been done previously and was independent of purchasing transactions once those military priorities were determined. And it goes without saying that Stimson was equally as committed as was Morgenthau to meeting the British needs for war materiel. In that respect, Morison had earlier quoted from Stimson's letter to the *New York Times*, published January 24, 1939: "Fascism with its moral deterioration, brutality, destructiveness of individual freedom of speech and thought, constituted probably the most serious attack ever made on democratic principals. To attempt to forestall the Fascist aggression by soft words or inaction was the counsel of confused thinking, emotion or, to speak plainly, undue timidity."[966]

Indeed, John J. McCloy, who was Stimson's closest aide in the War Department, would state unreservedly at a meeting in Morgenthau's office on the subject of aid to Great Britain, held the afternoon of March 3, 1941, "We have got a big [congressional] bill, three billion [and] eight [hundred million dollars], of which all but two or three hundred million [dollars] is for supplies, all of which supplies, practically speaking, *we want to have available to switch to the aid of any country whose defense is vital to ours*"[967] (italics added).

If we would proceed to a discussion of the separate provisions of the Morgenthau Plan: In the context of the seizure by the Russians of whole factories as reparations from East Germany—authorized by section IV.1. of the Potsdam Declaration signed by Truman in July, 1945[968]—it is probable that any economic damage to the Western Allies' zones of occupation resulting from the adoption of the provisions of the Morgenthau Plan curtailing coal mining and iron ore extraction and reduction, would have been containable. (After all, it will be remembered that by the first decade of the twenty-first century, the economy of the United States imports most of its raw iron and steel needs from other countries.)

It must be remembered that, ultimately, the differences between Morgenthau and Stimson were essentially in matters of degree. Otherwise, the basic approach of each was remarkably similar. In a sense, Morgenthau was recommending a replay of the French occupation of the Ruhr Valley in 1923, as Morgenthau himself admitted.[969] It was not the best of precedents but, in any case, one that was short-lived. By the end of the war in 1945, the damage to many of the German cities and manufacturing plants from Allied aerial bombing was enormous. In a real way, coal and iron ore production was a small part of the problem faced by the need for German reconstruction.

In that respect, Beschloss writes, "Just before VE-Day, [General] Clay assured McCloy that 'destruction of Germany's war potential' was no longer a serious problem: 'The progress of the war has accomplished that.' . . . After surveying the vast destruction across Germany, Clay wrote McCloy that some hunger was necessary to make Germans 'realize the consequences of a war which they caused' but not to the point where it results in mass starvation and sickness."[970]

The course the American government and its Western allies, Britain and France in their zones of occupation, decided upon was simple and honorable. It was to occupy West Germany with a light hand. (In that respect, it is not clear that even if the provisions of the Morgenthau Plan relative to interdiction of German iron and steel production in the Saar and the Ruhr valleys had been in effect, the basic approach to military government would have been appreciably different if at all. JCS 1067, the basic policy document governing military government, had been championed by Morgenthau.) General Lucius Clay, appointed the military governor of the areas of Germany occupied by the Western Allies, determined that his deputy must be identifiably Jewish, and he convinced Benjamin Buttenweiser, a private merchant banker in New York, to accept the position. The ensuing military government acceded to most requests of the nascent government of the German Federal Republic. But the key to the successful reconstitution of West Germany was the general attitudes of its inhabitants.

In the 1920s, a critical mass of German society was generally committed to an unspoken intent to evade the limitations on German military strength prescribed by the Treaty of Versailles. (In the eighteenth century such limitations had been imposed on the Polish Republic by its neighbors, Russia, Prussia, and the Hapsburg Empire, that would end by obliterating an independent Polish sovereignty by 1795.) The German democrats in the 1920s, who exercised control over the political organs of government, might be sincerely committed to a peaceable European future. The Kellogg-Briand Pact[971] signed by German Foreign Minister Stresemann embodied that purpose. But at the same time, the bureaucrats in the Ministry of War realized those unspoken popular attitudes that looked nostalgically back to the glories of the imperial, Wilhelmine era by encouraging, for instance, the creation of glider clubs to give future pilots nascent flight training, and by entering into secret agreements with the Red Army in the Soviet Union to arrange for the development of more-effective military equipment outside the limitations imposed by the Treaty of Versailles.[972]

General Clay reported to Washington in July, 1945, "that he had not yet seen any 'general feeling of war guilt or repugnance for Nazi doctrine and regime.' The Germans 'blame Nazis for losing the war, protest ignorance of the regime's crimes and shrug off their own support or silence as incidental and unavoidable.'"[973] The attitudes that General Clay described bear an unfortunate resemblance to the way many Germans felt in the interwar period that led to the Nazi years.

So, Morgenthau could write,[974] "This time we must be sure that the Germans do more than understand what we are talking about when we speak of the sanctity of life, the rights and duties of individuals, the equality of men and the place of the state as a servant of its citizens." He had warned,[975] "In the past these phrases were . . . without meaning for most Germans." He described the Weimar Republic somewhat unfairly as a "sham democracy which rushed for shelter to the protection of its worst enemies."[976] To him, the Weimar Republic "was hardly a sight to inspire enthusiasm for democratic ideals."[977] Still, Morgenthau was willing to concede, "Even in their fanaticism, Germans as a whole retain a certain practical sense."[978]

In a larger sense, 1945 proved to be a watershed year. The Social Darwinism that had pervaded the Western world's attitudes for perhaps three generations started to fade on April 15, 1945, when British troops entered Bergen-Belsen, the first of the Nazi concentration camps to be liberated by the Western Allies. There, anonymous, Anne Frank had died of typhus several months earlier, clad only in a blanket. Now, the pictures in newspapers of the emaciated prisoners in their striped garments being helped by British soldiers acted as a revelation.

Black writes: "[American General George] Patton forced the entire adult population of the town neighboring the Ohrdruf death camp [a subcamp of Buchenwald] to [walk] through . . . [where] almost all were speechless with horror." Black adds: ". . . they were well aware of the camp's existence and of Hitler's rhetorical reflections on Jews and other designated enemies. They had seen long trains of cattle cars packed with victims enter the camp, and never saw any inmates leave . . . Many vomited uncontrollably at the sight of the cadavers, skulls, dental fillings . . . children's shoes, ovens, gas chambers, and skeletons, living and dead. General Patton himself was physically ill."[979]

As Dr. David H. Marlowe, a former chief of military psychiatry at the Walter Reed Army Institute of Research is quoted as saying in 2005 (in connection with the stresses resulting from the continuing occupation of Iraq by American forces), "The great change among American troops in Germany during the Second World War was when they discovered the concentration camps. . . . That immediately and forever changed the moral appreciation for why we were there."[980]

Dwight Eisenhower, the Supreme Western Allied commander, would write:

[On April 12, 1945] I saw my first horror [concentration] camp. It was near the town of Gotha. I have never felt able to describe my emotional reactions when I first came face to face with indisputable evidence of Nazi brutality and ruthless disregard of every shred of decency. Up to that time I had known about it only generally or through secondary sources. I am certain, however, that I have never at any other time experienced an equal sense of shock.

I visited every nook and cranny of the camp because I felt it my duty to be in a position from then on to testify at first hand about these things in case there ever grew up at home the belief or assumption that "the stories of Nazi brutality were just propaganda." Some members of the visiting party were unable to go through the ordeal. I not only did so, but as soon as I returned to [General] Patton's headquarters that evening I sent communications to both Washington and London, urging the two governments to send instantly to Germany a random group of news-paper editors and representative groups from the national legislatures. I felt that the evidence should be immediately placed before the American and British publics in a fashion that would leave no room for cynical doubt.[981]

The moral bankruptcy of Social Darwinist perceptions of reality was starkly illustrated. It was not that persons inside and outside Germany had not known what was happening; it was just that for a variety of reasons, it had been disregarded and ignored. In an underlying sense, what was happening was seen in a Social Darwinist world as the natural order of things. In Germany, the disappearance of Jewish persons had been accepted both as the price for a seemingly miraculous recrudescence of German economic prosperity and its political power in the world, and because oppo-sition was personally dangerous—aside from anti-Semitic attitudes that Jews "deserved" what was happening to them.

Outside Germany, especially during the war years, there was the fear that any emphasis on Jewish suffering would harden and enflame anti-Semitic attitudes then widely prevalent and interfere with the war effort. There was, also, the consideration that claims of Nazi atrocities could backfire and have an adverse effect, as a result of the disillusionment after World War I, with what later proved to be false and propagandistic stories of German atroci-ties (such as the innocence of Nurse Edith Cavell, condemned to death for spying, and the mutilation of Belgian children).

So Beschloss, for example, writes: "Recalling World War I atrocity stories that had proven untrue, McCloy was not certain how much of the information about Nazi death camps he should believe. He felt that part of his job was to protect Stimson against special pleading. He told the British historian Martin Gilbert in the early 1980s about how much he had been 'bothered generally by Jewish requests throughout the war.'"[982] Certainly, the well-nigh-universal commitment of the American people during World War II to the necessity of victory over a Germany that had declared war against the United States, in this day and age after Vietnam and Iraq, must be regarded as near miraculous. However strongly attitudes of Social Darwinism and anti-Semitism were held, those attitudes started to fade with the specter of the surviving Nazi concentration camp prisoners—who were not primarily Jewish but political.

The American military government might set up book censorship in the occupied zones of Germany, but the first book that was submitted for approval for publication was a new edition of Heinrich Heine's poetry. Whatever suspicions might have been engendered about seeking to hoodwink the occupation forces, the book could have no harmful implications. For scores of years Heine's graceful lyrics had been belittled because these individually few lines had not the dimensions of a full-length work of art comparable to Goethe's monumental *Faust*—just as chamber music had come to be regarded in the late Victorian era as lacking in the importance and significance of orchestral compositions. With the advent of the Nazi hegemony over the German government on January 30, 1933, Heine's poetry had been banned because he was born of Jewish parentage. His poem "Die Lorelei" had been immensely popular in Germany and could not be ignored. And so when it was anthologized in the Nazi years, it was attributed to "Author Unknown." (Similarly, just after World War II ended, and through the last years of the Soviet Union, a young woman—one of three persons glorified as patriotic heroes who were hanged for sabotage in the early days of the Nazi occupation of Kiev—was identified by the Communist authorities as "unknown" because they knew she was Jewish.) There was no way the application to publish Heine's *Book of Songs* would be denied.

The Western Allies could only approve of the idea of surviving remnants of the Weimar Republic's democratic political establishment seeking to coalesce to create a political party structure to support a postwar government. So Konrad Adenauer, sensing the "lay of the land" and the benign protection afforded by the Western Allies' military government, brought together the survivors of the old Catholic Centrist Party—which had provided one of the last pre-Hitler chancellors, Heinrich Brüning—to form a newly christened "Christian Democratic Party." The party's name was probably taken from Alcide De Gasperi's already-existing Italian party of the same name. As Morgenthau had noted, the Weimar Republic had been corrupted and eaten away from within—failing in the first and fundamental function of any government, that is, self-preservation.

In that sense, in 1861, some contemporaneous Americans had argued in the North of the United States that the Southern states should be left to leave the Union peaceably. A legal conundrum was created because the provisions of Article I, section 8 [para. 15] of the United States Constitution[983] provided only that the Congress had the power to suppress insurrection, but not necessarily the power to respond to nullification of the prior acts of ratification of the Federal Constitution by the several state legislatures, and thereby accession to the new government created under it. The outgoing president James Buchanan could be said to have been particularly susceptible to that constitutional quandary, leading to a period of unsettled drifting in the opening days of the new year. In April of 1861, the uncertainty and the sense of drifting in Washington was abruptly brought to a close after Southern soldiers had fired artillery shells at the federal troops manning Fort Sumter in the harbor at Charleston, South Carolina. Reacting to the ensuing crisis, Abraham Lincoln, having only recently (on the preceding March 4th) been sworn in as the president of the United States, acted in terms of a kind of natural law implicit in the concept of government sovereignty—to preserve the Union.

And so, the Weimar Republic was a shame that could not speak its name.

Germany had started out in the twentieth century with seemingly unassailable advantages. The unification of the country under the suzerainty of the Prussian monarchy could be said to symbolize over two hundred years of sovereign expansion by a relatively minor, provincial, noble family, the Hohenzollern, on the eastern boundary of the Holy Roman Empire, that nominal and powerless political conglomerate led by the Hapsburgs, in which all German political jurisdictions were said to belong. Now, that powerless political abstraction had been succeeded by a nation that was one of the first powers in Europe. Its armies for some two hundred years had won wars, humbling other German states, the Polish Republic, Napoleon, Denmark, Austria, and finally even France. In Social Darwinist terms, it was newly constituted, a "young" country. It had wealth, and an industrial infrastructure that rivaled, if not exceeded, that of Great Britain. It had an army second to none. It led the world in scientific and musical achievements. It was run by Prussian military and civilian bureaucrats who were dedicated to excellence. Bismarck might dismiss his fellow Prussian gentry members derisively as "potato farmers," but they proved to be incorruptible government technicians inspired by the glittering achievements of their predecessors in service to the Prussian crown.

And then, in the twentieth century, the unthinkable happened. Imperial Germany went to war and ended by surrendering to the Western Entente powers, suing for peace. In the process, it lost lower Silesia—the jewel that Frederick the Great had wrested from Austria in the eighteenth century—to a newly reconstituted Polish Republic. The city of Danzig became an independent city-state nominally under the protection of the League of Nations. The provinces of Alsace and Lorraine, acquired by a newly unified Germany in 1871, were surrendered back to France. Following the precedent set by the newly established German Empire in 1871, which had demanded reparations from a defeated France, the French, in turn, on whose territory the war had been fought, demanded reparations.

There was one crucial difference between 1871 and 1920. In 1871, the French had been able to pay off the reparations in full in three years, due in part to the circumstance that the 1870s were a period of prosperity for the agrarian economy. The 1920s found Germany in the depression phase of the agrarian business cycle. The only way the Germans were able to pay reparations to France was to borrow the money from American sources, leading to default on the loans at the end of the decade. So Morgenthau could warn that "Germany cannot pay recurring reparations unless we do just that"[984]—namely, lend money to repair factories to produce exports to provide the money to make the reparation payments. He concluded, "The real test of the value of any reparation settlement is simple. Does it strengthen Germany's war-making potential? Then it is bad, no matter how profitable. Does it help our Allies without strengthening Germany? Then it is good."[985] (Morgenthau did not anticipate the Marshall Plan—although in fairness, one may say that there is no reason why he should have reasonably been expected to do so as his book was being written—prior to General Marshall's speech several years later, in what was a markedly different psychological and economic clime.)

In the 1920s, the agrarian depression caused severe economic distress to the landowning gentry in Pomerania and East Prussia, the latter now separated from the rest of Germany by the so-called

"Polish Corridor"—that had been lower Silesia—given to the newly reconstituted Polish Republic to provide it with access to the Baltic Sea, where the new port city of Gdynia was built. (The port facilities in German-ethnic Danzig were no longer considered sufficient for the newly flowering Polish nationalism of the period that required its own authentically Polish port facilities in good Social Darwinist fashion. Those considerations no longer continued to apply after World War II, when Danzig had become Gdansk.)

In East Prussia, landowners found themselves barely able to keep their heads above water financially. To their economic problems were added the political uncertainties resulting from the success of the anti-monarchist republicans in overturning the monarchy and setting up the Weimar Republic—just as the French republicans had succeeded in ousting Emperor Napoleon III, whom they held responsible for the debacle of defeat in 1871.

The Weimar republicans had been able to install Friedrich Ebert, a former saddle-maker, as their first German president, but the agrarian depression led to unsettled economic circumstances. (One may say that it had the same effect on the German economy of that period as does the price of imported oil on the measure of prosperity in the American economy since 1965—to take a date at random.) An irresponsible monetary inflation in 1923 destroyed much of the savings of the German middle class and created a nostalgia for the economic prosperity and seeming certainties of the pre–World War I imperial era. And just as in the case of the former Confederate States of America, after its defeat at the hands of the Union forces in the nineteenth-century American Civil War, sentiments of nostalgia for the luster of the defeated army (as it may never have been before hostilities began), inflated the prestige of Confederate generals over civilian leaders of the Confederacy (except for Jefferson Davis, the Confederate president, an ex–military officer himself). So in a Social Darwinist context, perhaps too many Germans in a miasma of sentimentality came to identify with the "honor" of the defeated Imperial army, leading to the legend that the republicans, who had overthrown the monarchy and created the Weimar Republic government, had "stabbed the army in the back," abandoning it by signing an unconditional armistice amounting to a treasonous surrender.

That fantasy ignored and obliterated the actions of newly arrived American soldiers who were responsible for overturning a tactical military situation, which, prior to their arrival, had evolved into essentially static trench warfare. By restoring fluidity and movement to the battlefields, the Americans had threatened to drive German soldiers across the Rhine River into Germany proper—as would happen in World War II.

That miasma of sentimentality for a "lost cause" led to the election as president of Paul von Hindenburg (born in Posen, presently Polish Poznan), the acclaimed victor at the second battle of Tannenberg fought in the vicinity of the Masurian Lakes during the opening days of August 1914, where an advancing Russian army was defeated and prevented from overrunning East Prussia. The election was a triumph for the Conservative Party, run by political activists from among the Prussian gentry— unfortunately a group of men, like so many others, who tended to think themselves smarter than they actually were—perhaps understandable in the contextual fantasy in which they operated: the nostalgia for the glories of the lost monarchy.

The German Communists, rallying behind a fantasy of eighteenth-century universality and the ennoblement of those who worked with their hands, might have been expected to provide political opposition, except that their leaders were subservient to Stalin's analysis of a political situation with which he was totally unfamiliar. They were committed to a fantasy characterized as the "dictatorship of the proletariat"—a facade masking the absolute control exercised by Stalin, who looked to Germany to play out the scenario visualized by Karl Marx: the collapse of the bourgeoisie. There was Lenin's grim joke: A capitalist will sell you the rope with which to hang him.

The onset of the Great Depression in 1929 led to massive unemployment with its political concomitant, the rise of the theretofore-fringe Nazi party led by Hitler—*perhaps more than anyone else committed to a belief in the implications of a Social Darwinist perception of reality*. That introduced another large block of Reichstag members disloyal to any acceptance of democratic governance. It left only the Catholic Centrist Party and the Social Democrats as a minority committed to a belief in a democratic form of government and an adherence to the ideals that formed the motivation for the creation of the Weimar constitution. In a sense, those democrats were both an anachronism in a Social Darwinist world and two generations ahead of their time. Their fate was similar to that of those Spanish republicans who overthrew the Spanish monarchy in 1931, and five years later found themselves faced with an army revolt supported by citizens nostalgic for the symbolism represented by the departed monarchy, who dubbed themselves the "nationalists."

The Weimar Republic in a moral sense, except for the Catholic Centrists and the Social Democrats, was infected with disloyalty if not outright treason in 1932, when it came to reelect Hindenburg as its president. In the absence of an effective majority in the Reichstag (the Nazis then controlled the largest, single party block of legislators, while the Communists were indifferent and unhelpful), Hindenburg had allowed chancellors Brüning of the Catholic Centrist Party, Papen, and lastly Schleicher to rule by decree. (Schleicher apparently had entered the officer corps and worked his way to flag officer rank before retirement and entry into the leadership of the Conservative Party.) Yeats's poem "The

Second Coming" seems to provide an eerie presentiment of the political crisis in which Weimar Germany found itself:

> Things fall apart; the centre cannot hold;
> . . . anarchy is loosed upon the world,
> The blood-dimmed tide is loosed, and everywhere
> The ceremony of innocence is drowned;
> The best lack all convictions, while the worst
> Are full of passionate intensity.

Hindenburg was subject to an inexorable decline in his energies due to the aging process; he was to die within two years of his reelection. Unable to focus concretely on the contours of the political crisis represented by the anarchic composition of the country's legislative body, Hindenburg was led to rely on the political judgment of Schleicher and Papen, the leaders of the Conservative Party. They concluded that the Nazis, then the largest block of the Reichstag members, were street ruffians who were ignorant of the subtleties and complexities of governance. If the president were to offer the chancellorship to Hitler, they reasoned, by including Papen as vice-chancellor, and other Conservatives constituting a majority of the cabinet ministers (that was premised on majority vote in a cabinet-directed government), this promised the prospect of a Reichstag majority.

That said, they looked forward to the Prussian bureaucracy in the person of Papen to make the essential decisions for an imagined politically impotent and cowed Hitler. So Hindenburg was convinced to appoint Hitler as chancellor on January 30, 1933. Schleicher's logic proved to be a monumental miscalculation that cost him his life during the Nazi Party purge in February 1934, a fate that almost included Papen as well. It most certainly ended Papen's illusions about political power—if he had continued to hold any by that date. Among those arrested during the Nazi

Party purge was Konrad Adenauer, who managed to convince those who examined him of his innocence. Luckily for him, he was unimportant enough so that he was released into retirement. (In 1944, in the aftermath of the failed attempt on Hitler's life, Adenauer would be rearrested and faced execution.) Former chancellor Brüning felt sufficiently threatened so that he went into exile in the United States, where he lived on Long Island outside of New York City under an assumed name.

During the Nazi era, those Weimar political figures who were not imprisoned in concentration camps (like Kurt Schumacher, later a leader of the post–World War II West German Social Democratic Party) or forced into exile, acted very unheroically, fading into the woodwork. Like Talleyrand, the French aristocrat who later served Napoleon, when asked what he did during the Jacobin Terror in 1793, they could reply, "I survived." Not for them were either the dangers of hiding Jews from deportation and death or the gallantry of the White Rose conspiracy. That conspiracy was left to a group of mostly young aristocrats and theologian Dietrich Bonhoeffer to try to retrieve the honor and moral integrity of their class by attempting the assassination of Hitler at his military headquarters in the forests of East Prussia. That they failed does not detract from their idealism. One can admire them while recognizing that their failure is symbolic of the bankruptcy of their class—its failure to fulfill its function in the twentieth century—that Prussian gentry which for some two hundred years had provided the members of the state bureaucracy that had enabled a minor, poverty-stricken polity to become a world-class nation.

Now, this remnant of Weimar Republic political survivors had the opportunity to rewind the reel and replay the film, to experience in life the chance given the characters—and, more particularly, the artist Dearth—in the second act of J. M. Barrie's most poignant play, *Dear Brutus*. Here was an opening to correct the mistakes that had led to the demise of democratic government in Germany. Shakespeare had said there was a tide in the affairs of men, and this remnant of Weimar Republic survivors was determined to take advantage of it.

Luck was with them. Everything fell into place.

The heartland of the Conservative Party of Hindenburg and Schleicher had been East Prussia, Silesia, and Pomerania. The Prussian gentry, their estates, the inhabitants, and the way of life practiced there were gone—swallowed up in Soviet conquests and divided between Poland and Russia with a concomitant expulsion of German ethnics. In that sense, reality came to follow Morgenthau's conjecture that some German nationals might have to emigrate in the future he envisioned for a postwar Germany—a prospect that had horrified Henry Stimson. So, Oscar and his family at the end of Günter Grass's novel, *The Tin Drum*, are waiting at Danzig—soon to become Gdansk—to board boxcars that may have transported European Jews to their deaths by gassing in half-underground chambers at Auschwitz in an earlier avatar.

The Nazis and their promised thousand-year empire had been discredited by defeat. Instead of the ruthless and ever-victorious *übermenschen* of 1941–42, the Nazis had been revealed as more the cowed mass of bewildered young men, exhausted and hungry, who obediently followed in ranks during the parade the Russians organized in Moscow in the summer of 1944, to march the German prisoners of war from one side of Moscow to the other on their way to the gulag. The American diplomat George F. Kennan watched and felt sympathy for them, even though, as he reminded himself, the Germans had treated far worse the hundreds of thousands of Russian soldiers who had fallen into their hands in the early days of the war.[986]

The Hohenzollern monarchy had been irretrievably sullied by its crown prince's accommodation to the Nazis.[987]

The West German Communists were ambushed by Stalin's ambitions. Stalin had not understood Germany in 1932, nor did he understand it in 1948. He was not content with the relatively strong Communist Party in Czechoslovakia that resulted in large part from the liberation of most of that country by the Red Army. The appearance of German troops in Prague in the spring of 1939 made it abundantly clear that Hitler's expansionist ambitions were insatiable and his word worthless. The Nazi occupation of the rump state of Czechoslovakia had made war inevitable. The Communist coup in Prague in 1948 not only vanquished a democratic Czechoslovak government, but it also destroyed the credibility of the West German Communists. And Stalin's successors completed the West German Communists' rout by instituting the Berlin blockade in 1962, which for some nine months prevented West German supplies from traveling on East German highways to keep the western sectors of Berlin, controlled by the United States, Great Britain, and France, supplied with food and other needs.

The Roman Catholic Church for its own reasons, perhaps unwittingly, also assisted the process by choosing to give passports under false names to those lesser Nazis who might have been expected to lead the Nazi "werewolves"—the guerrilla legions—that were feared would hide in the mountains of southern Germany. Instead, those putative guerrilla chiefs escaped to South America and the Middle East to live out their lives under aliases.

What legally and psychologically proved impossible in the late 1920s in Weimar Germany—the outlawing of any vestige of Nazi identification in word, dress, or deed—was imposed by the West German Federal Republic. Nazism in post–World War II West Germany came to evoke the same visceral feelings as Ku Klux Klan white sheets in the United States.

The Weimar Republic political remnant that now was left to govern West Germany would appear to have been committed to securing the political legitimacy that had eluded their predecessors in the 1920s. To that end, they chose as their capital the college town of Bonn. That purpose was facilitated because as a practical matter, the former capital of Berlin was unavailable. It was said that the choice was dictated in part because of its convenience to Chancellor Adenauer's home near Cologne/Köln—except that if his convenience was paramount, the capital should have been set in Cologne/Köln itself. Actually, his home was in a little village closer to Bonn. Bonn had the virtue of being the birthplace of the composer Beethoven—the democrat who had rewritten the dedication of his Third Symphony to refer to the *memory* of a great man when he learned Napoleon had chosen to become an emperor, and whose majestic Ninth Symphony included as its climax the universalism of the eighteenth-century poet Schiller's "Ode to Joy." Left behind was any Social Darwinist identification with the traditions of Prussian militarism.

The Weimar republican remnant was aided by a plan first proposed during the war by Jean Monnet,[988] and later publicized (and modified) by the French Foreign Minister Robert Schumann. This plan proposed the development of an economic union to regulate the iron and coal industries centered both east and west of the Rhine River, which led to the creation of the European Coal and Steel Community. The role of the Marshall Plan, initiated and supported by the United States, in bringing economic prosperity to the countries of Western Europe may not be discounted. The momentum slowly but surely also served to further the economic and political integration of Western Europe, by leading first to the eventual inclusion of the Benelux countries into the economic confederation accomplished by France and West Germany, and finally evolving into the European Union. The Marshall Plan was an expression of the American divergence from the Social Darwinist sentiments which had animated the Smoot-Hawley Tariff Act of 1930, which sought to bar foreign goods from the

American market, and the earlier Immigration Acts of 1921 and 1924 and the National Origins Act of 1929, which sought to limit the influx of Eastern and Southern European immigrants who were thought to be alien and socially inferior to the majority of the ancestry of the citizens of the United States.

In the quest for political legitimacy by the remnant of post–World War II Weimar democrats who were now governing West Germany, it was important to discredit the political philosophy of the prior government of Germany by Hitler and the Nazis, with its Social Darwinist focus on the persecution of the Jews. In this respect, over fifty years later, the German-born, Roman Catholic Pope Benedict XVI, on May 28, 2006, at Auschwitz during a four-day visit to Poland, would speak of "a ring of criminals [which] rose to power by false promises of future greatness and the recovery of the nation's honor, prominence and prosperity, but also through terror and intimidation."[989] (Roosevelt, had earlier characterized the governments of Germany and Japan as "[p]owerful and resourceful gangsters" in a "fireside chat" on 9 December 1941, after the Japanese attack on the naval anchorage at Pearl Harbor.) The pope would go on, "Deep down, those vicious criminals, by wiping out this [Jewish] people, wanted to kill the God who called Abraham, who spoke in Sinai and laid down principles to serve as a guide for mankind . . ."[990]

Intent on seeking to discredit the political philosophy of the prior government of Germany by Hitler and the Nazis, over fifty years before the words spoken by Benedict XVI, the Weimar Republic political remnant led by Chancellor Adenauer on its own initiative[991] started conversations with Nahum Goldmann, then head of the World Jewish Congress, to effectuate an agreement serving to recognize the enormity of the crimes of the Nazi regime.

Goldmann writes in his *Autobiography*,[992] ". . . to the credit of the German chancellor, it must be said he recognized the magnitude of the problem from the first." Morgenthau in his book had warned against seeking reparations that would be paid by securing loans from its former enemies[993] based on the experiences of the 1920s. The Western Allies, cognizant of the political havoc wrought by the requirement of reparations in the Versailles peace treaty, eschewed any thought of reparations for themselves (although the Russians had no qualms at taking whole factories from the East German areas they occupied to make up for the destruction that resulted from the initial successes of the German invasion in 1941, which made a battleground of Western Russia, Ukraine, and Belarus).

Yet, in 1950, the surviving Weimar republicans of West Germany, in the person of Adenauer, initiated conversations that were designed to accomplish exactly what had been abandoned by the Western Allies, namely, reparations. The role of Goldmann was at once to assist Adenauer to articulate the contours of his purpose, which was to legitimize the authority of his regime, and to increase the money that would be offered to an amount that could confer meaning to the gesture by the West German government. The West Germans ultimately agreed to the sum of one billion dollars. Goldmann admitted it "was a large sum of money for Germany at that time"—the year was 1952.[994]

What is fascinating in Goldmann's description of the negotiations that covered a period of some two years is that he describes Adenauer as a kind of fairy godfather, comparable to the role given to General Zhivago, the improbable offspring of an improbable liaison between the father of the hero and "a Caucasian princess" in Boris Pasternak's Nobel Prize–winning novel, *Doctor Zhivago*. General Zhivago in the novel is not shown to have any normal family relations and is apparently immune to the purge trials and the other political vicissitudes of life in Stalinist Russia. He appears at crucial points in the narrative almost miraculously to help his half brother, Dr. Zhivago, and later, to help the latter's natural daughter. So Adenauer is said by Goldmann to have "fulfilled his promises to the utmost, even when this involved great personal difficulties."[995]

In the early conversations, Goldmann writes, "I thought . . . the chancellor should recognize in the name of the Federal Republic, Germany's responsibility for National Socialist crimes and formally invite Israel and world Jewry to negotiate restitution . . . [O]n September 27 [1951] it was read with great solemnity by Adenauer to the Bundestag, which endorsed it unanimously."[996]

Implementing that declaration, a secret meeting was arranged in London on December 6, 1951, between Adenauer and Goldmann. After Goldmann had made his opening remarks to Adenauer, in which he also requested a letter to show the Israelis to convince them of Adenauer's sincerity, Goldmann writes, "Chancellor Adenauer was visibly moved and replied, 'Dr. Goldmann, those who know me know I am a man of few words and that I detest high-flown talk. But I must tell you that while you were speaking I felt the wings of world history beating in this room." (It was well that Adenauer, as he is quoted as saying, was "a man of few words," since he appears to have had a tin ear for metaphor. The "wings of world history" leaves something to be desired.)

Goldmann continues quoting Adenauer: "My desire for restitution is sincere. I regard it as a great moral problem and a debt of honor for the new Germany. If you will give me a draft of such a letter [to the Israeli Foreign Minister] after our talk I will sign it in the course of the day."[997]

(In his use of the phrase "new Germany," Adenauer would unknowingly reflect Morgenthau's writing that his publication, the *American Agriculturist*, was a "really new newspaper with new blood and new readers" in his letter dated February 7, 1924, to his father, then in Athens, Greece.[998] It would appear that the concept of "new beginnings" is a recurrent, optimistic, human need. The other side of the coin is the obsessive need to focus on an individual's or ethnic or national losses to the exclusion of all other considerations. Much of the romance of the American frontier in the nineteenth century may be traced to the urge to realize the promise of being able to escape from one's past and start over again. And so, American historian Jackson Turner described a major trauma in the American psyche when, with the admission of Arizona as a state into the Union in 1912, he declared an end to the American frontier. The sense of loss comported with the Social Darwinist idea of a constant threat from *others* to seek to take from one what was rightfully one's own.)

To return to the talks between Adenauer and Goldmann: At the end of their negotiations, when a subordinate West German official was contesting the numbers Goldmann was insisting on for Israel and the Conference on Jewish Material Claims against Germany, Goldmann writes, "[T]he chancellor immediately upheld my view and my suggestion that Germany could procure some of the goods through foreign exchange."[999]

Goldmann reports that later that evening, Adenauer was present at a dinner attended by the premiers of the German states. Goldmann writes, "At the end of the proceedings [Adenauer] rose and said he wished to make an important announcement. He had that evening reached a fundamental agreement with me. As chancellor he regarded his accord with world Jewry as an event no less important for Germany's future than the restoration of Germany's sovereignty. The premiers stood up and applauded."[1000]

It is useful to stop a moment and consider what Adenauer may have meant when he said "he regarded his accord with world Jewry as an event no less important for Germany's future than the restoration of Germany's sovereignty." In a real sense, it may be said to represent an abandonment of the attitudes implicit in the point of view represented by the term *Social Darwinism*. Psychologically, one facet of Social Darwinism implied a kind of "chip-on-the-shoulder" way of looking at the world—the sense that one's own kind of people were serving as a whipping boy for others. That sense of hurt is palpable in the quotations given earlier in these pages from Santayana, Eric Hoffer, and Halecki, and the remarks by Pilsudski at Vilna/Vilnius in 1920 as recorded by Henry Sr. It is the "battle" and the "struggle" that Hitler wrote about in *Mein Kampf*.

What Adenauer had accomplished was to cast away that sense of victimization and need to protect and fight for the interest of one's own group at all costs; that is, to be Eric Hoffer's "true believers," and to substitute an acceptance of a collective social responsibility for the group's actions. It represented a kind of humility that could lead to a sense of noblesse oblige. If one could say with Max Weber that capitalism represented the secularization of the Calvinist concept of a religious calling, then analogously, Adenauer may be said to have secularized the religious concepts of sin, acknowledgment, penance, and expiation that are so central to the theologies of Judaism and Christianity. So for Jews, the Day of Atonement is the single holiest observance in the Judaic liturgical calendar and for Christians, the Lenten season is the necessary and inescapable prelude to the glories of the Easter message.

And so the Luxembourg Restitution Agreement of 1952 was signed on September 10, 1952, by Adenauer, Goldmann for the Claims Conference, and the Israeli Foreign Minister, Moshe Sharett, for the government of Israel.[1001] That this was outside the borders of Germany represented an obvious effort to avoid offending Jewish sensibilities so soon after the Holocaust. Ironically, Adenauer was not able to convince a wing of his Christian Democrats to vote for the restitution agreement. It was carried by a vote in the Reichstag because the opposition Social Democrats recognized the necessity for the agreement. The moral dimension for the restitution agreement is spelled out in the summation of British prosecutor Shawcross at the Nuremberg Trial of Nazi leaders in 1946. There are two passages from Odd Nansen's diary that also sum up evocatively the moral dimension for the restitution agreement. Nansen starts one passage by writing, "There are no words left to describe the horrors I've seen with my own eyes."[1002] He continues,

> . . . the scene around me . . . was appalling. Dante's inferno couldn't be worse. There were more than a thousand Jews; that is, they had once been Jews and human beings, now they were living skeletons, beastlike in their mad hunger. They flung themselves on the [garbage] bins,[1003] or rather plunged into them, head and shoulders, several at a time, they scratched up everything, absolutely everything that was lying in them, potato peel, garbage, rottenness of every kind. They didn't see what they were eating, simply shoved it into their faces, clawed and tore at it, fought over it. They stuck fast in the [garbage] bins, taking [others] along when they straightened up again, and off they went like that, two or three skeletons combined into a strange caryatid sculpture. But the worst was that the whole time, without a break, the blows from rubber truncheons were hailing down on them. Young lads (SAW lads) thrashed away at them to their hearts' content. But they took no notice. The instant the tormentors turned away to hit out in another direction, they plunged into the [garbage] bins again. The blood was pouring off them, from their faces and hands and legs. Most were barefoot, and the clothes hung round them in shreds; more great wounds from blows shone through rents and openings in the clothes on their bodies.

. . . the tormentors were indescribable. They were only boys, but the act of striking intoxicated them and drove them wild. I followed them, I saw their faces as they struck, they were no longer human, they were living devils, possessed, transported with ecstasy. They struck whatever they saw, not merely those they saw in the [garbage] bins. They hurled themselves on the crowds like roaring lions, and struck out right and left. The wretched victims went down round them by dozens; that only inspired them, and they went on striking at them as they lay, trod upon them, kicked them, while the blood was streaming from mouths, ears, and wounds. Every time they needed a rest, they turned exultantly to their laughing and smiling comrades, laughed back, and gave the truncheon a limber, playful swing round their heads. Then they flew at it again.

A Jew who had been struck ten or twenty times tottered and fell down at my feet. He lay motionless, the blood was running out of his mouth and trickling from one ear. His eyes were bloody and the cheekbones swollen and cracked with blows. One of his lips was cleft and some teeth knocked out. He was barefoot and his feet were covered with frostbite. His trousers had slipped down, so that his matchstick thighs were visible, and through a rent in his shirt one could see his ribs. I bent over him, took him under the arms and raised him; he was light as a child . . . I dragged the Jew to the wall and managed to prop him up against it, and he came to again. He looked at me with such eyes—oh, God, such eyes; all the white was red, and the red was running down his cheeks—the brown pupils were dull as though a film had been drawn over them, and the big eyelids hung over them heavily. Some gurgling noises came from him, I thought he had difficulty breathing, I tried to strengthen him up; still the gurgling noises came, more regularly, it sounded as though he were being choked—but he was crying, crying like a child. A friend of his, who had been standing by for some time, came up and helped me hold him . . . reason, cold, odious reason, told me baldly that these men were doomed, nobody could save them, not even the best doctors in peacetime. They were too far gone, had already one foot deep in the grave.[1004]

The second of Nansen's passages reveals why the European Jews went naked as they were murdered in the death camps in Poland. Nansen writes,

A Norwegian who is an old inhabitant told me that in "the bad time" . . . one could go into the camp and sell a bit of sausage or ham, if one had any to spare, for twenty thousand dollars, for example. For there was money in unlimited quantities—dollars, pounds, rubles, and francs—in notes and gold. There were also precious stones, emeralds, rubies, pearls, diamonds—by the bucket—and all kinds of ornaments and treasures. But none of all these glories could be eaten! Even a multimillionaire might die of hunger, pitiful and helpless, side by side with the poorest and most wretched Ukrainian. The value of his millions became more and more illusory as famine preyed on him, while the value of the bit of sausage or ham rose and rose and burst all habitual standards—all "reasonable" limits—on its way to insanity!

But that calls for an explanation. Money? Jewels? Ornaments? Where did *they* come from?—And whom did they belong to?

From the great annihilation camps in Poland—Auschwitz, Lublin, and others—where hundreds of thousands upon hundreds of thousands of Jews were being killed, there came incessantly to Sachsenhausen railway trains full of clothing, footwear, and effects of the murdered Jews. A special squad of many hundreds of prisoners, among them my Norwegian friend, w[as] employed exclusively in ripping open these clothes and shoes, out at one of the factories to which the prisoners were "hired" from the camp. Sewn into the clothing they discovered fortunes in banknotes—and in the footwear, especially in the high heels of women's shoes, they found little treasures of jewels. Each day's "catch" was several tubs full of jewels and ornaments and great bundles of banknotes. One has to go back to one's childhood's fairy book, the *Thousand and One Nights*, for a counterpart to all that shining splendor. The robbers too are well represented; for who "owns" all that stolen property? The rightful owners have been put to eternal silence in the gas chambers of Poland, and no one can prevent the SS and the big "factory owners," Himmler, Göring, and Goebbels from taking over the goods. They too must live, and the D.A.W. (*Deutschen Austrüstungswerke*) find they can spare a little time from the production of armaments. Of course they charge a little for their trouble, both the head and the other SS men, one or two buckets of jewels a day, and a few piles of banknotes—then Himmler, Göring, and Goebbels get the rest—so they think.

But they forget the prisoners, who, in spite of strict control and the most intrusive body search at the end of every day's work, have no great difficulty in seeing to it that a considerable proportion finds it way out into the camp. Among the prisoners there are outstanding professionals in the criminal branch. Old jailbirds with experience and skill, they have little trouble in securing a colleague or two among the SS guards on a "commission basis." In brief: It wouldn't surprise me if the world's biggest swindles were taking place in Sachsenhausen. Everything is dead rotten, cold and soulless and horrible . . .[1005]

One may say that Nansen's descriptions illustrate the stark reality of what are abstract analyses in the words written by Santayana and Eric Hoffer, quoted in the introductory remarks at the beginning of this study.

It does not diminish Adenauer's moral integrity in the matter of the Luxembourg Restitution Agreement to recognize that whatever their personal moral codes, government leaders are motivated by other—political—factors as well in their determinations. Adenauer himself admitted as much when he described the agreement he had entered into with Nahum Goldmann "as an event no less important for Germany's future than the restoration of Germany's sovereignty."

So Ronald Irving concludes in his volume *Adenauer*.[1006] Paul Weymar, in his book *Adenauer: His Authorized Biography*,[1007] quotes Adenauer as telling Winston Churchill: "Today Germany is a shapeless mass which has to be remolded. What matters is whether this is done by good or bad hands." And Charles Wighton writes in *Adenauer—Democratic Dictator*,[1008] ". . . at the time of the anti-Semitic outrages at the beginning of 1960 . . . [h]e hoped, he is reported to have said, that the spirit of Nazism would die out with the older generation, and that Germany within the Atlantic alliance, would develop into a decent, democratic country." (Beschloss writes that Stimson told Morgenthau at lunch in the Pentagon on August 23, 1944, "that Germany must indeed be 'policed' for at least twenty years after World War II, until there was a new generation of Germans."[1009]) It would also appear that Adenauer's view of his generation of Germans was little different from that of Morgenthau's, except that Adenauer proved himself vastly different than the major political players in Berlin in 1932. (In a curious way, Adenauer's dismissal of his generation of

Germans is remarkably similar to Bismarck's nineteenth-century dismissal of the members of the Prussian gentry, of which he was one, as "potato farmers.")

On the question of government leaders' motivation, as noted, Beschloss in his study of the American government's decisions in the course of formulating a policy for postwar German redevelopment, cites John J. McCloy for the information that it was Franklin Roosevelt who made the ultimate American decision not to bomb the approaches to the Nazi death camps on the theory that the Germans would seek to score a propaganda coup by claiming that it was Americans who caused the deaths of European Jews.[1010]

Beschloss is somewhat dubious (as is Black) about the validity of McCloy's recollection at the age of eighty-six years, after some forty years of silence as to Roosevelt's connection with the matter. A possible explanation—assuming the accuracy of McCloy's assertion—is how the passage of time can change the way things are perceived. What in 1944 was viewed as a valid judgment in a Social Darwinist world, colored by anti-Semitism and necessitated by the exigencies of war, had come to be considered in moral dimensions. What had been acceptable as what seemed a relatively minor Hobson's choice had come to be unacceptable in a moral dimension some forty years later in a world that now gave greater importance to moral concerns than to Social Darwinist ideas of prevalence. At the end of his life, McCloy may have been responding in his remarks to the different world in which he then found himself, and so it had become important to set the record straight when an opportunity arose as he was being interviewed by Henry III.

To return to West Germany: The primary concern of the democratic, Weimar Republic survivors after 1949, who were now the government of West Germany, was to give reality to the legitimacy of their government. They could do that best by destroying any legitimacy that might cling to the Nazi regime among German voters. By acknowledging the moral stain that the Nazis had cast over Germany—and that was the effect of the Luxembourg Restitution Agreement—the government of the West German Federal Republic was taking a giant step toward destroying the political legitimacy of the prior regime and in the process creating its own legitimacy. In that purpose, the West German government succeeded wonderfully well.

While the war was winding down, Stimson (and those who agreed with him) had argued in Washington that acting in a nonpunitive manner offered the best chance to restore a society and a government in postwar Germany, which could then take its place in a peaceable world. Godfrey Hodgson, one of Stimson's more recent biographers, writes,

> Stimson was horrified. [The Morgenthau] plan would not only be foolish but in breach of the Atlantic Charter which had committed both the United States and Britain to allow "all States, great and small, victor or vanquished," access to trade and raw materials . . . The Morgenthau Plan, he argued, would involve a "chaotic upheaval" and would doubtless "cause tremendous suffering." It would be attributed to "mere vengeance" and shortsighted cupidity. It would be "an open confession of the bankruptcy of hope for a reasonable economic and political settlement of the causes of war."[1011]

Stimson's early biographer Morison writes, "[I]n the fall of 1944 he said, 'The question is not whether we want Germans to suffer for their sins.' The only question was 'whether over the years a group of seventy million educated, efficient and imaginative people can be kept within bounds' if they were 'reduced to a peasant level with virtually complete control of industry and science left to other peoples."[1012] Stimson was apparently willing to concede that the Ruhr should be placed under effective Allied control.[1013] Morison writes, continuing to outline Stimson's viewpoint, "To enforce poverty on a people who had been 'outstanding for many years in the arts and the sciences' would not only disrupt the economy, it would destroy the spirit of the victims and debase the victor. In fact 'it would be just such a crime as the Germans themselves hoped to perpetrate upon their victims—it would be a crime against civilization itself.'"[1014]

In a sense, Stimson may be attempting to apply the vision that animated Abraham Lincoln in his Second Inaugural Address when he spoke the words, "with malice towards none, and charity for all . . ." and the idea of "binding up the nation's wounds . . ." (In that respect, the great unanswerable question is how Lincoln would have reacted to the actions of the newly reconstituted Southern legislatures in adopting the "Black Codes" that sought to place limits on the liberty and activities of the former slave population.)

Another possible source that may have colored Stimson's attitude toward Germany is the Gospel parable of the prodigal son, who dissipated his inheritance and came home to be welcomed back into the family by his father. Indeed, Stimson in his diary records that at a dinner at Morgenthau's home on Monday, September 4, 1944, he told his host, "I think we can't solve the German problem except through Christianity and kindness."[1015]

For Stimson, in a Social Darwinist world, whatever their faults, the Germans remained members of the family of nations.

Richard N. Current in his study, *Secretary Stimson*,[1016] writes that planning "for the future of a defeated Germany began as early as March, 1943, when Roosevelt instructed Hull to consult about the matter with the British and with Stimson. The two Secretaries agreed upon a program, which Hull took to the Moscow conference in October, 1943. Their plan provided for unconditional surrender, occupation, denazification, dismantling of war industries, etc. It evaded the question of Germany's political future—the question whether Germany should be dismembered—but it recommended a 'tolerable standard of living' as necessary to 'make democracy work.'"

Current writes that Morgenthau found these recommendations much too mild, as did Roosevelt.[1017] Roosevelt thereafter appointed the three secretaries as a committee to produce a comprehensive plan. On September 5, 1944, the three men met in Hull's office, he being the senior cabinet officer. "Hull sponsored a State Department memorandum recommending the elimination of Germany as the dominant economic power in Europe with at least a subsistence standard of living. Stimson approved, except that he preferred a higher living standard. Morgenthau demanded the complete deindustrialization of the country, which would mean less than subsistence for the people."[1018]

In fact, what happened in Germany in the first months after occupation as described by Beschloss is that in connection with the appointment by President Truman of Byron Price, who had been Roosevelt's wartime censorship chief, to investigate General Clay's performance as administrator of the military government, Price was moved to argue that the approved daily food ration of 1,550 calories for Germans was not enough: "If starvation comes, as now seems likely, epidemics and rioting will not be far behind."[1019] Beschloss comments in a footnote: "In reply, Assistant Secretary Robert Patterson agreed that 1,550 daily calories was inadequate: 'The difficulty here has been that the level in Poland and Austria is no higher . . . and under the Potsdam Declaration, the Germans are not to be fed better than the people in the surrounding countries.'"[1020] Section III.15. of the Potsdam Declaration contained the language:

Allied controls shall be imposed upon the German economy . . .

(B) . . . to maintain in Germany average living standards not exceeding the average of the standards of living of European countries.[1021]

One may question—on the basis of the statements in Morgenthau's book—whether he intended either "the complete deindustrialization of the country" or "less than subsistence" for the Germans. Morgenthau would later write, "The postwar Reich will have to import some food after it is rebuilt for peace, but with improvement of small farms [the use of the term 'small farms' may reflect Roosevelt's commitment to the welfare of American farmers of the period and Morgenthau's own farming experience] and the consequent production of more hogs, the imports could be greatly reduced."[1022]

In any case, the high-water mark for the Morgenthau Plan came at the Quebec Conference between the president and Churchill that was held in the days after September 11, 1944. Apparently, the primary purpose of the conference had been to consider the economic problems Great Britain would face at the end of the war in Europe. Morgenthau was summoned by Roosevelt to participate in the discussion.[1023]

In that respect, Roosevelt and Churchill agreed to enter into negotiations that were conducted in Washington to stave off the anticipated post–World War II British insolvency. That purpose—post–World War II British financial needs—would be later satisfied (at least temporarily) by an understanding for an arrangement relating to anticipated British financial needs under the Lend-Lease agreement after the end of military activities in Europe and during the final phase of the war against Japan.[1024] Still later, a loan agreement, dated December 6, 1945, would be signed in Washington by Fred M. Vinson, Morgenthau's successor as secretary of the Treasury, for the United States, and by Lord Halifax, then the British ambassador, for the United Kingdom.[1025] One could analogize the succession of anticipated British financial crises in the 1940s to those the French franc suffered ten years earlier—however different their causes.

In the meantime, Churchill's scientific advisor Lord Cherwell, who was present at Quebec, had caught wind of the Morgenthau Plan and was enthusiastic about it. Hodgson believes at that point, Roosevelt was also for the Plan. Churchill was converted and he and Roosevelt initialed a version of it at Quebec.

Morison writes that "on the 20th of September [1944] Morgenthau returned to Washington to give Hull and Stimson an account of what happened [both as to the financial problems Britain faced and postwar Germany]. He did it 'modestly and without rubbing it in.' Churchill, when first confronted with the plan to dismantle Germany, 'blew up,' claiming it would 'tie the British nation to a dead corpse.' But later, under the persuasion of Roosevelt and Cherwell, he not only accepted the plan but dictated the celebrated memorandum which recommended converting Germany 'into a country primarily agricultural and pastoral in its character.'"[1026]

Roosevelt, on his return to Washington, apparently began to have second thoughts about the matter. Morison writes that when Roosevelt saw Stimson sometime later, "he grinned and looked naughty and said, 'Henry Morgenthau pulled a boner.' . . . 'Mr. President,' said the Secretary, shaking his finger, 'I don't like you to dissemble to me.' When Roosevelt asked what he was talking about, Stimson read him parts of the memorandum written at Quebec. Hearing this, Roosevelt was 'frankly staggered,' said he would never use a word like 'pastoral,' and added that he had 'no idea how he could have initialed this.'"[1027]

Afterwards, when the memorandum initialed by Roosevelt and Churchill at Quebec became public knowledge, there was widespread opposition to it both in Great Britain and in Washington. So the Morgenthau Plan was shelved, to become one more historical conception, an inchoate proposal that never became official policy. Its demise is, in large part, a tribute to Stimson's powers of advocacy.

All that is not to say that Morgenthau gave up his passionately held belief both in the dangers he believed Germany represented to the future of peace between nations and the need to contain the factors giving rise to that danger. Beschloss documents Morgenthau's continuing concern. The compilation of Morgenthau's book, *Germany Is Our Problem*, is clear evidence of that. The language of the book itself is a fascinating example of liberal American thinking in this period. Perhaps the most egregious example in Morgenthau's book of the liberal thinking of the time that would help give rise to the political anti-Communism of the late 1940s and 1950s in the United States is the following: "There is no record of a democratic country going Communist. But there have been all too many examples of democracy undermined by Fascism while its people were being deluded into the belief that Communism was the real danger. Germany, Italy and Spain are the glaring examples."[1028]

The second part of the quotation as to the dangers fascist thinking represented to democratic governance is beyond cavil. It is the first sentence of the quotation that is incorrect. The Bolsheviks' October Revolution did not overthrow Tsarist autocracy. That event took place in February, 1917. The October Revolution—John Reed's *Ten Days That Shook the World*—overthrew Kerensky's Provisional Government, which was democratically oriented and had arranged for the first universal general election in Russia before it was overthrown. That election created a Constituent Assembly which met after the October Revolution.

The Socialist-Revolutionary Party members proved to be the largest single component of that body and succeeded in electing their candidate Viktor Chernov as the chairman of the plenum session. The session lasted for a continuous thirty-six hours, during which Chernov steered the passage of a universal land distribution law before adjourning—what proved to be—*sine die*. (When the delegates returned to reconvene the Constituent Assembly, they found the Taurida Palace in then Petrograd, where it was to take place, surrounded by soldiers sent by Lenin preventing their reentry.)

Chernov was to die in New York City.

Perhaps the best original observation of the events of 1917 in Petrograd is N. N. Sukhanov's *Notes on the Revolution*. What should be the classic text on the Socialist-Revolutionary Party, Oliver Radkey's two-volume monograph,[1029] is marred by the circumstance that Radkey's unspoken hero is Lenin. (Lenin, in this respect, may be said to have acted in the context of the Social Darwinist idea of a fundamental need to ruthlessly outwit and prevail over the other Socialist factions then in Petrograd, in contrast to the commitment of Kerensky and the Socialist-Revolutionary Party leaders to democratic governance.) Along with Radkey's admiration for Lenin is a concomitant disparagement of most of the Socialist-Revolutionary leaders (although Radkey's personal political stance was surely right-wing). So Radkey, then a professor of history at the University of Texas, used transcripts of the early, 1922 "show trial" of the Socialist-Revolutionary leaders then still in the Soviet Union that found them guilty of counterrevolutionary treason and served as an excuse for their execution. More unfortunately, he also chose to use quotations from the published transcripts of Stalin's Purge Trials of the 1930s denigrating Socialist-Revolutionary Party leaders, *after* Khrushchev's Secret Speech to the Communists' Twentieth Party Congress in 1956, which exposed the fraudulent nature of those "trials."

To return to Morgenthau and Stimson: What is interesting in the success of Stimson's vision as to the means to reconstitute the political fabric of Germany is the ramification of his attitudes. Basically, what Stimson—and those who were in agreement with him on this point—were advocating was that a totalitarian or other non-democratic political society could be transformed into a democratic, rational, civilized society through the goodwill of a benign, democratically oriented, military government, which, by its example, could produce the desired result.

As has been suggested in this chapter, the actions and the character of the American military government in West Germany certainly contributed to a desired result there. But the desired result in West Germany was basically determined by the attitudes of the West Germans and that remnant of Weimar Republic political survivors who were able to become the government of West Germany and who, themselves, had a profound commitment to democratic governance.

The problem for the United States is that these political attitudes concerning American participation in foreign political transformations were accepted in Washington without giving them a second thought, and without understanding that the nature of a society and its local political leaders' attitudes were ultimately the dominant factors in any American attempt to reconstitute the political fabric of a society in a foreign land. The immediate political problem faced by the United States in the early 1950s was the Russian/Communist menace, both internally and on the world stage. So, for example, Jacobo Arbenz's efforts in Guatemala in Central America to effectuate some sort of land distribution that threatened the breakup of large, oligarchic landed estates, was seen in Washington in terms of the external Communist threat. Colonel Castillo Armas was encouraged to successfully overthrow Arbenz's government to keep the status quo intact.

More important, in 1954, at the Geneva Conference to ratify the French withdrawal from Vietnam—the latter a pledge that made Pierre Mendès-France the premier of France—John

Foster Dulles, then the United States secretary of state, insisted on the division of the country, Vietnam, that had been the principal part of French Indochina into two separate, political entities, with a plebiscite to take place in two years on the question of unification. The Viet Minh representatives were apparently convinced to agree to the partition on the theory that "Americans like elections." Dulles surely was influenced not merely by Stimson's belief in the beneficence of American political ideals but also by the fear, popular in the United States in this period, of the so-called "domino theory"—the thought that Communism was something of a political contagion that would spread from country to country in the underdeveloped areas of the world. (A few years later, after the success of Castro's revolution in Cuba, Che Guevara would attempt to implement the domino theory in Latin America with a dramatic lack of success, ending up shot to death in the highlands of Bolivia.)

So the plebiscite in Vietnam never took place. Instead, Ngo Dinh Diem was installed as president with American experts as advisors. Surely, Dulles had in mind an expectation that the results of the American military government experience in West Germany (and Japan) could be replicated in southern Vietnam. The American expert who had supervised the breakup of feudal estates in Japan, Wolf Ladejinsky, was given that task in Vietnam—surely with the expectation that land distribution would nurture loyalty to a democratic system of government and a hatred for the Communist land policies in the North. The latter was accomplished only in part, but not necessarily the former. (Ladejinsky found in Vietnam, unlike in Japan, that there was simply a lack of the necessary local bureaucratic infrastructure outside of Saigon to begin to accomplish the difficult task of land distribution. In crucial provinces, in addition to the absence of local officials competent to implement a land distribution program, the local governor might be a major landlord.)

The problem had to be that there was no local democratic tradition of governance in Vietnam. (In Korea it would take two generations to create an expectation of local democratic governance. Unfortunately, Vietnam lacked the geographic configuration given South Korea—the sea rather than the contiguous landmass—that permitted that period of political maturation.) Diem[1030] was basically an Annanese autocrat in the style of the old Annanese emperors who had ruled in Hué. He may have favored white, Western suits in the best colonial style, but he was no Weimar democrat. Philip E. Catton explains, "Diem was a modern nationalist, rather than a traditional mandarin, and it was his determination to push ahead with his own nation-building agenda that was a major source of the tension in U.S.-Vietnamese relations."[1031]

With the advent of John Fitzgerald Kennedy to the White House, there was an apparent disappointment with Diem and the results of the Vietnamese experiment. John H. Richardson wrote:

> Should the United States support a coup against Ngo Dinh Diem, the president of Vietnam? He was so unpopular that Buddhists were burning themselves in the streets and he seemed to be bungling the war effort. Nonetheless . . . there was no guarantee that the generals who wanted to overthrow him would be any better.
>
> With President John F. Kennedy on the fence, Averell Harriman and other powerful figures in the State Department pushed for the coup. The C.I.A. and the military opposed it . . .
>
> Just days after [the new American ambassador, Henry Cabot Lodge] arrived in Saigon, Lodge called for a "drastic change" in policy. But . . . the C.I.A. station chief was one of Diem's strongest supporters. In his cables to

Washington, he argued for patience, saying, ". . . there are few points of no return in Asia.'"[1032]

Kennedy may have interdicted American air support for the Bay of Pigs invasion of Cuba, which had the objective of overthrowing Fidel Castro and restoring the status quo ante—much in the manner of Castillo Armas's overthrow of the Arbenz government in Guatemala. Still, the failure of the United States to provide air support doomed the Cuban adventure to failure. But the real foreign policy debacle of the Kennedy administration was the decision to encourage the overthrow of Diem.[1033] It was, again, a decision made in terms of a preconceived notion of how things ought to be—without any understanding of the facts on the ground and what could reasonably be expected in Vietnam.

In its way, the encouragement of the overthrow of Diem in Saigon reflected the earlier overthrow on February 25, 1913, and subsequent murder, of Francisco Madero, the democratically elected president of Mexico, done with the covert encouragement of American ambassador Wilson.[1034] (To his credit, Woodrow Wilson [no relative], when he entered the White House, refused to recognize the ensuing Mexican government.) After the deaths of Diem and his brother Ngo Dinh Nhu in Saigon, the administration in Washington expressed what was apparently real shock at the unintended murders, but it was too late to undo what had been done. Diem's successors understood all too clearly that once they had acted to overthrow Diem, the society in which they operated would require his death. Otherwise, he would have made his way to Washington to argue his claim to return to power. If successful, it meant their demise in turn.

A good case could be made for Diem's return to power in Saigon because, whatever his inadequacies from an American point of view, he was probably the ablest of all the leaders who, after his death, came to rule Vietnam. Catton writes, "South Vietnam's new leaders proved even less capable than their predecessor."[1035] With Diem's death, whatever chance there was for the success of the American experiment in creating a viable government in Vietnam most probably vanished. Unfortunately, American involvement in Vietnam was not to cease for many long years.

If one would seek to find a moral to the story of the efforts in Washington in the years 1944 and 1945, to determine upon a policy to guide the reconstitution of Germany after the ending of World War II, it is probably to be found in the Yiddish saying, *Mentch trokht un Gut lokht*, which may be translated variously as "People scheme while God laughs," or, more piously, "Man proposes and God disposes."

End Notes

Introduction

1 *The New York Times*, Wednesday, October 15, 2003, "Honor the Uprooted Germans? Poles Are Uneasy," A3.

2 Historians are now exploring the extent to which nationalism among the ethnic groups in central and Eastern Europe after World War I reflected nothing so much as an exclusivity of particular ethnic groupings and a rejection of an eighteenth–century belief in the universality of the human species. For a summary of these ideas, see: *The New York Times*, Saturday, May 31, 2003, B9, columns 3–5, etc.; see, also: Kraushar, A., *Jacob Frank: The End to the Sabbatian Heresy* [tr. from Polish], ed. Herbert Levy, Lanham: University Press of America, 2001, "A Note for the General Reader," 2, n. 3: "This provincialism emerged in Central and Eastern Europe during the period of the First World War under the seemingly democratic concept of ethnic (or 'nationalist') self–determination as contrasted with the archaic, autocratic rule of Russia and Austria."

3 Ickes, Harold, *The Secret Diary of Harold Ickes*, New York: Simon & Schuster (1954), II.

4 *The New York Times*, Op–Ed, Wednesday, October 26, 2005, A27, "Future Shock at The Fed," col. 3.

5 Apparently, another factor might be considered. Harold Ickes noted in his *Secret Diary*, I:124, that Secretary Woodin "has wanted to resign but the President hasn't permitted it . . . the President said that he believed that Woodin was the best–loved man in the Cabinet." This suggests the president had not settled on a successor and was "playing for time" to come to a decision.

6 Morgenthau's fate, had he been brought up in Europe after World War I, is suggested by the short life of another young man, living in Warsaw, Poland, who also looked to spend his life as a farmer. Young Stanislaw Mesz was also the scion of wealthy parents. His father, Natan Mesz, was

an X–ray diagnostician in an era when X–rays were the sole diagnostic technique available to surgeons. Madame Mesz entertained regally. Her guests included a minor Polish general. In his uniform with a flag officer's medals, he graced her table with the aura of those Polish Eagles who, in 1920, routed the Red Army on the Central Front and recovered hundreds of square miles of territory once part of the historic Polish Realm. One imagines the general flattering the adolescent scion of the family, treating him as a grown–up and a personal friend with remarks suggestive of a special male intimacy.

After the German occupation of Warsaw in the autumn of 1939, before they started to clamp down on the Jewish population, the Mesz's middle child Janina and her husband, together with her younger brother, decided to try their luck traveling east to Soviet–occupied areas. No doubt, Dr. Mesz gave them generous amounts of money. During the winter of 1939–40, they found themselves in Brest–Litovsk, tolerated by the Soviet authorities so long as they had money. Apparently, their prospects looked bleak because they decided to send a radiogram to an American cousin with whom their father had kept up a correspondence over a period of years.

The young people found someone who could compose a message in English, asking for three American visas. Cruelly, the radiogram was somehow garbled. The American cousin understood it as requesting visas only for Janina and her brother. With the probable help of his congressional representative, the cousin secured the visas. Malevolence was stalking the streets and it seemed inconceivable to them that the absence of a visa for Janina's husband was due to anything more than dumb luck, correctable once they reached the New World. So neither used the American visas.

Later, Stanislaw was in a Soviet labor camp when he learned a Polish military contingent had been formed by the Russians, commanded by his parent's great friend, the general. If he left the camp, there was no return. However he rationalized his decision, Stanislaw left the camp and made his way to the Polish unit, where the general received him. Stanislaw asked to enlist under the general's command. The story that came back to Stanislaw's older sister after the war ended was that the general responded he would accept Stanislaw if he gave the general a piece of his mother's jewelry. (One of her lost bracelets was described to me. Its centerpiece was a huge square of clear amber, so prized in

Central and Eastern Europe, in which was visible a perfectly preserved ancient fly.)

Apparently, Stanislaw was so taken aback, he blurted out the truth without cosseting it in the expectation his mother would gladly give the general what he wanted once they returned to Warsaw. With that, the general dismissed him. Eric Hoffer writes, "There is a deep reassurance for the frustrated in witnessing the downfall of the fortunate" (*The True Believer*, New York: Harper and Row, First Perennial Library Ed. (Reset 1989), 98). The young man was cast into a dangerous and savage world that offered no refuge. With what little money remained from his father, he bought a can of lard, explaining to people as he slowly starved to death, he was keeping it to give to his mother.

7 ". . . life is animated for good and for ill, by ideas . . . and a scrupulous regard for reality is the necessary accomplice of any genuine intellectual pursuit." Guy Davenport. *The New Criterion*, 22:6 (February, 2005), 1.

8 *The New York Times*, Friday, June 13, 2003, A4, "Peenemunde Journal: Where Rocketry Is Honored, Rubble Is Remainder."

9 Mike Hawkins writes (*Social Darwinism in European and American Thought, 1860–1945*, Cambridge University Press [1997], 4): ". . . the expression 'survival of the fittest' was coined by Herbert Spencer rather than Darwin, and only adopted by the latter from the fifth edition of [*On the Origin of Species*] 1869 . . ." See, also: Hofstadter, Richard, *Social Darwinism in American Thought*, Boston: Beacon Press (1948/1992), 39.

10 For a brief discussion of Darwin's sense of social morality, see Hofstadter, *op. cit.*, 91.

11 *Op. cit.*, 199.

12 *Social Progress and the Darwinian Theory*, New York: G. P. Putnam's Sons (1916), various pages given by Hofstadter.

13 Hofstadter, *op. cit.*, 188.

14 Mahan, Alfred Thayer, *The Interest of America in Sea Power, Present and Future*, Boston: Little Brown & Co. (1898), 18.

15 Hofstadter, *op. cit.*, 197.

16 Von Bernhardi, Friedrich, *Germany and the Next War*, New York: Charles A. Eron (1914), tr. Allen H. Powles, 18, 19, 20. The first quoted translation actually used by Hofstadter is so free that it might be labeled "as suggested by."

17 *Ibid.*, 23.

18 *Ibid.*, 24.

19 Ciechanowski, Jan, *Defeat in Victory*, New York: Doubleday & Company (1947), 205.

20 *The Faulkner Reader*, New York: Random House (1954), 4.

21 Nansen, Odd, *From Day to Day*, New York: G. P. Putnam's Sons (1949), 413, December 14, 1944.

22 *The New York Times*, Tuesday, November 7, 2006, A3.

23 *The New Yorker*, January 8, 2007, "Die Weltliteratur" (tr. Linda Asher), 28, 30.

24 Hawkins, *op. cit.*, 304.

25 Hofstadter, *op. cit.*, 186.

26 Adams, Brooks, *The Law of Civilization and Decay*, New York: The Macmillan Co. (1896), ix.

27 See: Edman, I., ed., *The Philosophy of Santayana*, New York, Random House, Modern Library Ed. (undated), 382.

28 *Ibid.*, 383.

29 *Ibid.*, 386.

30 *Ibid.*, xl.

31 *Ibid.*, xl, xli.

32 Hoffer, Eric, *op. cit.*, 93–94, par. 68.

33 Dollard, John, *Caste and Class in a Southern Town*, Madison: The University of Wisconsin Press (repr. 1988).

34 Hawkins, *op. cit.*, 304.

35 Wilson, Edward O., *On Human Nature*, Cambridge, MA: Harvard University Press (1978), 111.

36 It seems endemic in the human species to try to integrate theories about the natural world with contemporary fashions in sociological ideas. A twenty–first–century author writes: "*moral* emotions make sense only as products of evolution" (italics added). He defines "moral emotions" by saying, "[P]eople simply *do* perceive sacredness, holiness or some ineffable good in others and in nature" (italics in original). Haidt, Jonathan, *The Happiness Hypothesis*, New York: Basic Books (2006), 98, xiii.

37 This distinction was explored by Jacques Barzun in his *Darwin, Marx, Wagner*, Boston: Little, Brown and Company (repr. 1946), 260–261.

38 The term *elect* is the technical term in Calvinist theology to denote those souls *predestined* for salvation who are distinguished from the common run of humanity. An essential element of this configuration of ideas involved a principle of uncertainty. One could not know if one was

one of the *elect* destined for salvation. One could only hope so, and act in one's life to preserve God's grace. Once the element of uncertainty was lost and people began to believe they were without question among the *elect*—like one thread taken from a seamless web—that faith began to fall apart and fade, viz., Puritanism in New England in the eighteenth century—a circumstance the divine Jonathan Edwards sought to contain with mixed success. (See: Morgan, Edward S., *The Puritan Family*, New York: Harper and Row [1966], 185.) Something of this principle of uncertainty appears in the Jewish folk concept of the *Lamed–Vuv*, the thirty–six souls in each generation whose humility, goodness, and holiness are said to save the world from perdition. Their anonymity is said to be so complete they are unknown even to themselves.

39 Hoffer, Eric, *op. cit.*, 91, par. 65.

40 Lindbergh, Anne Morrow, *The Wave of the Future—A Confession of Faith*, New York: Harcourt, Brace & Co. (1940).

41 *Ibid.*, 3.

42 *Ibid.*, 37.

43 *Ibid.*, 34.

44 *Ibid.*, 3.

45 *Ibid.*, 21.

46 *Ibid.*, 24. The reader will remember the title chosen for Dwight Eisenhower's book, *Crusade in Europe*, Garden City: Doubleday & Company (1948).

47 Hofstadter, *op.cit.*, 133.

48 James, William, *The Will to Believe*, New York: Longmans, Green & Co. (1897).

49 Hofstadter, *op. cit.*, 121.

50 Spencer, Herbert, *The Principles of Sociology*, New York: D. Appleton & Co. (3 vols. 1876–1907), II: 240–41.

51 Nansen, *op. cit.*, 387.

52 *Ibid.*, 320, October 11, 1943.

53 *Ibid.*, 398, September 18, 1944.

54 Hofstadter, Richard, *op. cit.*, 199.

55 See: Breuer, J. and Freud, S., *Studies on Hysteria* (New York: Basic Books, Inc. (1957), ed. and trans. James Strachey and Anna Freud, assisted by Alix Strachey and Alan Tyson, 125, "Case 4 Katharina").

56 Mann, Thomas, *The Magic Mountain*, New York: The Modern Library (1927), trans. H. T. Lowe–Porter, 895.

57 It would appear that the author was a "button–down woman of letters named Dominique Aury" who was a "longtime editor and translator at Gallimard, one of the most important publishing houses in France . . . [who] dressed in smart suits, appeared to wear little or no makeup, rubbed elbows with the likes of Camus and, in television interviews, projected an almost religious passion for the life of the mind." The book would seem to have been conceived because "[a]t 47, she worried that she was too old and not pretty enough to keep [her married lover] from straying." Her purpose—by seeking to involve him in a "non–clandestine" project—was apparently successful. *See*: Dargis, Manohla, Film Review: "Peering Behind the Mask of a Mysterious Erotic Novelist." *The New York Times*, E–5, c.1–4, Wednesday, 4 May 2005. On the other hand, an obituary article for Eliot Fremont–Smith, a former *Times* book reviewer, identifies the author as "Anne Desclos, a novelist and journalist." *The New York Times*, B–8, Friday, September 7, 2007, "Eliot Fremont–Smith, 78, Former Times Critic."

58 Réage, Pauline, *Story of O*, New York: Grove Press (1965), 197–198. The last sentences of the tale recount how Sir Stephen, having secured the complete subjugation of O, abandons her, and she, after seeking his permission, then ends her life—a conclusion that realizes the Social Darwinist ideal of prevalence over an *other*.

59 Ethnicity may be defined as those sociocultural qualities that fuse into a unique group identity with which members of the group are able to identify each other, and by which outsiders are able to identify members. Such qualities or attributes may include a particular language, religion, cuisine, dress, geographic location, customs, habits, literature, even beliefs and values. At various times this concept has been described by the words: *race*, *tribe*, *people*, and, in Eastern Europe, *nationality* (Kraushar, *op. cit.*, "A Note for the General Reader," 2). Stalin's theoretical contribution to the discussion of the nature of "nationalities" was that Jews were not a "true" nationality, since they did not constitute a majority of the population in any inclusive rural geographic area. The thought may not have been entirely original with Stalin. Shmuel Katz in his biography of Vladimir Jabotinsky, the ideological progenitor of the Likud Party in Israel, quotes from a pamphlet, *Nationalism in Our Day* by Karl Kautsky, a founder of the Second Socialist International, printed in 1903 in St. Petersburg in Russian translation from the original German, ". . . the Jews no longer exist as a nation, a nation [nation-

ality?] is inconceivable without a territory." (*Lone Wolf: A Biography of Vladimir Jabotinsky*, New York: Barricade Books (1996), I:59.)

60 See: Woodward, C. Vann, *The Strange Career of Jim Crow*, New York: Oxford University Press (1955), vii; Dollard, John, *op. cit.*

61 One brand of soap, Ivory, was advertised for decades during the first half of the twentieth century as "99 and 44/100s percent *pure.*"

62 In this respect, see: Greenberg, Jack, *Race Relations and American Law*, New York: Columbia University Press (1959), 344, for the rather mischievous observation that miscegenation provisions were generally placed next to the sections pertaining to incest in Southern states' penal codes in the decades before the United States Supreme Court ruled in 1954 that legislative provisions in state law referable to race were inherently unequal, an invidious discrimination and under the Fourteenth Amendment to the United States Constitution, thereby, a denial of the equal protection of the laws.

63 See: *Plessy v. Ferguson*, 163 U.S. 537, 551 (1896).

64 The "Prior History" on the first page of the court's decision (163 U.S. 537) includes the information: "on June 7, 1892, he engaged and paid for a first class passage . . ."

65 Still, note must be taken of the large, if losing, efforts of the Populist Party well into the first decade of the twentieth century to put forth candidates on a political platform emphasizing racial equality in the American South and elsewhere in the United States. See, e.g.: Woodward, C. Vann, *Tom Watson, Agrarian Rebel*, New York: The Macmillan Company (1938), 219–22, 239–40, 357–63, as to the failing efforts of Tom Watson, the Georgia Populist, to construct a Populist party election success in the face of the Social Darwinist breed of racism that enveloped the American South after 1890.

66 Hawkins, *op. cit.*, 109.

67 See: *Berea College v. Kentucky*, 211 U.S. 45 (1908).

68 Beschloss, *op. cit.*, 51, citing the *Morgenthau Diaries*, January 27, 1942.

69 Winkler, Allan M., *Franklin D. Roosevelt and the Making of Modern America*, The Library of American Biography, New York: Longman, Pearson Education, Inc. (2006), 10.

70 Parrington, Vernon Louis, *Main Currents in American Literature*, New York: Harcourt, Brace and Company (1930).

71 *Ibid.*, 256.

72 *Ibid.*, 257.

73 Beschloss, *op. cit.*, 137, 243.

74 *The New York Times*, May 25, 1961, "In The Nation," 36.

75 Morgenthau, Henry, III, *Mostly Morgenthaus: A Family History*, New York: Ticknor & Fields (1991), 439.

Chapter 1: The Founding Father

76 Morgenthau, Henry, III, *op. cit.*, 56. Henry, III's own volume takes the form of a family history over four or five generations, following its removal from a series of southern German villages, but it is really the story of one person's spiritual odyssey. Descended from a family whose religious roots in each successive generation became more and more attenuated, Henry, III describes how he recovered his family's spiritual heritage.

77 *Ibid.*

78 *Ibid.*, 54.

79 *Ibid.*, 55, 56.

80 *All in a Lifetime.* Garden City: Doubleday, Page & Co. (1922).

81 It would also lead to Henry, Sr.'s appointment in 1920 as an American representative to an international conference to establish the International Red Cross. Henry, III includes in his volume a picture of the representatives to this latter conference, with Henry, Sr. among the other conferees sitting stiffly at a conference table in the accepted pictorial stance of the period. His last international appointment would be to chair the commission that supervised the resettlement in Greece of Greek–speaking refugees displaced from the Aegean littoral of Turkey in the aftermath of the 1922 Greek invasion of the Anatolian plateau that was successfully repelled by the Turks. The ensuing treaty provided for a Greek–Turkish population exchange. (Kraushar, *op. cit.*, "A Note for the General Reader," 15.)

82 Morgenthau, Henry, Sr., *op. cit.*, 197.

83 *Ibid.*, 129.

84 *Ibid.*, 104. In the second decade of the twentieth century, Rabbi Wise and Reverend John Haynes Holmes, the minister of the Community Church (where the Free Synagogue had been welcomed to share the premises) practiced the Social Gospel forty years before that concept became fashionable. They were both forceful speakers always in the forefront of public issues. Reverend Holmes made so bold in those years

to publish a rather melodramatic novel focused on a *Jewish* president of the United States!

85 *Ibid.*

86 *Ibid.*, 120.

87 *Ibid.*, 159.

88 Ickes, *op. cit.*, II:221, Saturday, October 9, 1937.

89 *Ibid.*, 218.

90 Morgenthau, Henry, Sr., *op. cit.*, 107, 108.

91 *Ibid.*, 159.

92 *Ibid.*, 160.

93 Nevins, Allan, *Grover Cleveland*, New York: Dodd, Mead & Company (1932), 209, 210.

94 With the commencement of the Franco–Prussian War in 1870, the French emperor Napoleon III withdrew French troops guarding the papal lands from incursion by the soldiers of Italy, freeing the Italians to complete the consolidation of the Italian peninsula into a unified country, and leaving the Pope a "prisoner in the Vatican." The dispute was finally resolved in 1929 by Mussolini with the Lateran Treaty that created Vatican City as a politically independent territory.

95 Kraushar, *op. cit.*, "A Note for the General Reader," 14, 15. The Döenmeh, nominally Muslim, are apparently still extant in modern-day Turkey, having been expelled from Salonika as a consequence of the Greek–Turkish population exchanges after the failure of the Greek invasion of the Anatolian plateau in 1922. It was Salonika in the opening years of the twentieth century, then still a part of the Ottoman Empire, where the Young Turk Movement originated that deposed Sultan Abdul Hamid in 1908 and thereafter ruled the Ottoman Empire under a figurehead sultan.

96 Morgenthau, Henry, Sr., *op. cit.*, 161.

97 *Ibid.*, 162.

98 *Ibid.*

99 *Ibid.*, 188 (emphasis in original); Morgenthau, Henry, III, *Mostly Morgenthaus*, 119.

100 Halecki, Oscar, *A History of Poland*, New York: Barnes & Noble Books, reprint (1993).

101 *Op. cit.*, 282.

102 *Ibid.*, 296.

103 *Ibid.*, 297, 298.

104 It must seem inconceivable to one of Halecki's sensibilities that in 1997 the Polish Prime Minister, Buzek, was a Lutheran—and as such alien to the Roman Catholicism so inescapably an aspect of Polish, Social Darwinist identity—while the foreign minister, Gmerek, was of Jewish antecedents.

105 *Ibid.*, 306. Perhaps the Polish government imagined itself thereby the equal of Nazi Germany as might befit a signatory to the Ten Year Polish–German Non–Aggression Treaty of 1934 that Hitler was shortly to repudiate.

106 *Ibid.*, 297. This material is taken from Kraushar, *op. cit.*, 20–22, footnotes 36, 37.

107 Morgenthau, Henry, Sr., *op. cit.*, 356.

108 *Ibid.*, 372.

109 *Ibid.*, 372–374.

110 Morgenthau, Henry, *All in a Lifetime*, 374.

111 *Ibid.*

112 *Ibid.*

113 *Ibid.*

114 This was in keeping with a similar suggestion Henry, Sr. had made some five years earlier while he was still the ambassador in Turkey. In the nineteenth century the Ottoman Empire had been compelled to extend to European nationals so–called *capitulations*—that is, European nationals were exempted from the jurisdiction of local Turkish courts and prisons. In September 1914, the Ottoman government announced the abrogation of the capitulations, subjecting European nationals to Ottoman law and prisons, effective October 1, 1914. The American–supported educational institutions in Constantinople and elsewhere in the Ottoman lands were apprehensive as to the effects on those institutions and their personnel of the abrogation of the capitulations. Morgenthau had appealed to Enver Pasha, the Minister of War and one of the triumvirate who ruled Turkey. Enver Pasha responded with the assurance that the Turks had no hostile intentions toward Americans. Morgenthau asked him to visit Robert College in Constantinople on October 1, 1914, the day the capitulations were to be abrogated. Enver agreed. The gesture received wide publicity and no doubt prevented incursions into the American institutions thereafter (Morgenthau, Henry, *Henry I. Morgenthau, American Ambassador at Constantinople from 1913 to 1916*, Garden City: Doubleday, Page & Co. [1918], 47–48).

115 Morgenthau, Henry, *All in a Lifetime*, 377.

116 The Polish Nationalists of the period held formal adherence to the Roman Catholic creed to be an integral aspect of their ethnicity, and the Roman Catholic Church in that era discouraged its communicants from entering the precincts of other faiths.

117 Morgenthau, Henry, *All in a Lifetime*, 377.

118 *Ibid.*, 377, 378.

119 *Ibid.*, 378, 379.

Chapter 2: Of Birth and Growing Up

120 Morgenthau, Henry, III, *op. cit.*, 213.

121 Morgenthau, Henry, III, *op. cit.*, 214.

122 Morgenthau's bonding with his father remained strong throughout his father's life. Harold Ickes grumbled in his *Secret Diary* (Ickes, *op. cit.*, I:541, March 3, 1936), that the senior Morgenthaus were always the only guests at the annual formal dinners the presidential cabinet gave to President and Mrs. Roosevelt, except for very close White House staff members, General "Pa" Watson, the presidential aide, and "Missy" LeHand, his secretary, whose presence Ickes accepted and approved. Aside from invitations from the president himself to the White House, this cabinet dinner was the most exclusive social occasion in the nation's capital. Three years later Ickes found a valid reason for the senior Morgenthaus' presence at the dinner. He wrote one year objecting to the vice president's appearance, "the few guests have been those people who were most intimately associated with Roosevelt at the very beginning of the 1932 campaign—Mr. and Mrs. Morgenthau, Sr., Frank Walker, Steve Early, Marvin McIntyre, etc." (*Ibid.*, "The Inside Struggle," II:587–88, Sunday, February 26, 1939).

123 Morgenthau, Henry, III, *op. cit.*, 92.

124 Shriver & Weissberg, "No Emotion Left Behind," Tuesday, August 16, 2005, A15, cols. 1–5.

125 Morgenthau, Henry, III, *op. cit.*, 45. He explains this was his grandfather's brother.

126 Blum, John Morton, *From the Morgenthau Diaries*, Boston: Houghton Mifflin Company (1959), I:3.

127 Morgenthau, Henry, III, *op. cit.*, 214, 215.

128 Morgenthau, Henry, III, *op. cit.*, 215, 216.

129 Morgenthau, Henry, III, *op. cit.*, 215.

130 *Ibid.*, 216.

131 The settlement house occupied two adjoining buildings of what were, then, acres of eighteenth–century row housing in the area. Beginning in the 1930s, that evidence of eighteenth–century New York was demolished, along with the tenements that had infiltrated the area in the latter half of the nineteenth century, to provide space for new, subsidized public housing beginning with the ironically named "First Houses," so that today the Henry Street settlement buildings are virtually all that is left in the area of what was the eighteenth–century city.

132 *Ibid.*, 217.

133 The year is confusing in light of Henry, III's comment, quoted above, that his father left Cornell in the spring of 1911—unless one includes the period later, when Morgenthau went back to the Cornell Agricultural School after he had come to his decision to become a farmer. The year may reflect the common human error of writing the old year at the beginning of the new year.

Chapter 3: Love, Marriage, and Property

134 Blum, John Morton, *From the Morgenthau Diaries*, I:5.

135 *Ibid.*

136 Morgenthau, Henry, III, *op. cit.*, 217.

137 Morgenthau, Henry, Sr., *All in a Lifetime*, 148.

138 *Ibid.*, 148, 149.

139 *Ibid.*, 149.

140 Morgenthau, Henry, III, *op. cit.*, 217.

141 *Ibid.*, 218.

142 *Ibid.*, 217, 218.

143 Blum, John Morton, *From the Morgenthau Diaries*, I:5.

144 Morgenthau, Henry, III, *op. cit.*, 236. It would be only at the beginning of World War II, in 1939, that other opportunities for employment became available for household help, so that their ranks were rapidly depleted and salaries for those remaining in that employment category soon inflated.

145 Blum, John Morton, *From the Morgenthau Diaries*, I:6.

146 Ickes, *op. cit*, I:331.

147 Blum, *From the Morgenthau Diaries*, I:3.

148 Morgenthau, Henry, III, *op. cit.*, 215.

149 Tomasso di Lampedusa, Giuseppi, *Il Gattopardo*, Milano: Giangiacomo Feltrinelli Editore (2002), ottantesima edizione, 41.

150 Morgenthau, Henry, III, *op. cit.*, 431, 432.

151 *The New York Times Book Review*, Sunday, December 4, 2005, 52.

152 *Ibid.*

153 Morgenthau, Henry, III, *op. cit.*, 226, footnote.

154 Blum, John Morton, *Roosevelt and Morgenthau*, 7.

155 Morgenthau, Henry, III, *op. cit.*, 223.

156 *Ibid.*, 224.

157 *Ibid.*, 226.

158 *Ibid.*, 227.

159 *Ibid.*, 194.

160 Beschloss, *op. cit.*, 45.

161 Morgenthau, Henry, III, *op. cit.*, 245.

162 *Ibid.*, 244.

163 *Ibid.*, 245.

Chapter 4: Life in Dutchess County

164 Morgenthau, Henry, III, *op. cit.*, 253.

165 Blum, *From the Morgenthau Diaries*, I: xiii.

166 Morgenthau, Henry, III, *op. cit.*, 226.

167 Blum, *From the Morgenthau Diaries*, I:9.

168 Beschloss, *op. cit.*, 46.

169 *Ibid.*, footnote 1.

170 *Ibid.*, 46.

171 A lance corporal in the German army, Austrian by birth and citizenship until 1932, would choose to use those two words as the title of a book written by him in prison after the ending of the war then raging.

172 Hofstadter, *op. cit.*, 7.

173 Morgenthau, Henry, III, *op. cit.*, 229.

174 *Ibid.*, 239. The presence of a chauffeur would suggest that people in the early years of the twentieth century still thought in terms of traveling in a horse–drawn carriage requiring a coachman.

175 *Ibid.*, 229–230.

176 *Ibid.*, 207–208.

177 *Ibid.*, 36–38.

178 *Ibid.*

179 *Ibid.*, 230.

180 *Ibid.*

181 *Ibid.*

182 *Ibid.*, 231.

183 *Ibid.*

184 *Ibid.*, 232.

185 *Ibid.*

186 *Ibid.*, 232, 233.

187 *Ibid.*, 233.

188 *Ibid.*, 246.

189 Blum, John Morton, *Roosevelt and Morgenthau*, Boston: Houghton Mifflin Company (1970), 11.

190 It is not clear how Professor Blum comes by the year 1915, since in Morgenthau's letter dating from November/December 1914 (quoted in the preceding chapter 3), Morgenthau describes paying a call on Assistant Secretary of the Navy Roosevelt at his office in Washington, D.C., where they informally discuss how Henry, Sr.'s performance as ambassador to the Ottoman empire was evaluated by the State Department.

191 Beschloss, *op. cit.*, 49.

192 Morgenthau, Henry, III, *Mostly Morgenthaus*, 233.

193 *Ibid.*, 235.

194 *Ibid.*, 238–239.

195 *Ibid.*, 239.

196 *The New York Times*, B16, February 9, 1982.

197 Perhaps the most balanced view of the role of an independent press is given by Robert Caro in his biography of Robert Moses, when he describes how the idealism of young reporters led to their uncovering the scandals in Moses's conduct of New York City's urban renewal program in the late 1950s after Moses's enormous prestige at the time caused managing editors and publishers' initial skepticism.

198 Beschloss, *op. cit.*, 48.

199 Flynn, Edward J., *You're the Boss*, Westport: Greenwood Press (1947/1983), 78. Flynn, a longtime chairman of the Bronx County Democratic Party organization, writes: Roosevelt's "early history had been that of a reformer and insurgent in opposition to Tammany Hall."

200 Caro, *op. cit.*, 285.

201 *Ibid.*, 284.

202 *Ibid.*

203 *Ibid.*

204 See: Robert Moses's paid obituary notice in *The New York Times*, July 30, 1981, B17, "Funeral service Friday, July 31, 1981, 11 AM, at St. Peter's by the Sea Episcopal Church, Montauk Highway, Bay Shore, L.I."

205 Grondahl, Paul, *Mayor Erastus Corning: Albany Icon, Albany Enigma*, Albany: Washington Park Press (1997), 491.

206 Flynn, Edward J., *You're the Boss*, Westport: Greenwood Press (1947/1983), 232.

207 Caro, *op. cit.*, 285.

208 Morgenthau, Henry, III, *op. cit.*, 253.

209 Four–year gubernatorial terms would be enacted into law beginning with the 1942 election.

210 *Ibid.*, 249.

211 When it was eventually built, the Taconic never reached the aesthetic level of the landscaping of the parkways Moses built on Long Island.

212 *Ibid.*

213 *Ibid.*, 250.

214 *Ibid.*

215 *Ibid.*

216 Otto Kahn was a partner in the great merchant banking firm of Kuhn, Loeb & Co., and an eminent patron of the arts.

217 Morgenthau, Henry, III, *op. cit.*, xvi.

218 Morgenthau, Henry, III, *op. cit.*, 256.

219 *Ibid.*

220 *Ibid.*, 206.

221 *The New York Times*, "Hevesi Trial? Senate May Look to a 1913 Impeachment," Monday, October 30, 2006, B–7, columns 3–6.

222 Kennedy, Karen, National Register of Historic Places Registration Form OMB No. 1024–0018, (May, June 2001).

223 Letter to author dated May 22, 2006.

224 Morgenthau, Henry, III, *op. cit.*, 261.

225 *Ibid.*

226 See: Kennedy, Karen, National Register of Historic Places Registration Form OMB No. 1024–0018 (2001). After a long period of being regarded as hopelessly "dowdy," "old–fashioned," "out of date," the "Queen Anne" style is newly appreciated and—if not that style's floor

plan with its huge center hall, at least its architectural details, although perhaps bowdlerized, is now *comme il faut*.

227 *Ibid.*

228 Morgenthau, Henry, III, *op. cit.*, 261. As the Roosevelts had remodeled their own Queen Anne–style house in 1916 to add the library and change the facade to a Regency front, so Elinor Morgenthau hired a fashionable architect to transform her newly acquired building into an eighteenth–century Georgian Revival residence. (It would not be out of place among the suburban villas occupied by the likes of Scarlett O'Hara and Ashley Wilkes in the 1939 movie, *Gone With the Wind*.)

229 *Ibid.*, 262.

230 *Ibid.*

231 Beschloss, *op. cit.*, 47.

232 Morgenthau, Henry, III, *op. cit.*, 247–48.

233 Blum, *Roosevelt and Morgenthau*, 13.

234 See: Introduction

235 Flynn, *op. cit.*, 208.

236 Morgenthau, Henry, III, *op. cit.*, 169.

237 Beschloss, *op. cit.*, 48.

238 Morgenthau, Henry, III, *op. cit.*, 247.

239 *Ibid.*

240 Youngs, J. William T., *Eleanor Roosevelt: A Personal and Public Life*, New York: Pearson Longman (2006), 56.

241 Beschloss, *op. cit.*, 47.

242 Morgenthau, Henry, III, *op. cit.*, 248.

243 *Ibid.*, 257–259.

244 Beschloss, *op. cit.*, 47

245 *Ibid.*, footnote 3.

246 Morgenthau, Henry, III, *op. cit.*, 255.

247 *Ibid.*, 229.

248 Morgenthau, Henry, III, *op. cit.*, 256.

249 Freidel, Frank, *Franklin D. Roosevelt: The Ordeal*, Boston: Little Brown and Company (1954), 241, 242.

250 Slayton, Robert A., *Empire Statesman: The Rise and Redemption of Al Smith*, New York: The Free Press (2001).

251 *Ibid.*, 356.

252 *Ibid.*, 354.

253 *Ibid.*, 354, 355.

254 *Ibid.*, 355.

Chapter 5: In State Government

255 Slayton, *op. cit.*, 356.

256 Freidel, *Franklin D. Roosevelt: The Ordeal*, 233.

257 *Ibid.*, 250.

258 Davis, Kenneth S., *FDR: The New York Years*, New York: Random House (1985), 29.

259 Finan, Christopher M., *Alfred E. Smith, The Happy Warrior*, New York: Hill and Wang (2002), 187.

260 *Ibid.*

261 McCullough, *op. cit.*, 331.

262 Slayton, *op. cit.*, 356, 357.

263 Freidel, Frank, *Franklin D. Roosevelt*, New York: Little Brown and Company, First Paperback Ed. (1990), 54.

264 Slayton, *op. cit.*, 357.

265 Freidel, *Franklin D. Roosevelt: The Ordeal*, 54.

266 *Ibid.*, 259.

267 Black, *op. cit.*, 132.

268 Freidel, *Franklin D. Roosevelt: The Ordeal*, 262.

269 *Ibid.*, 264.

270 Black, Conrad, *Franklin Delano Roosevelt*, New York: Public Affairs (2003), 183.

271 Josephson, Matthew and Hannah, *Al Smith, Hero of the Cities*, Boston: Houghton Mifflin Company (1969), 398.

272 Davis, *op. cit.*, 47.

273 Josephson, Matthew and Hannah, *op. cit.*, 399.

274 So, for example, Black writes that Adolf Hitler, an *echt* Social Darwinist, "was viscerally repelled by Roosevelt's infirmity . . ." See: Black, *op. cit.*, 259.

275 Slayton, *op. cit.*, 356.

276 Schlesinger, Arthur Jr., *The Age of Roosevelt*, "The Crisis of the Old Order," Boston: Houghton Mifflin Company (1957), I:378, 379.

277 Black, Conrad, *Franklin Delano Roosevelt: Champion of Freedom*, New York: Public Affairs (2003), 182.

278 Lindley, Ernest K., *Franklin D. Roosevelt: A Career in Progressive Democracy*, Indianapolis: Bobbs–Merrill Company Inc. (1931), 19–20, cited in Freidel, *Franklin D. Roosevelt: The Ordeal*, 254, 255.

279 Black, *op. cit.*, 182.

280 Freidel, *Franklin D. Roosevelt: The Ordeal*, 255.

281 Beschloss, *op. cit.*, 48.

282 Morgenthau, Henry, III, *op. cit.*, 257.

283 Schlesinger, Arthur Jr., *The Age of Roosevelt*, "The Coming of the New Deal," Boston: Houghton Mifflin Company (1958), II:583.

284 *Ibid.*, 584.

285 *Ibid.*, 583.

286 Ickes, *op. cit.*, III:384–385, Sunday, December 1, 1940.

287. Schlesinger, *opcit*, II:237

288. *Ibid.*, II:537–8

289. *Ibid.*, 539

290 Morgenthau, Henry, III, *op. cit.*, 539.

291 Slayton, *op. cit.*, 355.

292 Schlesinger, *op. cit.*, I:383.

293 Black, *op. cit.*, 185.

294 Slayton, *op. cit.*, 355.

295 Freidel, *Franklin D. Roosevelt: The Ordeal*, 259.

296 Black, *op. cit.*

297 *Ibid.*, 185, 186.

298 *Ibid*, 186.

299 Slayton, *op. cit.*, 350.

300 *Ibid.*, 357.

301 Winkler, *op. cit.*, 46, writes, "In so doing, he may well have understood that he would never walk normally again and made a calculated decision to move on."

302 Black, *op. cit.*, 185.

303 Slayton, *op. cit.*, 357.

304 Morgenthau, Henry, III, *op. cit.*, 262.

305 Beschloss, *op. cit.*, 48. Beschloss writes that as part of his duties as advance man, Morgenthau "drove the candidate seventy–five hundred miles in an old Buick."

306 Slayton, *op. cit.*, 354.

307 Morgenthau, Henry, III, *op. cit.*, 264.

308 Slayton, *op. cit.*, 355. Slayton writes that in the period after Election Day, "Roosevelt made every effort to consult Smith, writing him for advice and then meeting with the governor in Albany to go over the state of the state in a mammoth four–hour session." Slayton goes on: "In his inauguration speech Franklin graciously observed, 'This day is notable not so much for the inauguration of a new Governor as it marks the close of a term of a Governor who has been our Chief Executive for eight years.'"

309 See: letter to his father dated March 23, 1924, above.

310 Blum, *Roosevelt and Morgenthau*, 10.

311 *Ibid.*, 13; Freidel, Frank, *Franklin D. Roosevelt: The Triumph*, Boston: Little Brown and Company (1956), 14, 37. The suggestion is of a piece with Morgenthau's earlier suggestion to Governor Smith to "call a meeting of upstate newspaper owners and farm leaders and give them the same talk he gave us," as Morgenthau reported in his letter to his father dated March 23, 1924. Morgenthau went on to write that Smith "said fine, please prepare a list for me, which we did." The appointment with the governor had come about, as Morgenthau had written in the same letter, because the *American Agriculturist* urged its "readers to sign a petition for general [rural] tax reduction. It was signed and sent to Gov[ernor] Smith [who] was sufficiently interested to send for Eastman [the editor] and myself."

312 Blum notes, "Roosevelt was wont to explain that [Morgenthau] was the only man he knew who had made a profit farming" (from the *Morgenthau Diaries*, I:15). As Henry, III confirms, Roosevelt's perception was incorrect. Like Roosevelt, Morgenthau's farming cost him money most every year.

313 Freidel writes that the members, agricultural experts at Cornell University, "met at their own expense and used the offices of Morgenthau's *American Agriculturist . . .*" Freidel, *op. cit.*, 37.

314 Morgenthau, Henry, III, *op. cit.*, 262.

315 *Ibid.*, 37, 38.

316 Freidel writes that Roosevelt "claimed that 18 out of the 21 members of his committee were Republicans." He adds, "This may very well have been, but they were not Republican politicians." Freidel, *Ibid.*, 14.

317 *Ibid.*, 38.

318 *Ibid.*, 39.

319 *Ibid.*, 39, 40.

320 Roosevelt Library. See: Box marked "Conservation."

321 College professors like nothing better than to be taken seriously by the political establishment.

322 Freidel, *Franklin D. Roosevelt: The Triumph*, 78.

323. *Ibid.*

324 Freidel, *Franklin D. Roosevelt: The Ordeal*, 151, citing letters—FDR to Morgenthau, December 6, 1928, Morgenthau to FDR, December 4, 1928, found in the Governor's Official File, Albany, New York.

325 It's interesting to note that computer keyboards no longer have the key showing a "c" with a diagonal line across it that appeared on typewriters in 1930 and signified the word "cents." Inflation has taken its toll.

326 Blum, *Roosevelt and Morgenthau*, 16.

327 Morgenthau, Henry, III, *op. cit.*, 263.

328 Blum, *Roosevelt and Morgenthau*, 17.

329 Morgenthau, Henry, III, *op. cit.*, 263.

330 *Ibid.*, 264.

331 Ickes, *op. cit.*, I:331, March 27, 1935.

332 Freidel, *Franklin D. Roosevelt: The Triumph*, 104.

333 Blum, *Roosevelt and Morgenthau*, 17.

334 *Ibid.*

335 *Ibid.*

336 McCullough, *op. cit.*, 871.

337 Morgenthau, Henry, III, *op. cit.*, 320.

338 *Ibid.*

339 Meltzer, Allan H., *A History of the Federal Reserve*, v. I, 1913–1951, Chicago: The University of Chicago Press (2003), 323–325.

340 *Ibid.*, 324.

341 *Ibid.*, n. 49.

342 *Ibid.*, 324–325.

343 *Ibid.*, 325, n. 52.

344 *Ibid.*, 324, n. 51.

345 Black, *op. cit.*, 277.

346 An example of the borrowers who went to the three banks in question for business loans is the author's uncle, who conducted an active wholesale business from 1920 through 1970 (surmounting the economic difficulties of the Great Depression in the 1930s). The business was incorporated as "Brooklyn Knit Sportswear Company, Inc." In his particular

business operation the incorporator was known as a "jobber," and relied on bank credit to finance his business operation. He sold women's sweaters and suits (in the 1920s) to sales outlets as varied as small neighborhood retail shops and large downtown department stores. He had the responsibility to decide on the next season's styles and colors, and to choose his subcontractors based on skill and price. When he started out, he no doubt used the styles of the company where he had been employed. Later, when his operation was large enough, he employed a "stylist," a designer who would simplify high–style designs, so that these could be manufactured cheaply enough to bring the product into a price range affordable to buyers at the lower end of the market—his business niche.

The next step was to choose the colors, that season's variations on the six primary colors. Virgin wool was then purchased (the grade consistent with the price range at which the finished product would be marketed). The quantity of wool purchased would be based on his estimate of expected sales that season. The next step was to send the wool to the dyer to be dyed in specified quantities for each color. Then the wool was sent to the knitting mill where it was knitted into the particular styles that had been decided upon earlier. Collaterally, cardboard boxes were ordered with printed covers showing an illustration and the name of the manufacturer. On a side panel was the information as to the style number, color, and size so that the boxed garments were available for easy retrieval. The boxes were delivered to the knitting mill where the knitted garment was folded and placed in the correctly labeled box. Only then was the boxed product delivered to the jobber's loft, where these were placed on shelves according to style number, size, and color.

The business employed traveling salesmen across the country who went to individual sales outlets seeking orders. (Some out–of–town retailers hired local New York buying services to do their ordering.) Retail orders would be assembled from the shelves in the jobber's loft by shipping clerks, then placed in cardboard containers for shipment by rail. Retailers had thirty days in which to pay for the goods purchased.

In the 1920s, the principal product was a "Chanel" three–piece, knitted suit. In the 1930s, these gave way to sweaters worn as a blouse and "twin sets"—a simple sweater worn with a cardigan, an open sweater that could be buttoned down the front but rarely was. (When the governor of Vermont, Howard Dean, was campaigning for a presidential nomination in 2004, his wife, a full–time physician, arranged to take one weekend off from her medical duties to appear at a campaign rally with him wearing the slightly unfashionable clothes suitable for a professional woman: a skirt and a twin set.)

Only after the retailers mailed in their checks to pay for the goods they had purchased, could the bank loans, borrowed to finance that season's separate manufacturing operations, be repaid.

347 Morgenthau, Henry, III, *op. cit.*, 263.

348 *Ibid.*, 262.

349 Black, *op. cit.*, 337.

350 Morgenthau, Henry, III, *op. cit.*, 251.

351 *Ibid.*, 265 (citing Blum).

352 Freidel, *Franklin D. Roosevelt: The Triumph*, 345.

353 *Ibid.*

354 *Ibid.*, 344.

355 *Ibid.*, 346.

356 Morgenthau, Henry, III, *op. cit.*, 267.

Chapter 6: Washington, D.C.

357 Morgenthau, Henry, III, *op. cit.*, 268.

358 Schlesinger, *op. cit.*, 38: that is, programs of reforestation, reduced sowing, and reduction in the quantity of produce made available for sale in the private market.

359 Freidel, Frank, *Franklin D. Roosevelt*, v. IV, "Launching the New Deal," Boston: Little Brown and Company (1973), 92.

360 *Ibid.*, 96.

361 Black, *op. cit.*, 206, 209.

362 Morgenthau, Henry, III, *op. cit.*, 267.

363 Freidel, *op. cit.*, IV:152.

364 Black, *op. cit.*, 262.

365 Morgenthau, Henry, III, *op. cit.*, 267.

366 Freidel, *op. cit.*, *The Triumph*, III:343.

367 Morgenthau, Henry, III, *op. cit.*, 272.

368 Schlesinger, *op. cit.*, II:45.

369 Meltzer, *A History of the Federal Reserve*.

370 Meltzer, *op. cit.*, 412.

371 *Ibid.*

372 Morgenthau, Henry, III, *op. cit.*, 272.

373 *Ibid.*, 273.

374 *Ibid.*, 268.

375 Black, *op. cit.*, 307.

376 *Ibid.*, 308.

377 Morgenthau, Henry, III, *op. cit.*, 271.

378 *Ibid.*, 270, 271. Ickes gives his version: "Henry Morgenthau, Jr., had been discussing a loan for some weeks with Boris E. Skvirsky, who represents Amtorg in this country . . . Then William Bullitt met Skvirsky in Morgenthau's office. Bullitt said: As you know, I am Assistant Secretary of State, but I am talking to you as private citizen William Bullitt. Bullitt showed him a draft of a letter that the President subsequently signed and asked Skvirsky what would be the reply of President Kalinin of Russia, if he should receive such a letter. Skvirsky's reply was that he would take it under consideration and give a reply later. A few days later there was another meeting in Morgenthau's office . . . Skvirsky said that as a private citizen he felt justified in saying that if such a letter as the one referred to should be sent to President Kalinin, the latter would reply . . . as appeared in a draft of a letter which Skvirsky then proceeded to show to Bullitt . . . Whereupon Bullitt took from his pocket an official letter signed by the President, this letter being a duplicate of the tentative one he had shown at the previous conference, and said to Skvirsky that in view of his assurances he was authorized to present that letter in behalf of the President of the United States. Then Skvirsky, on his part, produced an official letter signed by President Kalinin, and the deed was done" (Ickes, *op. cit.*, I:113–114, Monday, October 23, 1933).

379 *Ibid.*, I:117, Wednesday, November 8, 1933.

380 Black, *op. cit.*, 308.

381 *Ibid*; Schlesinger, *op. cit.*, II:66.

382 Meltzer, *op. cit.*, 8.

383 Schlesinger, *op. cit.*, II:238.

384 Freidel, *op. cit.*, IV:445.

385 *Ibid.*, 452.

386 Black, *op. cit.*, 298.

387 *Ibid.*, 298, 299.

388 *Ibid.*, 299.

389 Schlesinger, *op. cit.*, II:238.

390 *Ibid.*, II:238, 239.

391 *Ibid.*, II:239; Black, *op. cit.*, 309.

392 Black, *op. cit.*, 310.

393 Schlesinger, *op. cit.*, II:240.

394 Ickes, *op. cit.*, III:531, Sunday, June 8, 1941. Ickes' comment on Jones: "[Bernard Baruch] told Jesse Jones that he has altogether too much power. This was in reply to a request from Jones that Baruch help him get more powers from Congress. Jones told Baruch that he was as able as the President to exercise more powers. There certainly is nothing modest about Jesse."

395 Schlesinger, *op. cit.*, II:241; Black, *op. cit.*, 311.

396 Schlesinger, *op. cit.*, II:240.

397 *Ibid.*, II:241.

398 Black, *op. cit.*, 313.

399 Schlesinger, *op. cit.*, II:242.

400 *Ibid.*

401 Black, *op. cit.*, 312.

402 Schlesinger, *op. cit.*, II:242.

403 *Ibid.*; Black, *op. cit.*, 312.

404 Black, *op. cit.*, 332.

405 Morgenthau, Henry, III, *op. cit.*, 272.

406 Schlesinger, *op. cit.*, II:243.

407 Ickes, *op. cit.*, I:108, 109.

408 Morgenthau, Henry, III, *op. cit.*, 272.

409 *Ibid.*

410 Schlesinger, *op. cit.*, II:244.

411 Morgenthau, Henry, III, *op. cit.*, 240, 241.

412 Lundberg, Ferdinand, *America's 60 Families*, New York: The Citadel Press (1946), 279.

413 Meltzer, *op. cit.*, 9.

414 *Ibid.*, 25.

415 *Ibid.*, 430, "The 1933 act established a deposit insurance fund that became the Federal Deposit Insurance Corporation. . . ."

416 Meltzer writes, for example: "Delay [in making credit available by the Federal Reserve Board by lowering its discount rate] during the fall [of 1931] allowed a large part of the banking system to fail." Assets of those banks were in the form of bonds whose market value had declined, reducing the monetary worth of those assets below values that

supervising governmental agencies considered viable. "In two months, September and October 1931, the deposits of suspended banks rose to $705 million, as much as in the entire year 1932 yet to come. Nearly 30 percent of the bank suspensions between August 1929 and February 1933 came in the last four months of 1931 . . . The money stock [held by local banks] continued to decline, reflecting the additional increase in demand for currency" by members of the public who had lost confidence in the banking system, concluding it was "safer"—more useful— to preserve their money by placing it under the proverbial mattress than keeping it deposited in bank accounts. The other factor to which Meltzer attributes the bankruptcy of "a large part of the [American] banking system" was "the contractive policy of the Federal Reserve [System]" (Meltzer, *op. cit.*, 352).

Meltzer continues: "Despite worsening business and financial conditions, only two [Federal Reserve] banks reduced discount rates between the [Board] meetings on January 11 and February 24 [1932]. In late January, Richmond and Dallas lowered their rates from 4 percent to 3.5 percent. The system took no other expansive action despite a 20 percent decline in loans of member banks, a 3.5 percent decline in open market paper [certificates of loan indebtedness] outstanding and a 15 percent increase in the public's currency holdings during the last six months of 1931" [the last indicating a loss of confidence by members of the public in the solvency of banks]. "The buying [interest] rate on acceptances [i.e., purchases by the regional Federal Reserve banks of outstanding loans made by local banks] remained below the market [interest] rate, so the bill [or loan] portfolio [of regional Federal Reserve banks] declined, (*Ibid.*, 357).

"Concern at the New York and Chicago [Federal Reserve] banks about their gold reserves represents another failure of the Federal Reserve Act. Chicago acted as banks had acted before the act. The Federal Reserve Board did not force [the Federal Reserve] banks to pool their reserves, as the act intended. Knowing that it could not rely on support from other [regional Federal Reserve] banks, [the Federal Reserve Bank of] New York also acted to protect its gold reserve by first limiting, then ending, open market purchases [of local banks' certificates of indebtedness] . . . Purchases ended in early August [1932]" (*Ibid.*, 371).

Meltzer adds "seasonally adjusted data show that the stock of money [held by banks]—currency and demand deposits—increased during the summer and fall [of 1932]. Output responded to the increase in money. After falling to 47 in July [1932], the seasonally adjusted index of industrial production (August 1929 = 100) rose to 53 in October, an increase of more than 12 percent. It seems likely that had purchases [of local banks' certificates of indebtedness—"commercial paper" or "true bills" by regional Federal Reserve banks] continued, the collapse of the monetary system during the winter of 1933 might have been avoided" (*Ibid.*, 372, 373).

Meltzer concludes "[t]he banking crisis was not a sudden, unanticipated event. It developed over months, spreading from state to state, and when it was left unattended, spread fear throughout the country" (*Ibid.*, 379).

417 Then there was the precedent of the horrendous inflation that plagued Spain in the sixteenth century as a result of the annual convoys of Spanish galleons that carried shiploads of gold from the mines of Peru and Mexico to the wharves of Southern Spain. The value of money was cheapened by its plentitude.

418 *Ibid.*, 22.

419 *Ibid.*, 381.

420 Ickes, *op. cit.*, I:19.

421 Meltzer, *op. cit.*, 273, 274.

422 *Ibid.*, 415.

423 *Ibid.*, 426.

424 *Ibid.*, 458.

425 *Ibid.*, 534.

426 *Ibid.*, 459.

427 By the same token, "[a]s gold flowed into the United States [to take advantage of the increased monetary valuation Roosevelt had placed on the metal] the principal countries remaining on the gold standard—France, Belgium, Italy, and Switzerland—came under increasing deflationary pressure" due to the drain on their gold reserves" (*Ibid.*, 534).

428 *Ibid.*, 459.

429 *Ibid.*, 416.

430 Black, *op. cit.*, 332.

431 *Ibid.*, 334, 335.

432 Meltzer, *op. cit.*, 466.

433 *Ibid.*

434 *Ibid.*

435 Black, *op. cit.*, 356.

436 *Ibid.*, 428.

437 *Ibid.*, 8.

438 Ickes, *op. cit.*, I:294, 295.

439 *Ibid.*, 287.

440 *Ibid.*, 301.

441 *Ibid.*, 488.

442 *Ibid.*, 490.

443 *Ibid.*

444 *Ibid.*, 491–492.

445 Ickes, *op. cit.*, I:484.

446 Black, *op. cit.*, 362.

447 *Ibid.*, 373.

448 *Ibid.*, 535.

449 *Ibid.*

450 *Ibid.*, 493.

451 *Ibid.*, 497.

452 *Ibid.*, 492.

453 *Ibid.*, 497.

454 *Ibid.*, 497.

455 *Ibid.*, 499.

456 *Ibid.*

457 *Ibid.*

458 *Ibid.*

459 *Ibid.*, 536–537.

460 *Ibid.*, 537.

461 *Ibid.*, 537–538.

462 Ickes, *op. cit.*, I:596. While Ickes was envious of Morgenthau's social intimacy with Roosevelt, occasionally he makes a favorable comment— as at Roosevelt's second inauguration held January 20, 1936 in a pouring rain. Ickes was waiting in the Capitol for the ceremonies to begin when "a little later Henry Morgenthau came in. He had a flask of Scotch [whiskey] . . . He and I took a drink to fortify ourselves against the inclement weather that we were about to face" (*Ibid.*, II:51).

463 Meltzer, *op. cit.*, 502.

464 *Ibid.*, 503.

465 *Ibid.*

466 *Ibid.*, 504.

467 *Ibid.*

468 *Ibid.*

469 *Ibid.*, 504–505.

470 Edward Bernstein comments, ". . . Germany had seized the gold in the Bank of France, and everywhere else." Bernstein, Edward and Black, Stanley, *A Levite Among the Priests*, Boulder, CO: Westview Press (1991), 28; Black writes, "Huge costs and reparations were piled on France. . . ." Black, *op. cit.*, 559.

471 *Ibid.*, 505.

472 *Ibid.*

473 *Ibid.*, 506.

474 *Ibid.*

475 *Ibid.*

476 *Ibid.* Neither Roosevelt nor Morgenthau appears to have recognized the significance of the Banking Act of 1935 that, in law, set up a wholly independent central bank.

477 Slayton, *op. cit.*, 353–354; Black, *op. cit.*, 163.

478 *Ibid.*, 507.

479 Black, *op. cit.*, 381.

480 Meltzer, *op. cit.*, 507.

481 *Ibid.*, 507–509.

482 *Ibid.*

483 *Ibid.*, 510.

484 *Ibid.*, 510–511.

485 *Ibid.*, 512–513.

486 *Ibid.*, 513.

487 *Ibid.*, 515.

488 *Ibid.*, 517.

489 Black, *op. cit.*, 441.

490 Meltzer, *op. cit.*, 516.

491 *Ibid.*, 519.

492 *Ibid.*

493 Although the word *devaluation* was not used, rather the reference was to "floating" rates.

494 *Ibid.*, 540.

495 *Ibid.*, 541.

496 Blum, John Morton, *Roosevelt and Morgenthau*, Boston: Houghton Mifflin Company (1970), 85.

497 *Ibid.*, 542.

498 Ickes, *op. cit.*, II:84.

499 *Ibid.*, 85.

500 Meltzer, *op. cit.*, 542.

501 *Ibid.*

502 *Ibid.*, 543.

503 *Ibid.*, 544–545.

504 Ickes, *op. cit.*, II:142.

505 *Ibid.*, II:148, Saturday, May 22, 1937.

506 Morgenthau, Henry, III, *op. cit.*, 125, 126.

507 Blum, *Roosevelt and Morgenthau*, 518.

508 Ickes, *op. cit.*, Saturday, March 19, 1937, II:342.

509 *Ibid.*, II:343.

510 Ickes, *op. cit.*, II:497.

511 *Ibid.*, Sunday, February 26, 1939, II:391.

512 Black, *op. cit.*, 428.

513 *Ibid.*, 432.

514 *Ibid.*, 429.

515 Meltzer, *op. cit.*, 518.

516 *Ibid.*, 521.

517 *Ibid.*, 522.

518 *Ibid.*

519 *Ibid.*

520 *Ibid.*, 530, citing Blum, 1959, 393.

521 Ickes, *op. cit.*, II:272. Two years later, Ickes himself was the subject of an equally scabrous Gridiron Dinner lampoon in which he was pictured as the Disney cartoon character Donald Duck quacking answers to questions about Interior Department matters. The last question was what did he think of Harold Ickes and the quacking exploded. He was not amused on that occasion either (*Ibid.*, III:646).

522 *Ibid.*, II:269.

523 Morgenthau, Henry, III, *op. cit.*, 401.

524 In the 1930s, the concept of "public housing" was sufficiently new and experimental so that local housing authorities were run by civic–minded citizens whom local mayors appointed to serve as a public service. It

would take several decades for public housing commissionerships to come to be seen as a source of political patronage.

525 *Ibid.*, 284–285.

526 Meltzer, *op. cit.*, 530.

527 *Ibid.*, citing Blum, 1959, 400.

528 *Ibid.*, citing Blum, 1959, 405.

529 *Ibid.*

530 Black, *op. cit.*, 433.

531 Meltzer, *op. cit.*, 530, 531, n. 238.

532 Black, *op. cit.*, 434.

533 *Ibid.*, 434–435.

534 *Ibid.*, 435.

535 Meltzer, *op. cit.*, 531.

536 *Ibid.*, 524.

537 *Ibid.*, 531.

538 *Ibid.*, 532.

539 *Ibid.*, n. 242.

540 *Ibid.*, 532.

541 Morgenthau, Henry, III, *op. cit.*, 286.

542 *Ibid.*, 287.

543 *Ibid.*

544 Black, *op. cit.*, 493–495.

545 *Ibid.*, 494–495.

546 Meltzer, *op. cit.*, 545.

547 *Ibid.*, 533.

548 Ickes, *op. cit.*, III:430.

549 *Ibid.*, 546.

550 *Ibid.*, 574.

551 *Ibid.*, 573–74.

552 Blum, *Roosevelt and Morgenthau*, 313.

553 Black, *op. cit.*, 497.

554 *Ibid.*, 313–314.

555 *Ibid.*, 315–316.

556 *Ibid.*, 316.

557 *Ibid.*, 317.

558 *Ibid.*, 315.

559 Meltzer, *op. cit.*, 575.

560 Bernstein, *op. cit.*, 41.

561 Black, *op. cit.*, 613.
562 Meltzer, *op. cit.*, 548.

Chapter 7: The War Years and Beyond

563 Morgenthau, Henry, III, *op. cit.*, 297.
564 Meltzer, *op. cit.*, 590.
565 *Ibid.*, 585–86.
566 *Ibid.*, 586.
567 Morgenthau, Henry, III, *op. cit.*, 297.
568 *Ibid.*
569 *Ibid.*, 298–299.
570 *Ibid.*, 302.
571 *Ibid.*, 671.
572 Meltzer, *op. cit.*, 557.
573 *Ibid.*, 556.
574 *Ibid.*, 557.
575 *Ibid.*
576 *Ibid.*
577 *Ibid.*, 560.
578 *Ibid.*, 574.
579 *Ibid.*
580 *Ibid.*, 574–75.
581 *Ibid.*, 589; Blum, *Roosevelt and Morgenthau*, 450–51.
582 Blum, *Roosevelt and Morgenthau*, 431–32.
583 Meltzer, *op. cit.*, 589.
584 *Ibid.*
585 Blum, *Roosevelt and Morgenthau*, 446.
586 *Ibid.*, 450–51.
587 Meltzer, *op. cit.*, 590.
588 *Ibid.*
589 *Ibid.*, 588.
590 *Ibid.*, 590.
591 *Ibid.*, 587.
592 *Ibid.*, 591.
593 *Ibid.*, 591–92.
594 *Ibid.*, 592, n. 14.
595 *Ibid.*, 592.

596 *Ibid.*, 587.

597 Blum, *Roosevelt and Morgenthau*, 427–29.

598 *Ibid.*, 377.

599 *Ibid.*, 378.

600 *Ibid.*, 378–379.

601 *Ibid.*, 379.

602 *Ibid.*, 380.

603 *Ibid.*, 379.

604 Black, *op. cit.*, 729.

605 Meltzer, *op. cit.*, 593.

606 Blum, *Roosevelt and Morgenthau*, 384.

607 *Ibid.*, 385.

608 *Ibid.*, 386.

609 Bernstein, *op. cit.*, 35.

610 Meltzer, *op. cit.*, 613, and also, that page, n. 55.

611 Bernstein, *op. cit.*, 35.

612 Meltzer, *op. cit.*, 613.

613 Bernstein, *op. cit.*, 36–37.

614 Meltzer, *op. cit.*, 614.

615 Bernstein, *op. cit.*, 37.

616 Meltzer, *op. cit.*, 615.

617 Bernstein, *op. cit.*, 37–38.

618 *Ibid.*, 40.

619 *Ibid.*, 41.

620 *Ibid.*, 39.

621 *Ibid.*, 40.

622 *Ibid.*, 42.

623 Gardner, Richard, *Sterling Dollar Diplomacy*, Oxford: The Clarendon Press (1956), 174.

624 *Ibid.*

625 *Ibid.*, 174–75.

626 *Ibid.*, 175.

627 Beschloss, *op. cit.*, 99.

628 Ickes, *op. cit.*, II:389, Sunday, May 7, 1938.

629 Wyman, David, *The Abandonment of the Jews*, New York: Pantheon Books (1984), 107.

630 Morgenthau, Henry, III, *op. cit.*, 323.

631 Beschloss, *op. cit.*, 53.

632 Morgenthau, Henry, III, *op. cit.*, 323.

633 Wyman, *op. cit.*, 63.

634 Morgenthau, Henry, III, *op. cit.*, 343.

635 Beschloss, *op. cit.*, 43.

636 Wood, E. Thomas and Jankowski, Stanislaw M., *Karski: How One Man Tried To Stop the Holocaust*, New York: John Wiley & Sons (1994), 221.

637 *Ibid.*, 186–87.

638 *Ibid.*, 187.

639 *Ibid.*

640 Burt, Robert A., *Two Jewish Justices: Outcasts in the Promised Land*, Berkeley: University of California Press (1988), 102.

641 Baker, Leonard, *Brandeis and Frankfurter*, New York: Harper and Row, Publishers (1984), endnote, chapter 19, to p. 384; Frankfurter/Karski: Statement by J. Karski, "The Impact of the Holocaust on Judaism in America," American University, March 23, 1980. The statement is almost forty years later and represents a translation by the ambassador to Karski earlier, which can explain the labored sentence structure of Frankfurter's remarks.

642 Newton, Verne W. (Ed.), *FDR and the Holocaust*, New York: Oxford University Press (1996), 119 (Breitman).

643 Beschloss, *op. cit.*, 40. Beschloss then attempts to explain what, in retrospect, must appear a cruel and inhuman response.

644 Laqueur, Walter, *The Terrible Secret: An Investigation into the Suppression of Information About Hitler's Final Solution*, London: Weidenfeld and Nicolson (1980), 236.

645 Ciechanowski, Jan, *Defeat In Victory*, New York: Doubleday & Company (1947), 182.

646 *Ibid.*, 190.

647 Wood and Jankowski, , *op. cit.*, 201.

648 Morgenthau, Henry, III, *op. cit.*, 436; Wood and Jankowski, *op. cit.*, 252.

649 Bernstein, *op. cit.*, 30.

650 Morgenthau, Henry, III, *op. cit.*, 325.

651 See: chapter 3, above.

652 Blum, *Roosevelt and Morgenthau*, 12.

653 Morgenthau, Henry, III, *op. cit.*, 325.

654 The reader will remember that the Compromise of 1877 led to the inauguration of Rutherford B. Hayes as president of the United States and the removal of the last federal troops from the former Confederate States of America. With their departure ended the last Southern Republican state government administrations and created the "Solid South" for Democratic candidates to elective office for a century.

655 Wyman, *op. cit.*, 313.

656 Morgenthau, Henry, III, *op. cit.*, 325.

657 *Ibid.*

658 Wyman, *op. cit.*, 193.

659 *Ibid*, 194.

660 *Ibid.*, 201.

661 *Ibid*, 195–96.

662 *Ibid*, 196.

663 *Ibid.*

664 *Ibid.*, 196–197.

665 *Ibid.*, 197–198.

666 Morgenthau, Henry, III, *op. cit.*, 325–26.

667 *Ibid.*, 326.

668 Wyman, *op. cit.*, 186.

669 Beschloss, *op. cit.*, 54.

670 Wyman, *op. cit.*, 186–87.

671 Beschloss, *op. cit.*, 55; Wyman, *op. cit.*, 187.

672 Beschloss, *op. cit.*, 55.

673 Blum, *Roosevelt and Morgenthau*, 531.

674 Wyman, *op. cit.*, 187.

675 Morgenthau, Henry, III, *op. cit.*, 418–19.

676 Beschloss, *op. cit.*, 55.

677 Wyman, *op. cit.*, 203.

678 *Ibid.*

679 Beschloss, *op. cit.*, 55.

680 *Ibid.*

681 *Ibid.*

682 Wyman, *op. cit.*, 203.

683 Beschloss, *op. cit.*, 56.

684 *Ibid.*

685 Wyman, *op. cit.*, 203.

686 *Ibid.*, 204.

687 *Ibid.*, 205.

688 *Ibid.*

689 Black, *op. cit.*, 814.

690 Beschloss, *op. cit.*, 57.

691 Wyman, *op. cit.*, 198.

692 Blum, *Roosevelt and Morgenthau*, 532.

693 Wyman, *op. cit.*, 198.

694 *Ibid.*, 209, footnote.

695 *Ibid.*, 210.

696 *Ibid.*, 210–11.

697 *Ibid.*, 210.

698 *Ibid.*, 211.

699 *Ibid.*, 213.

700 *Ibid.*, 214–15.

701 *Ibid.*, 225.

702 *Ibid.*, 214, footnote.

703 *Ibid.*, 225.

704 *Ibid.*

705 Beschloss, *op. cit.*, 59.

706 *Ibid.*, n. 1.

707 *Ibid.*, 59.

708 *Ibid.*, 63.

709 *Ibid.*, 64.

710 *Ibid.*, 63.

711 *Ibid.*, 66.

712 *Ibid.*, 67.

713 *Ibid.*

714 *Ibid.*, 61.

715 *Ibid.*, 62.

716 Morgenthau, Henry, III, *op. cit.*, 334.

717 *Ibid.*, 335.

718 Bernstein, *op. cit.*, 42.

719 *Ibid.*, 43.

720 *Ibid.*, 43.

721 *Ibid.*, 42.

722 Morgenthau, Henry, III, *op. cit.*, 342.

723 Gardner, *op. cit.*, 113.

724 *Ibid.*, 134.

725 *Ibid.*, 135–36.

726 Bernstein, *op. cit.*, 47.

727 *Ibid.*, 43.

728 Gardner, *op. cit.*, 265.

729 *Ibid.*, 43–44.

730 *Ibid.*, 44.

731 *Ibid.*

732 *Ibid.*, 44–45.

733 Gardner, *op. cit.*, 118.

734 *Ibid.*, 136–37.

735 *Ibid.*, 137, citing *Foreign Affaires*, xiii (1945), 205.

736 *Ibid.*, 263.

737 *Ibid.*, 142–43.

738 Beschloss, *op. cit.*, 67.

739 Black, *op. cit.*, 937.

740 Beschloss, *op. cit.*, 67, n. 13.

741 Black, *op. cit.*, 966.

742 Morgenthau, Henry, III, *op. cit.*, 334.

743 Beschloss, *op. cit.*, 67.

744 *Ibid.*, 68.

745 *Ibid.*, 67.

746 *Ibid.*, 69.

747 Eisenhower, Dwight D., *Crusade in Europe*, Garden City: Doubleday & Company (1948), 276–77.

748 Morgenthau, Henry, III, *op. cit.*, 359, 360.

749 *Ibid.*, 361.

750 Beschloss, *op. cit.*, 70.

751 Blum, *Roosevelt and Morgenthau*, 566.

752 Beschloss, *op. cit.*, 71.

753 *Ibid.*

754 *Ibid.*, 71–72.

755 *Ibid.*, 71.

756 Eisenhower, *op. cit.*, 287.

757 Beschloss, *op. cit.*, 72.

758 Eisenhower, *op. cit.*, 287.

759 Blum, *Roosevelt and Morgenthau*, 567–68.

760 *Ibid.*, 568–69.

761 *Ibid.*, 569.

762 *Ibid.*

763 Morgenthau, Henry, III, *op. cit.*, 431.

764 Beschloss, *op. cit.*, 84.

765 Ferrell, Robert H., *The Dying President: FDR 1944–45*, Columbia: University of Missouri Press (1998), 36–37.

766 *Ibid.*, 27.

767 *Ibid.*, 71–72.

768 Black, *op. cit.*, 932.

769 Blum, *op. cit.*, 570.

770 Beschloss, *op. cit.*, 85.

771 *Ibid.* The reader may want to consider Beschloss's differing version of the subject of the above paragraph.

772 Eisenhower, *op. cit.*, 296.

773 Black, *op. cit.*, 931.

774 *Ibid.*, 933.

775 Beschloss, *op. cit.*, 89–90.

776 *Ibid.*, 92.

777 *Ibid.*, 93.

778 *Ibid.*

779 Ferrell, *op. cit.*, 27.

780 Bernstein, *op. cit.*, 46.

781 *Ibid.*, 333, citing the diaries of Stimson and Morgenthau.

782 *Ibid.*, 95–96.

783 *Ibid.*, 96.

784 Beschloss, *op. cit.*, 100.

785 *Ibid.*

786 *Ibid.*, 96, n. 7; 110.

787 *Ibid.*, 107. Hull's seeming "about face" may possibly lie in the circumstance that he was seriously ill (and would retire shortly), his former political ambitions faded. There was no longer need to hide the information that his late father–in–law was of German–Jewish origin. In a Social Darwinist, anti–Semitic world, this knowledge could be politically corrosive. Hull may have had regard for the man, perhaps even respect and affection.

788 *Ibid.*

789 Morgenthau, Henry, III, *op. cit.*, 374.

790 Beschloss, *op. cit.*, 108.

791 *Ibid.*, 109. By the end of the nineteenth century, the Germans and Austrians were not self–sufficient in food production. As with Britain (Gardner, *op. cit.*, 26), wheat was probably imported from Bukovina, Romania, and Ukraine. After the Armistice in November 1918, food was scarce in Berlin when the newly reconstituted Polish Republic flexed its muscles and enforced an agrarian blockade of Germany. The aborted peace treaty that Germany imposed on the nascent Soviet government in the early months of 1918 at Brest–Litovsk, required surrender of much of Ukraine to Germany. See also: comment, Beschloss, *op. cit.*, 232, n. 3.

792 See: Chapter 5 above.

793 Beschloss, 109.

794 *Ibid.*, 110.

795 *Ibid.*, 103.

796 *Ibid.*, 111, n. 15.

797 *Ibid.*, 111.

798 *Ibid.*, 115.

799 *Ibid.*

800 *Ibid.*, 118.

801 *Ibid.*, 117–19.

802 *Ibid.*, 117.

803 *Ibid.*, 121–132.

804 *Ibid.*, 135.

805 Blum, *From the Morgenthau Diaries*, I:10.

806 Beschloss, *op. cit.*, 147.

807 *Ibid.*, 164.

808 *Ibid.*, 168.

809 *Ibid.*, 165.

810 *Ibid.*, 176.

811 *Ibid.*, 193.

812 *Ibid.*, 192.

813 *Ibid.*, 193.

814 *Ibid.*

815 *Ibid.*, 193–94.

816 *Ibid.*, 194.

817 *Ibid.*, 195, n. 2.

818 Beschloss's interpretation of this dialogue is rather different from what is expressed here. See: Beschloss, *op. cit.*, 197.

819 *Ibid.*

820 *Ibid.*

821 *Ibid.*, 199–200.

822 Blum, *op. cit.*, 624.

823 McCullough, David, *op. cit.*, 334–35.

824 Beschloss, *op. cit.*, 201.

825 *Ibid.*

826 *Ibid.*

827 *Ibid.*, 202; Morgenthau, Henry, III, *op. cit.*, 412.

828 Morgenthau, Henry, III, *op. cit.*, 402.

829 *Ibid.*, 402–03.

830 Beschloss, *op. cit.*, 211.

831 Blum, *Roosevelt and Morgenthau*, 630; Beschloss, *op. cit.*, 212; Black, *op. cit.*, 1109.

832 Beschloss, *op. cit.*, 213.

833 *Ibid.*, 214.

834 Morgenthau, Henry, III, *op. cit.*, 403.

835 Blum, *Roosevelt and Morgenthau*, 632–33.

836 *Ibid.*

837 Beschloss, *op. cit.*, 220.

838 *Ibid.*

839 *Ibid.*

840 *Ibid.*, 224.

841 *Ibid.*, 221.

842 Morgenthau, Henry, III, *op. cit.*, 403–04.

843 Beschloss, *op. cit.*, 245.

844 Morgenthau, Henry, III, *op. cit*, 404–05.

845 *Ibid.*, 231.

846 Dunar, Andrew J., *The Truman Scandals and the Politics of Morality*, Columbia, Missouri: University of Missouri Press (1984), 99.

847 *Ibid.*, 98.

848 Beschloss, *op. cit.*, 233.

849 *Ibid.*, 236.

850 Beschloss, *op. cit.*, 236.

851 *Ibid.*, 242.

852 Gardner, *op. cit*, 201.

853 There is an obvious explanation for Truman's hesitancy to come right out and tell Morgenthau he was finished. Although Truman expected

to rely on Byrnes "experience" at Yalta, and perhaps even more on his "toughness" in negotiation with Stalin, Truman wanted Vinson's companionship in what promised to be a stressful experience, someone with whom he could relax and talk things over informally. So Truman could want Morgenthau to remain in place.

854 *Ibid.*, 247–48.

855 *Ibid.*, 248.

856 *Ibid.*

857 *Ibid.*, 249.

858 McCullough, David, *Truman*, New York: Simon & Schuster (1992), 404.

859 Morgenthau, Henry, III, *op. cit.*, 406.

860 McCullough, *op. cit.*, 404.

861 The reader will remember there are three or four possible versions of a possible rape visually told from differing points of view (with Japanese dialogue to increase a non–Japanese speaker's confusion).

862 It is evident in Truman's decision to attend the funeral of Tom Pendergast, Jr., after Truman became a national figure. Truman knew it would expose him to criticism in certain quarters because Pendergast was a felon, found guilty of criminal acts and sentenced to a federal prison.

863 Beschloss, *op. cit.*, 232.

864 Morgenthau, Henry, III, *op. cit.*, 407–08.

865 *Ibid.*, 406.

866 The colorful language in the Southern manner Truman used to describe Morgenthau after the latter left Washington, (Beschloss, *op. cit.*, 248–49) was not limited to Morgenthau. It would appear he talked that way about himself, telling Adlai Stevenson, "[I]f a knucklehead like me can be a successful president . . . I guess you can do it alright (sic)." (Schlesinger, Arthur, Jr., *Journals: 1952–2000*, New York: The Penguin Press (2007), eds. Andrew and Stephen Schlesinger, 27 (September 12, 1953) at a Democratic Party conference.)

867 Morgenthau, Henry, III, *op. cit.*, 302.

868 So Roosevelt had told Stimson, "Henry [Morgenthau] made a mistake"—at Quebec—except that Stimson had secured a copy of the memorandum Roosevelt initialed along with Churchill in September 1944 that spoke of a "pastoral" Germany, and Stimson confronted Roosevelt with it.

869 Beschloss, *op. cit.*, 250.

870 Morgenthau, Henry, III, *op. cit.*, 407.

871 *Ibid.*, 406.

872 *Ibid.*, 407.

873 *Ibid.*, 418–19.

874 Meltzer, *op. cit.*, 615.

875 Morgenthau, Henry, III, *op. cit.*, 411, 415.

876 Martin, Ralph G., *Golda*, New York: Charles Scribner's Sons (1988), 304–05, 318.

877 Morgenthau, Henry, III, *op. cit.*, 418.

878 Franklin Delano Roosevelt Library, Hyde Park, New York, Morgenthau documents, UJA box, "Meeting at Kaplan's home, Thursday evening, October 5, 1950" (carbon copy).

879 *Ibid.*, 7.

880 *Ibid.*

881 *Ibid.*, 2.

882 *Ibid.*, 5.

883 *Ibid.*, 6.

884 *Ibid.*, 1.

885 *Ibid.*

886 *Ibid.*, 2.

887 *Ibid.*, 6.

888 *Ibid.*, 7.

889 Morgenthau, Henry, III, *op. cit.*, 421.

890 *Ibid.*, 421–22.

891 *Ibid.*, 420.

892 *Ibid.*, 420.

893 *See:* Chapter 3, above.

894 In 1914, the concept of *ethnicity* had not yet evolved. The contemporaneous word was "race," with all the social malignancy that this Social Darwinist term implied.

895 Beschloss, *op. cit.*, 252.

896 *Ibid.*

897 Morgenthau, Henry, III, *op. cit.*, 435–36.

898 Beschloss, *op. cit.*, 252.

899 *Ibid.*, 423.

900 Beschloss, *op. cit.*, 152.

901 *Ibid.*, 425.

902 Beschloss, *op. cit.*, 153.

903 *Ibid.*, 150.

904 *Ibid.*, 151–52.

905 *Ibid.*, 152. The word *also* makes Beschloss's chronology difficult to follow. The negotiations with the British proceeded over a period of two years and ended with the Bretton Woods Conference in early July 1944. It is not clear that parallel discussions were carried out with the Soviet Union. If so, the Soviet delegation at Bretton Woods would not have had to protest to Morgenthau about the limit on their IMF drawing rights. Secondly, Beschloss identifies the secret Soviet agent with whom White spoke as one Nikolai Chechulin, whom he identifies as "a member of the Soviet delegation working with the Americans on the postwar economic system." The *postwar economic system* can only have reference to the IMF and the World Bank. There was nothing secret about that, especially if there was an official Soviet mission kept informed of the Anglo–American discussions in which White was concerned with limiting American exposure to foreign demands for loans. Morgenthau's European trip involved no formal diplomatic purpose on which to report to the Russians. Morgenthau might seek to advocate his views on the postwar reconstitution of an occupied Germany (White sought to temper the idea of flooding the coal mines), but Morgenthau's opinions were not state secrets. Beschloss's claim of White's subversive intent at that point in time is confusing.

906 *Ibid.*, 153, footnote 3.

907 *Ibid.*, 252.

908 *Ibid.*, 153.

909 The information that Chambers and his wife periodically returned to Esther Chambers's brother's home was supplied to the author some thirty–five years ago by Seymour Guttman, married to Esther Chambers's niece, and brother–in–law of Nathan Levine, Esther Chambers's nephew, to whom Chambers entrusted the "pumpkin papers" in 1938, when Chambers broke with the Communist Party and the espionage apparatus with which he was associated.

910 The three volumes are: Haynes, John Earle, and Klehr, Harvey, *Venona: Decoding Soviet Espionage in America*, New Haven: Yale University Press (1999), 125–26, 138–45; Romerstein, Herbert, and Breindel, Eric, *The Venona Secrets: Exposing Soviet Espionage and America's Traitors*, Washington: Regnery Publishing Inc. (2000), 29–30, 41–53; and

Weinstein, Allen, and Vassiliev, Alexander, *The Haunted Wood: Soviet Espionage in America*, New York: Random House (1999), 157–58, 161–69.

911 Haynes and Klehr, *op. cit.*, 139.

912 Beschloss, *op. cit.*, 152.

913 Haynes and Klehr, *op. cit.*, 139.

914 *Ibid.*

915 *Ibid.*, 140–41.

916 Halecki, Oscar, *A History of Poland*, New York: Barnes & Noble Books (1992, 1993), 331.

917 Romerstein, Herbert and Breindel, Eric, *op. cit.*, 42–43.

918 Black, *op. cit.*, 645, and 646–47 on Acheson's role.

919 *Ibid.*, 647.

920 Bernstein, Edward, *op. cit.*, 42.

921 *Ibid.*, 43.

922 *Ibid.*, 45.

923 Morgenthau, Henry, III, *op. cit.*, 427.

924 *Ibid.*, 439.

Chapter 8: The Morgenthau Plan for the Reconstruction of Germany

925 Morgenthau, Henry, Jr. *Germany Is Our Problem*. New York: Harper & Bros. (1945), 145.

926 *Ibid.*

927 Kennan, George F., *Memoirs 1925–1950*, Boston: Little Brown and Company (1967), 177.

928 Morgenthau, Henry, Jr., *op. cit.*, 146.

929 *Ibid.*, 159.

930 Morgenthau, Henry, III, *op. cit.*, 374; but see: Beschloss, *op. cit.*, 90; Blum, *Roosevelt and Morgenthau*, 576.

931 Morgenthau, Henry, III, *op. cit.*, 374–375; Beschloss, *op. cit.*, 103–104.

932 Morgenthau, Henry, III, *op. cit.*, 234, writes: "Everyone on both sides of my family had come to the United States from Germany. . . . My relatives through my parents' generation spoke German. . . ."

933 *Ibid.*, 31, n. Henry, III translates the last word as "potentates," but that word has faintly derisive connotations that would seem to contradict the tone of the rest of the quotation.

934 Morgenthau, Henry, Jr., *op. cit.*, 72.

935 *Ibid.*, 155.

936 Kennan, George F., *op. cit.*, 213, citing Feis, Herbert, *Churchill, Roosevelt, Stalin*, Princeton: Princeton University Press (1957), 287.

937 McCullough, David, *Truman*, New York: Simon & Schuster (1992), 450.

938 Morgenthau, Henry, Jr., *op. cit.*, 60.

939 Kennan, *op. cit.*, 438.

940 Schmitz, David, *Henry L. Stimson*, Wilmington: Biographies in American Foreign Policy No. 5 (2001), 179.

941 Aly, Götz, *Hitler's Beneficiaries: Plunder, Racial War, and the Nazi Welfare State*, New York: Metropolitan Books/Henry Holt (2007), tr. Jefferson Chase, 3.

942 Morison, Elton E., *Turmoil and Tradition: A Study of the Life and Times of Henry L. Stimson*, Boston: Houghton Mifflin Company (1960), 509.

943 *Ibid.*, citing Stimson's *Diaries*, September 10, 1940 and November 25, 1940; Cordell Hull's *Memoirs*, I:902; Watson, *Chief of Staff*, 300.

944 *Ibid.*

945 *Restatement of the Law of Contracts 2d*, St. Paul: American Law Institute Publishers (1981), sections 251 *et seq.*, II:276 *ff.*

946 Blum, *Roosevelt and Morgenthau*, 298–299.

947 *Ibid.*, 299.

948 *Ibid.*, 298.

949 *Ibid.*, 318.

950 *Ibid.*, 343.

951 *Morgenthau Diaries*, Roosevelt Library, Box 907, book 338, p. 35, December 10, 1940.

952 Bernstein, *op. cit.*, 41.

953 *Ibid.*

954 Black, *op. cit.*, 605.

955 *Morgenthau Diaries*, Roosevelt Library, Box 907, book 338, p. 102, December 10, 1940.

956 Black, *op. cit.*, 608–09.

957 Blum, *Roosevelt and Morgenthau*, 349.

958 *Ibid.*

959 *Ibid.*, 351.

960 *Ibid.*

961 *Ibid.*, 351–52.

962 *Ibid.*, 352.

963 *Ibid.*, 357.

964 *Ibid.*, 358.

965 Morison, *op. cit.*, 509.

966 *Ibid.*, 470, 471.

967 *Morgenthau Diaries*, Roosevelt Library, Box 907, book 378, p. 123 (p. 4 of the transcript).

968 Morgenthau, Henry, Jr., *op. cit.*, 213.

969 *Ibid.*, 86.

970 Beschloss, *op. cit.*, 272.

971 See: *The General Pact for the Renunciation of War*, Washington: United States Printing Office (1928).

972 Evans, Richard J., *The Coming of the Third Reich*, New York: The Penguin Press (2004), 98–99, 136.

973 Beschloss, *op. cit.*, 273.

974 Morgenthau, Henry, Jr., *op. cit.*, 144, 145.

975 *Ibid.*, 145.

976 *Ibid.*, 130.

977 *Ibid.*

978 *Ibid.*, 146.

979 Black, *op. cit.*, 819.

980 *The New York Times*, Saturday, November 26, 2005, "The Struggle to Gauge a War's Psychological Cost," A1, A8, col. 5.

981 Eisenhower, *op. cit.*, 408–09.

982 Beschloss, *op. cit.*, 61.

983 Washington, D.C.: United States Government Printing Office (1987), Bicentennial Edition, 4, 5.

984 Morgenthau, Henry, Jr., *op. cit.*, 80.

985 *Ibid.*, 88.

986 Kennan, George F., *op. cit.*, 197, 198.

987 Evans, Richard J., *op. cit.*, 267–68.

988 Blum, *Roosevelt and Morgenthau*, 573: "A proposal made by Jean Monnet to internationalize the Saar Basin and have joint control by some international body and to permit the Germans to work there but not run it."

989 Black, *op. cit.*, 693.

990 *The New York Times*, Monday, May 29, 2006, "A German Pope Confronts the Nazi Past at Auschwitz," A7, col. 2.

991 Goldmann, Nahum, *Autobiography*, New York: Holt, Rinehart & Winston (1969), 255.

992 *Ibid.*, 254.

993 Morgenthau, Henry, Jr., *op. cit.*, 80.

994 Goldmann, *op. cit.*, 258.

995 *Ibid.*, 261.

996 *Ibid.*, 256.

997 *Ibid.*, 260.

998 See: Chapter 4 above.

999 Goldmann, *op, cit.*, 270–71.

1000 *Ibid.*, 271–72.

1001 *Ibid.*, 273.

1002 Nansen, *op. cit.*, 437.

1003 The translator uses the term *dustbins* but that seems a Briticism. The meaning that Nansen would appear to intend—in an American sense— is best conveyed by the use of the word *garbage*.

1004 Nansen, *op. cit.*, 438, 439, dated February 12, 1945.

1005 *Ibid.*, 316, 317.

1006 Irving, Ronald, *Adenauer*, London: Pearson Education (2002), 198.

1007 Weymar, Paul, *Adenauer: His Authorized Biography*, New York: E. P. Dutton & Company, tr. Peter De Mendelssohn, (1957), 425.

1008 Wighton, Charles, *Adenauer: Democratic Dictator*, London: Frederick Muller Limited (1963), 310.

1009 Beschloss, *op. cit.*, 89.

1010 See: Beschloss' discussion on this point, 64–67.

1011 Hodgson, Godfrey, *The Colonel: The Life and Times of Henry Stimson, 1867–1950*, New York: Alfred A. Knopf (1990), 265.

1012 Morison, *op. cit.*, 606, citing Stimson's *Diary*, August 25, 1944; Brief for Conference with the President, August 25, 1944; Harvey Bundy, "Memorandum of Conference with the President," August 25, 1944; Stimson, Memorandum to Franklin D. Roosevelt, September 15, 1944, in *Diaries*.

1013 Morgenthau, Henry, III, *op. cit.*, 374–75.

1014 Morison, *op. cit.*, 606.

1015 Quoted in Beschloss, *op. cit.*, 105.

1016 Current, Richard N. *Secretary Stimson*. New Brunswick: Rutgers University Press (1970), 216, 217.

1017 *Ibid.*, 216.

1018 *Ibid.*, 217.

1019 Beschloss, *op. cit.*, 274.

1020 *Ibid.*

1021 Morgenthau, Henry, Jr., *op. cit.*, 220, taken from *The New York Times*, August 3, 1945, and cited for comparison with his text.

1022 *Ibid.*, 61.

1023 Morison, *op. cit.*, 608, n. 11; Blum, *Roosevelt and Morgenthau*, 551.

1024 Blum, *op. cit.*, 552–54.

1025 The text of that agreement is found among the notes to Title 22, section 286–l, of the *United States Code Service*.

1026 Morison, *op. cit.*, 609, footnote 12, citing Stimson's *Diaries*, September 20, 1944, John J. McCloy's notes of the meeting in Hull's office, September 20, 1944. Also, Hull's *Memoires*, II, 1614.

1027 *Ibid.*, citing Stimson's *Diaries*, 3 October, 1944; conversation with John J. McCloy, September 14, 1955.

1028 Morgenthau, Henry, Jr., *op. cit.*, 98, 99.

1029 See: Radkey, Oliver H., *The Agrarian Foes of Bolshevism*, New York: Columbia University Press (1958); *The Sickle Under the Hammer: the Russian Socialist–Revolutionaries in the Early Months of the Soviet Rule*, New York: Columbia University Press (1963).

1030 More properly, "Ngo," since in Asiatic societies one's family name comes first and then one's given names—although for Americans he will always remain "Diem."

1031 Catton, Philip E., *Diem's Final Failure: Prelude to America's War in Viet Nam*, Lawrence: University Press of Kansas (2002), 2.

1032 *The New York Times*, August 7, 2005, 12WK, cols. 2–6, Richardson, John H., "The Spy Left Out in the Cold."

1033 *Ibid.*

1034 Ross, Stanley R., *Francisco I. Madero, Apostle of Mexican Democracy*, New York: Columbia University Press (1955), 307–329.

1035 Catton, Philip E., *op. cit.*, 4.

References

Books

Adams, Brooks. *The Law of Civilization and Decay.* New York: The Macmillan Company, 1896.

Aly, Götz. *Hitler's Beneficiaries: Plunder, Racial War, and the Nazi Welfare State.* New York: Metropolitan Books/Henry Holt, tr. Jefferson Chase, 2007.

Arendt, Hannah. *Eichmann in Jerusalem* (rev. & enl. ed.). New York: Penguin Books, 1994.

Baker, Leonard. *Brandeis and Frankfurter.* New York: Harper and Row, 1984.

Barzun, Jacques. *Darwin, Marx Wagner.* Boston: Little, Brown and Company, 1946.

Bernhardi, Friedrich von. tr. Allen H. Powles. *Germany and the Next War.* New York: Charles A. Evon, 1914.

Bernstein, Edward and Stanley Black. *A Levite Among the Priests.* Boulder, CO: Westview Press, 1991.

Beschloss, Michael. *The Conquerors.* New York: Simon & Schuster, 2002.

Birmingham, Stephen. *Our Crowd: The Great Jewish Families of New York.* New York: Harper and Row, 1967.

Black, Conrad. *Franklin Delano Roosevelt, Champion of Freedom.* New York: Public Affairs, 2003.

Blum, John Morton. *From the Morgenthau Diaries.* Boston: Houghton Mifflin Company, 1959–67.

Blum, John Morton. *Roosevelt and Morgenthau*. Houghton Mifflin Company, 1970.

Breuer, J. and Freud, S., ed. and tr. James Strachey and Anna Freud, assist. by Alix Strachey and Alan Tyson. *Studies in Hysteria*. New York: Basic Books, 1957.

Burt, Robert A. *Two Jewish Justices: Outcasts in the Promised Land*. Berkeley: University of California Press, 1988.

Caro, Robert. *The Power Broker: Robert Moses and the Fall of New York*. New York: Random House, Vantage Books Ed., 1975.

Catton, Philip E. *Diem's Final Failure—Prelude to America's War in Viet Nam*. Lawrence: University Press of Kansas, 2002.

Ciechanowski, Jan. *Defeat in Victory*. New York: Doubleday & Company, 1947.

Cossens, James Gould. *By Love Possessed*. New York: Harcourt, Brace & Company, 1957.

Current, Richard N. *Secretary Stimson*. New Brunswick: Rutgers University Press, 1970.

Davis, Kenneth. *FDR: The New York Years*. New York: Random House, 1985.

Dollard, John. *Caste and Class in a Southern Town*. Madison: University of Wisconsin Press, 1988.

Dunar, Andrew J. *The Truman Scandals and the Politics of Morality*. Columbia: University of Missouri Press, 1984.

Eisenhower, Dwight D. *Crusade in Europe*. Garden City: Doubleday & Company, 1948.

Evans, Richard J. *The Coming of the Third Reich*. New York: The Penguin Press, 2004.

Faulkner, William. *The Faulkner Reader*. New York: Random House, 1954.

Ferrell, Robert H. *The Dying President: FDR 1944–45*. Columbia: University of Missouri Press, 1998.

Finan, Christopher. *Alfred E. Smith: The Happy Warrior*. New York: Hill and Wang, 2002.

Flynn, Edward J. *You're the Boss*. Westport: Greenwood Press, 1947/1983.

Freidel, Frank. *Franklin D. Roosevelt*. New York: Little Brown and Company (First Paperback Ed.), 1990.

———. *Franklin D. Roosevelt*. Boston: Little Brown and Company—v. I "The Apprenticeship" (1952); v. II "The Ordeal" (1954); v. III "The Triumph" (1956); v. IV "Launching the New Deal," 1973.

Gardner, Richard. *Sterling Dollar Diplomacy*. Oxford: The Clarendon Press, 1956.

Goldmann, Nahum. *Autobiography*. New York: Holt, Rinehart & Winston, 1969.

Greenberg, Jack. *Race Relations and American Law*. New York: Columbia University Press, 1959.

Grondahl, Paul. *Erastus Corning: Albany Icon, Albany Enigma*. Albany: Washington Park Press, 1997.

Haidt, Jonathan. *The Happiness Hypothesis*. New York: Basic Books, 2006.

Halecki, Oscar. *A History of Poland*. New York: Barnes & Noble Books, repr. 1993.

Hawkins, Mike. *Social Darwinism in European and American Thought 1860–1945*. Cambridge: Cambridge University Press, 1997.

Haynes, John Earle and Harvey Klehr. *Venona: Decoding Soviet Espionage in America*. New Haven: Yale University Press, 1999.

Hodgson, Godfrey. *The Colonel: The Life and Times of Henry Stimson, 1867–1950*. New York: Alfred A. Knopf, 1990.

Hoffer, Eric. *The True Believer*. New York: Harper and Row, Fr. Perennial Libr. Ed., 1989.

Hofstader, Richard. *Social Darwinism in American Thought, The New Yorker*. Boston: Beacon Press, 1948/1992.

Ickes, Harold. *The Secret Diary of Harold Ickes.* New York: Simon and Schuster—v. I "The Thousand Days" (1953); v. II "The Inside Struggle" (1954); v. III "The Lowering Clouds," 1955.

Irving, Ronald. *Adenauer.* London: Pearson Education, 2002.

James, William. *The Will to Believe.* New York: Longmans Green & Co., 1897.

Josephson, Matthew and Hannah. *Al Smith, Hero of the Cities.* Boston: Houghton, Mifflin and Company, 1969.

Kautski, Karl. *Nationalism in Our Day*, pamphlet printed in Russian trans. St. Petersburg (1903), cited in: Katz, Shmuel, *Lone Wolf: A Biography of Vladimir Jabotinsky*, New York: Barricade Books, 1996.

Kennan, George F. *Memoirs 1925–1950.* Boston: Little, Brown and Company, 1967.

Kraushar, Alexander. *Jacob Frank: The End to the Sabbatian Heresy.* Lanham: University Press of America, tr. from Polish, ed. and anno. with an intro. by Herbert Levy, 2001.

Kundera, Milan. "Die Weltliteratur," *The New Yorker*, tr. Linda Asher, January 8, 2007, 28, 30.

Laqueur, Walter. *The Terrible Secret: An Investigation Into the Suppression of Information About Hitler's Final Solution.* London: Weidenfeld and Nicolson, 1980.

Lindbergh, Anne Morrow. *The Wave of the Future—A Confession of Faith.* New York: Harcourt, Brace & Co., 1940.

Lundberg, Ferdinand. *America's 60 Families.* New York: The Citadel Press, 1946.

Mahan, Alfred Thayer. *The Interest of America in Sea Power, Present and Future.* Boston: Little, Brown & Co., 1898.

Mann, Thomas. *The Magic Mountain.* New York: The Modern Library, tr. H.T. Lowe–Porter, 1927.

Martin, Ralph G. *Golda.* New York: Charles Scribner's Sons, 1988.

McCullough, David *Truman*. New York: Simon and Schuster, 1992.

McDonald, Forrest. *The American Presidency: An Intellectual History*. Lawrence: University Press of Kansas, 1994.

Meltzer, Allen H. *A History of the Federal Reserve*, v. I: *1913–1951*. Chicago: University of Chicago Press, 2003.

Morgan, Edward S. *The Puritan Family*. New York: Harper and Row, 1966.

Morgenthau Henry, Jr. *Germany Is Our Problem*. New York: Harper & Bros., 1945.

Morgenthau, Henry, Sr. *All in a Lifetime*. Garden City: Doubleday, Paige & Co., 1922.

———. *Ambassador at Constantinople from 1913–1916*. Garden City: Doubleday, Paige & Co., 1918.

Morgenthau, Henry, III. *Mostly Morgenthaus: A Family History*. New York: Ticknor & Fields, 1991.

Morison, Elton E. *Turmoil and Tradition: A Study of the Life of and Times of Henry L. Stimson*. Boston: Houghton, Mifflin Company, 1960.

Nansen, Odd. *From Day to Day*. New York: G. P. Putnam's Sons, 1949.

Nasmyth, George. *Social Progress and the Darwinian Theory*. New York: G. P. Putnam's Sons, 1916.

Nevins, Allan. *Grover Cleveland*. New York: Dodd, Mead & Company, 1932.

New Testament: *Gospel of St. Luke*.

Newton, Verne W. (ed.). *FDR and the Holocaust*. New York: Oxford University Press, 1996.

Parrington, Vernon Louis. *Main Currents in American Literature*. New York: Harcourt, Brace and Company, 1930.

Proust, Marcel. *Remembrance of Things Past [A la Recherche du Temps Perdu]*, tr. C.K. Scott Montcrieff. New York: Random House, 1932.

Radkey, Oliver H. *The Agrarian Foes of Bolshevism*. New York: Columbia University Press, 1958.

———. *The Sickle Under the Hammer: the Russian Socialist–Revolutionaries in the Early Months of the Soviet Rule*. New York: Columbia University Press, 1963.

Réage, Pauline. *Story of O*. New York: Grove Press, 1965.

Restatement of the Law of Contracts 2d, St. Paul: American Law Institute Publishers, 1981.

Romerstein, Herbert and Eric Breindel. *The Venona Secrets: Exposing Soviet Espionage and America's Traitors*. Washington: Regnery Publishing, 2000.

Ross, Stanley R. *Francisco I. Madero, Apostle of Mexican Democracy*. New York: Columbia University Press, 1955.

Santayana, George. *The Philosophy of Santayana*. New York: Random House, Modern Library Edition, ed. I. Edman, undated.

Schlesinger, Arthur, Jr. *Journals 1952–2000*. New York: The Penguin Press, eds. Andrew and Stephen Schlesinger, 2007.

———. *The Age of Roosevelt*. Boston: Houghton, Mifflin Company—v. I "The Crisis in the Old Order" (1957); v. II "The Coming of the New Deal," 1958.

Schmitz, David. *Henry L. Stimson*. Wilmington: Biographies in American Foreign Policy No. 5, 2001.

Slayton, Robert A. *Empire Statesman: The Rise and Redemption of Al Smith*. New York: The Free Press, 2001.

Spencer, Herbert. *The Principles of Sociology*. New York: D. Appleton & Co., 3 vols., 1876–1907.

Tomasi di Lampedusa, Giuseppi. *Il Gattopardo*. Milano: Gianciacomo Feltrinelli Editore, ottantesima ed., 2002.

Weinstein, Allen and Alexander Vassiliev. *The Haunted Wood: Soviet Espionage in America*. New York: Random House, 1999.

Weymar, Paul, tr. Peter De Mendelssohn. *Adenauer: His Authorized Biography*. New York: E. P. Dutton & Company, 1957.

Wighton, Charles. *Adenauer—Democratic Dictator.* London: Frederick Muller Limited, 1963.

Wilson, Edward O. *On Human Nature.* Cambridge: Harvard University Press, 1978.

Winkler, Allan M. *Franklin D. Roosevelt and the Making of Modern America.* The Library of American Biography, New York: Longman, Pearson Education, Inc., 2006.

Wood, E. Thomas and Stanislaw Jankowski. *Karski: How One Man Tried to Stop the Holocaust.* New York: John Wiley & Sons, 1994.

Woodward, C. Vann. *Tom Watson: Agrarian Rebel.* New York: The Macmillan Company, 1938.

Woodward, C. Vann. *The Strange Career of Jim Crow.* New York: Oxford University Press, 1955.

Wyman, David S. *The Abandonment of the Jews: America and the Holocaust (1941–1945).* New York: Pantheon Press, 1984.

Articles from the New York Times

"A German Pope Confronts the Nazi Past at Auschwitz," May 29, 2006, A7.

Dargis, Manhola. "Peering Behind the Mask of a Mysterious Erotic Writer," May 4, 2005, E5.

Fremont–Smith, Eliot, obituary of, September 7, 2007, B8.

Grant, James, "Future Shock at the Fed," October 26, 2005, A27.

"Hevesi Trial? Senate May Look to a 1913 Impeachment," October 30, 2006, B7.

Krock, Arthur, "In the Nation," May 25, 1961, 36.

Moses, Robert, paid obituary notice, July 30, 1981, B17.

Potsdam Declaration, Text of, August 3, 1945.

Provincialism of post–World War I nationalism in newly emergent European countries, May 31, 2003, B9.

"Results of Secret Nazi Breeding Program: Ordinary Folks," November 7, 2006, A3.

Review of Philip Roth's *oeuvre* in the "Library of America" series, *The New York Times Book Review*, December 4, 2005, 52.

Richardson, John H., "The Spy Left Out in the Cold," August 7, 2005, 12 WK.

Shriver and Weissberg, "No Emotion Left Behind," August 16, 2005, A15.

Sorkin, Andrew Ross, "Summer Story Lines Have Legs," August 26, 2008, C1.

Sunstein, Cass, re: Franklin Roosevelt's use of multiple subordinates to review problems, *The New York Times Book Review*, January 25, 2004, 16.

"The Struggle to Gauge a War's Psychological Cost," November 26, 2005, A8, c. 5.

Truman's Presidential Diary, July 11, 2003, A14, cs. 3, 4.

Whitney, John Hay, obituary of February 9, 1982, B16.

U.S. Government Documents

Constitution of the United States, Bicentennial Ed., Washington: Government Printing Office (1987).

National Register of Historic Places Registration Form OMB No. 1024–0018 (May, June 2001), prepared by Karen Kennedy.

Henry Morgenthau, Jr., Diaries, Hyde Park: Roosevelt Library, Box 907, book 338, pp. 35, 102; book, 378, p. 123.

Henry Morgenthau, Jr.'s Letters to his Father, Hyde Park: Roosevelt Library.

The General Pact for the Renunciation of War, Washington: United States Printing Office (1928).

Treaty (Loan Agreement) between the United States and the United Kingdom, dated December 6, 1945, United States Code Service, Title 22, section 286–l, (*see:* notes for text of treaty).

U.S. Supreme Court Decisions

Berea College v. Kentucky, 211 U.S. 45 (1908).
Plessy v. Ferguson, 163 U.S. 537 (1896).

Index